STORIES
EMPLOYERS TELL

STORIES EMPLOYERS TELL

RACE, SKILL, AND HIRING IN AMERICA

PHILIP MOSS AND
CHRIS TILLY

A VOLUME IN THE MULTI-CITY STUDY OF
URBAN INEQUALITY

RUSSELL SAGE FOUNDATION | NEW YORK

The Russell Sage Foundation

The Russell Sage Foundation, one of the oldest of America's general purpose foundations, was established in 1907 by Mrs. Margaret Olivia Sage for "the improvement of social and living conditions in the United States." The Foundation seeks to fulfill this mandate by fostering the development and dissemination of knowledge about the country's political, social, and economic problems. While the Foundation endeavors to assure the accuracy and objectivity of each book it publishes, the conclusions and interpretations in Russell Sage Foundation publications are those of the authors and not of the Foundation, its Trustees, or its staff. Publication by Russell Sage, therefore, does not imply Foundation endorsement.

Library of Congress Cataloging-in-Publication Data

Moss, Philip I.
  Stories employers tell : race, skill, and hiring in America / Philip Moss and Chris Tilly.
      p.   cm. — (A volume in the multi-city study of urban inequality)
  Includes bibliographical references and index.
  ISBN 0-87154-609-4
  1. Career development—Social aspects—United States.   2.
Minorities—Employment—United States.   3. Discrimination in
employment—United States.   I. Tilly, Chris.   II. Title.   III. Multi-city
study of urban inequality.
  HF5549.5.C35   M674   2001
  331.13'3'0973—dc21   00-050999

Text design by Suzanne Nichols.

RUSSELL SAGE FOUNDATION

112 East 64th Street, New York, New York 10021
10 9 8 7 6 5 4 3 2 1

The Multi-City Study of Urban Inequality

The Multi-City Study of Urban Inequality is a major social science research project designed to deepen the nation's understanding of the social and economic divisions that now beset America's cities. It is based on a uniquely linked set of surveys of employers and households in four major cities: Atlanta, Boston, Detroit, and Los Angeles. The Multi-City Study focuses on the effects of massive economic restructuring on racial and ethnic groups in the inner city, who must compete for increasingly limited opportunities in a shifting labor market while facing persistent discrimination in housing and hiring. Involving more than forty researchers at fifteen U.S. colleges and universities, the Multi-City Study has been jointly funded by the Ford Foundation and the Russell Sage Foundation. This volume is the sixth in a series of books reporting the results of the Multi-City Study to be published by the Russell Sage Foundation.

To our parents, who taught us the importance of working to end racial inequality.

To Milton and Tatyana

To Chuck and Louise

Contents

About the Authors

PHILIP MOSS is professor in the Department of Regional Economic and Social Development at the University of Massachusetts, Lowell.

CHRIS TILLY is University Professor of Regional Economics and Social Development at the University of Massachusetts, Lowell.

IVY KENNELLY is visiting assistant professor of sociology in the School of History, Technology, and Society at the Georgia Technological Institute.

JOLEEN KIRSCHENMAN is research associate of Distressed and High Yield Investments at Citadel Investment Group, LLC in Chicago, Illinois.

Acknowledgments

This was a big research project, and there are lot of people to thank. We gratefully acknowledge funding from a number of sources. First and foremost was the Russell Sage Foundation, which provided generous research support, including a year in residence for Chris Tilly as a Visiting Scholar. Russell Sage, in the persons of Eric Wanner, Nancy Casey, Reynolds Farley, Suzanne Nichols, and David Weiman, also kept up the pressure and encouragement that carried us through the project. We also thank the Ford Foundation, the Rockefeller Foundation, the Social Science Research Council, and Chancellor William Hogan of the University of Massachusetts at Lowell for funding support.

We owe a large debt of gratitude to Joleen Kirschenman, who was an equal partner with us on research design, data collection, and coding, and took the lead on project management during the data collection phase. She also participated in the early phases of analysis and did the lion's share of coding. Joleen, along with Ivy Kennelly, wrote parts of chapter 5 and parts of chapter 2 as well.

A large and able team of research assistants aided us in conducting and analyzing the face-to-face employer interviews. The team included graduate students at the University of Georgia, the University of Massachusetts at Boston, the University of Massachusetts at Lowell, the University of Michigan, and the University of California at Los Angeles. Tuck Bartholomew, Nancy Beale, Laurie Dougherty, Devon Johnson, Sherry Russ Lee, Michael Lichter, Julie Press, and Susan Turner conducted employer interviews; Dougherty also helped with data analysis and management. Ivy Kennelly was data czar during the critical years of data collection, and assisted in coding and data analysis. Sandra Gary, Kim Nicholas, and Amy Kelly transcribed tapes. Joleen Kirschenman and Robert Smith, as well as the two of us, coded qualitative data. Don Aldin, Urska Cvek, M. K. Park, and Bryan Snyder helped with data management. Paula Maher and Hong Xu assisted with library research, and

Cheryl Seleski and David Grant provided additional research support. We also appreciate the efforts of Sheldon Danziger, who helped with project supervision at the University of Michigan, and Larry Bobo and Melvin Oliver, who did the same at UCLA—in all cases without compensation.

Harry Holzer, who oversaw the Telephone Employer Survey, generously helped us understand and use it. The Survey Research Division of the Institute for Public Policy and Social Research at Michigan State University, and in particular project manager Karen Clark, administered the several hundred additional telephone interviews that supplemented Holzer's data set. Tom Hertz cleaned, recoded, and documented the combined data set.

We received feedback on various elements of this work from too many people to keep track of. We particularly want to thank the many members of the Multi-City Study of Urban Inequality research team, and above all Alice O'Connor, who provided very helpful feedback on an early draft of the manuscript, and Harry Holzer, who has offered many thoughtful comments over the years. We would also single out Kathy Bradbury, Daniel Cornfield, Sheldon Danziger, Sandy Darity, and Marie Kennedy, who offered constructive guidance at important junctures. We got ideas from seminar audiences at the Allied Social Science Associations, the American Sociological Association, the Association for Public Policy Analysis and Management, the Annie E. Casey Foundation Jobs Initiative, the Boston Center for Community Economic Development, the City University of New York, Cornell University, Columbia University, the Eastern Economic Association, the Eastern Sociological Society, Harvard University, the New England Study Group at the Federal Reserve Bank of Boston, the John D. and Catherine T. MacArthur Foundation, the Massachusetts Institute of Technology, the NAACP Legal Defense Fund, the New School for Social Research, Queens College, the Russell Sage Foundation, the Social Science History Association, the University of Massachusetts at Boston, the University of Massachusetts at Dartmouth, the University of Massachusetts at Lowell, and the University of Michigan. Last, but not least, two anonymous reviewers offered extremely valuable critiques of the draft manuscript.

Finally, we would like to thank our long-suffering families. Kathy Bradbury, Willie and Tanya Moss, and Marie Kennedy made this work possible with their love and support.

PHILIP MOSS
CHRIS TILLY

1

RACIAL INEQUALITY IN THE LABOR MARKET: MARKET FORCES OR DISCRIMINATION?

Interview 1

Interviewer: What's the most important thing in deciding whether you hire somebody?

Respondent (personnel administrator, a white woman, at a large Los Angeles–area organization): You need to have the skills, that's the most important. And then the impression that that applicant makes on me in the screening process. Is that person going to fit in?

Interviewer: One thing that we hear from employers is that they find significant differences in the workforce in different groups of people. Between whites, blacks, Hispanics, Asians, between men and women, between natives and immigrants.

Respondent: I don't see any difference. If you have the skills, a person is motivated to learn those skills, I really don't see a difference.

Interviewer: One of the reasons that we ask is that we know that minority applicants, particularly blacks, are having a difficult time in the labor market.

Respondent: Well, yes, I think that the unemployment of minorities in general is based on old prejudices that still exist. And again the only thing that I have seen as a difference, and my own assistant administrator is black, is the issue of the manner of speech.

Interview 2

Interviewer: Have you had any other problems with managing diversity?

Respondent (department head, a black woman and the only black manager in the same organization): Issues do come up. People do get annoyed with each other, or with the situation, and racism frequently enters into the quotient. There is a pervasive view that the management is racist, and that if you have so many women and minorities in clerical jobs, it's because they're low-paying, and that they intend to keep them that way precisely because of that.

Interviewer: There's one more thing I wanted to ask about the diversity issue. We know from research that black men, and black women, and other minorities, have been doing badly in the labor market recently.

Respondent: I think it's very simply racism. Where you have a management that is primarily white, and where the conception of how a person should deal with any given situation comes from the ideal vision in the white manager's mind, of what they have grown up with and known. To find a person of color, any color, coming in, who doesn't quite meet that model, they tend to select someone else white, given another person with the same skills. There is some real challenge with understanding the African [American], certainly, and I'm sure other groups as well, as something other than as a servant.

Interview 3

Interviewer: Have you ever felt at any time in the past that others at your place of employment got promotions or pay raises faster than you because of your race or ethnicity?

Respondent (black woman employed in a clerical job at this organization until a year and a half ago): Yes.

Interviewer: What happened that made you feel that way?

Respondent: Because other, white people got a raise, and I didn't. One white employee got three raises in one year. I feel strongly that I was forced out of my job after nineteen and a half years—just six months short of my twenty years, which would have qualified me for a pension. I feel bitter because in spite of the fact that I was a union steward, and personally saved other employees' jobs, I was not able to save my own job.

A debate rages in the United States about the sources and significance of continuing racial inequality: Are the ongoing disadvantages faced by African Americans, Latinos, and other people of color principally the result of impersonal market forces or of continuing, pervasive discrimination? Media pundits, political leaders, and scholars have weighed in with varied views, and the terms of the debate play out somewhat differently depending on whether the subject is housing segregation, school quality, or jobs. But the central question of market forces versus racism is a common theme.

In the case of the labor market, the subject of this book, the dialogue sounds a little like the quotes that open this chapter. "If you have the skills, I really don't see a difference," say those who argue that market forces are central. If blacks and Latinos suffer from lower wages or higher unemployment, they must not have the schooling and skills needed to succeed in today's economy. Market forces have escalated skill requirements, based on new technology and stepped-up competitive pressure. The skill problem, some would add, is overlaid with a geographic one: African Americans and Latinos are concentrated in central cities, but the low-skill jobs that best match the abilities of many people of color have shifted to the suburbs—again, because manufacturers and retailers have responded to market forces.

"It's racism," goes the counterargument; "management is racist." Businesses are slow to hire or promote people of color, and quick to fire them, because of managers' stereotypes and biases. If businesses have fled the inner city, the reasons lie in prejudice rather than economics. Of course, most advocates of the importance of discrimination would not deny that lagging skills pose a problem for many black and Latino job seekers—just as those pointing to market forces would not deny that some employers still discriminate. It's a question of which exerts a more powerful effect on racial inequality. The policy implications are serious: How much effort and resources should we as a society devote to overcoming discrimination, and how much to strengthening opportunities for education and training?

This book will not resolve the debate. In our analysis of interviews with large numbers of employers in the Atlanta, Boston, Detroit, and Los Angeles areas, we found evidence that employers hire whites and Asians instead of blacks and Latinos because of average skill differences among the groups, and choose where to locate their businesses based on

3

where costs are lowest. We also found evidence that managers hold negative stereotypes of blacks and, to a lesser extent, Latinos, and act on these stereotypes by discriminating in hiring. And the interviews suggest that factors such as an exaggerated fear of urban crime shape location decisions. There is something for everyone in these research results.

But what about the question of the relative size of the impacts of market forces and discrimination? Here we have reached a different conclusion from any we anticipated at the outset of the research. Our interviews do not answer this question, and we have concluded that this and most other current labor market research cannot completely answer it. The reason is that stereotypes, on the one hand, and assessments of worker skills or of the suitability of a business location, on the other, are tightly wrapped together in a single package. Not one employer told us, "I don't like blacks" or "I prefer to hire someone from my own ethnic group." But many, many managers made statements like "Blacks are less reliable" or "Immigrants work harder." Nobody said, "I didn't want to start up my business in a Latino neighborhood," but plenty claimed, "If we located in the inner city, we'd still need to attract a workforce from the suburbs." Statements like these combine objective assessments of workforce skills with racial stereotypes, and it is very hard to draw the line between the two.

One obvious answer to this dilemma is to counterpose employer statements about racial groups or neighborhoods with direct information about those racial groups and neighborhoods. But this runs into both measurement and conceptual problems. If a manufacturer says, "Blacks don't have the basic math I need in a worker," we may be able to show that three-quarters of black high-schoolers in the metropolitan area can solve the math problems she is talking about, but that does not tell us whether she is describing the blacks in her applicant pool accurately. More critically, returning to the chapter's initial quote, who determines what is an appropriate "manner of speech" for a particular job? How should we measure how "reliable" a group is, on average? And if we manage to measure "reliability" through indices such as tardiness and absenteeism, are we detecting differences in skill, or differences that result from disparate pay, working conditions, and respect from managers faced by each racial or ethnic group?

We are confident that these problems can be surmounted, through a combination of better social science and the ethical and political discussions needed to resolve issues like the appropriate workplace requirements for "manner of speech." But our key objective in this book is far more modest: to depict the way prejudice and rational economic decision making are tangled together in employers' perceptions. We seek both to document this entanglement in some detail and to explore how it differs according to circumstance. Along the way, we provide a great deal of related information about employer perceptions and actions in urban labor markets.

How We Came to "Stories Employers Tell"

Our journey to this book began in 1990, when the Social Science Research Council commissioned us to write a literature review surveying the influences of labor *demand*—what kinds of jobs are being created, where, and what kinds of workers employers seek to fill those jobs—on concentrated urban poverty. At that time, the central concern animating research on urban labor markets was the "underclass"—groups of low-income people, disproportionately people of color, who remained cut off from the labor market.[1] At that time the social science consensus held that African Americans as a whole continued to make great strides in labor markets, as they had over the course of the century. As blacks moved out of the South and into urban areas, and achieved higher levels of education, their wages rose apace (Smith and Welch 1989). Civil rights laws and affirmative action seemed to clinch this progress: black managers and professionals became increasingly common. The wages of black and white male college graduates had become nearly indistinguishable; black women's wages surpassed those of white women (Freeman 1976; Wilson 1978). Given this generally rosy picture, attention naturally turned to those left behind by this trend toward racial economic convergence. "Underclass" research focused on concentrated, persistent (indeed, often intergenerational) urban poverty—affecting whites, blacks, and Latinos, but particularly prevalent among black inner-city populations in northern cities (Wilson 1987). It stressed nonmainstream behavior such as prolonged nonemployment among men, welfare dependence among women, and participation in criminal activities in the underground economy. The central research questions were how concentrated poverty populations had become detached from labor markets, and how they could be reintegrated into the workforce.

Many "underclass" researchers sought to explain why inner-city blacks were dropping out of the labor market. We, along with some other researchers, posed the question differently: What was shutting these potential workers out of the labor market? Our timing was good. A flurry of economic research around that time revealed that convergence in black and white wages had ended, and that a new divergence had begun. The wage gap between young black and white men began to widen again; the employment gap was already growing and would continue to do so (Bound and Freeman 1992). Among young women, white women's wages pulled ahead of blacks', and black women, who a decade earlier were more likely than white women to be employed, became less likely than their white counterparts to be employed by the early 1990s (Bound and Dresser 1999; Corcoran and Parrott 1999). Young black workers suffered these wage and employment setbacks, even though blacks continued to draw closer to whites in educational attainment and test scores (Bound and Freeman 1992; Jencks 1991). Indeed, wages diverged particularly dramatically between young black and white men *with a college degree* (Bound and Freeman 1992). Latinos have also experienced economic backtracking, although their situation has been less well studied (Hinojosa-Ojeda, Carnoy, and Daley 1991; Corcoran, Heflin, and Reyes 1999).

The recession of 1990 to 1991 hit African Americans particularly hard. Among the 35,000 corporations large enough to report employment to the Equal Employment Opportunity Commission (which cumulatively account for more than 40 million workers), black employment dropped by nearly 60,000 between 1990 and 1991, while employment of whites, Latinos, and Asians *climbed* by amounts ranging from 55,000 to 71,000 (Sharpe 1993). Conversely, the booming economy of the late 1990s and early 2000s brought some renewed narrowing of black-white wage and employment gap (Freeman and Rodgers 2000), but this progress toward equality has been small and, most likely, temporary.

The fact that both wage and employment gaps widened between blacks and whites (men and women alike) tells us something important. If black employment fell relative to whites but wages rose—the story of men from the 1950s through the 1970s—economics tells us that the explanation could be a shift in labor supply. When one group becomes scarcer relative to another (assuming they are not perfect substitutes in the eyes of employers), we expect the relative "price" of this group to rise as employers bid wages up. Decreased labor supply of African American men, in turn, could result from black men holding out for better jobs than America was prepared to offer them (arguably a reasonable response on the part of black men to the promise of equal opportunity) or the lure of criminal activity, among other possibilities. But when relative employment and relative wages for blacks both slump, the explanation must lie in decreased demand. Fewer businesses are bidding (or businesses are bidding less) for the services of young black men and women.

We explored these new developments in our literature review (Moss and Tilly 1991, 1993a). But the evidence of declining demand for black labor brought us face to face with a new question, a variant of the one we posed at the beginning of this chapter: *Why* are businesses not bidding for black labor as much as in the past? Again, one set of answers stresses impersonal market forces. Even though average black educational attainment has climbed, skill requirements may have soared even higher, leaving blacks behind. And job growth has shifted from cities to suburbs distant from where most African Americans live. Another set of explanations emphasizes heightened discrimination, perhaps encouraged by a political backlash against affirmative action.

Plenty of evidence points to the continued vigor of racial prejudice and discrimination in the United States. Few whites any longer answer yes to survey questions expressing old-fashioned white supremacist sentiments, such as supporting segregated schools or agreeing that whites should receive preference over blacks in access to jobs—both of which received majority support as recently as the 1940s. At a deeper level, however, many whites still harbor negative stereotypes of blacks. A majority of 56 percent of whites rate blacks as less intelligent than whites, and 78 percent view blacks as more likely to prefer living off welfare than whites (Bobo and Kluegel 1991). Whites hold similar, though somewhat more attenuated, negative opinions of Latinos. Shifting the focus from opinion to action, audit studies send out "testers," members of different racial groups with matched qualifications, to apply for jobs. Audit studies in Chicago and Washington, D.C., have consistently shown that blacks and Latinos are less likely than non-Hispanic whites to gain an interview or be offered a job (Bendick, Jackson, and Reynoso 1994; Fix and Struyk 1993). In four audit studies involving 1,247 "tests" (pairs of job applications) between 1989 and 1992, non-Latino whites encountered better treatment or a better outcome 20 to 31 percent of the time, whereas blacks and Latinos did better only 3 to 11 percent of the time; putting the numbers together, whites were three to eight times as likely to do better. Most critical, of course, is whether applicants received a job offer. Although only a small minority of applicants received an offer, that percentage was 15 to 22 percent among non-Latino whites and 4 to 8 percent among African Americans and Latinos; employers were three to four times as likely to offer whites the job (Bendick, Jackson, and Reynoso 1994, table 2).

Blacks and Latinos (along with Asians and whites) certainly *believe* that they face discrimination in the workplace. In the Multi-City Study of Urban Inequality Household Survey, a survey of almost nine thousand adults in the Atlanta, Boston, Detroit, and Los Angeles metropolitan areas, 19 percent of blacks and 14 percent of Latinos stated that they had experienced workplace discrimination based on race or ethnicity *in the last year* (see table 1.1). (Considerably smaller percentages of Asians and whites also reported such discrimination.) Furthermore,

TABLE 1.1 *Percentage of Persons Reporting Experiences of Racial or Ethnic Discrimination at the Workplace, by Race-Ethnicity*

	Black	Latino	Asian	White
Experienced workplace discrimination in last year	19.4	14.4	6.0	5.6
Passed over for raises or promotions	24.3	8.7	2.8	6.5
Answering yes to either discrimination question	31.8	18.4	7.8	9.5

Source: Calculated by the authors from the Multi-City Study of Urban Inequality Household data.
Note: Sample of adults from Atlanta, Boston, Detroit, and Los Angeles areas. Black, Asian, and white categories exclude Latinos.

24 percent of blacks and 9 percent of Latinos said that at some time in the past they had been passed over for raises and promotions due to race or ethnicity. Taking into account the overlap between these two groups, a total of 32 percent of blacks and 18 percent of Latinos reported some experience of labor market discrimination.

As a follow-up to the question about raises and promotions, respondents who reported discrimination were asked, "What happened that made you feel that way?" The answers make painful reading. A few answers were perfunctory ("Because it happened"). But the rest unfold a raw litany of perceived abuse. We present an extensive sampling of their words, because they provide an essential backdrop to employers' accounts in the rest of the book.

About half of those who reported being passed over said they knew of members of other racial groups (typically whites) with less experience, ability, or seniority who had received pay increases or promotions before them:

> They flunked inspectors in exams and they still made it. They were promoted without qualifications because they were white.

> You can notice it in my work area. There are only two Hispanics there, and they've been at the same grade for many years, whereas other employees with less years have been promoted faster because they are the supervisor's pet. The higher-up jobs are all white males. The next level is all white females. The minorities are the lowest paid.

> It's all women in my job category. The higher-level and -paying jobs are all held by white women. No black women have ever been promoted.

> My supervisor is a young white man with little experience or training—I'm teaching him.

Stories of someone who trained a current or future supervisor are remarkably common. In a few cases, the respondent worked with payrolls, and therefore had hard data about the salaries of employees in different racial groups.

Although whites were most often mentioned as the beneficiaries of workplace discrimination, respondents at different times pointed to almost every ethnic group but their own. A black respondent complained that the bosses favored "whites, Hispanics, and Asians"; a Latino said that "the Asians, the black Americans, the whites get promoted"; at one workplace a white complained that managers mistreated "anyone who wasn't Japanese—even the Chinese." Particularly common were statements that linked racial preferences to other kinds of favoritism—based on friendship, family, flirtation, shared national origin, or other ties. Here are some illustrative examples:

> This guy, he's an Italian, same as my boss and her boss. This guy, he was here a week or two after I got here. He got a raise before I did, which I didn't think was fair. Now he's supervising over the crew that's been there much longer than me and him.

> A lot of nepotism exists there among the whites. They tell their family members about job openings.

> A white girl who's twenty-two, shapely, and has long hair got promoted to thirty thousand dollars right away.

> There were people at that job who got promotions and pay raises because they fit into the club—straight white male—not based on merit. The boss made a comment about how it depended on who would play golf with him.

> People are equally qualified, but certain people always make it. I don't think it's racist, it's who you know—networks.

Even more vivid than the Multi-City Study responses, because they allowed for longer conversations, were a pair of New York City and Boston focus groups conducted by Boston-based Jobs for the Future, a research and policy organization. In these discussions, young African American men from the inner city cast a cynical eye on employers. In Boston, for instance, a discussion of qualifications sought by employers quickly turned to issues of racial bias (Jobs for the Future 1995a, 13–18):

> *Focus Group Moderator:* What do you think employers are looking for, when you walk through the door? What type of person are they looking for?

Respondent (respondents are all young, inner city black men): Hard working. Neat, clean, hard working.

Respondent: Easy tempered. Well, somebody who's going to keep their temper in check.

Respondent: Qualifications. Experience that would pertain to whatever.

Moderator: What else do you think they're looking for? . . .

Respondent: White workers.

Moderator: Why do you think white workers?

Respondent: Because they think we don't know what we're doing, that's how they see it. If you're white and the guy's white, he's going to want someone of his own blood, because he's white.

In the New York focus group, participants voiced frustration about the uphill struggle to find a job (Jobs for the Future 1995b):

We all have our needs and all, so, in order to satisfy our needs we have to go and work. It's disheartening when we go out and we do not find work. When we go to different organizations to look for work, a lot of times whites do not want to hire us, unless it's for a low-paying job. (4)

A lot of whites comes from suburbia, where they're in middle class and even upper middle class, so their starting point is at a better starting point than for us. Because many of us come from the city and in the city there aren't as many opportunities as there are up in suburbia. (12)

They acknowledged that when it comes to jobs with limited skill requirements, they are competing with immigrants who are willing to settle for less:

The people with the green cards, they're willing to work for lower pay than we are. Because they're coming over here with nothing, so they're going to take anything—they'll take $2.00 an hour. (9)

Even after landing a job, they talked about being tested, disrespected, and mistreated—held to a different standard because they were black:

First of all, I feel that they're going to test you. When you're first walking in the door and you've got the job, we're all being tested, the brothers, because they want to find out how much can you accept. "Well, let me see his breaking point." (24)

Because, I do notice when I'm doing my type of work, right, when a black person sees it, "wow, that's really good." When a white person sees it, they don't feel that blacks can do that and should be doing it. So, it's negative. (26)

When I was working for this company and somebody else came in and he was white and I noticed, because I looked at his paycheck, that he was getting more than me, so I went to the employer and said, "How come I'm not getting more money?" (14)

I felt I was doing a good job as steward and everything, and they said, because I didn't come in with the experience and all like that, they gave it to another guy. This guy came in, boom, and he didn't really have experience. Different color, more money and everything off the bat. Now, that just knocks my self-esteem down. (12–13)

Despite these hard-bitten attitudes, the men said they were unprepared for the level of racism they encountered when starting a job:

Moderator: Now, when you guys first started with your position, what were you least prepared for when you got there? . . .

Respondent: Racism.

Moderator: You were least prepared for racism.

Respondent: Corporate racism.

Moderator: What's the difference?

Respondent: They don't say it to you. It's more implied. It's more the things they ask you.

Respondent: You know what it is, you look at those professional people, and you wouldn't think that they could act the way they act. You're in a professional place, a law firm that makes a billion dollars a year, all these people they're laughing in your face and behind your back.

Moderator: Vincent, what were you least prepared for?

Respondent: I was least prepared for somebody thinking I'm stupid because I'm black.

Moderator: [Addressing another focus group participant] What were you least prepared for when you started your job?

Respondent: I'm not going to say racism, but to me, it was more like the favoritism. Because everybody supposedly goes through the same process to get a position, but once you're in, it's, like, "Well, this is my boy. He's going to be able to do things and I'm going to cover for him." (32–34)

Most likely, some of these firsthand reports of discrimination represent misperception of employer decisions based on merit (or, in any case, on criteria other than race). But as Lawrence Bobo and Susan Suh (1995) pointed out, social psychology predicts that people will tend to *under*report experiences of discrimination, since describing such bias means admitting a lack of control over one's own fate. In this context, the high frequency with which blacks report workplace discrimination—nearly twice as often as Latinos, and three times as often as whites—takes on particular significance.

Still missing from this body of evidence are the voices of employers. When it comes to hiring, what do employers have to say about what they believe, about what they do, and about why they do it? We wanted to capture an "employer's-eye view" of the processes that cumulate into labor demand.

Talking to Employers

As we pondered our next steps, sociologists Joleen Kirschenman and Kathryn Neckerman were pioneering the use of in-depth, face-to-face employer interviews to explore employers' perceptions of various racial groups, as part of the Chicago Poverty and Urban Family Life Study (Kirschenman and Neckerman 1991; Neckerman and Kirschenman 1991). This was the research tool we were groping for. We adopted their approach in a two-city pilot study looking at Detroit and Los Angeles. Then we joined with Joleen Kirschenman to carry out a considerably larger set of face-to-face employer interviews in the same two cities, plus Atlanta and Boston, as one part of the Multi-City Study of Urban Inequality (Johnson, Oliver, and Bobo 1994). In the meantime, as another part of the Multi-City Study, economist Harry Holzer conducted a telephone survey of employers in the same four cities, much larger in scale than the labor-intensive Face-to-Face Surveys (Holzer 1996). These three surveys yielded the data we draw on for this book.

We chose to carry out in-depth, face-to-face interviews precisely because we wanted to understand how employers look at the world. We were particularly interested in "how" and "why" questions. How do employers view applicants of varying backgrounds? Why are they increasingly choosing suburban locations? How do they evaluate the varied information that they gather in the screening process, and under what circumstances do they change their recruiting or screening procedures? Why are managers seeking stronger social skills as well as technical ones? And so on. We both had experience using in-depth interviews to investigate labor market dynamics. Moss and his colleagues employed this approach to study work organization in the fishing industry, among other topics (Doeringer, Moss, and Terkla 1986). Tilly used it to look at the use of part-time employment in insurance and retail businesses (Tilly 1996). So it was a natural next step to team up with Kirschenman to conduct in-depth employer interviews to learn more about employment barriers to workers of color.

We describe the Telephone Survey and the two Face-to-Face Surveys in more detail in the next chapter, but here we explain how we use the data to get at our central questions about labor demand. We came away from the earlier literature review with questions about what had *changed* in labor demand to increase the disadvantage of black and Latino job seekers, particularly about whether discrimination had changed or worsened. But talking to employers at one point in time is not a terrific way to learn about change over time. Instead, we focused our inquiry on closely related questions: How widespread is racial discrimination in the labor market, and how does it happen? To keep the project manageable, we limited the scope to the initial hiring process. Retention and promotion are also crucial, of course, but our goal was to learn in depth about one set of hurdles. We also narrowed our attention to jobs requiring no more than a high school degree. Looking at the reasons why there are few black surgeons or Latino attorneys would require focusing more on medical and law schools than on hospitals and law firms. Our question, instead, was what were the obstacles to workers of color in entry-level jobs with modest skill demands.

The surveys asked managers to address four major topics, corresponding to four types of potential obstacles we had identified in our literature review:

(1) What skills do employers seek, and how is this changing?

(2) How do employers make location decisions, and what role do perceptions of urban areas play in this process?

(3) How do employers perceive workers of color as prospective employees?

(4) How do employers recruit and screen applicants?

One can potentially learn about each of these topics by means other than interviewing employers, but it's hard to beat speaking to employers directly to get answers to these questions. The face-to-face interviews focused more single-mindedly on this set of queries than the Telephone Survey, which was designed by Harry Holzer to tackle other questions as well.

The combination of the large Telephone Survey and the smaller In-Depth Surveys is a powerful one, since each type of data has comparative advantage for particular types of questions. The Telephone Survey allows us to generate statistics such as the frequency of specific types of skill demands by employers and the representation of people of color in jobs with differing skill demands, both of which we examine in chapter 3, and the spatial distribution of entry-level jobs, which we discuss in chapter 5. The large sample and extensive set of variables also permit multivariate analysis to test hypotheses and scrutinize relations among a number of variables, for instance, the effect of different recruiting methods on the likelihood of a minority hire, which we explore in chapter 6.

Face-to-face, qualitative interviews are truly the "stories employers tell." These expansive conversations give us the opportunity to probe the meaning of complex concepts that are difficult or impossible to capture in quantitative codes. Further, the interviewer can develop a rapport with the interviewee in a qualitative interview that helps in gathering data on sensitive topics—and the role of race in hiring is most definitely a sensitive topic. Finally, because the responses are open-ended, qualitative interviews can uncover unanticipated responses, for example, how some employers use dependence on public transportation as a warning signal to avoid inner-city job candidates, which we report in chapter 5. Despite prioritizing qualitative results from the Face-to-Face Surveys, we also made the sample sufficiently large and representative of the four metropolitan areas to support some statistical analyses, such as exploring the connection between managers' stated perceptions of workers of color and the business's odds of hiring a person of color, as we do in chapter 4. And to get a full picture of each business, we interviewed up to three people: a top executive, a personnel or human resource official, and a frontline supervisor.

These point-in-time surveys cannot directly track changes over time in hiring. But we, as well as Holzer, wanted to learn what we could about such changes. So all the interviews included retrospective questions, asking each manager about how skill needs on the job have evolved, how the company has changed its hiring procedures, and whether the company has moved. In the face-to-face interviews, we were interested in learning about the causes and consequences—specifically, the consequences for hiring of people of color—of changing skill demands, shifts in the organization of work, and relocation. To this end, we designed our sample of firms to ensure that adequate numbers of businesses making each of these kinds of changes were included.

Our analytical strategy for understanding these data has three main elements. The first is *description*. Simply describing the characteristics of these large samples of employers from four diverse metropolitan areas yields a bounty of interesting results. This holds particularly for descriptions of managers' perceptions, which are seldom measured. Drawing on the in-depth interviews, our goal is to document the variety of employer responses, not just their central tendency. And we seek to describe not just the "which" and "how much" answers, but also the "why's" and "how's." Thus in chapter 4 we size up employers' explanations for why, as they see it, black workers are not up to par; in chapter 6 we learn how employers get around official, formal hiring processes to give jobs to the candidates they want.

Comparison is the second element of our analytical strategy. We consistently compare patterns across Atlanta, Boston, Detroit, and Los Angeles, and contrast city businesses with suburban ones. In some cases, we make added comparisons, such as looking at how managers' perceptions of various racial groups as potential workers differ depending on the race of the manager, and depending on the job to be filled. The final analytical task is examining *associations* between variables. In particular, we repeatedly look at whether and how different factors are associated with the probability of hiring someone of a particular race and gender.

Two serious problems confront our research design. For one thing, despite the fact that the interviews are confidential, the managers may not have been open with us. Some or even all of them may have tailored their answers to be socially desirable, adjusting what they said based on what they thought the interviewer wanted to hear. The other problem is that we have no independent information about the people or neighborhoods that the employers told us about. Our main remedy for these shortcomings is to draw on multiple sources of evidence from within the Employer Surveys. We compare results from the telephone and in-depth interviews; we contrast views of executives, personnel managers, and supervisors; we juxtapose different employers in a given locality or industry; we measure employers' stated perceptions against their actions. All these comparisons are helpful, but nonetheless we wrestle with the two problems throughout the book. As some consolation, we conclude that we can learn a lot from employers' subjective views, even if we can't fully determine how accurate they are.

The Plan of the Book

We set out to discover the extent and mechanisms of racial discrimination in entry-level hiring. We did find evidence that discrimination contributes importantly to hiring outcomes, and we did learn how this happens. But we ended up learning, above all, that employer biases are intricately interwoven with legitimate judgments about the skills of workers and the qualities of neighborhoods. Fortunately, this interweaving does not prevent us outright from drawing further conclusions. For instance, a central finding in chapter 4 is that skill assessment and prejudice overlap most in the area of social skills. We also discover that employers are demanding higher levels of such social skills, as documented in chapter 3. This combination leads to a straightforward prediction that racial discrimination should be on the rise. It also points to possible policy solutions, including stronger antidiscrimination enforcement, but also programs to teach managers better methods for evaluating and managing a diverse workforce, as discussed in chapter 7.

Before launching into our findings, in chapter 2 we describe our data in more detail and profile the four metropolitan settings for our research. The four core chapters, 3 through 6, take on the four major questions we posed. Chapter 3 examines the skills employers seek, and how those skill needs are changing. In chapter 4, the longest in the book, we explore managers' stated perceptions of racial groups, as well as to what extent negative perceptions translate into discriminatory actions. Chapter 5 undertakes a parallel investigation, reviewing the images employers hold of the inner city and tracing connections between these images and business location decisions. We probe the recruitment and screening procedures employers use—and their impact on who gets hired—in chapter 6. Finally, in chapter 7, we sum up our conclusions, briefly consider what employers in the surveys had to say about government and public policy, and make our own policy recommendations.

The barrier to employment for people of color with limited skill in urban America is not a monolithic bar, like the old Jim Crow laws of the South or the racial covenants that kept nonwhites from owning homes elsewhere. Rather, the "stories employers tell" reveal that the obstacles grow out of dozens of small decisions by each employer: where to locate, how to define and design each job, how and where to recruit, what methods to use for evaluating candidates, what to look for in a pre-employment interview, and so on. At each step, disadvantages for inner-city blacks and Latinos arise both from problems rooted outside the labor market—inadequate schooling, segregated residential patterns—and from employer discrimination. Overcoming this set of disadvantages will require efforts on many fronts. We hope that this book's analysis of employer perceptions and decisions will help stimulate these badly needed efforts.

2

THE SCOPE OF THE STUDY: DATA, METHODS, AND THE FOUR CITIES

Our investigation of the labor market difficulties experienced by urban minorities relies on information supplied by employers located throughout the metropolitan areas of Atlanta, Boston, Detroit, and Los Angeles. In this chapter we describe in more detail the three Employer Surveys from which we draw our data. Following this, to set the context for the results discussed in coming chapters, we provide a snapshot of the recent history of industrial and demographic change in each of the four cities.

Surveys of Employers

There is more than one way to interview employers. As we noted in the previous chapter, we analyze two types of interviews. We draw in part on a Telephone Survey of managers responsible for hiring at 3,510 firms. But primarily, we base this book on two smaller sample in-depth, Face-to-Face Employer Surveys—extended conversations with prespecified questions, but open-ended answers and ample opportunity for impromptu follow-up questions.

The Telephone Survey was designed and for the most part conducted by economist Harry Holzer of Michigan State University.[1] The managers, at companies located in the Atlanta, Boston, Detroit, and Los Angeles metropolitan areas, were interviewed between 1992 and 1995, with a 69 percent response rate for screened firms. Roughly 800 firms were successfully interviewed in each city. The survey questions addressed the characteristics of the business, of the last person hired, and of the job that that person filled. Respondents were asked about frequency of performance of certain tasks, recruiting and screening procedures, other hiring requirements, and the race and gender of the worker hired, as well as of job applicants, employees, and customers. Holzer wrote about the results of this survey in *What Employers Want:*

Job Prospects for Less Educated Workers (1996). In this book, we replicate some of his findings on a slightly expanded data set, and also report new findings from these data.[2]

We conducted the first set of face-to-face interviews with seventy-five managers at fifty-six firms (including multiple respondents at some businesses)—automobile-parts manufacturers, insurance carriers, department stores, and local government—during 1991 and 1992. We refer to this pilot study, funded by the Social Science Research Council, as the SSRC study. We limited our attention to four industries in order to get a well-rounded sense of how hiring dynamics unfold within an industry. We also confined the study to the Detroit and Los Angeles areas.

The second, full-scale Face-to-Face Survey, which we coordinated with our colleague Joleen Kirschenman, comprised 365 conversations with managers at 174 firms already interviewed in the Telephone Survey. We refer to this four-city survey, part of the Multi-City Study of Urban Inequality, as the Multi-City Study. The firms were roughly equally distributed among the Atlanta, Boston, Detroit, and Los Angeles urban areas. Response rates in both the SSRC and the Multi-City Study surveys were about two-thirds. Interviews were taped and transcribed. Transcripts from the Multi-City Study were coded and entered into a qualitative text database to facilitate analysis.

Graduate students carried out almost all of the second wave of interviews, which took place from 1994 to 1996. A different team of one to three students conducted interviews in each metropolitan area. This division of labor made the project possible, since we could not have arranged and conducted 365 interviews across four metropolitan areas by ourselves. However, it also had costs. Some interviewers stuck closely to the questionnaire, whereas others wandered from time to time. Some questioners gave up more easily, at times, when managers avoided questions about differences among racial groups, whereas others pursued the questions like bulldogs. We suspect, based on review of the transcripts, that the difference between infrequent negative assessments of blacks' social skills in Boston and much more frequent criticisms in Atlanta and Los Angeles is more the result of varying interviewer styles than of true differences in employer perceptions.

In this book, we use fictional names for a few businesses from whom we quote repeatedly: "Michigan Utility," "Jack's Junkyard," "Value King Stores," and the like. But since it would be pointless and confusing to invent names for all 174 Multi-City Study and 56 SSRC businesses, we most often ground quotes with just a one- or two-word description of the company.

In all of these surveys, the great majority of interviews targeted jobs requiring no more than a high school education, and the results reported in this book are limited to these lower-skill jobs. Our objective is to examine jobs to which even relatively unskilled inner-city workers could—in theory—have access. In the face-to-face interviews, we sought to converse with up to three managers per workplace: a top exec-utive (where possible, the CEO), a human resource or personnel official responsible for hiring into the relevant sample job, and a frontline man-ager who oversees sample jobholders. In the smallest businesses, these three roles overlap—in fact, the proprietor often does all three, reducing the number of interviews to one. In a few firms with complex manage-ment structures—for example, ones that use temporary agencies or sub-contractors to staff the sample job—we were compelled to conduct more than three interviews, following the chain of command in the temporary agency or other contractor as well as in the core corporation. The upshot was that at 174 firms we interviewed 365 respondents, aver-aging 2.1 informants per business. Interviewers also did their best to get a plant or office tour, and recorded observations of the surroundings.

The Telephone Employer Survey and the four-city In-Depth Em-ployer Survey, in combination with the four-city Household Survey yielding the quotes about experiences of discrimination in the previous chapter, constitute the Multi-City Study of Urban Inequality, funded by the Russell Sage and Ford foundations, with additional financial support for the In-Depth Employer Survey coming from the Rockefeller Founda-tion (Johnson, Oliver, and Bobo 1994). The Multi-City Study undertook three main topics of investigation in the four urban areas where it was based: racial residential segregation, interracial attitudes, and labor mar-kets. Though the Employer Surveys were anchored most firmly in labor market issues, we also connected our research to the other two areas by asking how employers view workers and communities of color.

The Employer Surveys were not simply conducted in parallel with the extensive Household Surveys in each metropolitan area, but were directly linked to them. In the Telephone Survey, about one firm in three surveyed was the current or last employer for a household respon-dent. (The remainder were drawn from business directories purchased from Survey Sampling, Inc.) The sample for the In-Depth Survey con-sisted entirely of household-linked employers already contacted through the Telephone Survey. That is how we are able to quote from managers and an ex-worker at the same business at the outset of chapter 1. Each survey focused on a "sample job," making it the subject of a large share of questions—and the sample job was none other than the job category of the household respondent. (In Telephone Survey firms not drawn from the Household Survey, the sample job was the last job the business hired for, limited to jobs requiring no more than high school.) To select firms for in-depth interviews from the much larger telephone interview sample, we stratified on the occupation of the sample job and the presence or absence of three key types of change that seemed likely to affect employer hiring choices: technological change or organizational change that affected the skills required for the sample job, or a recent relocation. This stratified sampling scheme ensured that we would speak to employers who were grappling with important workplace changes. In theory, the sampling design allows us to reweight any findings to approximate the totality of jobs requiring no more than high school in the Atlanta, Boston, Detroit, and Los Angeles areas. But given the small total sample size of 174 observations, we have chosen simply to report unweighted descriptive statistics.

Basing the Employer Surveys in four cities grounds each interview in a specific metropolitan context. These four places provide fascinating contrasts in labor market climate and racial-ethnic mix. Atlanta is a booming Sunbelt service-sector growth pole, famous for offering opportunity to the African American middle class, but still riven by black-white inequality. The Boston area, a high-technology and financial center still recovering from a deep recession when we conducted our interviews, has seen dramatic growth of Latino and Asian groups in recent years, overshadowing slower expansion of the black population. Detroit combines a deeply depressed, overwhelmingly black Rustbelt hub with economically dynamic, predominantly white suburbs and an economy that remains centered on consumer durables, especially the automobile. In Los Angeles, immigrant-staffed apparel workshops rub shoulders with giant aerospace corporations and Pacific Rim financial titans in a dizzyingly multiethnic patchwork spread across seemingly endless suburban sprawl. We now turn to each city in some greater detail.

A Tale of Four Cities

Interviewer: So how do you see the area around Waltham [a mainly white, middle-class suburb northwest of Boston] as a place to do business?

Respondent (white male chief executive of educational institution): It's very dynamic. There are eleven thousand high-tech jobs in Waltham today compared to ten thousand in Cambridge. There is a demographic sector called Metrowest between here and Framingham and Natick. It has an economic average of family income, individual income, rivaling Fairfield County in southern Connecticut. So it's very prosperous. There's three million square feet of office space in Waltham. There's Polaroid. We have Microsoft. We have several Raytheon installations. It's dynamic.

Interviewer: Can you tell me a little bit about Needham [affluent, mainly white suburb southwest of Boston] as a place to do business?

Respondent: (white male owner of cleaning shop): It's a nice town. It's relatively affluent and the demographics, one of the reasons I'm here is it's, I believe the number is around eighty percent white-collar. It's kind of an affluent Mayberry.

Interviewer: What is Lawrence [extremely poor, largely Latino satellite city northwest of Boston] like as a place to do business?

Respondent: (white, non-Latino male financial officer of manufacturing firm): Right now it's an issue for us. It's all crack houses and prostitutes out here. And it's tough for us right now bringing customers in.

We are interested in two kinds of variation: differences *within* each metropolitan area, as highlighted by these three quotes from Boston-area businesspeople, and variation *across* the four urban complexes. A look at the demography of the four cities underscores the variation they contribute to our study. Table 2.1 shows population and race information for each metropolitan area and central city in 1990. We see the large concentration of blacks in the central cities of Detroit and Atlanta, and the more diverse central cities of Boston and of Los Angeles, whose Latino central-city population dwarfs the other cities. We see the contrasts in the fraction of a metropolitan area's black population that lives in the central city, from a high of 83 percent in Detroit to Atlanta's low of 39 percent.

Table 2.1 also shows the segregation index. This measure, based on census block residential composition, represents the percentage of either blacks or whites who would have to be relocated to another block to achieve zero segregation (random dispersion of the population with respect to race).[3] Like other U.S. metropolitan areas, all four of these cities are highly segregated. But the patterns and trends of segregation differ. Detroit, with the highest segregation level, saw a slight increase in segregation between 1980 and 1990, whereas racial segregation in the other four areas is lower and falling.

In presenting profiles of the four areas, we flesh out the cross-city differences as well as describing the map of economic and racial variation within each area. Because it presents the extreme case in table 2.1, we start by profiling Detroit.

TABLE 2.1   *Population and Race in Four Metropolitan Areas*

	Atlanta	Boston	Detroit	Los Angeles
Metropolitan area				
Population (1000s)	2864	3748	3913	8863
Percentage Black	26.0	6.2	24.0	11.2
Percentage Hispanic	2.0	5.0	1.9	37.8
Percentage Asian	1.8	3.1	1.4	10.8
Central city				
Population (1000s)	394	574	1028	3485
Percentage Black	67.1	28.0	75.5	13.9
Percentage Hispanic	1.8	10.8	2.8	39.9
Percentage Asian	0.9	5.3	0.8	9.8
Percentage living in the central city				
Total population	13.9	15.3	26.3	39.3
Black	38.5	63.1	83.2	49.1
White	7.8	11.0	7.7	36.6
Black-white segregation index[a]				
1980	79.0	76.3	88.7	80.1
1990	72.6	70.4	88.8	71.4

Source: U.S. Department of Commerce 1990. The metropolitan areas for the purposes of these numbers are very close to, but slightly different from, each city's metropolitan statistical area (MSA). In each case, the metropolitan area in the table corresponds to the area from which all the Multi-City Study surveys were drawn. See Harry Holzer (1996), chap. 1, n. 10, for a definition of the metropolitan area used in this table.

[a]The Black-White Segregation Index is the index of dissimilarity as calculated and reported by Reynolds Farley and William Frey (1994). A value of 0 represents completely random dispersion of the population by race, while a value of 100 represents a situation in which every block in the metropolitan area was entirely white or entirely black. The average score for metropolitan areas in 1990 was 64.3 and 68.8 in 1980.

Detroit: The Black-White Line

Industrial suburbanization in Detroit was launched by Henry Ford in the early 1900s, accelerated during the 1940s, and surged again in 1967 with white flight following Detroit's riot. (See map 2.1 for a breakdown of Detroit and the surrounding area.) The current map of industrial activity in the Detroit area shows concentrations of manufacturing and industrial parks along every major road or highway leading out of Detroit, but relatively few within the city itself (SEMCOG 1984).

The deindustrialization of the U.S. auto industry began at the outset of the 1980s, taking a heavy employment toll especially in Detroit and in the "Downriver" area southeast of the city. Nonetheless, the pulse of southeastern Michigan is still set by the auto industry—the Big Three (General Motors, Ford, Chrysler) joined by newcomers such as Mazda, with a plant in Flat Rock, at the southern extreme of Wayne

MAP 2.1   *Detroit Metropolitan Area*

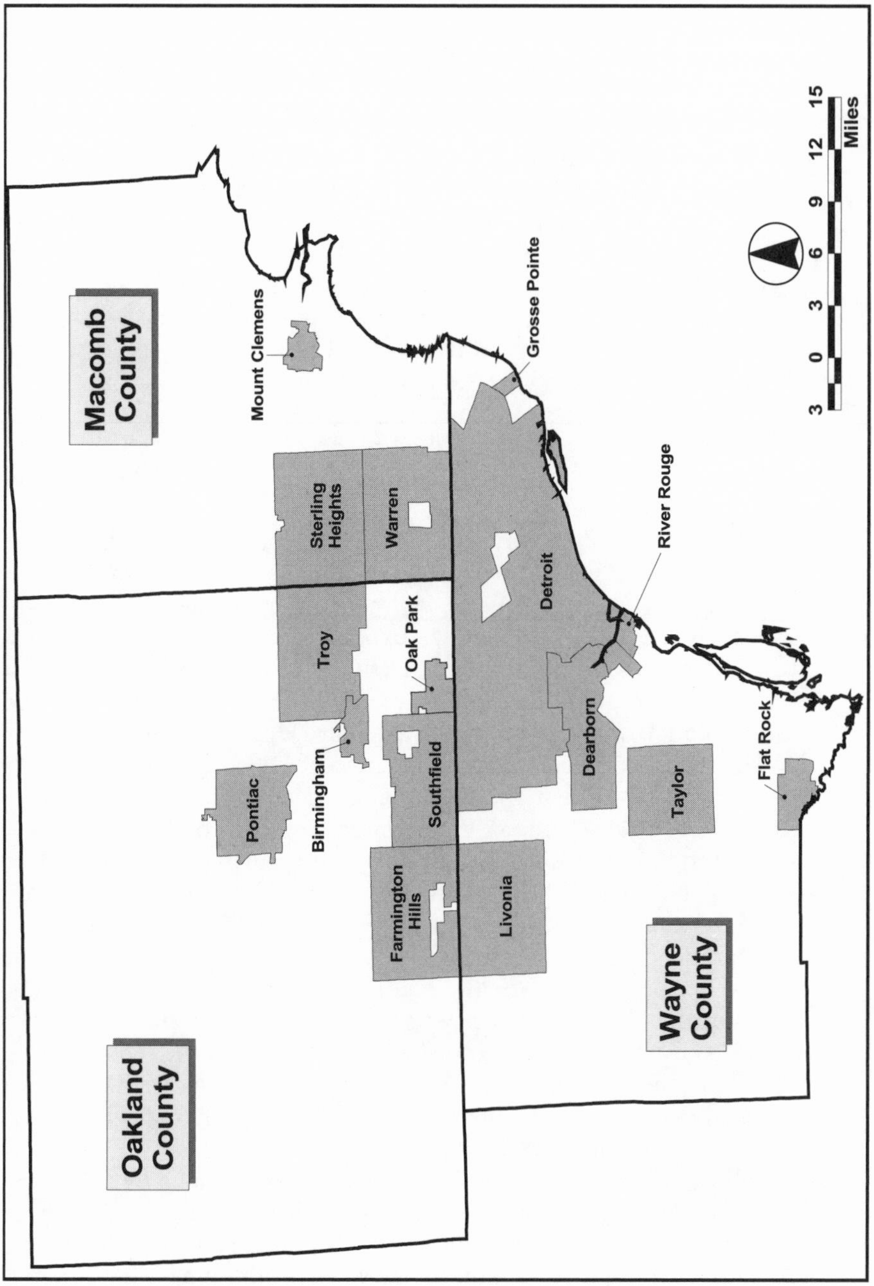

Oakland County

Macomb County

Mount Clemens

Sterling Heights

Warren

Troy

Oak Park

Pontiac

Birmingham

Southfield

Farmington Hills

Livonia

Detroit

Grosse Pointe

River Rouge

Dearborn

Taylor

Flat Rock

Wayne County

3 0   3   6   9   12   15
                              Miles

Source: U.S. Department of Commerce, Bureau of the Census.

23

County. One legacy of auto's sway is the high rate of union membership: in the Detroit metropolitan area, 21 percent of workers are union members (and 31 percent in the city proper), compared with 19 percent in Boston and Los Angeles, 16 percent nationwide, and a mere 8 percent in right-to-work Atlanta.

Overlying the industrial landscape is a starkly segregated racial geography. Detroit, perhaps more than any other city in the United States, has the image of "chocolate city, vanilla suburbs," in musician George Clinton's phrase (put to academic use by Farley et al. [1978])—an African American central city surrounded by nearly lily-white communities. The Detroit metropolitan area was the most segregated of the forty-seven U.S. metropolitan areas with populations of one million or more in 1990, and the only one to increase its level of segregation between 1980 and 1990 (Farley and Frey 1994). While 76 percent of Detroit residents were black, only 5 percent of the residents of the remainder of the three-county area of Wayne, Macomb, and Oakland were (Farley et al. 1993). Put another way, the numbers in table 2.1 indicate that 83 percent of blacks in the metropolitan area lived in Detroit and 93 percent of whites lived outside it. A long history of resistance to integration by white communities helps explain these dramatic contrasts. The racial differences are compounded with class: in 1990, Detroit poverty rates were four times as high as in the surrounding area, and median family income was less than half as great (Moss and Tilly 1993b).

The racial and economic divergence of Detroit from its suburbs began in the 1940s, when the first major wave of industrial suburbanization coincided with the arrival of large numbers of black migrants responding to the explosive growth of manufacturing during World War II. Whites in Detroit met the black influx with hostility that periodically flared into violence, boiling over in 1942 in the violent resistance to the construction of the Sojourner Truth public housing project for blacks, and in the race riot of 1943. Exclusionary homeowner compacts and attacks on black in-migrants persisted in large sections of Detroit into the 1960s, prompting an outcry from a civil rights movement grounded in the churches and unions (Darden et al. 1987). Nonetheless, African Americans continued to move in, while whites, along with industrial and commercial employers, moved out.

Following the riot of 1967, both whites and blacks fled the city, but given differing degrees of access to the suburbs, whites exited at much greater rates. From one-third of Detroit's population in 1960, blacks became a majority by 1970. But the city was imploding, declining from a peak of 1.6 million in 1952 to just over 1 million in 1990. Even more tellingly, the city of Detroit tumbled from 42 percent of the three-county area's population in 1960 to 24 percent in 1990 and 22 percent in

1995 (Darden et al. 1987; Moss and Tilly 1993; Rusk 1999). Detroit's share of assessed value shrank from 50 percent in 1960 to 16 percent in 1980, 7 percent in 1990, and 6 percent in 1995 (Darden et al. 1987, 21; Rusk 1999, 60). Perhaps the most graphic symbol of this disinvestment is the boarded-up hulk of Hudson's downtown department store—once the anchor of Detroit's downtown commercial district, but closed in 1983—surrounded by abandoned commercial and office buildings. Detroit's first African American mayor, Coleman Young, widely (and, in our opinion, sometimes unfairly) seen as antagonistic to white suburbs and businesses, won office in 1973 only to preside over this decline. Young served five terms and was succeeded in 1993 by Dennis Archer, another African American with a more moderate image.

While the disparity between city and suburb in the Detroit metropolitan area is stark, it is no knife edge. Within each of the two halves of this divide can be found significant racial variations (fudge ripples within the overall chocolate-vanilla pattern, if you will), as well as striking class differences. Detroit proper can be divided into three concentric rings, following a classification by the City Planning Commission (City of Detroit 1978; Hill 1984). The rings start from the southern center of Detroit, fronting on the Detroit River to the southeast. The "inner city" includes the central business district, the "revitalized" riverfront area (including the landmark Renaissance Center), but also the poorest and most deteriorated residential areas. It combines riverfront gentry, white and black, with desperate black inner-city poor. The "middle city" includes the large majority of Detroit's black population. This area, while not as poor as the most stricken inner-city areas, is struggling with poverty, deterioration, and abandonment, and its economic indicators fall each decade. Finally, "outer city" comprises the northwest, north, and northeast periphery of Detroit. The outer city includes the main remaining white or mixed neighborhoods, and the most economically advantaged areas of the city—in some cases relatively indistinguishable from the surrounding suburbs. However, over the last decade these relatively privileged outer city areas have shrunk to a very small fringe. In 1970, 29 percent of Detroit's census tracts had 20 percent or more of the population in poverty, but this proportion soared to 48 percent in 1980 and 75 percent in 1990 (Kasarda 1993).

We can also usefully distinguish among the three counties that make up Detroit's suburbs. Macomb County, to the northeast, is a blue-collar area with a strong segregationist history. Although it gained much manufacturing employment during the early shift to the suburbs (1940 to 1970), it has benefited least of the three counties from the more recent "edge city" growth of high technology, service, and commercial centers outside the city. Overall, Macomb County's black population remains a tiny 1.5 percent. The county's largest community, Warren, just north of Detroit, has a history of bitter resistance to integration. In 1970, Warren citizens voted to forfeit HUD funds rather than allow the development of integrated housing. In the 1992 Detroit Area Study, a majority of blacks and whites still agreed that Warren residents "would be upset" if a black family moved into that area, and the 1990 black population was a mere 0.7 percent (Farley et al. 1993). Sterling Heights, just north of Warren and second in size among Macomb's cities, has even fewer African Americans, 0.4 percent. Macomb does include a few black enclaves: black populations climbed into the double digits in Mt. Clemens and the tiny village of New Haven (Wayne State University 1991).

Oakland County, to the northwest of Detroit, is the most prosperous of the three counties and also the most open to black in-migration. Oakland County claims to be "the business center of southeastern Michigan," and the numbers back it up: by 1988, the 24.8 million square feet of office space in place or under construction in Southfield, the county's business heart, exceeded the total in Detroit (Chafets 1990, 139). Indeed, one-fifth of the Fortune 500 companies have world, national, or regional headquarters in Southfield (Darden et al. 1987, 34); in 1988 Oakland County was the second wealthiest county in the United States, lagging behind only Manhattan (U.S. Department of Commerce 1988).

Southfield and the smaller Oak Park, both of which border Detroit and have large Jewish populations, have the reputation of being open to African Americans. By 1990 Southfield's population was 29 percent black, and Oak Park's 34 percent, placing them among the most integrated cities in the area. The northern city of Pontiac, at 42 percent black, is viewed by many as a mini-Detroit; housing values there fell 10 percent between 1980 and 1990 despite rising values countywide (Wayne State University 1991). On the other hand, thriving Troy, Oakland County's runner-up to Southfield as a business center, was rated as hostile to blacks by majorities of blacks and whites in the Detroit Multi-City Study household survey, and its black population languishes at 1 percent (Farley et al. 1993). And overall, African Americans make up only 7 percent of Oakland County's population (Wayne State University 1991).

Finally, the remainder of Wayne County (excluding Detroit itself) spreads to the east, west, and south of Detroit. Wayne County takes in a diverse swath: the posh Grosse Pointe bedroom communities, the deindustrializing Downriver suburbs such as Ecorse, River Rouge, and Taylor to the south, and new corporate growth poles, such as the Fairlane planned community created within Dearborn in the early 1970s, or "automation alley," the high-tech industrial corridor stretching west from Detroit to Ann Arbor along I-94. There are even two small majority-black communities, Highland Park and Inkster—the latter created by Henry Ford as a segregated community for his black workforce at the same time as he founded Dearborn for his white workforce. Such is the variety that leads Joe Darden et al. (1987, 37) to describe Wayne County as "the region in microcosm."

Mirroring the region, Wayne County remains quite segregated. Excluding 76 percent black Detroit, the rest of the county's black population stands at 7 percent. Livonia, the county's largest city after Detroit, located only two miles from Detroit's western frontier, has a black population of 0.3 percent. Dearborn, Detroit's neighbor to the southwest, has a reputation for intransigent resistance to black entry, spearheaded by white supremacist mayor Orville Hubbard from 1941 to 1973. Despite Hubbard's exit from the political stage, only 0.6 percent of the population of Dearborn was black in 1990, and 90 percent of black respondents agreed that Dearborn residents would be upset if a black family moved in (Farley et al. 1993). Dearborn, a middle-class community slightly less wealthy than Southfield, was rated a considerably more desirable place to live than Southfield by whites and considerably less desirable by blacks.

The three-county area is stitched together by a transportation system consisting primarily of freeways radiating from downtown Detroit. Public transit links between Detroit and surrounding areas are notoriously bad, reflecting many of the communities' history of resistance to black access.

In summary, the racial and class map confronting Detroit-area employers has two levels. At a high level of aggregation, Detroit is black and poor, whereas the suburbs are white and relatively affluent. However, these smooth generalizations disaggregate into more textured differences. Detroit's struggling middle city, mainly working- and middle-class blacks, is flanked by the more desperate inner city and by the whiter, wealthier outer city. The suburbs are not monolithically white: witness the relatively mixed Southfield and Oak Park and majority-black Inkster and Highland Park. Nor are they monolithically prosperous: deindustrialization has hit hard at Macomb County and at the Downriver towns of Wayne County. As we examine how employers themselves map the Detroit metropolitan area, we must keep a sharp watch out for both levels of cognitive—and actual—geography.

Atlanta: The Line Moves North

As the capital city of the New South, Atlanta is transforming its landscape. The Atlanta metropolitan area has experienced tremendous economic growth over the past two decades and has earned the reputation of being a mecca for African American opportunity—at least for those in the middle class. Nonetheless, racial and economic inequality remains deeply embedded in the geography of the Atlanta region.

Table 2.1 shows that blacks are not confined to the central city as in Detroit, and the segregation index for Atlanta is noticeably lower as well. Nonetheless, the Atlanta metro area is markedly divided between majority-white areas in the northern suburbs and majority-black areas in the southern suburbs and inner city (see map 2.2). Jobs and population are growing at a rapid clip in the north, while growth in the southern suburbs has been spottier and the inner city struggles to remain viable. Historically, Interstate 20, which cuts across metro Atlanta horizontally just south of downtown, was the defining line between black and white, and consequently between south and north. As the population of the metro area has increased over the past three decades, the black-white dividing line has moved increasingly north, to where it now roughly separates the southern two-thirds of the city of Atlanta from the northern third and beyond (Bayor 1988; Rutheiser 1996). As African Americans have pushed farther north, whites have also increasingly gone farther north to develop the suburbs outside Atlanta's perimeter (Interstate 285) as far as thirty miles from downtown. This bifurcation of space is facilitated by the sharp resistance of northern suburban homeowners to the extension of the mass transit system, MARTA, into their counties—a move that could provide African Americans from the city and the southern suburbs access to expanding job opportunities in the north. Northern suburban homeowners have also rebuffed efforts to develop modestly priced housing in these high-income areas.

Fulton County, which extends from the north of the Atlanta metro area through the bulk of the city down to the southwest corner, reflects some of the larger trends in the metro area because of its size and span. In the southern half of Fulton County, the African-American population has grown from just over 15 percent in some areas in 1980 to at least 75 percent in 1990 (Rutheiser 1996). In the northern half of that county, however, African Americans continue to comprise less than 15 percent of the population (Rutheiser 1996). This county includes the largest numbers of low-income and high-income households in the metro area, and class corresponds heavily with race (U.S. Department of Commerce 1992). In true southern spirit, north Fulton residents have even recently begun to push for secession from the county, claiming that their taxes are disproportionately being spent on the south side.

The population in the city of Atlanta itself has declined almost 19 percent since 1960, including a drop of more than 7 percent between 1980 and 1990 (though the population rebounded slightly over the 1990s). This is particularly striking because population in the surround-

MAP 2.2   *Metropolitan Atlanta*

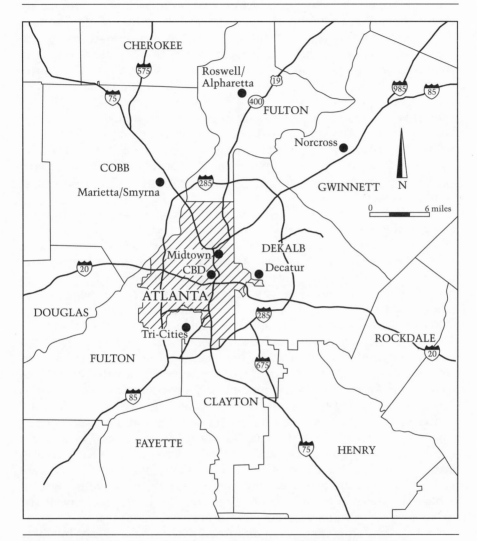

Source: Cartographic Research Laboratory, Department of Geography, Georgia State University, 1999.

ing counties experienced double-digit and in some cases even triple-digit percentage growth over the 1980s (Hartshorn and Ihlanfeldt 2000).[4] Despite the population outflows, the city's racial balance has remained fairly constant, with African Americans consistently making up about two-thirds of the city's population from 1980 to 1992 (U.S. Department of Commerce 1988, 1994). However, like Fulton County, the city is bi-furcated by race and geography. White Atlanta households' incomes averaged $61,691 in 1989, nearly $40,000 above black households' average of $22,322 (Hartshorn and Ihlanfeldt 2000). In fact, despite the metro area's prosperity, the number of census tracts with 20 percent or more in poverty increased from 56 in 1970 to 91 in 1990—almost all majority black neighborhoods (Rusk 1999). White residents are concentrated in the northern part of the city, and African Americans in the south. Despite this separation, Atlanta maintains its reputation as "the city too busy to hate." Atlanta-area residents were asked (in the Multi-City Study of Urban Inequality) whether Midtown residents (in the northern, whiter area of Atlanta) would welcome a black family or be upset, and only 9 percent of those with an opinion responded that Midtowners would be upset.

Outside the city all metro counties have experienced growth, especially in the northern suburbs of Gwinnett, Forsyth, and Cherokee. Employers we spoke to highlighted the growth. The CEO of a real estate firm, for instance, joked that the Atlanta area "is growing so rapidly that if you go on a three-day vacation you've completely lost touch with what's going on by the time you get back." The regional manager of a home improvement company echoed the sentiment for the northern suburbs in particular: "You can't find anyplace around here that's not just going out and bulging at the seams." It is noteworthy that fast-growing Gwinnett, Forsyth, and Cherokee counties are all over 90 percent white. The counties experiencing the least growth since 1980, DeKalb and Fulton, also have the highest proportions of African Americans. As blacks have increasingly settled outside the city of Atlanta, DeKalb County (east of Atlanta) saw a dramatic rise in its black population, climbing from 27 percent to 42 percent black; Fulton County remained steady at around 50 percent black. Decatur, in DeKalb County just east of Atlanta, is over 75 percent black, and very few Atlanta metro-area residents predicted that Decatur residents would be upset if a black family moved in—about 6 percent, the lowest for any of the Atlanta areas for which this question was posed.

Other outlying counties remain overwhelmingly white, but here as well the black percentage has grown, if only slightly. Cobb County to the northwest, notorious for its conservative politics, crept up from less than 5 percent black in 1980 to almost 10 percent in 1990, although its northernmost section is still almost all white. Marietta and Smyrna, just northwest of Atlanta, form the urban hub of the county, and have seen moderate increases in their black populations. In contrast with the responses for Midtown and Decatur, 29 percent of Atlantans stated that Marietta-Smyrna residents "would be upset" by the arrival of a black family. The percentage is even higher—31 percent—

in Norcross, northeast of the city in a white, wealthy area of Gwinnett County just past the edge of an expanding African American population within the county. Overall, blacks still account for only a tiny 5 percent of Gwinnett County's population. Atlantans predicted the most negative reaction of all—50 percent said that residents would be upset if a black family moved in—in Roswell-Alpharetta, north of the city in booming northern Fulton County.

The Latino and Asian populations of the Atlanta region remain small, only about 50,000 apiece (about 2 percent of total population) in the entire nine-county region as of 1990. However, their robust growth rates between 1980 and 1990 (134 percent for Latinos and a dramatic 331 percent for Asians) appear to be harbingers of future importance for these groups.

Originally developed as a transportation center (a railway hub), Atlanta has always had a largely service-based economy. Thus the decline of manufacturing and the rise of services that occurred across much of this country's urban space did not have the same fallout here as in many northern cities. Moreover, the city of Atlanta actually added more than five thousand manufacturing jobs between 1980 and 1995, bucking national trends and notching a small (less than 1 percent) increase in manufacturing employment as a percentage of the city's total. However, neighboring areas eclipsed manufacturing growth in Atlanta proper, so that Atlanta's share of the region's manufacturing jobs dipped from 33 percent to 18 percent. Similar trends marked all major industries (Smith 1997). Indeed, while the "center of Atlanta" has not emptied as it did in Detroit, Atlanta is no longer solely centered around its downtown. The airport anchors the south; government, education, and professional sports dominate the old downtown area; the new retail, restaurant, and nightspot epicenter lies largely in a predominantly white area called Buckhead in the northern part of the city; and the primary new center of industry, business growth, technological innovation, and economic expansion lies in the northern suburbs. "The center of Atlanta is moving north," in the words of a manufacturing manager. Areas east of the city have also boomed, as a department store manager explained:

The way Atlanta's grown, the perimeter used to be like this [gestures] and Atlanta was right in the middle. Well, now the perimeter is way out here [to the east] and [Route] 285 doesn't ring it like it used to. Well, this store [east of the city] is right in the heart of Atlanta.

This all points to Atlanta's multinodal, rather than simply inner-city-suburban character. "They have these little mini-downtowns all over," as a top executive at a nonprofit agency put it.

Boston: Black Plus Latino-Asian
Inner Cities

The mix and geography of Boston-area jobs have changed markedly over the last several decades. Traditional manufacturing (textiles, shoes, and leather), once Boston's mainstay, declined from the 1920s onward, and Boston proper has had little manufacturing since the end of World War II. Outside of Boston, the decline in traditional manufacturing was initially offset by an expansion of defense-related manufacturing during and after World War II, concentrated around aircraft production that came to a halt in the early 1970s. Computer manufacturing industries boomed in the late 1970s and early 1980s, and related software and instrument industries remain vital. In recent decades, manufacturing has taken place well outside the city, either in satellite cities fifteen to forty miles from Boston or dispersed along distant highways that circumscribe the city. Meanwhile, the economy of the City of Boston has been fueled by a growth in sectors such as legal services; finance, insurance and real estate; and health care (Harrison and Kluver 1988; Porter 1994).

The consequence of this transformation of jobs in the city coupled with the suburbanization of higher income and more highly educated populations is that city residents with relatively low educational credentials have faced continued erosion of job opportunities. Between 1970 and 1990, the fraction of jobs in Boston held by persons without a high school degree plummeted from 29 percent to 7 percent (Porter 1994). By contrast, the fraction of city residents over age twenty-five without a high school degree was 28 percent (among people of color, the fractions are much larger—33 percent for blacks, 47 percent for Latinos, and 38 percent for Asians).

Beyond Boston is a set of residential suburbs, the most affluent of which are to the west and northwest, and a set of smaller, far less affluent industrial cities (see map 2.3). The residential suburbs supply the commuters who dominate the job market in Boston (in 1989, 77 percent of jobs in the city were held by commuters [Dougherty 1993]). Some neighboring industrial cities have become linked to the Boston economy, such as Quincy to the southeast (a recent location for low-level support jobs in the financial, insurance, and real estate industries) and Cambridge to the north (where manufacturing jobs have given way to a boom in upper-end high-technology service jobs complementing Cambridge's well-known area of specialization, higher education services). Other cities cut and fashioned by the industrial revolution of the nineteenth century, such as Lowell and Lawrence, thirty miles to the north of Boston, have struggled through most of this century. And in a ring around Boston, the well-known high-tech industrial complexes dot the landscape.

The public transportation system of Boston is quite extensive. Subway and buses link the various parts of the city, the border cities and towns, and the inner residential suburbs. Most of the outlying cities are on commuter rail lines. Travel from the subway and rail lines without a car becomes more difficult, of course, as one moves farther away from the city.

How does race map to the economic geography of greater Boston? In the decades prior to the 1980s, the nonwhite population of the greater Boston area was primarily black and living within the city of Boston. Further, blacks were concentrated in a very few neighborhoods close to the central city, mainly Roxbury and the South End. In 1980, 8 percent of the population of the Boston metropolitan area was nonwhite, and blacks comprised 4 percent—half of the total nonwhite population.[5] Within the city of Boston, however, blacks constituted 22 percent of the population and 75 percent of the nonwhite population. The segregation of blacks within the City of Boston, and the resistance to black access by white neighborhoods, were spotlighted in the mid-1970s by the difficult and at times violent course of court-ordered school desegregation (Lukas 1985). Only a few communities—all working-class cities—outside Boston had substantial communities of color in 1980, notably Cambridge (11 percent black), Lawrence (16 percent Latino), Chelsea (14 percent Latino), and Lowell (5 percent Latino) to the north, and Brockton (9 percent black) to the south.

During the 1980s, the overall picture of spatial demography changed significantly. By 1990, greater Boston had become much more racially diverse, with a pace and extent of change exceeding the nationwide average. The proportion of blacks did not change greatly. The black population, still the most populous nonwhite group in the greater Boston area, as table 2.1 shows, grew primarily in areas where it was already concentrated: Boston (mainly in the low-income neighborhoods of Roxbury, Mattapan, and North Dorchester), Cambridge, and Brockton (where the increase was sizable: from 9 percent of its population up to 23 percent).

It was the inflow of Latinos and Asians that dramatically altered the terrain. Dominicans, Central Americans, Puerto Ricans, and Southeast Asians immigrated to the area in large numbers. Latinos almost doubled their population over the decade of the 1980s, reaching 5 percent of the total Boston metropolitan area in 1990.[6] The Asian population more than doubled and made up 3 percent of the greater Boston population in 1990. Latinos in Boston have settled particularly in areas that were primarily black (Roxbury and North Dorchester, as well as predominantly white Jamaica Plain), climbing from 6 to 11 percent of the population of the city itself between 1980 and 1990. The most rapid growth among Latinos, however, occurred in Lowell, Chelsea, and Lawrence. The frac-

MAP 2.3   *Greater Boston Social Survey Study Area, 1993 to 1994*

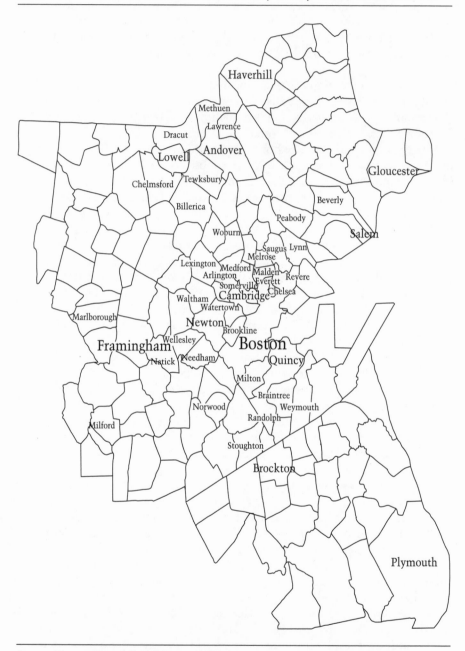

Source: Greater Boston Social Survey 1995.
Note: Named cities and towns of 25,000 population or more in 1990.

tion of the Lowell population that is Latino doubled, from 5 percent to 10 percent, between 1980 and 1990. Chelsea's population vaulted from 14 percent Latino in 1980 to 31 percent Latino in 1990, and the Latino population of Lawrence exploded from 16 percent in 1980 to almost 42 percent in 1990. The census's tendency to undercount minorities suggests that the actual figures are even higher than those reported.

Southeast Asian populations have expanded in some Boston neighborhoods, but the largest jump in the numbers of Asians took place in Lowell and surrounding areas. From less than 1 percent of the Lowell population in 1980 (primarily Vietnamese), Southeast Asians made up an estimated 20 percent in the late 1980s. The 1990 census reported a figure of 11 percent, in part due to out-migration after the region's economy crashed in 1988 and 1989, though this figure is also likely to be depressed by undercounting. The majority of Southeast Asians in Lowell are Cambodian, and in 1990 Lowell had the second largest population of Cambodians in the United States (behind Long Beach, California). Southeast Asians as well as Latinos in Lowell were absorbed both into some of the traditional lower-skilled manufacturing industries and, to a degree, into the higher-tech electronics assembly industries.

Overall, Boston-area Latinos and Asians appear to have developed a greater geographic diffusion than have blacks. One measure is that affluent blacks still overwhelmingly live in Boston, while more affluent Asians and Latinos are more likely to be in the suburbs, mimicking patterns for more affluent whites. Among white and Asian households with incomes in excess of $75,000 who live in either Boston or its contiguous suburbs, about 60 percent live in the suburbs. The figure for Latinos is 38 percent, and for blacks it is only 18 percent.

One index of the racial climate in the various neighborhoods and suburbs of Boston is the extent to which Boston-area residents expect current residents to be upset by a black, Latino, or Asian family moving in. Large majorities agreed that the residents of wealthy, very white Newton, to the west, would be upset if a black or Latino family moved in—64 percent in the case of a black family and 71 percent if the family were Latino. The numbers were quite similar for gritty, working class, and overwhelmingly white South Boston, which has a long and sad history of racial attacks and harassment against people of color. Large minorities—over 40 percent—felt that an Asian family would be unwelcome in both places as well. Fewer Bostonians expected families of color to be unwelcome in Cambridge, but despite Cambridge's liberal reputation and recent surge in demographic diversity, 36 percent of Bostonians predicted that Cambridge residents would be upset by a black family moving in, with lower figures of 32 percent for a Latino family and 17 percent for an Asian one. Boston-area residents attributed the greatest tolerance of diversity to the outlying mill towns of Lowell (where 16 percent felt residents would be upset by the arrival of a black family) and Brockton (where 26 percent predicted a negative reaction). Interestingly, in Lowell, where the rapid 1980s influx of Southeast Asians sparked a backlash, including the sole "English-only" referendum in Massachusetts, a slightly greater percentage expected residents to be upset at the arrival of an Asian family than a black or Latino one.

In sum, the city of Boston facing employers is still majority white (58 percent in 1990) but significantly less so than a decade earlier (68 percent), with minority populations concentrated in identifiable inner-city neighborhoods. The larger Boston area that employers view holds a few pockets of minority concentration close to the city—notably in Chelsea, Cambridge, and Lynn, the working-class cities along the northern border—plus large concentrations of varied groups of people of color in some more distant old manufacturing cities, including Brockton to the south and Lowell and Lawrence to the north. These latter satellite cities are large enough to form their own patterns of racial geography with surrounding suburbs, but they are linked to the greater Boston-area economy as well.

Los Angeles: What Is the Inner City?

The seemingly straightforward task of describing the objective contours of a particular urban space becomes bewildering when one arrives at Los Angeles (Waldinger and Bozorgmehr 1996). However, the urban sprawl and demographic diversity that make Los Angeles famous are relatively recent developments. Early suburbanization in the 1910s and 1920s created streetcar suburbs at the end of the Red Car lines, but massive suburbanization awaited mass automobile ownership, the construction of freeways, and the outward shift of industrial activity in later decades—particularly from the 1950s onward (Laslett 1996). And for most of this century, the bulk of Angelenos were white, native-born, and Protestant—despite the city's origins as part of Spain's network of colonies (Davis 1990).

Today, Los Angeles's ethnic diversity is such that journalists routinely describe Los Angeles with phrases like "the most ethnically diverse [metropolitan area] in the nation" and "the face of the future" (Bennett 1991). This picture changed dramatically even in the twenty years between 1970 and 1990. The Los Angeles County population, 71 percent white and Anglo in 1970, was in 1990 just over 40 percent Anglo, with an almost equal percentage (37 percent) Latino and sizable black and Asian groups (each 11 percent) as well (Grant 2000, figure 1).[7] This demographic seesaw reflects massive population movements: between 1970 and 1990, the population of the county added 2 million, but the non-Latino white population declined by 1.4 million. African Americans held steady at about 10 percent of the county's population, growing at a 26 percent rate, equal to that of the county as a whole between 1970 and 1990. But the number of Latinos surged by 238 percent and the Asian population exploded by 426 percent. These changes reflect migration patterns (whites and, to a lesser extent, blacks moving out, Latinos and Asians moving in), but also differing age structures and fertility rates.

Interestingly, Los Angeles's residential segregation remained moderate in the early part of this century. Despite the existence of ghettos and barrios, between 1880 and 1920 Mexicans and African Americans were relatively dispersed across the city. However, by 1917 whites began to adopt racial covenants barring home sales to people of color, particularly in the southern and western parts of the city (Laslett 1996). Discrimination against Mexicans was exemplified by the 1942 Sleepy Lagoon incident, in which the Los Angeles Police Department arrested twenty-two young Mexican Americans involved in an altercation and told the grand jury that "Mexicans [were] inherently criminal and biologically prone to violence" (Sanchez 1993, 266, cited in Laslett 1996, 57). And Japanese Americans, the largest Asian ethnic group at the time, were placed in internment camps and had their property confiscated—in many cases permanently—during World War II. Despite these vicious instances of discrimination, however, Latinos and Asians began to settle widely across the metropolitan area in the postwar decades.

African Americans remained more concentrated. Blacks fought bitter legal and political battles to gain access to areas such as Watts. They won a signal victory when the Supreme Court ruled in 1948 (in a case involving black home buyers in Watts) that racial covenants were illegal, but various forms of resistance by white realtors, bankers, and sellers were not definitively outlawed until the Open Housing Act of 1968 (Laslett 1996). Even more recent opposition by homeowner associations to new development—typically under environmental banners—often primarily reflects an interest in keeping neighborhoods racially and socioeconomically homogeneous. Mike Davis (1990) graphically described the race and class character of the gated residences of the wealthy, the walled subdivisions of the middle class, and the surveilled shopping areas and public spaces.

In 1970, the Los Angeles black-white dissimilarity index stood at 90 out of a possible 100, indicating virtually complete separation of these two groups (only Chicago and Gary, Indiana, were more segregated) (Grant 2000; Massey and Denton 1993). As table 2.1 indicates, this stark segregation had moderated to a degree by 1980, and again by 1990,

MAP 2.4   Los Angeles Metropolitan Area

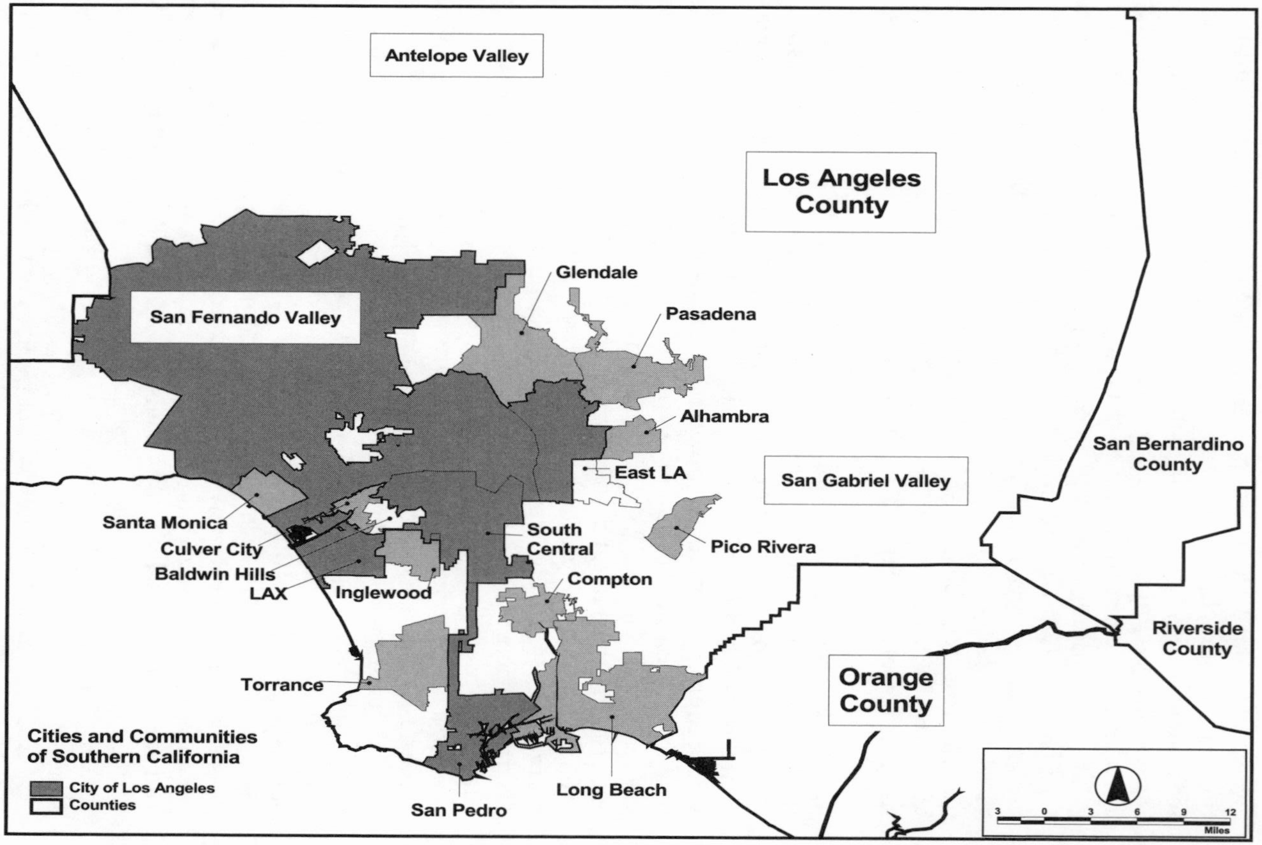

Antelope Valley

Los Angeles County

San Bernardino County

Riverside County

San Gabriel Valley

Orange County

Glendale

Pasadena

Alhambra

East LA

Pico Rivera

South Central

Compton

Long Beach

San Fernando Valley

San Pedro

Santa Monica

Culver City

Baldwin Hills

LAX

Inglewood

Torrance

Cities and Communities
of Southern California

City of Los Angeles

Counties

3 0 3 6 9 12
Miles

Source: U.S. Department of Commerce, Bureau of the Census.

though blacks remain the most spatially segregated ethnic group in Los Angeles. "Racial Lines Blur," declared an *L.A. Times* headline on the 1990 census results (Clifford and Roark 1991). The proportion of Anglos living in majority-Anglo neighborhoods dropped from 47 percent in 1980 to 30 percent in 1990; the proportion of African Americans living in predominantly black neighborhoods fell even more dramatically, from 35 percent to 13 percent—reflecting both Latino and Asian in-migration to historically black neighborhoods and black dispersion.

The two main centers of black residence remain South Central Los Angeles and, secondarily, the Pasadena area. Ted Watkins, president of the Watts Labor Community Action Committee, characterized South Central by saying, "This is one of those 60 percent unemployment communities. It's like looking at the problems in Bangladesh or something, and then realizing you're in South Central L.A." (interview with authors, May 21, 1991). In recent years, however, more well-off African Americans, along with whites, have shifted north and east to San Bernardino and Riverside counties (Clifford and Roark 1991). Given a list of seven Los Angeles areas, Angelenos predicted that blacks would be most welcome in Baldwin Hills (a predominantly black, middle-class community) and least welcome in Glendale (65 percent white, and north of the city), where almost half supposed that current residents would react negatively to black newcomers. About 30 percent or more of area residents stated that a black family would be unwelcome in all areas *except* Baldwin Hills and majority-white Culver City (the remaining areas include two predominantly white communities, the overwhelmingly Latino Pico Rivera, and Asian-Latino-white Alhambra).[8]

An expanding Latino population—in which Mexicans and Mexican-Americans are increasingly joined by Central Americans and others—has begun to overtake the black majority in South Central Los Angeles. South Central, virtually all black in 1970, had in 1990 equal shares of blacks and Latinos. Latinos have settled far from the traditional East Los Angeles barrio, challenging Anglo strongholds in the San Fernando Valley and elsewhere. Nonetheless, Latino-white segregation has actually grown in recent decades, while black-white segregation declined. Typically, Los Angeles–area residents were about half as likely to predict that a Latino family would be unwelcome in selected communities as to predict that a black family would be unwelcome. (The major exceptions were Latino stronghold Pico Rivera, where only 5 percent thought Latinos would be unwelcome, compared with 29 percent for blacks, and majority-black Baldwin Hills, where respondents were more than twice as likely to predict a negative reaction to Latinos as to blacks.)

Asian (along with Middle Eastern) immigrants now inhabit the once all-white, middle-class neighborhoods in the San Gabriel Valley. Asians have also crowded into downtown, Long Beach and neighboring communities, and Cerritos and La Mirada along the border with Orange County to the southeast. Los Angeles residents saw Asian newcomers as being more welcome than blacks or Latinos in all the selected neighborhoods, except Pico Rivera and Baldwin Hills. The Los Angeles Asian population has also become increasingly multiethnic. Japanese, the largest Asian ethnic group as of 1970, have been left behind by Chinese, Filipinos, and Koreans, with Vietnamese, Asian Indians, and the residual category of "other Asians" (including a large Cambodian community based in Long Beach) catching up quickly (Cheng and Yang 1996).

Anglos maintain their exclusive enclaves along the coast—Santa Monica, Malibu, Brentwood—but increasingly have moved north into the Antelope Valley and east into San Bernardino and Riverside counties. As with Latinos and Asians, it is risky to view non-Hispanic whites in the Los Angeles region as a unitary group, since the category in 1990 included 82,000 foreign-born Armenians, 63,000 foreign-born Iranians, and 400,000 other foreign-born whites, including a large Russian population (Sabagh and Bozorgmehr 1996).

African Americans, the poorest racial-ethnic group in the county in 1979, were edged out for that dubious distinction by Latinos in 1989 (Moss and Tilly 1993b, table III.3). Both groups experienced grim poverty rates, almost 50 percent greater than the Los Angeles County average, more than 2.5 times as high as the Los Angeles Anglo population (Asians fell in between), and nearly twice the nation's 13 percent poverty rate (for persons) in 1989. Furthermore, poverty rates for blacks within the city of Los Angeles were essentially unchanged over the ten-year period; the percentage of Latinos in poverty rose markedly.

In 1989 blacks' median family income lagged behind Latinos' by a tiny $200 a year (Moss and Tilly 1993b, Table III.4). This represented a narrowing of the gap between black and Latino families over the previous ten years—but relative to non-Latino whites, almost all of the narrowing took place via Latino incomes falling rather than black incomes rising. Both groups' medians stood at around 60 percent that of whites; Asians' median income was considerably higher at 96 percent of whites'.

The Los Angeles economy was fueled first by agriculture, then by the discovery of oil in the 1890s. The economy lacked a substantial industrial base until the early 1940s, when war in the Pacific motivated a defense-based economy, focused on aerospace and shipping, that spurred rapid growth. Even at the outset, industrial development took place far from downtown, in the corridor stretching south into San Pedro and Long Beach. Industrial as well as residential location were and remain "polynucleated and decentralized," in the words of Edward Soja, Rebecca Morales, and Goetz Wolff (1983). Moreover, the industrial surge of the 1940s to the 1960s dissipated as industrial locations dispersed and services overtook manufacturing. Professional services replaced durable-goods manufacturing as the leading industrial sector in Los Angeles County (Grant 2000).

One aspect of this shift was painful deindustrialization. Our interviewees ticked off the major plant closings: Ford, Chrysler, General Motors, Goodyear, Firestone—most of them concentrated around South Central Los Angeles (Soja, Morales, and Wolff 1983). Data from 1980 and 1990 for durable manufacturing and motor vehicles and equipment in particular confirm that for these industries, employment in the city of Los Angeles was in freefall. Los Angeles County urban employment stagnated relative to the rapid overall job growth (nearly 34 percent in ten years) the suburbs experienced (Moss and Tilly 1993b). In the early 1990s the previously booming aerospace sector, rocked by defense cuts, undertook massive layoffs.

Where did the jobs go? Some of the losses simply tracked losses in market share by key U.S. industries, such as auto. In other cases plants fled farther into the suburbs, to states with less stringent environmental regulations and less burdensome workers' compensation costs, or, in many cases, below the border. The maquiladora region of Mexico, where wages run $4 a day and environmental regulations are barely enforced, exercises a powerful attraction for Los Angeles manufacturers. Urbanist Rebecca Morales told us that many automotive-parts manufacturers maintained plants on both sides of the border, shifting production back and forth as convenient (see Hinojosa-Ojeda and Morales 1992). Union official Robert Lennox told of an organizing drive at a plant where compensation was minimal: only $4.50 an hour, with no benefits. "But," he said, "the company has already said if [the workers] vote in the union, they'll probably move to T. J. [Tijuana]. Their major competitor is already there" (interview with authors, May 15, 1991).

Despite losses in traditional manufacturing, three other groups of industries have grown rapidly. First, a cluster of finance, insurance, business command and control functions, and business services has expanded both along a growing spine of high-rise buildings anchored in downtown and in the suburbs, An increasing share of these jobs gravitated to the suburbs. Of the four specific industries we chose to focus on in the SSRC survey, insurance is the only one that enjoyed employment growth in Los Angeles between 1980 and 1990, but over 100 percent of the growth took place in suburban Los Angeles County (Moss and Tilly 1993b). Second, high-technology industries—chiefly aerospace and electronics—have sprouted. However, these businesses have sited almost exclusively in outlying areas: Orange County, the LAX corridor near the airport, and the San Fernando Valley—the "outer cities" (Soja, Morales, and Wolff 1983) or "technopoles" (Scott and Drayse 1991). Third, there has been a resurgence of low-wage, labor-intensive manufacturing and service industries, fed by Latino and Asian immigration. The decade from 1980 to 1990 saw employment jump in nondurable manufacturing such as apparel (+31,000), retail (+145,000, but with a 15,000 decline in department stores, which followed the purchasing power farther out into the suburbs), and personal services (+53,000) (Moss and Tilly 1993b). New immigrants dominate these workforces.

Soja, Morales, and Wolff argued that in Los Angeles we see a combination of both Sunbelt and Frostbelt dynamics. The original "center" of industry from South Central to San Pedro and Long Beach echoes Detroit's decline, while the growth of high-technology industry emulates Silicon Valley and the addition of low-skilled, exploitative manufacturing resembles Hong Kong and Singapore. This fragmented economic development contributes to the fragmented character of the region's physical space and to the socioeconomically polarized character of its population.

These four city profiles depict very different urban complexes. However, a common thread in all of them, as in any city in the United States, is continuing racial inequality and a legacy of racial and ethnic tensions. The profiles set the stage for employers' accounts of how and whom they hire. We now turn to analysis of the answers gathered from employers in these four cities. The next chapter asks what skills employers demand, how skill needs have changed, and how different skill demands affect the prospects of workers of color.

3

THE SKILLS EMPLOYERS SEEK

Interviewer: Some employers have told us that the way that jobs and skill needs have changed over time, differences between black and white workers actually matter more than they used to. Do you find that to be true?

Respondent: I think that you'll notice that the majority of the skilled positions are white people. So in that respect there's a widening of the gap there. It's like the information system highway they're talking about. You're either going to be computer-literate and get on the information highway or you're going to be left behind. (*Hotel manager*)

This Atlanta hotel manager is not alone in his opinion. Common wisdom holds that an important source of the labor market difficulties of young African Americans and Latinos is that they do not have the skills for today's jobs. The jobs that have been created over the last twenty years or so, it is argued, require "new" skills, driven in large part by computers and computer-related technology. Manufacturing and other entry-level jobs that provided some reasonable income and security with relatively less demand for skills and credentials have been shrinking away, the story continues. The widely observed escalation of earnings inequality is posited to be the result of these shifts in skill demands. The final step in the argument is that blacks and Latinos have less or poorer quality education and hence fall short on these new skills, leaving them out of the new economy. The "digital divide" is therefore the key to the growing racial divide.

How serious are skill barriers to workers of color in low-skill jobs—those requiring no more than a high school education? We argue in this chapter that skills do create important dividing lines, though computer skills are only part of the story in this set of jobs. However, in the following chapter we go on to show that employers' "skill" distinctions often incorporate racially discriminatory attitudes, complicating any assessment of the impact of skill differences on the labor market fortunes of racial and ethnic groups.

In order to tackle this question, an important first step is dividing skills into two categories, hard skills and soft skills. We define *hard skills* as cognitive and technical abilities. They include basic skills such as reading, writing, arithmetic, and grammar; more abstract abilities such as problem solving or ability to learn; and technical abilities ranging from computer know-how to construction skills. The story of the digital divide is an account of escalating hard-skill requirements.

Although most scholarly and media attention has focused on hard skills, we and others who interview employers also hear a lot about soft skills—those that are social or behavioral. The term *soft skills* dates back to a 1972 U.S. Army training manual (Fry and Whitmore 1972, cited in Conrad 1999), but the term came into widespread use in the early 1990s. Definitions of the term vary (Conrad 1999). We define *soft skills* as skills, abilities, and traits that pertain to personality, attitude, and behavior rather than to formal or technical knowledge. We group them into two clusters, based on how employers described to us the skills required to perform entry-level jobs. The first cluster, *interaction*, involves ability to interact with customers, coworkers, and supervisors. This cluster includes friendliness, teamwork, ability to fit in, and appropriate affect, grooming, and attire. The interaction category is related to, but goes beyond, concepts of "emotional labor" (Hochschild 1983; Wharton 1993) and "nurturant social skills" (England 1992; Kilbourne, England, and Beron 1994). Oral communication poses a difficulty for the distinction between hard and soft skills, since it includes both hard skills such as grammar and vocabulary, and soft skills such as friendliness and judgments about when it is appropriate to use slang.[1] A second cluster of soft skills, *motivation*, takes in characteristics such as enthusiasm, positive work attitude, commitment, dependability, integrity, and willingness to learn.

Based on these definitions, it is immediately apparent that there are two serious conceptual problems with assessing a prospective worker's soft skills. For one thing, any assessment of soft skills is inherently subjective. Friendliness or work ethic, representing as they do states of mind, simply cannot be measured with the same precision as, say, ability to use a word-processing program or to calculate percentages. Indeed, though some human resource consultants have expended considerable effort in developing psychometric questionnaires to capture soft skills (Paajanen 1997; Paajanen, Hansen, and McLellan 1993), most employers continue to rely on the rough-and-ready technique of the pre-employment interview to assess these aspects of applicants, as we shall see in chapter 6. Managerial attitudes toward potential workers therefore color most assessments of soft skills.

The second conceptual problem is even more critical. Soft skills are profoundly dependent on context. How successfully a worker interacts with customers, coworkers, and supervisors depends decisively on how these other parties view and treat the worker. Pay level and his or her treatment by managers shape a worker's level of motivation. We would argue that for these dimensions of worker performance, the worker's context is *at least as important* as any intrinsic characteristics of the worker. Indeed, this problem spills over to some extent to hard skills as well. As Charles Darrah (1994) pointed out, in most work settings successful performance of even narrowly defined technical tasks depends crucially on a set of relationships with other workers and managers.

Thus, although soft skills include learnable capacities that deserve the title "skill," they inevitably also include a large dose of context-driven behavior. And when employers size up potential workers' soft skills, they add their own attitudes to the mix. In short, *soft skills* is a misnomer. However, as we and others have found, *employers genuinely view interaction and motivation as skills* (Cappelli 1995). So, as part of our effort to provide an employer's-eye view of the workplace, we use the term here. We present managers' discussions of soft skills in their own words, but examine these discussions critically to see what we can learn about actual worker skills, employer attitudes, workplace contexts, and the interaction among all three.

In the remainder of this chapter, we look in depth at the skills employers seek. In addition to summarizing the key findings of other researchers, we pose three main questions based on our own data:

- Which skills are in growing demand in our relatively low skill sample?
- Because blacks and Latinos lag behind whites in average educational attainment and other measures of skill, we would expect skill requirements to constitute a significant barrier to job access for workers of color. Which hard-skill requirements appear most important in determining the race of the person hired for a job? In particular, how important is computer knowledge compared to other requirements?
- We suspect that soft skills deserve more attention. How important are interaction and motivation as hiring criteria? To what extent are demands for these characteristics rising? How do soft-skill requirements affect the likelihood of hiring persons of various racial and ethnic groups? Because employer assessments of soft skills (and, to a lesser extent, hard skills) centrally incorporate the employers' own

attitudes, we defer analysis of how managers view the skills of various racial and ethnic groups for the following chapter.

Brave New Workplace?

Evidence from a variety of sources indicates that skill demands are rising in U.S. workplaces. Because skill itself is difficult to measure in large-scale survey data, it rarely is. Most of the statistical analyses rest on the assumption that level of education is reasonably synonymous with skill. More educated people are assumed to be more skilled, and therefore, more use of employees with more education (controlling for relative supply) means there must have been an increase in the demand for skill on the job.

An important piece of evidence about skill demands comes from the price side—the earnings of college-educated workers relative to high school-educated workers. This premium has soared. Men with college degrees (but no more advanced degree) earned 36 percent more than high school-educated men in 1979, down from 39 percent in 1973. The bonus rose to 67 percent by 1997. For women, the trend was from 48 percent in the early 1970s down to 34 percent in 1979, then doubling to 68 percent in 1997. The reason for the continued rise in the education premium is not that college-educated employed workers have enjoyed substantial increases in after-inflation pay. It is that the real, after-inflation wages of high school- and less than high school-educated workers nosedived over this period (−12 percent over the period for high school, −26 percent for less than high school [Mishel, Bernstein, and Schmitt 1999]).[2]

At the same time, the share of employment of more educated workers has increased within occupations and within industries. In a supply-demand framework, the fact that both relative price and relative quantity have gone up indicates an increase in demand. Some analysts claim, however, that the focus on educational attainment is misleading. Economists Frederic Pryor and David Schaffer (1999) argue compellingly that, far from suffering a shortage of college graduates, the United States is experiencing a surplus: the number of college grads has outstripped job slots requiring college, and millions of graduates are spilling over into jobs for which they are nominally overqualified. However, they still conclude that skill demands have outrun supply. They reason that demands for *cognitive ability* have exceeded supply. Educational credentials are an imperfect indicator of cognitive ability, and they suggest—based on somewhat thin evidence—that the college graduates in lower level jobs are those whose actual skills do not reflect their credentials.

Even if educational attainment does not fully capture cognitive ability, education-linked evidence still points to a broad and deep process of skill upgrading. Industries that employ more educated workers have grown relative to those that do not. Within industries, occupations that require more education have become more important, and within occupations, the share of workers with more than a high school education has increased (for example, Berman, Bound, and Griliches 1994; Murphy and Welch 1993). Some of the studies have attempted to decompose the effect of within-industry increases in the use of more educated labor and the across-industry compositional shift. These studies are fairly uniform in arguing that the within-industry rise is the more important explanation for the overall increase in the use of more educated labor (Kodrzycki 1996).

Several authors have surveyed the research on skill upgrading *within* job categories (as opposed to the effects of a changing *mix* of jobs) in the United States (Cappelli 1996; Handel 1994; Mishel and Teixeira 1991). Analysts have used several sources of data, including the *Dictionary of Occupational Titles*, the census, and specialized data that rate jobs in order to set compensation levels. The results indicate that the degree of skill upgrading has been moderate and uneven.

Employers themselves fairly consistently report increased need for skills (Cappelli 1996; Holzer 1996; Moss and Tilly 1996; Murnane and Levy 1996; Osterman 1995). Most of the studies report modest increases in skill demands, and none reports dramatically increased demand for computer or other technological skills. The weight of the evidence points to increased demands at the level of basic skills—reading and writing, soft skills such as motivation and communication, and, to some degree, team and group problem-solving skills.

Finally, Richard Murnane and Frank Levy showed that controlling for a person's mathematics or reading skill while a high school senior eliminates a substantial portion of the growth in the college-to-high-school wage premium in a later period (for women essentially all, and for men about one-third). This indicates to them that it is basic high school-level skills that are increasingly in demand, and employers are relying more and more on college completion as a screen to get the people who are more likely to have them.

There has been much less analysis of changes in the demand for hard-to-measure social or behavioral traits. Certainly the job mix has shifted toward industries and occupations that involve contact with customers. Retail and service industries, totaling 36 percent of non-agricultural employment in 1979, climbed to 48 percent by 1999. Among occupations excluding higher-skilled managers and professionals, sales and service employment rose more modestly, from 32 percent to 37 percent over the last twenty years (calculations by authors from U.S. Department of Labor 2000). Peter Cappelli (1995) concluded that the "skill shortages" decried by employers in the first half of the 1990s referred primarily to issues of worker motivation. Quantitative evidence for growing soft-skill demands within job categories is limited. Paul Osterman (1995), based on a large, representative survey, reported that behavioral traits are important hiring criteria for blue-collar jobs (one of the two top criteria in 82 percent of cases, and the top criterion in about half). However, he found that among the 40 percent of employers reporting rising blue-collar job complexity, only one in seven cited increased demand for interpersonal skills or responsibility.

What is driving demands for higher levels of skill? Technological change, as captured by greater use of computers and computer-driven processes, has received the lion's share of the attention. At a 1994 conference on earnings inequality sponsored by the Federal Reserve Bank of New York, participants (including a broad spectrum of economists working on the issue, along with a number of top corporate executives) were asked to rate the relative importance of various explanations for increasing earnings inequality. Technological change dominated. The panel believed, on average, that technological change was responsible for 60 percent of the change in the distribution of earnings compared to 10 percent for international trade and 30 percent for a grab-bag of other causes (Klitgaard and Posen 1995). As of 1999, two leading economists in the field declared that "The [economics] profession seems to be near consensus" that skill-biased technological change is driving increased demand for skilled labor (Berman and Machin 1999, 3). Alan Krueger (1993), in a frequently cited paper, found that people working with computers were paid a significant amount more, on average, than those who were not working with computers. He also found that the likelihood of a person using a computer rose with his or her level of education, and the payoff to the use of computers rose with education as well. The fractions of workers using computers rose between 1984 and 1989, but the premium paid to workers who use them did not diminish, leading Krueger to infer that the technology of computer use was driving demand for workers with computer skills faster than the supply was increasing.

Several authors have leveled serious criticisms at the work of Krueger and other researchers emphasizing computer technology as the driving force behind the rising skill demand and widening earnings inequality in the United States (Card and Lemieux 1999; Mishel, Bernstein, and Schmitt 1999; Mishel, Bernstein, and Schmidt 1997; Howell 1997; Handel 1997; DiNardo and Pischke 1996; Moss, forthcoming). In fact, John DiNardo and Jörn-Steffen Pischke (1996), using German data, demonstrated that although there is a higher wage associated with using a computer at work, similar rewards accrue to working with a handheld calculator, a pen, a pencil, or working sitting down! They conclude that all these variables signal the presence of ability not otherwise measured in the data—but these indicators could equally signal high social status. This result casts doubt on computer use as the major force behind rising skill demands and rising relative wages for skilled work. Moreover, David Howell and colleagues noted that the main surge in skill demand took place by the early 1980s, *before* microcomputer use became widespread (Howell, Duncan, and Harrison 1998). And case studies of the implementation of computers and other new technologies in the United States (Handel 1994; Cappelli 1996) show wide variation in the impact on skills, including upskilling, deskilling, and simply skill transformation without a clear increase or decrease in skill.

Consequently, researchers have advanced other explanations for rising skill demands (as well as for growing disparities in the distribution of wages). Peter Cappelli (1996), noting that a significant fraction of firms report high-performance work activities, such as teams or employee participation, inferred that these forms of organization are likely to be associated with more skill needs, and therefore, because these organizational developments are relatively new and spreading, skill needs must be rising. We and others have also stressed firms' changes in work organization and competitive strategies (Howell 1997; Howell, Duncan, and Harrison 1998; Moss, forthcoming; Tilly 1997). The changes in competitive strategies are themselves due in part to increased globalization. There are also industry-specific drivers of competitive strategies from industry to industry, as we elaborate later in this chapter.

The counterpoint to all the evidence for increasing skill demands in the workforce is the continuing educational disadvantage of African Americans and Latinos. Although blacks have been closing the education deficit and until recently, the standardized test score gap between themselves and whites, they fall short of whites on average educational attainment and other measures of skill (Jencks 1991). Latinos, unlike blacks, have fallen *farther* behind Anglos in college completion, though Latinos' rate of college completion has continued to increase slowly (Harrison and Bennett 1995). Latinos' educational disadvantage stems primarily from the recent large influx of Latin American immigrants with low levels of education. George Borjas (1994) attributed declining earnings of successive cohorts of Latino immigrants to diminishing levels of education.

What do we conclude from this survey of research on skill demand? Skill needs are indeed rising. It is not simply a story of technology and high-tech skills, and rising skill is not restricted to jobs at the top of the job ladder. The rise in skill demand appears to be moderate, and to involve in large part basic cognitive and technical skills, and to a lesser extent behavioral skills. Most of the research does not really measure skill directly, and focuses, by inference, on technical skills. In particular, this research gives little attention to the importance of and rising demand for behavioral, or soft, skills. The gaps in this literature point to a need for data from employers—crucial actors in defining skill needs. We turn now to our employer-based findings.

What Skills, Tasks, and Credentials Do Employers Want?

Our focus is on entry jobs for which inner-city workers with a high school education or less could potentially qualify. The Telephone and Face-to-Face Employer Surveys offer a more detailed look at what employers are demanding of entry-level hires—what tasks workers will perform, what skills they should possess, and what credentials employers screen for in judging applicants. The surveys also gathered information about increases in skill demands. For each employer, we focus on a "sample job"—a typical job requiring no more than a high school education.[3] The results paint a daunting jobscape for many blacks and Latinos, since on average they possess less education and skills than their white counterparts.

Quantitative Data on Skills

What tasks do employers require entry-level workers to perform? The quantitative Telephone Survey asked employers the frequency with which certain tasks—such as talking face to face or on the telephone to customers, reading instructions at least a paragraph long, writing paragraphs or memos, doing arithmetic, or working with computers[4]—are done on the sample job. The results are presented in table 3.1. All the tasks, except writing, are performed daily on at least half of the jobs reported. The results also show that most jobs require these tasks either everyday or essentially not at all. Note that two of these tasks (talking face to face or on the phone to customers) require both soft and hard skills.

Harry Holzer, who conducted the Telephone Survey and first analyzed the data, broke down the frequency of task performance by occupational category, and showed that while the top category of professional-managerial jobs has the greatest frequencies of daily task use, all occupation groups have substantial task requirements—with half or more jobs requiring each task in almost all cases. This is true even for the lowest-paid category, service workers, except in the case of com-

TABLE 3.1   *Frequency of Task Performance*

	Daily	Weekly	Monthly	Almost Never	
Talk face to face with customers	58.4%	7.2%	2.1%	32.0%	N = 3,137
Talk on the phone with customers	53.1	7.2	2.4	37.1	N = 3,138
Read instructions	54.1	20.8	6.8	17.8	N = 3,139
Write paragraphs	30.6	16.8	9.6	42.8	N = 3,139
Do arithmetic	64.6	11.8	4.1	19.0	N = 3,139
Use computers	51.0	5.4	2.5	40.9	N = 3,139

Source: Multi-City Telephone Employer Survey.

puter use (Holzer 1996, 48–49 and table 3.2). He also showed that the frequency of task use is higher in the primary central city of the metropolitan area, in comparison to the suburbs and other areas (other central cities in the metropolitan area, and municipalities with at least 30 percent of their population black). Clearly there appears to be a strong need for cognitive and social skills to handle the daily tasks on entry-level noncollege jobs, particularly in central-city areas where the concentration of minority, less educated workers resides.

What credentials do employers want of their entry-level employees? Table 3.2 shows the credentials that surveyed employers reported they require. The level of required credentials is high. Most of the credentials are required for approximately two-thirds to three-quarters of the available jobs. The most frequently required credential is a high school diploma, while the least sought is prior vocational or other training (although even this certification is required by 30 to 40 percent of available jobs). The results also indicate that a higher proportion of employers in the primary central city require each of the hiring credentials, except for the case of vocational training. Holzer also shows that in every job category almost every credential is required by half or more of the employers, with the exception of the training requirement for sales, laborer, and operative jobs, which is relatively infrequent (25 to 35 percent of such jobs) (Holzer 1996, table 3.6).

Table 3.3, replicating calculations by Holzer, drives the point home. Very few of the jobs reported in this survey require none of the job tasks analyzed or none of the credentials. If the pool of jobs is expanded by adding the jobs that require only talking to customers, the situation improves somewhat but remains fairly bleak. The same is true when the stock of jobs is augmented to include those that require only a high school degree or, further, by including those that require only the high

TABLE 3.2   *Hiring Requirements by Primary Central City, Suburb, and Other Central Cities*

Requirements for Hiring	Primary Central City	Suburbs	Other Central Cities
All Metropolitan Areas			
High school diploma	74.5%	70.4%	68.1%
General experience	72.6	68.4	67.3
Specific experience	66.8	59.4	57.9
References	73.2	71.6	72.3
Vocational or other training	41.8	38.9	32.3
	N = 810–14	N = 1,835–40	N = 485–87
Los Angeles			
High school diploma	67.0	66.7	68.9
General experience	71.3	70.3	75.3
Specific experience	71.7	66.5	73.1
References	64.5	68.1	69.7
Vocational or other training	39.6	42.9	44.9
	N = 224–26	N = 574–76	N = 87–88
Boston			
High school diploma	80.3	74.6	61.4
General experience	77.5	71.0	72.0
Specific experience	68.9	57.9	60.4
References	81.3	80.7	80.2
Vocational or other training	43.4	43.6	29.3
	N = 145–46	N = 504–5	N = 147–48
Detroit			
High school diploma	73.2	70.6	71.6
General experience	75.7	62.3	59.3
Specific experience	66.1	51.4	47.8
References	61.2	64.4	63.2
Vocational or other training	38.5	28.3	27.4
	N = 127–28	N = 479–82	N = 106
Atlanta			
High school diploma	78.1	70.5	71.2
General experience	70.1	70.9	64.1
Specific experience	62.6	61.5	53.9
References	81.2	77.0	73.3
Vocational or other training	44.1	41.4	31.1
	N = 314	N = 271–73	N = 146–47

Source: Multi-City Telephone Employer Survey.
Note: "Other central cities" also include any municipality other than the primary central city that has a black population of 30 percent or more.

TABLE 3.3   *Percentage of Jobs with Few Tasks and Requirements, by City and Suburb and Other Central Cities*

	Primary Central City	Suburbs	Other Central Cities
Perform none of major tasks daily	5.8	8.0	8.6
Perform none of major tasks except talking to customers	12.7	14.0	14.5
Requires no high school diploma, training, experience, or references	4.1	6.3	5.9
Requires only high school diploma	6.8	9.1	7.9
Requires only high school diploma and general experience	9.4	12.6	11.6
	N = 814	N = 1,840	N = 488

Source: Multi-City Telephone Employer Survey.
Note: "Other central cities" also include any municipality other than the primary central city that has a black population of 30 percent or more.

school degree and some general experience. More jobs become available, but the amount is still relatively small—increasing from around 5 percent to around 10 percent of the jobs. (And recall that this set of jobs already excludes any jobs requiring college education!) Importantly, the fraction of available jobs is in all cases lower in the central cities than in their suburban areas, as less skilled workers, particularly less skilled minority workers, are more likely to live in the central city. In addition, jobs with few or no requirements pay from 20 to 33 percent less per hour than the average noncollege entry job in these four cities (not shown).

Beware of supposing that a required credential constitutes a completely insurmountable barrier. Tom Hertz, Chris Tilly, and Mike Massagli (2001) examined the subset of the Telephone Employer Survey data that can be linked to interviews with employees, and found that underqualification as well as overqualification are surprisingly common. Comparing employer with employee interviews about the *same job*, they discovered that many incumbent workers lack some supposedly required credentials: 4 to 5 percent of workers lack "required" education or general experience, and a much larger 28 to 29 percent lack requisite training or job-specific experience (table 3.4).

While the underqualification numbers testify to the flexibility of employers' requirements, however, they do not greatly alter the powerful odds against job seekers with limited skill. Taken together, tables 3.1

TABLE 3.4   *Percentage of Workers Underqualified or Overqualified for the Jobs They Hold*

	Underqualified	Overqualified	
Credential			
Education	4.9	24.4	N = 2,839
Training	27.6	21.1	N = 773
General experience	4.6	23.2	N = 633
Specific experience	28.8	11.2	N = 555

Source: Analysis by authors of Multi-City Study of Urban Inequality–linked employer-employee data described in Hertz, Tilly, and Massagli (2001).
Note: Sample size is much larger for education, which is based on data from the Multi-City Telephone Employer Survey alone, than for other variables, which are based on Telephone Survey data linked to Multi-City Study Household Survey data.

through 3.3 tell a sobering story. The hurdle to qualify for entry-level jobs, especially in central cities, appears to be high. This indicates that less educated minority workers, in particular, face a potential skills mismatch—jobs that overwhelmingly require skills that they do not possess—in their local labor markets.

To the degree that rises in skill demands outstrip the supply of skills among these groups, this mismatch is likely to worsen. The results in table 3.5 suggest that employers are indeed escalating skill demands apace. Our data do not take into account changes in the supply of skills in the labor force, but the rising skill demands appear to threaten a growing mismatch, at least for the near term.[5] Employers were asked whether the skills needed to perform the sample job had changed over the last five to ten years. If they reported a change, they were asked whether skills were rising or declining and, if rising, why they were rising. Less than half (40 percent) of all employers reported a change in the level of skills required on the sample job. But, among those who did report a change, essentially all reported a rise in skills. Basic reading, writing, and numeric skills—hard skills—are most frequently cited as the kind of skills that are rising. Very close behind are the social and verbal skills—soft skills—or a combination of both sets of skills. According to the surveyed employers, the greater need for skills derives most often from the introduction of new technology or organizational change.

The pattern of skill change across occupations is similar, but with some notable differences. Employers report greater skill increases for clerical occupations, apparently driven by the widespread introduction of computers into clerical work. As might be expected, blue-collar occupations are relatively more likely to require more basic skills, and cus-

TABLE 3.5   *Proportion of Employers Reporting a Change in Skills Sought for the Sample Job*

	All Jobs	Clerical	Customer Service	Blue-Collar	Other
Report a change in skills	39.8%	52.3%	32.7%	34.1%	44.0%
Of those reporting a change					
Skills risen	96.3	97.1	96.1	95.3	96.4
Skills declined	3.1	2.5	3.0	4.3	2.9
Of those reporting a rise in skills					
What kind of skills					
Basic reading, writing, numeric	29.2	27.2	19.6	38.5	29.9
Social and verbal	26.6	20.4	44.6	20.0	24.3
Both	23.9	27.4	21.1	21.8	25.4
Other	17.8	24.2	13.2	16.1	16.8
Reasons for the rise					
New technology	83.1	94.3	70.3	78.8	85.6
Computers	71.7	92.3	63.2	48.2	79.6
New products	46.9	43.3	46.2	58.4	40.3
Higher product quality	62.5	57.7	51.8	73.9	64.4
New services provided	66.2	66.3	76.1	55.2	68.6
More customer contact	56.4	53.9	74.7	40.5	58.4
Organizational change	77.1	76.8	79.0	76.2	75.9
	N = 3,132	N = 528	N = 789	N = 910	N = 836

Source: Multi-City Telephone Employer Survey.

tomer service jobs are relatively more likely to demand greater social and verbal skills.

Table 3.6 displays, for each type of increased skill need, the fraction of employers who cited various reasons for the increase. Not surprisingly, employers most often attributed heightened basic skill needs to utilization of new technology, particularly computers, and to a lesser extent new products or a need for higher product quality. On the other hand, those reporting greater needs for social and verbal skills pointed most often to new services, more customer contact, or organizational change which frequently involves more use of teams and a broader span of interaction across the organization. Employers who reported *both* types of increased skill demands cited almost every reason (except more

TABLE 3.6   *Percentage of Employers Citing Various Reasons for Increased Skill Needs, by Type of Skills That Increased*

	Among Employers Who Reported Increased Need For		
	Basic Reading, Writing, Math	Social and Verbal	Both
Percentage who cited as a reason			
New technology	88.0	70.3	88.4
Computers	75.4	59.0	77.7
New products	46.6	45.1	49.4
Higher product quality	65.1	57.0	69.3
New services provided	57.7	74.0	71.3
More customer contact	46.2	71.1	63.4
Organizational change	73.3	80.4	84.3
	N = 318–47	N = 279–301	N = 283–94

Source: Multi-City Telephone Employer Survey.
Note: Employers were able to indicate multiple reasons for a skill increase.

services and greater customer contact) more often than either group of employers who noted only one type of skill upgrading.

Because of the attention that has surrounded computer use as a potential source of skill increase and skill mismatch, we examine that connection a bit further. Among jobs that require daily use of computers, 48 percent saw a boost in skill requirements—1.27 times the 38 percent of all jobs reporting such increases (though still not quite a majority of cases). Only 2 percent of computer-using jobs saw a *decrease* in skills (though this is slightly higher than the percentage of other jobs in which skills declined). Finally, among the jobs necessitating daily computer use and that experienced a rise in skill needs, 29 percent reported an increased need for basic skills, 27 percent reported a greater demand for social and verbal skills, 24 percent reported more need for both basic and social and verbal skills, and 19 percent indicated that more of other skills were called for. These percentages are nearly identical to those for all jobs (see the third panel of table 3.5). Thus, in employment entailing daily computer use, as for other jobs, the increase in skill needs is nearly as likely to be for soft skills as for basic hard skills.

How seriously should we take employers' claims about skill increases? After all, they have read as many headlines about the new economy as the rest of us, and might feel obligated to assert that their companies have not been left behind. However, table 3.7 suggests that, at

TABLE 3.7   *Correlations Between Reported Changes in Skills and in Screening Methods (p-Values in Parentheses)*

	Screening Changed	At Least One Screen Used More Often	At Least One Screen Used Less Often	Interview Used More Often
Skills increased	0.26	0.22	0.23	0.20
	(0.0000)	(0.0000)	(0.0000)	(0.0000)
Basic skills increased	0.18	0.15	0.15	0.14
	(0.0000)	(0.0000)	(0.0000)	(0.0000)
Social or verbal skills increased	0.230	0.203	0.213	0.191
	(0.0000)	(0.0000)	(0.0000)	(0.0000)
Skills decreased	0.05	0.06	0.04	0.04
	(0.0057)	(0.0024)	(0.0108)	(0.0139)

Source: Multi-City Telephone Employer Survey.
Note: Employers were able to indicate both types of skill increase. P-values of .05 or less indicate statistical significance at the 5 percent level. Variables were nonmissing for 3,075 to 3,510 observations, depending on the variable.

least in the aggregate, the employers are talking about real changes. A few minutes *before* being queried about changes in the skills sought for the sample job over the past five to ten years, respondents were asked if they had changed the way they screen applicants for this job, over the same time period. If their responses are internally consistent, we would expect to find a positive correlation between reports of skill changes and reports of changes in selection methods.

As table 3.7 indicates, there are indeed good-sized (and highly statistically significant) positive correlations between increases in skill and changes in screening procedures. Heightened skill demands are equally correlated with *more* use of various screening methods and with *less* use of various screening methods; employers typically reported that they use some methods more and others less than before. The association between skill upgrading and altered selection methods is greater for increases in social and verbal skills than for escalations in basic reading, writing, and numeric skills, in part because employers were particularly likely to make more use of pre-employment interviews in cases where they sought stronger social skills. Interestingly, businesses with *decreasing* skill requirements were also more likely than "no change" firms to report changes in screening, though this correlation is much weaker than for those with skill increases.

Skill Change in the
Face-to-Face Interviews

Interviewer: How has this [the skills required on the job] changed over the last ten years?

Respondent: Oh, a lot. Just by the type of equipment that we have installed in the facilities, number one. Number two, the outlook of the corporation as it relates to the involvement of the worker, whereas before the management guy had to always do all of the thinking and planning.

[T]he workforce that you used in the past was acceptable for what you were trying to do at the time. Today if that same mentality persists, that same educational level persists, then those people will not work out in this business. I mean, you have to look at things like a desire for lifelong learning.

They've got to be customer-oriented because they've got to understand that if we don't satisfy the customer, then we're not in business. They've got to be adaptable to new technologies and new processes. They've got to be able to communicate verbally and in writing, and a lot of people can't do that today. (*manufacturing personnel official*)

In-depth conversations with employers reiterated the widespread nature of skill increases, filling in details not visible through the multiple-choice responses in the Telephone Survey. These discussions also illuminated the complexity of skill requirements, in particular, offering a window on soft skills.

As described in chapter 2, we conducted two rounds of in-depth interviews. A first round, the Social Science Research Council interviews, surveyed 56 businesses in Detroit and Los Angeles to plumb deeply into conditions in four specific industries. The second round, the Multi-City Study of Urban Inequality interviews, expanded to include Atlanta and Boston as well, and incorporated 174 firms from a broad cross-section of industries.

In both studies, we asked interviewees to identify the most important qualities they look for in hiring entry-level workers. Both surveys echo other findings about the importance of soft skills (Cappelli 1995). The profiles of the most important skills sought by each industry in the SSRC study are informative.[6] As the first panel of table 3.8 shows, interaction skills are by far the most important qualification in retail. Motivation and hard skills received roughly equal emphasis in auto parts

TABLE 3.8   *Most Important Qualities Looked for in Entry-Level*
Employees: Frequency with Which Each Category Was
Mentioned, by Industry

	Hard Skills	Interaction	Motivation	All Soft Skills	
By industry (SSRC sample)					
Auto parts manufacturing	58.0%	32.0%	63.0%	79.0%	N = 19
Retail clothing	22.0	78.0	39.0	74.0	N = 15
Insurance	67.0	67.0	78.0	100.0	N = 8
Public sector	100.0	60.0	60.0	100.0	N = 15
Total (Multi-City Study sample)					
Mentioned at all	53.6	56.0	51.2	84.0	N = 125
Mentioned first	24.8	39.2	36.0	75.2	N = 125

Source: SSRC In-Depth Employer Survey; Multi-City In-Depth Employer Survey.
Note: Unit of analysis is the firm. Respondents frequently mentioned more than one category.

and insurance. Only in the public sector were hard skills mentioned as often as soft skills. Thus, soft skills are already very important in the industries we have studied closely. Overall, fully 86 percent of SSRC respondents included soft skills in their list of the most important hiring criteria, and almost half mentioned soft skills first in that list (with retailers particularly likely to cite soft skills first, and manufacturers particularly unlikely to do so).

In the larger, more diverse Multi-City Study sample, the results were similar (table 3.8, second panel). Small majorities of employers mentioned hard skills, interaction, and motivation when asked to identify the most important skill or qualification sought. Respondents at 84 percent of firms mentioned at least one of the two forms of soft skills, and a remarkable 75 percent mentioned soft skills *first* in their description of the most important skills. Interaction skills lead the pack by a slim margin, in terms of both any mention and first mention.

In many cases, the requirements entailed by interaction and motivation are fairly basic. As clichéd as it may seem, numerous managers in retail and service environments boiled down the requisite interaction skills to "a smile":

Interviewer: Out of all those things [criteria for hiring a cashier], if you had to narrow it down to one important thing that you look for, what would you say that is?

> *Respondent:* The smile on that individual's face. An individual that's friendly and carrying a smile, you can deal with them. In this business you don't have to be real smart starting off. *(Peachtree Foods, Atlanta area)*

And in manual jobs, "motivation" often translates into showing up for work:

> *Interviewer:* What kinds of skills and qualities do you look for?

> *Respondent:* We look for someone who basically has their personal life together. You have to have somebody that you can rely on, who will get to work every day, call in when they're not going to show up, not come in drunk or having stayed up all night and not been to bed so that they could hurt themselves here, or stuff like that. As I say, their personal lives have to be stable to the point where they can maintain a constant effort to make it to work. We call it "making it to work." *(factory owner-manager)*

Numerous employers reprised this emphasis on reliability in the form of steady attendance and timely arrival at work. In fact, when we asked employers about workforce issues or problems, an overwhelming 84 percent of the Multi-City Study sample raised concerns about reliability. "That's 90 percent of our battle," stated one manager ruefully, "getting them to come to work on time every day." Another window on this issue from the Telephone Survey was a question asking employers how often workers were fired for tardiness or absenteeism. Among all jobs, 38 percent said "very often" or "sometimes"; for jobs that do not require high school, the total was 54 percent.

In looking at the qualifications employers rated most important, in table 3.8, it is somewhat surprising that managers did not cite hard skills more often. Recall, however, that our questions in both surveys focused on low-skill jobs. As one manager put it, "to be honest, this isn't rocket science. So we're looking more for dependability." Expressing a view that we heard over and over again, a public-sector respondent explained that:

> Technical skills, you can teach almost anybody how to do anything. That's important, but it's not the most important. Because you can have a really good guy who knows how to do everything who's never here because he's absent all the time, or you can have a guy who's mediocre who will do anything for you, and he's here every time, and he's better than the guy who's not here.

A restaurateur stated a position even more strongly tilted toward soft skills rather than job knowledge:

Times are kind of tough for people who are coming in from another restaurant, they worked there for years, and they were trying to do it the same way as the other place, and that isn't the way it works. I think it creates more of a teamwork if I get people in with less experience and train them my own way. They all have to be on the same page, heading in the same direction, and helping each other out. If they don't do that, then the service definitely suffers.

While relatively few employers voiced this proprietor's outright antipathy toward accumulated experience, many agreed that attitude trumps technical facility in large numbers of low-skill jobs.

Note that because of the conversational nature of the face-to-face surveys, employers' description of the most important qualification was sometimes ambiguous—making it difficult to reduce the results to simple categories. Consider, for instance, the following set of interchanges with the receiving manager at a manufacturing facility, discussing inventory control jobs:

Interviewer: What about skills? Do you look for anything particular in people?

Respondent: Well, what we try to find is somebody, first of all, who has the capacity, the ability to assimilate instructions and training.

. . .

Interviewer: And what do you look for in the very entry-level positions?

Respondent: First and foremost is somebody that understands the team concept. The other one is the ability to be flexible.

. . .

Interviewer: So what's the most important part of the process in making your decision? What stands out in your mind—"I'll hire that person"?

Respondent: I think a willingness to do the work first of all.

In sequence, this manager has identified hard skills (ability to learn), interaction ("understands the team concept"—more interactional than conceptual, in our view), and motivation, all as "first." We coded all three as *mentioned* as "the top qualification," and coded motivation as *first mention*, because the manager gave that response to the most pointed posing of the question. This coding system certainly accommodates more complexity than a single multiple-choice response, but still does not do justice to a cognitive reality in which the manager seems to be describing a broadly conceived willingness and ability to do what is needed to work well with others. And the cognitive complexity expands exponentially when more than one respondent was interviewed at an employer (as in the large majority of cases). The numbers reported in table 3.8 are one cut through this complexity.

In terms of incidence of skill *changes*, the face-to-face interview samples generally confirm the results from the larger Telephone Survey. For example, consistent with the Telephone Survey data, employers in the Multi-City Study survey most commonly reported no change in skill requirements. In the SSRC survey, the proportion citing skill upgrading was slightly higher—about half of the employers reported a rise in skill needs. But the qualitative data from the face-to-face interviews tell us that there is often more to skill changes than meets the eye. In some cases, employers stated that there had been no skill changes, but later described precisely such changes! Consider this interchange with the president of a small manufacturing company.

Interviewer: Have there been any changes in the kind of things you're looking for in a worker? Has that remained kind of constant?

. . .

Respondent: Yeah, we're still doing essentially the same thing we did thirty-one years ago.

. . .

Interviewer: Has technology affected the way these people do business, work?

Respondent: Yeah, it's unbelievable. Technology has changed our business. Technology has changed the way that we deal with our product.

Interviewer: Has it changed the kind of qualities that you're looking for in a worker? Has it affected what you need to look for?

Respondent: To a degree. Anybody that comes in here, if they were lucky enough at the time, that their school had computers and things of this type, it's just an asset for them to have, and that's technology right there.

A growing need for computer skills was the most common skill change reported in the face-to-face interviews, congruent with the reports of technologically driven skill rises in the Telephone Survey. However, a substantial minority of respondents described computerization without any resulting increase in the skills sought. "It takes about ten minutes" to train file clerks how to use the computers, one Atlanta manager reported. A Boston construction supply wholesaler had just spent $250,000 on a new computer system, but was not looking for anything different among clerical hires, because "if it's not broke, don't fix it." Others commented that it has been easy to train people to use computers and other new automated equipment. In fact, the human resource director at a bank commented that she doesn't look for computer familiarity in new hires "because our computers are different. I mean all systems are different. They have to learn our system and that's what they're trained in." Similarly, some managers observed that general workforce skills had changed in step with the business's technical requirements, or even ahead of them:

We only got our computer system three years ago. By the time we got it, everybody else has got it working someplace else, [so the employees] know more than we do.

[Most applicants already know how to use a computer] because as an infant now they toddle up to the microwave, and press a few buttons, and cook their hot dog. They have all of those games they play on TV. It's not a problem for them. They learn it real fast.

In some cases, computerization has spelled deskilling. As we will examine in more detail later in this chapter, most retailers commented that "smart" cash registers have actually made the cashier's job easier and diminished the need for mathematical skills. And the data-entry supervisor at a consulting firm noted that computers have gotten easier to use.

Moreover, in some cases computerization has tremendous workforce impacts that have nothing to do with skill. In a fascinating secondhand story, a Los Angeles mortgage company executive recounted:

Two to three years ago the [name of bank], their mortgage company decided that they were going to equip all of their salespeople with laptop computers. Rather than fill out the loan application longhand and deliver it to the processor for closing, they were going to be required to enter the information. They had a 95 percent turnover in their sales force. They just quit. It's because of the different attitudes about using the computer at that time. Typing is women's work, and the male loan officers considered it beneath them. Demeaning.

(He went on to add that male attitudes had changed, and that now his sales force is "begging for us to buy them computers.")

In addition to reports of greater needs for computer-related skills, we heard repeatedly about three other kinds of rises in technical or hard-skill requirements. First, many businesses have placed new emphasis on basic skills such as numeracy and literacy, often in response to new equipment, new worker involvement in quality control processes such as statistical process control, or new standards for customer or worker safety, all of which may require reading written instructions or keeping written records.[7] For instance, a Los Angeles-area auto parts manufacturer recently introduced computerized numerical control (CNC) machines, as well as new foundry machinery. This manufacturer now requires machinists to have basic math to program CNC machines, and both machinists and foundry workers need reading skills to consult operating manuals. Many other businesses newly select for the basic skills employees need to monitor, record, analyze, and report their own output. This new requirement is most typically imposed in manufacturing settings, but some service-sector employees have made analogous adjustments. A department store now looks for high school-level reading and math because their employee incentive pay program requires timing and counting operations and filling out report sheets. Changing technology also interacts with changing regulation: two hospitals recently added reading requirements to housekeeper jobs in order to comply with right-to-know laws regulating workers' use of hazardous chemicals. Interestingly, the new literacy requirements do not necessarily demand English. The auto parts manufacturer and one of the two hospitals mentioned provide written materials in Spanish as well.

Second, employers told of a need for workers to handle a broader range of tasks, or to possess a more analytical overview of how their tasks fit into broader processes. Secretaries, for instance, are no longer typists but "information managers" at a small nonprofit organization in Detroit. "We're changing the way we do business," remarked a manager at a Boston-area government agency that we call Public Agency X. "[Clerical] people are going to have to be able to do two or three and four jobs and be able to move within that."

Third, a variety of industry-specific changes call for added skill: home care aides need added technical knowledge because managed care is inducing hospitals to discharge sicker patients, the director of a Boston agency told us. In line with the literacy requirements for some janitors, custodians in a Detroit-area public facility must contend with more sophisticated equipment and new requirements for handling hazardous waste and chemicals. A personnel official explained:

Respondent: I think more training and more responsibility has to be taken by the district and by the employees themselves, in terms of making themselves aware of what it is they have to do. It's not a mindless job, let's put it that way. They have to pay attention to detail and be aware of what they're doing.

Interviewer: More so than in the past?

Respondent: Yes, because things are so much more, they can get into trouble mixing chemicals wrong now, or get the district into trouble just by throwing away a diaper or some bloody article, by not putting it in the hazardous waste container—that nobody had ever heard of ten years ago.

More frequent than any of the hard-skill shifts except for computer literacy, however, were heightened demands for *soft* skills. Managers of retail, service, and clerical workers spoke of greater needs for the interaction skills involved in customer service—in some cases linked to a *declining* need for hard skills:

They've [computers have] taken a lot of the basic thinking process out of it. Y'know, a lot of it the computers do for you, so probably communication skills [are what's needed] (*grocery store manager*).

At one time we [had] more people [in] what we consider operational functions. They unloaded trucks, they straightened up the stock room, they worked in office areas. But with the computer systems now in place, our goal is to get more and more people on the selling floor to take care of our guests. And let the computers do a lot of the things that once happened (*clothing retailer*).

It's becoming more and more important that people have good communication skills and they're people-oriented, along with having your basic typing and word-processing skills as well. There's not that many secretarial jobs anymore where you just sit in front of a computer and type all day (*hospital administrator*).

The employers' descriptions of the new interactional imperative were often quite emphatic. "It's a radical change," a Los Angeles hospital manager commented about the new stress on "guest relations, customer service" among nursing aides. "It's like going from zero to one thousand." She added, "It used to be the other way around. The clinical skills were at the top." She and other managers related these new needs back to competitive pressure and to a competitive strategy designed to win over customers—to make these businesses "a fun place to shop and to work," in the words of one Detroit retailer. Less commonly, managers expressed a need for stronger interaction skills stemming from the adoption of "team" forms of organization.

Employers also talked about accentuated requirements for motivation. At a bakery, following automation "they actually need less skills to do the job, but I think they're a little more conscious of the quality of the work they do now." A car dealer says he looks more than before for workers who "give a damn about who's the customer," a supervisor of equipment service people wants more of "a can-do attitude, will-do, 'Let's go out there and knock those calls out.'" As these snippets suggest, businesses' push for more motivation is often tied to the same customer satisfaction goals as the drive for better interaction skills. Even in a consumer durable factory, the human resource director said he needs someone who is "more customer-oriented"—meaning someone who is motivated to think about the quality the customer seeks.

While reported growing soft-skill demands reinforce a widely reported pattern of skill upgrading, they do not necessarily imply that the *total* job mix in these workplaces is shifting toward higher-skill jobs. Managers report escalating social-skill requirements in the *least* skilled jobs in particular industries. These jobs should be viewed as one part of a broader mix of jobs. Employers typically explained heightened demands for motivation by noting that workers now have to take on more tasks formerly handled by management (coordination, problem solving, taking initiative, monitoring), in a context where many of these companies are "getting lean" by stripping away layers of middle management. Thus, businesses assign more skills to the lowest-level workers, but do so by shifting tasks that were formerly performed by more highly skilled workers. So, for example, the hospital housekeeper who adds patient liaison functions takes on tasks formerly shouldered by aides or even nurses. If this shift is used to free up aides or nurses for more complex tasks, the result is skill upgrading throughout the related set of jobs. On the other hand, if this means that the hospital uses more housekeepers and fewer aides and nurses, the net result may be a reduction in the average level of skill in the workforce.

Similar skill-*shifting* processes seem to be at work in some of the instances of augmented hard-skill requirements, as well. An insurance company, for instance, has expanded one of its major frontline clerical jobs from pure data entry to underwriting assistance, transferring work down the skill chain from underwriters. At a Detroit area scrap recycling facility we have dubbed Jack's Junkyard, a manager talked about his new hiring objectives:

> The way that I put it to the crews that I have now, I want people who can think. I don't need bodies, I don't need somebody I can just stick outside with a shovel. I want somebody that I can put outside with a shovel, that knows what they are doing and that can think about what they are doing and I don't have to have a supervisor standing right next to them telling them, "when you are done putting this pile of black stuff over here, take the pile of red stuff and put it in a pile over here." We've gone from having maybe twelve supervisors down to the operations managers and one other supervisor.

In fact, the manager added, he prefers to hire "somebody with some college," since "generally they think a lot better and are a little faster on their feet and they are also available if you want to advance into a better job."

The implication is two-edged. On the one hand, the bar for access to entry-level jobs is raised, posing a greater relative barrier for inner-city workers of color. On the other, workers who do gain access to many of these entry-level jobs will experience broader skill development and more chance for mobility than previously.

As in the Telephone Survey, we were most confident about reported skill changes when employers also noted changes in hiring procedures. For instance, the vice president for human resources at an insurance company commented,

> We are more concerned about making sure that those people who come to work for us not only have the right basic skills to do the job, but also share our value system. And so we are trying to redesign all of the human resource systems to focus on our business philosophy and the values that articulates. Recruiting and selecting is one of the first areas we change.

Other current or planned changes in hiring practices ranged from newly requiring a high school degree to explicitly asking about teamwork experiences in the pre-employment interview. More typically, however, the employers have simply placed more emphasis on certain criteria without fundamentally altering hiring and screening methods.

To flesh out the overall skill requirement patterns and their causes, we examine changing skill demands separately in all four industries of the SSRC study, in some detail. Reported skill changes differed markedly by industry: for example, nearly two-thirds of retail and insurance employers pointed to soft-skill increases, compared to around one-quarter of their manufacturing counterparts, mirroring the gap between customer-service and blue-collar jobs that we saw in table 3.8. In these industry narratives, we focus on soft-skill changes, but discuss hard skills as well, where relevant.

Skill Changes in Auto Parts Manufacturing

Greatly increased competitive pressures are being felt everywhere in the auto industry, including among parts manufacturers.[8] The big three U.S. automakers (Ford, General Motors, and Chrysler) are directly orchestrating pressure on parts suppliers, leading two-thirds of the suppliers in our SSRC sample to seek higher skills in entry-level jobs. Most frequently, the suppliers are demanding heightened basic hard skills: numeracy and literacy. However, increased soft skills—in this industry, most often expressed as initiative, flexibility, team skills, and communication skills—play a significant role as well.

Competitive pressure takes two forms, the "old" competition and the "new" competition (Best 1990). Old-style competition stresses cost reductions, usually through downsizing and speedup of various kinds. The CEO of a small steel fabrication company commented,

> There's no question that the heyday of this kind of business is over. And with all the downsizing and loss in share of the big three, with the narrowing of margins—you know, twenty years ago, this was a hell of a business to be in. And you know, from the people standpoint, we cannot tolerate poor performers and substandard performers. If we're going to survive and if we're going to be a company with forty or fifty people, they all have to be good, as far as I'm concerned.

However, suppliers also feel ("new") competitive pressure to increase quality, as expressed through the quality certification programs operated by the big three automakers—of which Ford's Q1 ("Quality is Job One") certification is the best known. The larger first-tier suppliers who sell directly to the auto manufacturers are in turn applying quality certification programs to their lower-tier suppliers. Suppliers at all levels have responded to quality demands both by strengthening quality control within existing production methods and also, in some businesses, by attempting to reorganize production to emphasize team production and employee involvement. Many of the supplier firms have escalated their requirements for basic skills among new hires, in some cases newly demanding a high school diploma.

While managers at the majority of manufacturing companies were embarked on a quest for greater technical or basic literacy and numeracy skills, a number sought more soft skills as well. These businesses were particularly oriented to quality improvement and to Japanese-style management innovations. In particular, they planned greater use of teams with broader job descriptions for each team member, requiring more flexibility from employees.

As the human resources manager for a metal-stamping plant put it, "We're in the process of restructuring the entire management, flattening the organizational chart, empowering—truly empowering—hourly teams to handle the basic, day-to-day operations of the plant." This meant that in the future, they would be looking for employees with the

> ability to fit in to the environment we're going to create. We want people that can step up and take responsibility and accountability for their actions, can function in an environment that requires them to coordinate a lot of information with other departments and other people. All employees will be on a team, setting their own objectives and key measurables in their area, and then working through a continuous improvement process.

A human resources manager at an alloy-casting plant indicated he was looking for

> self-motivated individuals, good work habits, past teamwork or total quality [management] knowledge is a plus—[that's the] direction in which we're looking at. A lot of hiring used to be based on 90 percent experience, 10 percent attitude or work ethic. I see that changing due to the [emphasis on] teamwork and total quality. I would almost say it's 50 to 60 percent being experience and the other 40 percent being attitude, work ethic, teamwork.

Skill Change in Retail

In retail clothing, heightened emphasis on customer service has led companies to screen more carefully for soft skills when hiring for sales associate and salesclerk jobs.[9] Almost all informants spoke of a concerted effort to increase the level of customer service. One chain's human resource director summarized the swings in emphasis across retail:

> The way that retailing was run in the thirties and maybe forties, you had counters and you had associates, like, every three feet of those counters. Then either in the fifties or certainly in the sixties and seventies there was a move away from higher staffing levels to lower staffing levels and more clerking as opposed to selling. What we were trying to do in the mid-eighties was to make a mark and a niche for ourselves in the market by running counter to that trend. And I think that [counter]trend continues

for our organization. From what I read about what's going on in the industry as a whole, there continues to be a move toward more service.

The pressures toward increasing customer service are straightforward. On the one hand, the successful high-service models of Nordstrom's and Neiman-Marcus beckon. On the other hand, deep discounters such as WalMart have reduced the space for price competition. Commented a regional personnel representative for a discount chain we will call Value King:

> In this economy if you go into a store and somebody treats you poorly, you go right next door. And the store next door has got the same product for the same price. There's no consumer loyalty like there used to be. So that consumer loyalty and the loss of it is a big reason why we have to pay more attention to customer service.

In turn, the attempt to upgrade customer service leads retailers to stress new qualities in the process of hiring salesclerks, who make up the vast majority of their workforce—60 to 90 percent of the employees in the stores we visited. Of the store-based retail sites (one other site was a warehouse), two-thirds reported heightened emphasis on soft skills, and half were specifically looking for stronger customer-service skills.

Value King exemplifies these changes. In 1989, the chain adopted a new program called "fast, fun, and friendly," designed both to cut down on employee turnover and to enhance service. A Value King store-level personnel manager reported that as part of this program, corporate management wants her to hire "bubbly, outgoing, friendly people. The generic All-American Boy and Girl." The regional personnel representative agreed: "I tell my personnel managers, 'If they don't smile, don't hire them.' I don't care how well educated they are, how well versed they are in retail, if they can't smile, they're not going to make a customer feel welcome. And we don't want them in our store."

This represents a change, according to the store personnel manager: "Before [fast, fun, and friendly], I think, more or less, 'get a body in the store' was the phrase that was used." She added that the new approach emphasizes narrowly defined productivity less, friendliness more. Most other Value King personnel managers gave similar accounts.

Informants at other chains sounded the same themes. A store manager from one chain remarked that following a shift toward self-service in the 1970s, "in the eighties we tried to go back and got more customer service oriented and we are striving every single day to get more and more and more customer service oriented."

The vice president for human resources of another retailer noted that rather than focusing on job applicants' familiarity with operational tasks, his company is now "looking for people with good communication skills, enthusiasm, high energy levels, someone very interested in retail, someone who likes the product that they're going to be selling. All of those kinds of issues really come up more often in an interview than they would have five or six years ago."

Retailers' growing emphasis on service-related soft skills is particularly striking in contrast to the *reduction* in the need for hard skills in salesclerk jobs. Of retail respondents in the SSRC sample commenting on mathematical and machine operation skill requirements in these jobs, 62 percent reported declining skill demands, while 15 percent reported no change. Falling skill requirements were attributed to optical scanning equipment and cash registers that prompt the cashier for input—"the same kind of thing that you see in McDonald's," according to one manager. Interestingly, two regional personnel representatives told us of companywide attempts to raise the hiring standard to require a high school education, but the store managers and store personnel managers in their regions appeared blissfully unaware of these initiatives.

Skill Changes in Insurance

The computer revolution has led insurance companies to seek computer familiarity in a growing proportion of their entry-level clerical workforce. But in addition to this change in hard skills, the insurers have upgraded their soft-skill requirements for clerical jobs in ways that are less visible, but equally influential in the hiring process.[10]

The story of soft-skill escalation in insurance begins, as in auto parts and retail, with intensified competitive pressure. Although the details have varied by specific sector within the insurance industry, in general financial deregulation has led to an erosion of the boundaries between insurance and other financial services, and overcapacity in many insurance lines—what one manager called "something similar to what the S&Ls have gone through."

The insurance companies we spoke to have responded with three kinds of steps. First, some insurers have downsized. Second, companies have striven to increase customer service. Informants at the majority of the insurers cited rising customer-service standards. A typical comment: "Customer service is a big issue in the nineties, and if we can't keep up with that we'll lose out to the competition." Respondents defined "customers" to include insurance agents and employees in other parts of the firm, in addition to policyholders themselves. A manager from a property and casualty company noted that "because of the legislative environment that we work in, prices are pretty much the same," so that an agent will choose the policy to sell based on "the company that is going to get him the quickest quote, that's going to get him the paper the quickest, that will be fair and consistent if there is a claim and will provide that agent and business owner with information to make him a wiser insurance buyer."

The third step insurers have taken is work reorganization. Human resource officials sprinkled their comments with references to total quality management and continuous improvement. Three of the eight companies were in the process of reorganizing from functionally based departments to multifunctional "teams," "pods," or "donuts":

> We are moving to what I'll call a team environment, where instead of having a giant department of underwriters and a giant department of typists and a giant department of clerks and file people, we'll have a team set up with one or two of each position combined to service by state or a territory or agents, that have last names, say, A to L.

In turn, these operational changes have led to two major changes in employee-selection criteria, even for entry-level clericals: employees who can handle broader jobs and who are well suited to customer contact. (As we noted earlier in the chapter, many respondents in the larger and more industrially diverse Multi-City Study described very similar changes in clerical jobs.) Illustrating the issue of job breadth, one human resource official stated, "We look for an individual who has a wider paintbrush, if you will." Another explained:

> Now every policy has twenty different pieces inside it. So for a clerical entry-level employee, it's not like it was twenty years ago. They have to be able to do maybe more things in their head at one time. And to remember more pieces of the puzzle and understand the total product versus, you know, just processing this piece of paper.

Interestingly, though the ability to handle a complex or varied set of tasks is a hard skill, managers seeking to meet this need search for a mixture of hard *and* soft skills. In the managers' words, increased complexity drives them to look for a clerical employee who is more "self-directed" or "self-motivated to achievement"; personnel departments are trying to detect "ability to learn" and "a positive attitude." In other words, a greater requirement for a hard, conceptual skill compels managers to look for stronger soft skills as well.

In addition, the insurers seek employees who can relate well to customers—even for routine clerical jobs. Due to broader jobs, greater orientation to customer service, and adoption of scanning technology that greatly reduces the need for data entry and paper file handling, "There used to be people that never had to answer the phone and didn't have to interface with the customers. But the way the work is designed now, there are very few jobs that do not involve that kind of interface."

Another human resource manager added that in hiring, "on a scale of one to ten it [customer relations] is a 9.99. There is much more emphasis now being placed on it."

Customer service in insurance is multifaceted, but one important aspect sounds a great deal like "fast, fun, and friendly": "if you're nice to people and you speak well on the phone and you sound happy and all that smile-in-your-voice kind of stuff."

Some managers argued that all these changes in competitive strategy and hiring qualifications are linked:

> We are not unlike the entire total quality management revolution in this country. We are now trying to focus more on trying to find out what our customers' needs are and satisfying those needs. When you couple that with a need to be as lean as possible in order to cut overhead, you find jobs being multifaceted and people who used to move paper now move paper and answer phones and might do some correspondence. So the skill needs have changed over time.

Skill Changes in the Public Sector

Public-sector agencies do not confront the fierce competitive pressures of auto part manufacturers, retail stores, and insurance companies. Nonetheless, the public sector faces budget reductions and demands for greater productivity and quality. Managers told us that cost and productivity pressures are driving some public-sector agencies to seek higher-skilled labor, lower-cost labor, or both.[11] Public agencies are often emulating private-sector firms in improving customer service and quality.

Most likely to adopt new strategies are those parts of the public sector most similar to the private sector: public utilities and contracted-out public-sector operations. However, some traditional government agencies themselves are downsizing, stressing customer service, and changing work organization in ways that affect the skills they seek. Overall, two-thirds of respondents reported that they were looking for people with greater skill levels. While some noted a greater need for hard skills, *all* mentioned a need for greater customer skills.

A Detroit-area public utility provided the clearest example of how increased cost and productivity pressure lead to greater hard-skill demands. A top human resource official mentioned the utility's customer-service needs, but the major issue was downsizing to boost productivity and reduce costs. Their strategy was to combine blue-collar jobs (folding lower-level jobs into somewhat higher-level ones) and make greater demands on existing workers. In order to staff these more demanding jobs they were raising the test-score requirements for hire.

Most other respondents cited quality and customer service as the primary issues driving increased skill needs. The manager of employee services at a Los Angeles–area utility stated,

> I think that there is more emphasis on lower-level people being more involved in the running of an organization or being aware of what needs to be done and using their initiative. Customer service has suddenly become, I don't know why, but suddenly they discovered it's important. And in doing so I think that we have to look for people who are, if not skilled in speaking to people, at least have the basic courtesy so they can be trained to work with the public or whoever their customers are, whether they're internal or external customers. I think you have a greater need for someone to be interested and trainable than you might have before.

Customer service is becoming more important in government bureaucracies, as well. The personnel chief for a local government agency reported changes similar to those described in hospitals and insurance companies earlier in this chapter:

> We don't see a word-processing pool in very many places anymore, like you used to. [Now managers] want interpersonal skills because these people are now in there, one or two people in a section doing PC work, telephones and stuff, so more independence. They don't have a supervisor watching everything they do. A lot of them [are] working now with the public one on one. And so they got to make some judgments that they might not have [had] to make in the past when they were all holed up in a room doing clerical work.

Several public hospital managers talked about a new stress on customer service in housekeeping and dietary jobs. Though the jobs are entry-level, these employees come into frequent contact with patients. Managers are increasingly scrutinizing potential customer-interaction skills during the pre-employment interview. Private contractors, who are handling a growing range of outsourced public agency functions, expressed similar concerns. The district manager for a company that provides contracted housekeeping and dietary services to hospitals stated,

> Health care is starting to become user-friendly and what's happening is they [housekeepers] are having to become more customer-oriented with that process. The entry-level housekeeper is going to have to be a little bit more pleasant when they come to clean the room because one of the things that happens is a lot of times the patient knows nothing about the

medical terminology or what's wrong, but they do know what is clean and they do know what is comfortable. And so that emphasis is put on the housekeeper to greet the patient, "How are you doing?"—this type of thing. That's big in health care right now, How can we be more friendly to our customers? And that competition there for the health care buck is just tremendous right now.

He predicted that housekeeping jobs would get upgraded to patient liaison positions, providing some services to the patient as well as mopping the floor. As a result, he noted, "Communicative skills, personal appearance, now are becoming more of an issue when we recruit. Again, presentation skills. Some type of knowledge of friendliness in an interview. Do you like the person, could you like them?"

Skill Changes Across the Four Case Studies

Strikingly, respondents in all four case-study industries attributed the rise in soft-skill needs—and many of the increased hard-skill requirements as well—to heightened competitive pressure (or its equivalent in the public sector: increased fiscal and political pressure). Indeed, some of the competitive challenges appear to be sufficiently similar across industries that managers emulate best-practice techniques from remarkably distant industries. Given these commonalities, it's not surprising that widening the scope of our examination to the manifold Multi-City Study sectors yielded some of the same basic findings.

The Racial Consequences of Skill Requirements

What are the racial consequences of high and rising skill requirements? The context for this question is a highly charged public discussion on the role of ability in economic success. A growing chorus of intellectuals tell us that the United States is increasingly becoming a meritocracy. People's rewards—jobs, income, social standing—depend more and more, we are told, on their abilities. Free enterprise, technological dynamism, and widely available education have swept away invidious distinctions of race, ethnicity, gender, and parents' social class.

Perhaps the most forceful, if flawed, depiction of the new meritocracy appeared in Richard Herrnstein and Charles Murray's 1994 book, *The Bell Curve*. "The twenty-first century will open on a world in which cognitive ability is the decisive dividing force," they tell us. "Social class remains the vehicle of social life, but intelligence now pulls the train" (25). Herrnstein and Murray attracted controversy by claiming not only that economic success now depends chiefly on intelligence but that differences in cognitive ability are primarily, and increasingly, genetically determined. Consistent with this viewpoint, they argued that a large and increasing share of the gap between blacks and whites in employment and income is due to genetically based differences in intelligence.

Few other social scientists appeal to genetic differences to explain earnings inequality. But many agree with Herrnstein and Murray that ability is the key. Reflecting on the growing gap between high-wage and low-wage men, and the smaller but also expanding gap between high-wage and low-wage women, economists point to a growing payoff to education (especially higher education) and experience—meaning that those who have the most education and experience earn much more, and those with the least education and experience earn much, much less. Economist Alan Krueger noted that 45 percent of the increase in wage inequality among men during the 1980s and 1990s can be statistically accounted for by greater rewards to education and experience (Task Force on Reconstructing America's Labor Market Institutions 1999).

Recent analyses of racial wage differences have also emphasized ability rather than discrimination. Ronald Ferguson (1996), June O'Neill (1990), and Derek Neal and William Johnson (1996) all pointed out that the average wage difference between black and white young men can be nearly completely accounted for (in a statistical sense) by the difference in their scores on the Armed Forces Qualifying Test, a battery of cognitive examinations.

There are plenty of ways to poke holes in all these statistical results. Few would contest the claim that racial and ethnic differences in education and skill contribute in important ways to disparities in wages and employment. But many question the contention that differences in cognitive ability—let alone inherited cognitive ability—explain virtually all the racial differences in economic status. To start with, even if one takes intelligence tests at face value, Herrnstein and Murray's results "demonstrating" the preponderant role of inherited ability in determining occupation and wage levels turn out to depend greatly on the details of how they set up their analysis. With small changes the results reverse, and social environment trumps parents' test scores (their measure of genes) (Levine 1999). Moreover, many question the degree to which tests fairly measure intelligence (Steele and Aronson 1995) or even whether intelligence can be captured in one or a small number of measures (Gardner 1983). Samuel Bowles and Herbert Gintis (1995) argued that the majority of the payoff to schooling rewards noncognitive traits such as socialization to workforce norms (and found no evidence that the returns to the cognitive component of education have risen over time). In general, evidence for rising returns to cognitive test scores is mixed: analysis based on a math test shows an increase (Murnane, Willett, and Levy 1995), whereas research based on a vocabulary test does not (Hauser and Huang 1997). Moreover, the correlation between jobs' skill demands and hourly wages remains quite low among non-supervisory workers (Howell and Wolff 1991).

Turning to the statistics of black-white wage differences, it turns out that test scores are highly correlated with socioeconomic background. In this context, even accounting for 100 percent of the wage difference between black and white young men becomes less impressive, since it is not clear to what extent the test reflects ability and to what extent it simply reflects socioeconomic status (Levine and Painter 1999). Controlling for other factors in addition to test scores (years of education and psychological assessments are two examples) restores a substantial black-white male wage differential, indicating that something more complicated than a simple ability difference is involved (Darity and Mason 1998). More important, the major gap in economic fortunes between black and white men is due to divergent rates of employment, not differing wage rates.

The results from our Employer Surveys will not resolve these statistical debates. However, they make a compelling case for two propositions. First, where skill requirements are greater, representation of blacks and Latinos is lower. And second, when employers assess potential workers' skills, those assessments often integrally incorporate the employers' racial biases or stereotypes. So although racial differences in employment and wages stem in part from genuine skill differences, they reflect largely unconscious discrimination as well. We take up the first proposition in the remainder of this chapter, and address the second one in the chapter that follows.

Race, Gender, and Skill: How Skill Requirements Disadvantage Particular Groups

What is the association between stated skill requirements and the race and gender of the person hired into the job? Table 3.9 shows the association between the need for certain job tasks or the use of particular hiring credentials and the proportion of new hires in each of six race, ethnicity, and gender groups (white, black, Latino, by male and female).[12] Rather than directly reporting the proportion falling in each demographic group given a particular task or qualification, we divide each such proportion by that group's share of all jobs. For example, white men were the last

TABLE 3.9 *Gender and Race of New Hires by Daily Task Use and Hiring Requirement Index of Representation (1.0 = Proportional to Share of All Jobs)*

	White Men	Black Men	Latino Men	White Women	Black Women	Latina Women
All jobs	1.00	1.00	1.00	1.00	1.00	1.00
Daily tasks						
Talk face to face with customers	0.91	0.91	0.71	1.11	1.17	1.06
Talk on the phone with customers	0.77	0.68	0.45	1.38	1.09	1.06
Read instructions	1.04	0.87	0.85	1.06	0.96	1.03
Write paragraphs	0.85	0.85	0.55	1.27	1.00	1.03
Do math	1.09	0.82	0.77	1.12	0.87	0.87
Use computers	0.75	0.66	0.43	1.39	1.13	0.93
Requirements for hiring						
High school diploma	0.98	0.87	0.57	1.17	1.03	0.94
General experience	1.03	0.89	0.88	1.08	0.93	0.91
Specific experience	1.05	0.86	0.93	1.03	0.95	1.01
References	1.00	0.99	0.92	1.04	0.95	0.94
Vocational or other training	1.13	0.83	0.95	1.01	0.81	1.09
	N = 702–4	N = 273–76	N = 280–82	N = 961–69	N = 291–96	N = 188–90

Source: Multi-City Telephone Employer Survey.

hire in 26.0 percent of all jobs in the sample, but only in 23.7 percent of jobs involving face-to-face conversations with customers. We divide 23.7 by 26.0, and report the result, 0.91, indicating that white men are underrepresented in these jobs. More generally:

- An index below 1 indicates underrepresentation of this demographic group in jobs with this requirement or task
- An index greater than 1 denotes overrepresentation.

Recall that none of the jobs analyzed here requires more than a high school education—so this is a low-skill job pool to start with. What's striking is that there is both a strong gender component and a strong racial component to the hiring patterns. Within racial and ethnic groups, *virtually every task requirement and credential is associated with greater probability of hiring a woman*. The only exceptions are requirements for job-specific skills (for whites) and vocational training (for whites and blacks), both relatively uncommon requirements. The gender gaps yawn particularly wide for jobs whose incumbents must "talk on the phone with customers," "write paragraphs," and "use computers." Clearly, part of what we are picking up here is the familiar segmentation of women into clerical jobs and men into manual jobs, but the results are powerful nonetheless.

The racial sorting is also quite sharp. Within gender, almost every task requirement and credential is correlated with *reduced hiring of blacks and Latinos* relative to non-Latino whites. The most notable exceptions are the task of speaking face to face with customers (in which black men are represented equally to whites, and black women are overrepresented relative to their white counterparts) and jobs requiring vocational training (which Latinas are more likely to hold than white women). But jobs requiring reading, using math or computers, or a high school diploma manifest large racial tilts within gender groups. The combined effect of racial and gender sorting is particularly devastating to black and Latino men.

A comparison of the effects of job tasks versus the effects of hiring credentials suggests that occupational segregation by gender accounts for much of the observed gender differences. Two job tasks—using computers and talking on the phone with customers—do more to boost white and black female percentages, and widen the difference between white and black women and their male counterparts, than any of the hiring credentials. These two tasks are the ones most associated with clerical and customer-service jobs, where occupational segregation by gender is high. On the other hand, reading paragraphs and doing math, which are less specific to a particular occupational category, only slightly increase the probability that a woman will be hired, and the gender effects of experience requirements are small to negligible.

We are particularly interested in how computer use affects the race and ethnicity of the person hired. Looking within gender, computer tasks do not have a racial impact that differs greatly from the impact of other tasks. For example, the representation gap between white and Latino men associated with computer use is nearly identical to the gap found with requirements for writing, performing math, and talking to customers on the phone.[13] The same is true for the gap between white and black women. For black men, the disadvantage relative to white men in computer-using jobs is dwarfed by the disadvantages found in jobs requiring reading or math skills. Only in comparing Latina women with white women does the computer effect stand out as larger than the effects of other tasks.

It is also instructive to compare tasks requiring primarily soft skills (talking face to face or on the phone with customers) with those requiring mainly hard skills (the remainder of the tasks, as well as the high school credential requirement). Within gender groups, a requirement to speak face to face with customers daily does not have large impacts on the race or ethnicity of the person hired—with one exception, Latino men, who are far less likely to be hired than white men. In fact, black women are overrepresented relative to white women where face-to-face customer contact is required. On the other hand, the task of speaking on the phone to customers, selects strongly against blacks and Latinos— about as strongly as a high school degree requirement or as many of the tasks requiring hard skills. Presumably the difference lies in the fact that jobs involving face-to-face contact emphasize service, whereas jobs entailing telephone conversations are more likely to emphasize communication and information. So this first cut does not appear to demonstrate that soft-skill requirements in general make it substantially less likely that a black or Latino applicant will be hired. Rather, requirements for particular types of soft skills (and hard skills) appear to matter most.

In addition to asking about required credentials, the large-scale employer survey asked about the educational level of the person most recently hired, so that we can examine this directly. We expect high school dropouts to be at a disadvantage relative to high school graduates in general, and for this effect to be larger when jobs require more tasks or higher levels of credentials. Table 3.10 confirms this expectation and explores how the pattern varies by gender. Within the categories of high school graduates and dropouts, the gender difference mirrors the effects shown in the previous table. Men are less in evidence when any of the job tasks are necessary, and, correspondingly, women increase in numbers when this is the case. Women are more strongly represented than

TABLE 3.10   *Gender and Educational Level of New Hires by Daily Task Use and Hiring Requirements Index of Representation (1.0 = Proportional to Share of All Jobs)*

	Male High School Graduate	Female High School Graduate	Male Dropout	Female Dropout
All jobs	1.00	1.00	1.00	1.00
Daily tasks				
Talk face to face with customers	0.89	1.09	0.93	1.21
Talk on the phone with customers	0.81	1.20	0.43	0.95
Read instructions	1.00	1.04	0.57	0.63
Write paragraphs	0.91	1.14	0.03	0.63
Do math	0.99	1.03	0.67	0.89
Use computers	0.86	1.18	0.40	0.58
Requirements for hiring				
High school diploma	0.89	1.14	0.47	0.63
General experience	1.02	1.02	0.63	0.68
Specific experience	1.02	1.02	0.57	0.63
References	1.00	1.02	1.13	0.79
Vocational or other training	1.07	0.98	0.40	0.79
	N = 1206–11	N = 1436–39	N = 117–19	N = 77–78

Source: Multi-City Telephone Employer Survey.

men when the high school diploma is required, and among high school dropouts, experience credentials also favor women.

But the real story here is the contrast between high school graduates and dropouts. The situation for men who lack a high school degree is stark. Daily tasks of reading, writing, math, computer use, or telephone conversation thin the ranks of high school dropouts by one-third or more—in the case of writing, driving their representation down to 3 percent of its workforce-wide level. Aside from references, credential requirements have a similar screening effect on male dropouts. In contrast, for male high school graduates the task and credential requirements have negligible to small negative effects—reducing male high school grads' presence by at most one-fifth—or even small positive effects.

The contrast between women high school graduates and dropouts is also striking. All six task requirements increase the probability of hiring a female high school graduate. All except talking face to face with a customer and doing math *decrease* the chances of hiring a female high school dropout. Whereas every credential requirement except training screens *in* women with a high school diploma, every such prerequisite screens *out* women who lack the diploma—at rates similar to their male counterparts. In this particular comparison, educational differences overwhelm gender effects.

Note that though jobs "requiring" the high school diploma are less likely to employ dropouts, they do not exclude them altogether. In a small, but non-negligible 2.6 percent of high school-requiring jobs, the last hire was a high school dropout. Put another way, 26 percent of recently hired high school dropouts occupy jobs that nominally call for a high school diploma! As we discussed in connection with table 3.4, there is plenty of evidence in these data that firms' requirements have some built-in flexibility.

Conclusion

We started the chapter by posing a set of questions about skills in the jobs under study. Let us return to these initial questions to review what we have learned.

• Which skills are in growing demand?

Even in this sample, restricted to jobs requiring no more than a high school degree, skill requirements are relatively stiff. Large majorities of jobs entail a variety of tasks, each requiring some type of skill, and multiple credentials. Only a minority of jobs—but a substantial minority, 38 percent—saw skill increases over the past five to ten years. Skill increases were most widespread among clerical jobs, among which a bare majority (51 percent) of employers reported skill rises. Increases in basic skills and boosts in social and verbal skills were about equally common in the Telephone Survey. Greater demands for basic skills most often coincided with increased use of computers or other new technology; heightened soft-skill requirements were more often driven by organizational change, new services, or added contact with customers. Like the Telephone Survey, the face-to-face interviews pointed to increased requirements both for basic skills, particularly computer-related ones, and for soft skills. The industry-level case studies indicate that although availability of computer technology helped drive some skill increases, managers explained many heightened requirements—especially for interaction abilities and motivation—as a business response to stepped-up competitive pressures.

• Which hard-skill requirements appear most important in determining the race of the person hired for a job?

All hard-skill requirements have sizable impacts on the likely race (and educational level and, in most cases, gender) of the person hired. Credential requirements have more modest effects, with the high school requirement overshadowing other credentials. Almost every task or credential requirement is associated with *reduced* hiring of blacks and Latinos relative to whites of the same gender. Daily computer use does not stand out from other tasks in this regard, except that it vastly reduces the probability of hiring a Latina woman relative to that of hiring a white, Anglo woman. This is consistent with face-to-face interviews, which tell us that the skill impacts of computer use are quite mixed.

- How important are interaction and motivation as hiring criteria? To what extent are demands for these characteristics rising? How do soft-skill requirements affect the likelihood of hiring persons of various racial and ethnic groups?

Majorities of respondents in both face-to-face surveys pointed to soft skills as the most important qualities they sought. As a number of interviewees stressed, this is due in part to modest hard-skill requirements in this sample of jobs. The Telephone Surveys also bring home that most of the jobs involve daily customer contact. Again, heightened demands for social and verbal skills were about as common as increased basic skill requirements in the Telephone Survey. Each of these two types of skill escalation was reported by about half of the managers who noted any skill increase, or about 20 percent of all businesses. One of the two soft skill–intensive tasks in the Telephone Survey, speaking daily *by telephone* to customers, excludes blacks and Latinos to an extent comparable to hard-skill requirements. The other, speaking *face to face* to customers, does not.

This evidence distances us from the "digital divide" story of racial inequality in three ways. First, as other studies of skill demands also show, the United States has seen a rising tide of skill requirements, but nothing like a tidal wave. Second, while computers have driven some skill increases, they should be viewed as one factor among many, and not the primary one barring African Americans and Latinos from the jobs with modest skill requirements that are the focus of this study.

Third, soft skills beg for more attention. Employers typically rate soft skills as their top need in these low-end jobs, and report growing soft-skill requirements almost as often as they report greater needs for basic skills. The face-to-face interviews offer a particularly promising window for learning more about how managers view soft skills. But as we observed at the outset of the chapter, the notion of "soft skills" brings with it two serious conceptual problems: the subjectivity inherent in assessing such qualities and the extreme degree to which performance in these areas is sensitive to social context. For this reason, in the next chapter we consider both employer perceptions of the skills of various racial and ethnic groups *and* employers' racial attitudes. The two phenomena are so closely linked that they must be examined jointly.

4

EMPLOYER PERCEPTIONS OF
RACE AND SKILL

Interviewer: Some of the other managers we've talked to have noticed differences between black workers and white workers. Do you agree with that?

Respondent (white male Atlanta-area fast food restaurant owner): Yeah, there's some. Usually whites are a little bit more focused, a little friendlier, and the ones I've had here probably a little bit more dependable. Blacks probably overall make better workers. They're faster, they have more dexterity. They seem to be able to work a little bit longer. They do a more thorough job. White kids are usually more educated. It doesn't mean they make better workers.

Interviewer: I know that you mentioned earlier that Asians were really good workers?

Respondent: Dependability, reliability, responsibility, and all that kind of stuff. Attitudes. They never talk back to you or anything. They have that, and work habits probably stand out more than anything. Not all of them, but the majority of them. All of them are ambitious. Every one I've had has been contemplating going to college, or they are in college, and a lot of them working two and three jobs. They are determined to make it. A lot of these people over here don't want to do anything.

Respondent (white female supervisor in Michigan Utility): I think that for whatever reason, a higher percentage of minority employees are not as dependable and do not, performancewise, make it sometimes. I think it gets right back to the family or lack of family, and the support or lack of support, or expectations that single parent or double parents place on the kids. And maybe as the kids see or don't see their own parents working, every day, and leaving at seven-thirty to get to work by eight o'clock, so they know that this is something you do. There's lots of reasons for it, but I think it's culturally based and maybe societal.

In the simplest models of human capital theory, a worker's probability of being employed and his or her wage depend directly on his or her potential productivity. This potential productivity, in turn, is a function of accumulated skill. Racial groups differ in average educational attainment and other skills, so this theory predicts employment and wage differentials as a consequence. But the employer quotations leading off this chapter suggest that it is critically important to examine the employer *perceptions* that underlie assessments of employee skills. To what extent are assessments of various racial or ethnic groups as "more focused," "friendlier," "faster," or "not as dependable" shaped by stereotypes?

Here we squarely confront issues of bias and discrimination. Gary Becker (1957), in his classic treatise on economic discrimination, pointed out that discrimination can take varied forms. In *pure discrimination*, an employer acts on an aversion to a particular group, offering that group lower wages, fewer jobs, or a combination of the two. *Employees* or *consumers* can also drive discrimination by the employers. For example, if majority-group employees dislike working with minority-group employees, they may accept jobs involving such contact only if offered a higher wage (or they may be less productive at any given wage level). In this case, even if the employer feels no personal antipathy toward the minority group, he or she is under economic pressure to exclude members of that group, or to reduce their wages to offset the required higher wage (or lower productivity) of majority-group employees. A similar process can take place when customers prefer to avoid contact with workers of a particular racial or ethnic group.

Edwin Phelps (1972) and Kenneth Arrow (1972, 1973) moved beyond Becker's notion of a "taste for discrimination" (a distaste for contact with members of a given group) by suggesting that employers may engage in *statistical discrimination*. That is, given the impossibility of measuring individual productivities in advance, employers may discriminate against whole classes of people based on (correct or incorrect) perceptions of the average productivity (or variation in productivity) of these classes. In this situation, if employers underestimate the true average productivity of, say, blacks relative to whites, they will treat blacks as a group unfairly, offering them lower wages or fewer employment opportunities than their productivity merits. Even if employers *correctly* estimate the average productivity of racial groups, they will offer unduly low wages to individual black applicants whose actual productivity exceeds the average (though this will be offset in the aggregate by offering overly high wages to black applicants whose productivity falls below the average). Others (Aigner and Cain 1977) have suggested that employers' main concern may not be the lower average productivity of a group, but rather the perception that some groups include higher proportions of very poor employees. In this theory, employers avoid hiring from these groups to reduce the risk of a catastrophic hire. Models of statistical discrimination depend on the assumption that individuals have productivities at least somewhat independent of context.

While mainstream economists *assume* that employers are motivated by the drive to maximize profits and by unexplained "tastes" (their own and those of employees and customers), social psychologists attempt to *explain* discriminatory tastes and perceptions. Henri Tajfel and John C. Turner (1986) put forward the *social identity* theory of prejudice. They posited that an individual self-image is grounded in part on that individual's image of the social categories of which he or she is a member. Since people prefer to see themselves positively, they will tend to view their own group positively relative to other groups—translating into prejudice against the other groups. And indeed, experimental evidence indicates that people do tend to rate their own group more positively than others, even when the groups are artificially constructed in an experimental setting and even when they have little or no empirical evidence for differences between the groups (Brown 1995). A related notion, the *similarity-attraction* hypothesis, posits that people use demographic traits to infer similarity in attitudes, which is an important basis for attraction (Tsui, Egan, and O'Reilly 1992). Moreover, once stereotypes of particular groups are formed, they are quite resilient. People remember information that confirms stereotypes more readily than information that contradicts them, and tend to view behavior that departs from the stereotype as exceptional or situational. However, prejudice toward one's own group and against other groups is most pronounced for dominant or high-status groups (such as whites); lower-status groups may be more likely simply to identify less with their group as an alternative strategy for maintaining a positive self-image (Brown 1995).

More sociological theories emphasize the roots of social identity in material interests and history of conflict, expressed through widely held norms. For example, Herbert Blumer's (1958) *group position* theory points to a dominant group's sense of entitlement to resources or status, coupled with a perceived threat by a subordinate group to such entitlements. More generally, *realistic conflict* theory (Sherif 1967) holds that bias arises when groups pose a threat to each other's status or resources. John Duckitt (1992) suggested that the notion of "realistic conflict" could readily be extended to situations in which dominant groups may face no threat, in which prejudice may serve purposes of justifying exploitation or scapegoating. Charles Tilly (1998) located the origin of discrimination in segregated social networks that form the basis for allocation of resources such as jobs, "solving" organizational problems at the expense of subordinating one group to another; such discrimination becomes entrenched when endorsed by authoritative social actors.

Finally, some social scientists have made a case for more complex, multifactor explanations of discrimination that combine features of a number of these simpler models. Economist Ray Marshall (1974) proposed an *institutional* theory of discrimination that combines economic, historical, social, and psychological factors in the context of group bargaining. Sociologist Gordon Allport (1954) listed "historical, sociocultural, situational, personality, phenomenological, and stimulus object" levels of explanation (Duckitt 1992, 44). Duckitt (1992) scaled this list back to four levels: universal psychological processes, social and intergroup dynamics, mechanisms of transmission of attitudes, and determinants of individual differences in prejudice.

In contrast with the somewhat timeless flavor of economic theories of discrimination, sociologists and social psychologists have noted a shift in the nature of racial prejudice in the United States (and elsewhere) over the last several decades. This shift has variously been described as a movement from "old-fashioned" to "modern" or "symbolic" racism (McConahay 1986; Sears 1988), from "blatant" to "subtle" racism (Pettigrew and Meertens 1995), or from "Jim Crow" to "laissez-faire" racism (Bobo, Kluegel, and Smith 1997). While the particulars of these concepts differ, all stress a movement away from openly stated aversion, assertions of biological inferiority, and support for outright separation of racial groups. Instead, newer versions of racism target the perceived "excessive" demands and privileges of subordinate groups, assert or imply cultural or social inferiority of these groups, and oppose policies designed to aid them. Other researchers have observed that as more overt forms of racism become less common, racism more often takes an "aversive" form, entailing subconscious discomfort or anxiety about contact with members of another group, rather than conscious hostility (Gaertner and Dovidio 1986).

In analyzing the determinants of racial and ethnic wage differences, economists have devoted considerable research effort to statistically separating out the effect of labor market discrimination from the effects of differences in education, experience, and ability (Cain 1986). However, sociological and social psychological research suggest that U.S. employers typically state prejudicial views of racial and ethnic groups *in terms of skill*; they speak the language of "modern" or "laissez-faire" racism, making it difficult to distinguish prejudice from accurate perceptions of skill differences. In-depth interviews indicate that many U.S. employers rate Latino and, especially, black workers as less preferred, and offer skill as an explanation. In face-to-face interviews with employers in Chicago, Joleen Kirschenman and Kathryn Neckerman found that many employers rate black workers worse than others and few rate them better. In fact, employers described a racial gradation, placing Anglos above Latinos, and Latinos above blacks (Kirschenman and Neckerman 1991; Neckerman and Kirschenman 1991). Roger Waldinger (1997) reported similar results from interviews of Los Angeles hotel and restaurant managers. Two other sociologists, Shirley Harkess and Carol Warren (1994), likewise found that some manufacturing managers in an unidentified southern city expressed negative views of blacks, though the fact that their interviews took place in 1979 and 1980 makes them of less immediate interest. Somewhat farther afield, British researchers have also probed negative employer attitudes of racial minorities in their own national context (Jenkins 1986; Lee and Loveridge 1987).

Research in social psychology and organizational demography (Tsui, Egan, and O'Reilly 1992) complements these field studies. Surveys consistently find an expressed preference for coworkers who are homogeneous by race and other characteristics (Tajfel and Turner 1986; Shellenbarger 1993), and in fact homogeneous groups outperform other groups along some dimensions (Jackson 1991). Racial and other demographic differences in a superior-subordinate pair are linked to discomfort and less favorable performance evaluations of the subordinate (Ford, Kraiger, and Schechtman 1986; Greenhaus, Parasuraman, and Wormley 1990; Kraiger and Ford 1985; Sackett and DuBois 1991; Tsui and O'Reilly 1989). This suggests that negative employer assessments of workers of color, at least assessments by white managers, are likely to be shaped by managerial aversion as well as actual worker performance. And social identity theory suggests that black and Latino managers may distance themselves psychologically from inner-city workers, potentially contributing as well to negative assessments (Brown 1995).

A final question posed by the social psychological research inquires: Under what circumstances do prejudicial attitudes translate into action? Numerous experimental studies, summarized by John Duckitt (1992), document that the step from stated attitude to action is far from automatic.

While some social scientists concluded that there is no reliable link between prejudicial attitudes and discriminatory actions (Wicker 1969), Duckitt made a compelling case that in many studies this link was obscured by attitude scales based on "old-fashioned" racism (and therefore mismeasuring modern prejudice) and/or single, narrowly defined actions (which fail to capture a person's broader propensity to act). Analyses that corrected for these problems, he pointed out, *do* tend to demonstrate a correlation between prejudice and discriminatory actions. Experiments that varied conditions further revealed that subjects engaged in discriminatory actions more often when surveillance and the cost of discriminating were low. Finally, Duckitt affirmed that prejudicial attitudes and actions are mutually reinforcing: engaging in discrimination can strengthen bias, as well as the other way around (Simpson and Yinger 1985).

We approach our own data on employer views of workers of color with several propositions and questions:

- We expect negative employer views of workers of color—as incumbent workers or as potential workers—to be common. We expect such negative views to be couched in terms of skills, particularly soft skills. We are interested in learning how employers *explain* these skill problems.

- We predict that employers' views will vary by the gender of the workers being discussed, the manager's race or ethnicity, the type of job being discussed, and the manager's position within the firm (top executive, human resource official, or direct manager of the workers in question). Joleen Kirschenman (1991) reported more positive employer perceptions of black women than of black men, so we expect to replicate this finding. Predictions about the other three types of variation are less clear. We anticipate that managers' perceptions will be shaped by the degree of contact they have with each group, their degree of sympathy with each group, and the degree to which they are concerned about each type of worker performance. We expect employer attitudes to go beyond simple antipathy toward black or Latino workers to encompass managerial views about the *appropriate types* of employment for particular racial and ethnic groups, and assessments of the *alternative workforces* available for a particular job.

- Since we lack independent evidence about the skills of workers or applicants, we cannot directly test the accuracy of employers' perceptions. However, we pose several questions that shed some light on this issue. What evidence do employers themselves cite in characterizing workers from various racial and ethnic groups? How common are obvious stereotypes? What do the interviews tell us about how the observed soft skills of workers depend on context rather than the workers' intrinsic qualities?

- We expect to find a correlation between negative employer attitudes toward workers of color and reduced hiring of these workers.

Throughout, we focus in most detail on employer attitudes toward blacks, since these attitudes appear to be particularly charged and since we gathered more information about perceptions of black workers than of other groups.

What Are Employer Attitudes Toward Workers of Color?

Telephone Survey Results: Worker Ratings and Ethnocentrism

The Employer Surveys offer us an opportunity to find out directly about employer perceptions of various groups' skills. Two sets of questions in the Telephone Survey bear on these perceptions. The first set asks employers to rate the performance of the last hire (whose race and gender are also reported). The second inquires about the relative performance of whole groups of workers. Both show only modest differences in employer perceptions of workers in various race and gender categories.

Averages of individual performance ratings for the last person hired appear in table 4.1. Ratings shown are divided by the rating for "a typical employee's performance," so that 1.0 corresponds to the typical worker. Like the children in Garrison Keillor's mythical Lake Wobegon, all race and gender groups perform above average—at least, above the average current employee. Though rating differences among race and gender groups appear small, a number are significant at the 10 percent level or better. Black and Latino men and white women all earn significantly lower ratings from employers than do white men. On the other hand, racial differences among women and gender differences among nonwhite groups are not associated with perceived performance differences. In addition, there were no differences in *median* ratings (median ratings for all the groups shown was 1; not shown), indicating that the differences in means are driven by extreme values. Note that these ratings apply to *hired* workers, and therefore are likely to understate employer perceptions of differences among groups of applicants.

Table 4.2 records what managers said over the telephone about *general* differences in task or job performance by men, women, racial and ethnic groups, and inner-city residents. The most dramatic result here is that *very* few employers ventured to agree that there are performance differences by gender, race or ethnicity, or area of residence—whether due to political correctness, fear that survey results would fall in the hands of the Equal Employment Opportunity Commission, or a sincere belief that there are no significant performance disparities. The landslide against stereotyping is most overwhelming in the case of (un-

TABLE 4.1   *Mean Performance Rating, by Race and Gender, of Last Hire (1.0 = Performance of a Typical Worker)*

	White	Black	Latino	Asian	All Racial and Ethnic Groups
Men and women	1.06	1.04	1.03**	1.05	1.05
	N = 1492	N = 552	N = 379	N = 87	N = 2,510
Men only	1.07	1.04*	1.03**	1.07	1.06
	N = 660	N = 260	N = 218	N = 48	N = 1,186
Women only	1.04***	1.04	1.03	1.03	1.04††
	N = 832	N = 292	N = 161	N = 39	N = 1,324

Source: Multi-City Telephone Employer Survey.
*Significantly different from whites at the 10 percent level.
**Significantly different from whites at the 5 percent level.
***Significantly different from men at the 5 percent level.

specified) racial and ethnic differences: only 5 percent of respondents replied "yes" or even "maybe." Making distinctions by gender or area of residence appears to be more acceptable, with 20 percent in each case opting for "yes" or "maybe."

Breaking down these stated opinions by race and gender of respondent is instructive. Men are considerably more likely than women to agree to general statements about differences in work performance, particularly differences by gender or residence. Latinos and, especially, Asians are far more prepared to agree to gender or racial differences than are whites or blacks. However, when it comes to the "inner city," which is often used as a synonym for black and/or Latino neighborhoods, it is *whites* and Asians who most often pinpoint a difference in workforce quality.

The radical differences in perceptions by race and gender of respondent suggest that the responses to these questions are politicized. They are colored, to a greater or lesser extent, by what respondents see as socially desirable responses. The numbers seem particularly suspect when compared with the ratings of individual workers, in which employers *do* report differing perceptions, on average, of different race and gender groups.

The Telephone Survey also asked employers to gauge whether customers, employees, or other employers in the industry prefer to deal with people of their own race or ethnicity. The results are reported, broken down by the location of the employer, in table 4.3. Overall, about 20 to 23 percent of employers reported ethnocentric preferences by customers, employees, or other employers. About a third of employers re-

TABLE 4.2   Employer Generalizations About Job Performance by Race, Gender, and Inner-City Residence (Percentage)

	All Respondents	Respondent Race and Ethnicity				Respondent Gender	
		White	Black	Latino	Asian	Male	Female
Some Tasks Are Performed Better by Men, Others by Women							
Yes	18.1	17.1	19.7	23.3	29.8	22.1	13.4
Maybe	2.0	1.8	3.0	1.5	7.4	2.2	1.8
No	79.9	81.1	77.4	75.2	62.8	75.6	84.8
	N = 2,675	N = 2,186	N = 198	N = 123	N = 97	N = 1,434	N = 1,241
Some Tasks Are Performed Better by Members of Some Ethnic or Racial Groups							
Yes	4.3	3.9	3.5	6.5	13.6	4.8	3.7
Maybe	0.9	0.7	1.3	0.0	5.8	1.1	0.8
No	94.8	95.4	95.3	93.5	80.6	94.1	95.5
	N = 2,719	N = 2,227	N = 203	N = 121	N = 97	N = 1,463	N = 1,256
On Average Inner-City Residents Are Weaker Job Applicants or Employees							
Yes	16.1	16.7	10.6	9.7	18.2	20.7	10.9
Maybe	4.2	4.4	4.5	1.6	4.0	4.0	4.3
No	79.8	78.8	85.0	88.7	77.8	75.3	84.8
	N = 2,601	N = 2,114	N = 203	N = 116	N = 97	N = 1,376	N = 1,225

Source: Multi-City Telephone Employer Survey.
Note: Within each panel, each column totals to 100 percent. "Don't know" and refusal responses omitted.

TABLE 4.3   *Proportion of Employers Reporting Ethnocentrism by Customers, Employees, and Other Employers*

	All Employers	Primary Central City	Suburbs	Other Central Cities
Employers reporting Customers prefer to deal with employees of their own race or ethnic group	19.7%	23.0%	19.0%	16.6%
Employees prefer other employees of their own race or ethnic group	23.2	28.0	21.8	20.0
Other employers in your business prefer employees of their own race or ethnic group	21.4	24.6	20.6	19.4
Any of the types of ethnocentrism	31.6	36.7	29.9	29.8
	N = 2,449–3,152	N = 641–817	N = 1,407–1,844	N = 401–91

Source: Multi-City Telephone Employer Survey.
Note: "Other central cities" also include any municipality other than the primary central city that has a black population of 30 percent or more.

ported at least one of the forms of bias. Looking across location in the metropolitan area, perceptions of ethnocentrism are reported with the greatest frequency among central-city employers. These results do not differ dramatically across cities (not shown). Los Angeles and Detroit employers were somewhat more likely to report prejudice among employees and customers. In Los Angeles, this may be due to the tendency of the workforces of many firms to develop into ethnic enclaves. As we noted in chapter 2 and will elaborate in chapter 5, Detroit has a particularly sharp geographical demarcation between blacks and whites, corresponding to the boundary between city and suburb, and a marked social divide among blacks and whites as well. The contrast between city and suburb along ethnocentrism measures was largest for Los Angeles and Boston.

In addition, employers were polled about the racial composition of their customers. We compared the customer composition of businesses that reported customer racial preferences with those that did not. Non-Hispanic whites account for the majority of customers from both groups

(55.8 percent in businesses reporting customer ethnocentrism and 61.2 percent in those that do not), suggesting that customer ethnocentrism is primarily *white, non-Latino* ethnocentrism. Businesses that reported customer ethnocentrism have higher than average representation of black and Latino customers. One potential interpretation is that white, Anglo consumers and employers are most sensitive to workers' race in businesses located in "transitional" or "border" neighborhoods where a broader mixture of racial groups mingle. For whites in segregated suburbs, the issue simply may not be salient. But other interpretations are possible: the difference may be due in part to ethnocentric preferences by black and Latino customers, perhaps based on experiences of discrimination from white employees or, in the case of Latinos, on language issues.

A comparison between these results and those in table 4.2 is interesting. A much higher fraction of employers report a negative perception of other races or ethnicities on the part of *others* than they do a negative assessment of other races or ethnicities *themselves*. This contrast underscores the point that the answers to both sets of questions are influenced by the respondents' willingness to be candid about questions of race during a telephone interview. While the problem of socially desirable responses plagues any survey, it is likely to affect a Telephone Survey more severely than a face-to-face one. Face-to-face interaction creates greater rapport and trust, and the open-ended format enhances this rapport and allows respondents to explain statements that they might fear would be misunderstood. We turn now to the face-to-face interviews for additional evidence.

Employer Perceptions of Demographic Groups in the Face-to-Face Survey

In-depth interviews provide an important vantage point for learning about employer perceptions. Multi-City Study interviewers asked managers whether they saw differences in skill or worker quality among whites, blacks, Latinos, and Asians.[1] The questioning focused on differences between black and white workers, particularly in Atlanta and Detroit, where other racial and ethnic groups are relatively small. The SSRC survey focused even more narrowly, contrasting black men with other workers, particularly whites.

Many employers did describe such differences. It is important to note that the *largest* group of respondents consisted of those who answered, "I don't see any differences" or "I don't know" (sometimes citing the fact that their workforce is too segregated to assess different groups). We will return to this "silent majority" later in the chapter. We focus here on the numerous managers who did identify racial skill disparities. We contend that the views employers hold in this regard are partly an accurate perception of the skills that many less educated workers of color bring to the labor market, but also—especially in the case of soft skills—partly stereotype and partly cultural gap.

Just what is the extent of negative attitudes about the different race and ethnic groups of workers reported in the Multi-City Study face-to-face interviews? The answer is given in tables 4.4 and 4.5. Table 4.4 presents the percentage of our 365 *respondents* who reported each of a variety of attitudes, broken down by metropolitan area. However, workers are not hired by individual managers, but by businesses. One might suppose that negative attitudes by any major decision maker in the business would disadvantage applicants of color or, alternatively, that the barrier would be significant only when a majority of managerial gatekeepers share such views. To address these concerns, we aggregate individual responses up to the level of the *firm* in table 4.5, broken down by firm location within the metropolitan area. Both the percentage of firms in which *any* respondent expressed such an attitude and the percentage of firms in which a plurality of *50 percent or more* of respondents expressed the attitude are displayed in table 4.5. We analyze these employer attitudes separately for each major ethnic or racial group, first considering blacks (as well as statements about "minorities" more broadly) and then Latinos, Asians, and immigrants in general.

Employer Views of Black Workers

As tables 4.4 and 4.5 document, negative employer views of black workers' skills were frequent, consistent with other studies based on employer interviews. We explored three dimensions of employers' characterizations of black skills: hard skills and the soft skills of interaction and motivation. Managers more often identified shortcomings in interaction skills and, especially, motivation than deficits in hard skills among black workers.

To begin with, consider employers' ratings of black workers' hard skills—reading, writing, math, and so on. Referring to table 4.4, approximately 20 percent of all respondents had something disparaging to say about the hard skills of black workers or applicants. In Detroit and Atlanta, cities where blacks are the primary minority group, 31 percent and 29 percent of the respondents made such statements. The responses collected at the firm level, presented in table 4.5, indicate that about 25 to 30 percent of firms across metropolitan locations have a plurality of respondents who believe black hard skills are relatively poor. These percentages are much greater than the proportions of employers who made corresponding statements about Latinos or Asians. Thus, in our survey,

TABLE 4.4   *Percentage of Individual Respondents Reporting Particular Perceptions in Face-to-Face Interviews, by Metro Area*

	Atlanta	Boston	Detroit	Los Angeles	Total
Employers who said					
About blacks					
Blacks have lagging hard skills	28.9	9.9	31.1	16.3	20.3
Blacks have lagging interaction skills	20.0	4.0	18.0	18.4	14.6
Blacks have lagging motivation	40.0	15.8	32.8	45.9	33.4
Black women are better than black men	5.6	0.0	8.2	5.1	4.0
Black men are better than black women	0.0	2.0	1.6	1.0	1.1
Blacks are better workers	3.3	—	1.6	2.0	1.7
About Latinos					
Latinos have lagging hard skills	1.1	7.9	—	10.2	5.4
Latinos have lagging interaction skills	—	—	—	4.1	1.1
Latinos have lagging motivation	2.2	7.9	—	9.2	5.4
Latinos are better workers	5.6	14.9	1.6	26.5	13.4
About Asians					
Asians have lagging hard skills	—	2.0	—	4.1	1.7
Asians have lagging interaction skills	—	—	—	2.0	0.6
Asians have lagging motivation	—	—	—	1.0	0.3
Asians are better workers	3.3	8.9	—	14.3	7.4
About immigrants					
Immigrants have a stronger work ethic	5.6	18.8	3.3	20.4	13.1
	N = 90	N = 101	N = 61	N = 98	N = 350

Source: Multi-City In-Depth Employer Survey.

employers have particularly negative assessments of blacks' hard skills. Negative views of black hard skills are more common in the primary central city than in the suburbs and in other central cities in the metropolitan area. Because relatively more blacks are employed in the primary central city and, therefore, employers there are more familiar with black employees, this finding may be evidence that such gaps are real.

TABLE 4.5   *Percentage of Firms Where Respondents Report Particular Perceptions in Face-to-Face Interviews, by Location*

	Primary Central City	Other Central Cities	Suburbs	Total
Firms where respondents said				
About blacks				
Blacks have lagging hard skills				
At least one respondent	39.7	32.4	29.0	33.7
Half or more of firm respondents	27.9	29.4	23.2	26.2
Blacks have lagging interaction skills				
At least one respondent	29.4	17.6	29.0	26.7
Half or more of firm respondents	19.1	17.6	18.8	18.6
Blacks have lagging motivation				
At least one respondent	54.4	52.9	46.4	50.6
Half or more of firm respondents	38.2	47.1	37.7	39.5
Black women are better than black men				
At least one respondent	13.2	5.9	2.9	7.6
Half or more of firm respondents	10.3	5.9	2.9	6.4
Black men are better than black women				
At least one respondent	1.5	5.9	1.4	2.3
Half or more of firm respondents	—	5.9	1.4	1.8
Blacks are better workers				
At least one respondent	1.5	5.9	4.3	3.5
Half or more of firm respondents	1.5	2.9	2.9	2.3
About Latinos				
Latinos have lagging hard skills				
At least one respondent	11.8	8.8	8.7	9.9
Half or more of firm respondents	4.4	8.8	4.3	5.2
Latinos have lagging interaction skills				
At least one respondent	2.9	—	1.4	1.7
Half or more of firm respondents	1.5	—	1.4	1.2
Latinos have lagging motivation				
At least one respondent	14.7	8.8	5.8	9.9
Half or more of firm respondents	7.4	8.8	2.9	5.8
Latinos are better workers				
At least one respondent	16.2	26.5	21.7	20.3
Half or more of firm respondents	16.2	20.6	14.5	16.3
About Asians				
Asians have lagging hard skills				
At least one respondent	2.9	2.9	4.3	3.5
Half or more of firm respondents	1.5	2.9	2.9	2.3

TABLE 4.5   *Continued*

	Primary Central City	Other Central Cities	Suburbs	Total
Asians have lagging interaction skills				
At least one respondent	1.5	—	1.4	1.2
Half or more of firm respondents	—	—	—	—
Asians have lagging motivation				
At least one respondent	—	—	1.4	0.6
Half or more of firm respondents	—	—	—	—
Asians are better workers				
At least one respondent	13.2	17.6	11.6	13.4
Half or more of firm respondents	13.2	17.6	10.1	12.8
About immigrants				
Immigrants have a stronger work ethic				
At least one respondent	14.7	29.4	18.8	19.2
Half or more of firm respondents	11.8	29.4	13.0	15.7
	N = 68	N = 34	N = 69	N = 172

Source: Multi-City In-Depth Employer Survey.
Note: "Other central cities" also include any municipality other than the primary central city that has a black population of 30 percent or more.

Alternatively, however, it may simply be that suburban employees simply do not think about black workers as much.

In some cases, employers made narrow criticisms of blacks' hard skills. For example, at Michigan Utility, the human resource director stated that blacks pass the exam at a much lower rate than whites. More often, managers combined faultfinding about the hard skills *and* soft skills of black applicants or workers. For example, the manager of clerical workers at a Boston hospital stated,

> I think [minorities'] education is maybe on a lesser level. This is not a racial remark, but I can still say that I think that the white secretaries that I have are much more professional. I'm not sure it's fair to say more "intelligent" but they certainly present themselves that way. They are more higher-caliber.

This manager mixed comments on hard skills (education, intelligence) with evaluations of soft skills (professionalism, self-presentation). In similar fashion, a hospital manager in Los Angeles lamented,

> I would have to say that as far as qualifications, the literacy level of the Caucasian is higher. And I'm talking about verbal communication. I'm

talking about written communication. I see that on the reports that I have to read. I can tell where the report came from. With some of the Hispanics, of course, that's because English is the second language. And with African Americans some of it, I feel, is cultural. There's a certain speech quality. That doesn't mean they, certainly, weren't capable, but it's ingrained.

An Atlanta grocery store manager, describing applicants who "tend to be more black," complained, "They come in usually with very little skills and very little training. They really don't have anything to offer, other than just being a body, a person."

In fact, employers' criticisms of blacks' hard skills often shaded over into discussions of soft skills. Recall that employer assessments of "soft skills" may be distant from any objective representation of workers' skills, because of the subjectivity of such assessments and the context sensitivity of worker behavior along these dimensions. Nonetheless, it is instructive to review what employers said about soft skills. We first consider interaction skills, then motivation, and finally examine managers who made *positive* statements about blacks' soft skills.

Almost 15 percent of respondents complained about blacks' ability to interact well with others in the workplace. The percentage of respondents in Boston who reported negative perceptions of blacks' interaction skills (and of blacks' motivation skills) is substantially less than the proportion in the three other cities.[2] At the firm level, approximately 27 percent of firms had at least one respondent offer such a view, and 19 percent of firms had half or more respondents with this perception of blacks' interaction skills. In the smaller and less representative SSRC sample, 32 percent of businesses had at least one respondent who faulted the interaction skills of black men in particular (not shown). Negative comments on blacks' interaction skills touched on a variety of issues. To start with, numerous managers complained that many African Americans don't know how to apply for a job. The human resource director of a Los Angeles–area department store, for example, complained that few black or Latino men "come in a suit and present that professional image that I need for [commission sales]. They just don't know how to get a job." Quite a few managers, including the Los Angeles hospital manager quoted earlier, also remonstrated African Americans for using a "black" dialect, a problem particularly in jobs involving customer contact. A manager at a retail chain store in Detroit explained that for employers like her, it is important that your language not identify you as black: "I don't want to know when I pick up the phone whether you are black or white."

Respondents' negative comments about blacks' interaction skills went beyond speech patterns. Standard stereotypes about black hostility or oversensitivity abounded, as managers described blacks, and black men in particular, as defensive, combative, or having a difficult "attitude." We discuss further in the next chapter the well-documented stereotype that whites hold about hostility and violence among blacks. The content of employers' comments ranged widely. At one extreme, a Latino store manager in a black area of Los Angeles, who hires mostly Latinos, flatly stated, "You know, a lot of people are afraid, they [black men] project a certain image that makes you back off. They're really scary." When asked how much he thought was perception and how much reality, he responded, "I think 80 percent is reality." Other respondents stated that managers see black men as difficult to control. For example, the black female personnel manager of a Detroit retail store commented:

> Employers are sometimes intimidated by an uneducated black male. Their appearance really isn't up to par, their language, how they go about an interview. Whereas females, black or white, most people do feel, "I could control this person." A lot of times people are physically intimidated by black men. The majority of our employers are not black. And if you think that person may be a problem, [that] young black men normally are bad, or [that] the ones in this area [are], you say, "I'm not going to hire that person, because I don't want trouble."

A white female personnel official from a Los Angeles area public-sector agency department offered a related perspective, laying part of the blame on white supervisors:

> There's kind of a being-cool attitude that comes with walking down the street a certain way and wearing your colors, or challenging those who look at you wrong, and they come to work with an awful lot of that baggage. And they have a very difficult time not looking for prejudice. If a supervisor gives him an instruction, they immediately look to see if it's said different to them because they're black. Or if something goes wrong in the workforce, they have a tendency to blame the race, their being black. And I also think that part of the problem is that the supervisors and managers of these people have their own sets of expectations and their own sets of goals that don't address the diversity of these people, and it's kind of like, "Well, hell, if they're going to come work for me, they're going to damn well do it my way." And my own personal feeling is that a lot of these young black men who are being tough scare some of their supervisors. And so rather than address their behavior problems and deal with the issues, they will back away until they can find a way to get rid of them. We have a tendency to fear what we're not real familiar with.

Other managers agreed that blacks are overly sensitive to discrimination, and/or have expectations that exceed their merits as workers. "It's that old adage, you know, 'The world owes me a living and here I am—give it to me,' type thing," remarked a supervisor of nursing aides in the Los Angeles area. "Even some of them don't want to be told what to do." "With the black workforce for some reason, I've had people say that they weren't being treated fairly," chorused the human resources director of a Boston-area manufacturer. The head cashier at an Atlanta-area grocery store complained,

> With some of the part-timers you have had a problem where a black associate was asked to clean the bathroom or do some type of cleaning, they basically told us that their grandmother, grandfather, did that when they were a slave and now in this era they shouldn't have to do that anymore.
>
> And so you kinda gotta watch what you say so that they don't get offended. With a black person you've got to be mainly serious most of the time, you can't crack a joke without making sure you don't say the wrong things. But whereas if I was around the white people or Oriental, we crack jokes and even if they are putting down our race and things like that, it was a joke, nothing more, no harm done, you know, whereas if it was done in the presence of a black person they get easily offended.

Furthermore, some employers deplored blacks' tendency to congregate in cliques and share stories of perceived discrimination—"the grapevine gets going in the wrong direction," as one Atlanta manager put it.

Turning to the issue of motivation, another recurrent soft-skill stereotype depicted blacks as lazy, unmotivated, or undependable. This, too, is a stereotype of African Americans held widely by whites (Hacker 1992; Majors and Mancini Billson 1992; Peffley and Hurwitz 1998; Fiske 1998). Among employers interviewed face to face in the Multi-City Study, one-third of the respondents expressed a negative view of blacks' motivation. Aggregated to the level of the firm, 40 percent had half or more respondents voice disparaging views of the motivation of blacks. About 50 percent of firms had a least one respondent offer this type of sentiment. As with employer views about hard skills, more primary central city than suburban employers voiced pejorative attitudes about black motivation and work ethic. Again, this differential between the primary central city and suburb might be interpreted as evidence for the accuracy of employer views or for the greater salience of these issues for urban employers. In the SSRC sample, respondents at 40 percent of firms voiced perceptions of black men as unmotivated employees.

As with interaction, comments about black workers' motivation varied widely in substance, but in general were more sharply negative than those about interaction. A Latina female personnel officer of a Los Angeles retail distribution warehouse whose workforce is 72 percent Latino and only 6 percent black stated outright, "Black men are lazy. Who is going to turn over? The uneducated black." The white male owner of a small Detroit-area plastic parts plant (46 percent black, 54 percent white) said that in his experience, black men "just don't care." "Black kids don't want to work" was the opinion of a white male owner of a small auto parts–rebuilding shop in Los Angeles whose workforce is entirely Hispanic women. "Black men are not responsible," added a Latina personnel supervisor for a Los Angeles auto-parts manufacturer located next to a major black neighborhood but with a workforce that is 85 percent Latino and less than 1 percent black. Other typical comments asserted that black workers "tend to work a little slower," "are not as dependable," "have more of an 'I don't care' attitude," "don't really want to work," "are lazy" or are "not as dependable" as immigrant workers because "their job is not as important to them."

Negative views of blacks' interaction skills and motivation were mixed with a smaller number of positive views. About 2 percent of our respondents voiced such positive perceptions, including a slightly higher percentage (3.3 percent) in Atlanta. This is small, indeed, compared with a cumulative total of 46 percent who made negative comments about blacks' hard or soft skills, but it is informative to examine the substance of the positive statements.

Some managers viewed black workers' assertiveness as understandable or even positive. Said the African American director of a Detroit-area social service agency,

> Because of things that we've gone through that maybe people more in the mainstream or majority don't go through, we're just a little more testy, and sometimes people in the majority take that to mean that we don't like them or we're aggressive or real pushy or mean or something.

A white production manager in a Boston-area consulting firm voiced a similar sentiment:

> Those people who have been the underdogs, they are stronger fighters than the people who have had an easy road of it. And perhaps this is where antagonism is created, but it's understandable. If you are an underdog, you're going to fight to do better. And if you're on the other end of the stick, where it's been very easy for you to progress and to achieve and to become successful, you can feel very threatened.

More widespread are employers who see black workers as needing the job more, and therefore more willing to work hard, do menial tasks, and stay at a job longer. Not surprisingly, employers in the suburbs and in other central cities (where the nearby workforce tends to be more affluent) were more likely to hold this belief than their counterparts in the primary central city (see table 4.5). Managers who lauded blacks as harder workers typically offered lower-paying jobs. At establishments where at least one manager described blacks as better workers, the average starting wage lagged a substantial $1.10 behind the pay level at other firms. The wage gap was 66 cents in cases where half or more of the respondents made such statements. The number of firms yielding praise of blacks as better workers was quite small, making these estimated differences rather imprecise. However, we will see in chapter 5 that businesses that spoke highly of *inner-city* workers show an even greater wage disadvantage, and one that is highly statistically significant.

The white manager of an Atlanta-area fast food restaurant reported a striking difference between the white and black workers he was able to hire:

> I find the workers in the suburbs to be, if they are white, to be lower-educated. They don't have communication skills. In the store that I am at now and the ones that I worked at in predominantly black neighborhoods, they tend to be higher-educated. They have a better work ethic in general. The middle-class kids that we did have, they didn't want to work as hard because they didn't have the drive. If you are having to pay bills and pay your own tuition, there is a certain incentive that you have to work. If Mom and Dad are paying the bills and when they write the checks in front of you, why do you have to work hard?

A white manufacturing supervisor agreed, reflecting back on his experience hiring at a department store in a previous job:

> Initially the people from the more affluent areas, whether they be white or black, but primarily they were white, from an interviewing and presentation standpoint they were much more polished. So [you would think], "Hey, this is a great person, let me put them on the floor." They can work in the designer area, whatever, and present themselves very well. Whereas the group from the lower-income areas, which were primarily black, may not present themselves as well at first or may not be as polished or whatever. So you may think, "Well, for this particular position this [upper-income] person presents, better, so we'll go with this person." But the lower-income person may need the job more and may be the more solid employee. If you hire both of them, the lower-income person, the black person or whatever, may stick around longer and be a much more solid citizen than the upper-income person, because [the upper-income person is] always looking for something else to go to.

Some employers thought their black employees were more inclined toward friendly customer service than their white employees. This sentiment was offered by more than one home health agency manager, and also by a Detroit-area dry cleaning manager: "If the truth be told, my black employees are much friendlier on the counter, they make a little bit more of an effort. Yeah, they smile a lot more and they are much more pleasant. They just try harder for the job, I guess."

In short, although substantial minorities of employers criticized blacks' sense of entitlement and lack of commitment, smaller minorities described blacks as willing to settle for less and work hard at the worst jobs. These statements come predominantly from low-wage employers comparing blacks with white, suburban youth.

Cross-city comparisons reaffirm the importance of comparison groups in shaping employers' assessments of black workers. Employer testimonials to African Americans as hard workers who need a job came primarily from low-wage employers in the Atlanta and Detroit areas; their comparison group is often white suburban youth, who do *not* need the job as much. Atlanta and Detroit have not experienced immigration flows from Latin America and Asia on the scale of Boston, let alone Los Angeles; indeed, rural African Americans rather than rural foreigners constitute a major source of immigrant labor for low-wage Atlanta employers. The absence of Boston employers who praised the work ethic of African Americans—and the greater number in Los Angeles who denounced their work ethic (Los Angeles respondents were about half again as likely to complain about blacks' motivation as were their Detroit counterparts, in both SSRC and Multi-City Study data)—is presumably related to the availability of even needier immigrant workforces in those metropolitan areas.

Customer and Employee Attitudes Toward Black Workers

In addition to employers' own perceptions of black workers, they may respond to the attitudes of nonblack customers or employees. Recalling Gary Becker's discussion of employer reaction to customer or employee prejudices, we looked for employer concerns about these attitudes. The face-to-face interviews uncovered many such concerns among employers, particularly in the retail sector. Though no manager indicated approval for customer or employee prejudices, a number talked about adapting to these prejudices in their hiring and placement of black workers. In fact, in a subset of the SSRC retail sample in which we made a point of asking about the issue, respondents at seven out of ten retail stores admitted efforts to race-match employees to store clienteles.

The issue of customer attitudes was brought home forcefully by the personnel director of a chain department store located in an integrated suburb of Detroit. The majority of employees in the store are black, and to avoid driving away a white clientele, he said, "we are forced to have an Affirmative Action program for nonminorities in this particular store." In fact, the store had shifted away from walk-in applications to recruiting in the store (or by mail) from the store's customer base. Other Detroit-area retailers reported similar issues, as with this manager of a home-improvement chain store near Detroit,

> *Respondent:* You do get customers coming in and they'll tell you, "You need to hire more whites," or if the line is long at the register, the guy will blame it on the black girl behind the register.

> *Interviewer:* Do you think that's true about this neighborhood more than, say, Mount Clemens or Eight Mile [areas on the border of the city of Detroit]?

> *Respondent:* Yeah, I think here because you do have a little more of the upscale and you get more of the older, senior shoppers that are still from the old school—you know, "White or no way."

The manager of a Detroit-area dry cleaning establishment echoed the problem, explaining, "I've had a few customers come in and tell me, too, 'Well, I don't want this one waiting on me.' And I will say, 'Why?' 'Well, she's black and I don't want her touching my clothes.' I say, 'Well, it doesn't rub off, you know. It doesn't make any difference.'"

We heard about customer prejudices beyond Detroit and beyond retail businesses. The white female personnel manager at a Los Angeles store said, "At [a store she was posted at previously] we had a lot of customer complaints because it's primarily white and we were always getting complaints that there were all black employees and it's because they were black. That would be the first thing the customer would bring up was 'black.' It was because they were black that they didn't do their job right."

The manager of a home health agency in Boston stated that customers sometimes complain about the race of an aide, and added: "The clients, absolute vast majority, it's whites not wanting blacks. In my time I have not heard of any black client refusing a white caregiver."

The manager of a second home health care agency in Boston repeated this sentiment: "Our patients, not a lot of them but every organization has a certain patient population that says, 'I don't want Hispanics. I don't want blacks.' So we deal with that. And that's tough, because you could have the most compassionate home health aide and here she is black and the patient has a certain, you know. . . ."

A white attorney in Detroit told a similar tale about clients of his law firm, saying that, although blacks appear comfortable with him, "I think I have some white clients who would be very uncomfortable with a black attorney." Another attorney in Los Angeles stated flatly that she would not hire a black receptionist because her clients would object. In some cases, businesses' clients are themselves employers. The site manager at a Public Agency X in the Boston area, which deals with employers, reported:

> You have people right now who are afraid to hire black males, because they think there is a certain level of violence associated with black males. Some employers don't even do business with us because they realize the office is in [a primarily black neighborhood]. We have employers who play little games, who don't actually work with this office. They'll work with another office.

Finally, in one instance—an Atlanta pest-control firm—the manager reported *black* customers' aversion to black employees: "The black customers prefer white people. They tell us that all the time. They don't trust their own kind."

Reports of problems with the attitudes among fellow employees came up repeatedly in the face-to-face interviews. Several respondents cited racial aversion as an explanation for racial homogeneity among their employees. This occurred most frequently in Los Angeles, where managers particularly reported friction between Latinos and blacks. One example is the local manager for a business that handles contracted housekeeping services. His workforce at a Los Angeles-area hospital was almost entirely Latino and not receptive to blacks, whereas the contractor's housekeeping team for another nearby firm was almost entirely black, even though it was managed by a Latino. He commented: "When you are talking black-Hispanic differences, the black on the job will tend to feel very isolated because the Hispanic individuals cluster together, they speak their native language, and you or I or a black person would feel outside of that group automatically."

Accounts of white employees resisting association with black employees surfaced as well, but in most cases the respondent added that such attitudes are not tolerated in the firm. For example, the Latino service manager at a firm in Los Angeles recounted: "I mean, I had a guy come here once, he came in and he refused to ride with a black technician. You know, we have them ride to get experience. [This technician said,] 'I won't ride with [the black technician].' 'Well, then, you don't have a job.'"

Employer Explanations of
Black Skill Levels

Employers who criticized blacks' skills advanced a number of theories to explain these perceived skill problems.[3] Respondents who noted *hard-skill* differences attributed them above all to educational attainment or school quality. A Boston public agency official griped:

> Well, do I see any differences [between workers of different racial or ethnic groups]? Only in the skills level. Again, it goes back to the school system. Whites have abandoned it. It's a minority school system. Those kids who are going through the school system have a different level, a lesser level, of skills than the kids who don't. There's no question about that.

We further explore employers' condemnation of city schools—particularly in Boston—in chapter 5.

The list of reasons given for lagging soft skills is much longer. The most frequent items on the slate were the influences of family structure, the welfare system, and inner-city life. But we also heard from managers who specifically pointed to class rather than race as the key factor shaping blacks' social skills. And some employers noted the dependency of soft skills on workplace context, implicitly or explicitly raising the question of whether they are skills at all.

Employers frequently portrayed black families as not placing sufficient stress on the value of work and education. The opinion of this manager at County Construction in the Atlanta suburbs is representative:

> I think that sometimes they have been raised where a lot is not expected of them, and I think that lends itself to their poor self-confidence and them thinking that they're not capable of it. It's hard to take a person who's lived in an environment where neither of their parents worked and they got along just fine, and then you try and tell them that you've got to work to succeed, and it's something that they just haven't been taught.

The quote above refers to "neither of their parents." More frequent, however, was the view that blacks are likely to have had single mothers, who failed to instill in them a work ethic (or other positive values, such as desire for education) while growing up.[4] Remarks from a manufacturing plant manager exemplify the perceived association between single parenthood and lack of a strong work ethic:

> I think there's a higher percentage chance if you go in the inner city that a black person is going to come from a single-parent home where there has not been any values taught or work ethic, that type thing. But where a

black person has come from what I call a quote "normal" home, there is no difference, okay?

The regional vice president of an insurance firm described *hard-skill* consequences of single-parent upbringing as well:

> When you find that a large number of those people [blacks] are unemployed, I think it's because either they don't want to be employed or they're not college-educated. They're high school-educated or less, and they don't have the technical skills required to get a decent job. And that could come from family background or lack of nurturing. Single-parent family could come into that, because education may not be as strong.

In Los Angeles, the comparison goes beyond black and white. This transportation company manager clearly feels that being raised by single mothers is part of the reason blacks are less attractive job candidates than the alternative sources of labor in Los Angeles, Hispanics and Asians:

> One of the key elements of the business code is the word "respect" and the second word is "responsibility." We have found because of family values that, for instance, the Asian worker has a very strong sense of responsibility and respect. We have found a little closer sense of responsibility because of the family value with the Hispanic. We have found less of that being prevalent in the black, and principally because they don't have the same strong family value. In the economic environment of Los Angeles as a whole, if an Asian applies for a position, you can say in most cases they have come from a family where the mother and father are still living together. In the Hispanic you can say that. In the black you cannot say that.

Many employers also expressed the belief that blacks are more likely than other groups to depend on public welfare, and this contributes to their poor work habits. Most frequently, employers suggested that welfare undermined blacks' upbringing or, in the case of women, their current seriousness about work:

> I have interviewed where I was stunned that their [black women's] expectations were, expecting to be given something for nothing. I believe [it's due to] their environment where there's more of the matriarch, and it's more of the welfare system. More of the black races are on that system where they have children so that they can get more money. And I have interviewed a few of the young ladies who don't see a goal in mind. They don't have any vision of what they could do. It is a day-to-day survival. (*Los Angeles-area hospital manager*)

They're trying to get the blacks to get their self-esteem back and basically the biggest problem with a lot of people, not just blacks, is the welfare system. Because you've got third- and fourth-generation people on welfare. They can't remember when the last person in that family went to work for a day. (*Boston-area candy factory manager*)

A welfare mentality to me is people that don't give a damn. After you've been beaten down and beaten down for so long, then they really don't give a damn. That person feels like, they already don't have a goal in life. They just want a job. They don't care as far as satisfying the customer. They're under no pressure as far as bills go, 'cause the government is taking care of them, so if you ride them too hard they quit. (*personnel director at an Atlanta-area fast food restaurant*)

Our respondents frequently explained blacks' (and, to a lesser degree, Hispanics') labor market problems as a result of growing up in inner-city areas. As we describe in more detail in the following chapter, managers envisioned the inner city as a place where there is a concentration of negative causal factors such as inferior schools, single-parent families, poor role models, and welfare dependence. So we often heard accounts that wove together these various factors. For instance, a custodial supervisor in a Detroit-area public agency said:

Respondent: In some situations perhaps by the environment in which they [blacks] were raised, they are at a disadvantage coming from single-parent families or broken homes or see their parents be on some type of aid.

Interviewer: Do you think that's more true among your workers here [in a community immediately adjacent to Detroit] than at Macomb [County, north of Detroit, where the respondent previously employed a white workforce]?

Respondent: Yes, I don't know if it's because it's a poorer area and it's put more strain on families and people where they couldn't hold the family together.

Another Detroit-area manager, a senior administrative assistant at the regional headquarters of "ShopKwik," a retail chain, offered a similar analysis: "Well, it's the way that they're brought [up]—I mean, there's gangs out on the streets. There's people hijacking cars and it's the way that, if your mom is not home and you're on welfare, what type of a life can those kids have?"

Single motherhood, reliance on welfare, and inner-city residence are disproportionately present among *low-income* families, not just black families. And quite a few managers, particularly in Detroit, did link blacks' perceived skill problems to class rather than race. As a white manager at a Detroit publishing concern put it, skill disparities are "more a reflection of—the people of that race might fit into this socio-economic structure, and therefore they reflect the values of that socio-economic structure."

A white supervisor at a Detroit nonprofit stated the case even more strongly:

See, my thing is the whole, the income level. I wish we would have a day where people would understand how the income level affects work ethics. Because I think they look at it from a racial view. And maybe there are some tie-ins, but I just am bound to confront that race stuff. It's like, have you looked at every other possibility before you went immediately and said it's race?

An African American manager at a government federal agency office in Detroit concurred:

Black and white, I would think it was more a matter of economics, which would tend to be black and white [laughter]. But I don't think black and white is the issue. I think it's those that come from lower-income levels have lower expectations of themselves and do not necessarily do as well. They don't expect to do as well as those who have lived a middle-class or better life, regardless of the color, have different expectations and then they bring that with them. So with Detroit being primarily black and low-income level in general, then it could appear to be black and white.

The white vice president of operations at an industrial real estate company in the Los Angeles area agreed in part, but suggested a more complicated story that involves attitudes spawned by poverty and the complementary problem of management prejudice toward blacks:

I think it could be a combination of their attitude and the way they look at going into a position, and I think you can look at it also on the management's end as prejudice that is still remaining in the minds of a lot of the owners. I think it's a twofold situation. I think there is a history to overcome with the black employee. That they're lazy. I think a lot of times that there are black employees that have that feeling themselves. That they have probably come up out of the poverty without a lot of initiative given behind them. So they go in with the attitude that it is owed to them.

A number of our informants took a quite different line of argument, however. Instead of blaming poor soft skills on blacks' social environments or families, they maintained that such qualities—and particularly motivation—are created within the workplace and labor market. That is, they pointed to the importance of *context*—both current and earlier in someone's work history—in shaping soft skills. As a black human resource official of a Detroit-area insurer expressed it:

> I think business drives the work ethic. If business is lax, then people have casual attitudes about their jobs. You are one thing up to the point of entering the business world, but then you are something else. I'm not the same person I was fifteen years ago. I had to take on certain thoughts and attitudes whether I liked it or not.

Several others agreed that motivation is more a function of management than of the workforce. When asked about racial differences in the work ethic, a white manager of contracted public-sector workers mused, "I think it's how you motivate each group. Two or three years ago I would have probably said, Well, the black race isn't as motivated as the Oriental or the Hispanic. But I've seen that if you motivate, that you have to motivate each group differently."

A white public-sector human resource official added that work ethic may vary by job:

> If I take security, or I take the basic labor jobs, I'm not so sure that when they were Caucasian-dominated, twenty years ago, that people weren't leaning on a shovel and gold bricking. Many times the classifications we normally associate with being more lazy or finding ways to avoid work are the entry-level, lower-skilled ones. And now those happen to be dominated by blacks and, to a lesser extent, Hispanics.

The black human resource director at an Atlanta-area motel gave a similar account. Asked if there was a racial difference in work quality or work ethic, he responded, "Nah, nah. I think that if they made more, I think they would work a lot better. It's money." And a white Los Angeles hospital executive likewise explained workforce differences by the nature of the jobs held:

> One of my departments is entirely black, and we find their style to be less professional. The radio's going, the workplace is sloppier, there's always food. They have an increasing need to work overtime to get their work done. They have the most boring and tedious jobs, so there's a certain amount of tolerance. That they kind of need to do what makes the day the most enjoyable, to put up with the work and stick around for these boring jobs.

A few respondents also argued that workers can readily be trained to relate well to customers. Even a store manager who commented that "it does take a certain kind of person" to be "fast, fun, and friendly" (the slogan of the Value King chain, discussed in chapter 3), added, "but if you work with a person, I think that you could pretty much [get them to] be fast, fun, and friendly."

Although most of these employer comments referred to blacks, we encountered a particularly striking example of the ability of employers to shape worker attitudes in a Latino community. By coincidence, our SSRC sample included two department store distribution warehouses located in the same Latino neighborhood in the Los Angeles area. In one case, personnel officials complained sarcastically about employee laziness, their propensity for theft, the presence of "gang bangers" wearing their gang colors, and even the poor personal hygiene of the workforce. Turnover in this warehouse stands at 25 percent, even after personnel beefed up screening to select for more stable employees. In the second warehouse, however, turnover is 2 percent. Although this warehouse also employs large numbers of present and past gang members, managers have successfully imposed a dress code that bans the wearing of colors. The key to the remarkably low turnover, according to the vice president for human resources, "is simply locating your operation in an area where you don't have an awful lot of competition, and what competition you do have, you meet or exceed all pay and benefits they offer."

Indeed, this warehouse pays its entry-level workers from 50 cents to $2.50 more per hour than its competitor does. The contrast suggests that efficiency wage models, which posit that higher pay will elicit greater effort from workers, help explain worker attitudes (Akerlof and Yellen 1986). A manager at Atlanta-area County Construction described the principles involved. After complaining about laziness, tardiness, and transportation woes among his entry-level workers, he explained how the business is addressing these problems:

> The biggest strategy is money speaks. We went through a big, major change in our pricing structure here lately, as far as what we start off people. You go to [another business that competes for workers] and you get paid $4.50 an hour. We start entry-level people off at $7.50 an hour. We feel like if we offer you more money, we're offering you good money as far as an entry-level person with no experience, and we expect our money's worth.

As all these examples illustrate, differences in workers' soft skills may be real, yet be effects as well as causes of unequal treatment.

Employer Views of Latinos, Asians, and Immigrants

When asked about "differences between blacks, whites, Latinos, and Asians," most respondents zeroed in on the distinction between blacks and whites. We heard much less about Latinos and Asians, in part because in two of the metropolitan areas under study—Atlanta and Detroit—these groups remain small. When managers did speak to Latinos' and Asians' skills, positive comments outnumbered negative ones—the reverse of the situation for blacks. This is particularly true with regard to soft skills. Since relatively few employers made *any* comment about Latino and Asian skills, it is useful to compute the ratio of positive to negative comments in order to facilitate comparison with employers' views of blacks. For blacks, the ratio of respondents indicating blacks are better workers to those stating that blacks are worse workers (in terms of hard skills or soft skills) was a minuscule .04, meaning that for every respondent with a positive viewpoint there were 25 with negative things to say. For Latinos, positive statements slightly outnumbered negative ones, yielding a ratio of 1.32. For Asians, the ratio was 2.92: nearly three laudatory respondents for each critical one. After reviewing criticisms of Latino and Asian skills, we will turn to analysis of the positive statements.

Start once more by considering hard skills. As table 4.4 shows, only 5 percent of all respondents criticized Latinos' basic and technical skills. This percentage was considerably higher—over 10 percent—in Los Angeles, where Latinos are the major group of people of color. Asians came in for very little criticism. The responses collected at the *firm* level, presented in table 4.5, indicate that while a plurality of respondents at 26 percent of firms criticized black hard skills, the percentage judging Latinos this way was a lower 5 percent, and the percentage for Asians lower still.

"I have to say the Hispanics, most of them don't pass the [math] test," commented a Boston-area bank manager. More commonly, however, employers pointed to language problems with Latino, Asian, and other immigrant groups. The personnel director at a Boston-area factory lamented:

> I think a lot of the [ethnic groups], especially Hispanic, are not prepared to go into the workforce. Language. Simple math skills, basic reading skills. Some of them have the initiative to go to school and learn the language. Others do not, and it's a big problem. It's a horrendous problem because we're looking at entry-level people, we're looking for people to train on their job. And to train to run a machine, for instance, the drilling machine. We're going to get maybe a high school grad or even less, and we find that it's almost impossible to hire some people, because there's no standards when these people come into the country.

In a Los Angeles nursing home chain, Asians' difficulty with English raised very concrete issues: "Facilities have been written up for language. Like a building I had in [location]. They were cited because the residents couldn't talk to some of the staff members because their English was so poor that they couldn't communicate."

Aside from difficulties with language, no employers disparaged the hard-skill levels of Asian workers. On the contrary, we frequently heard the stereotype of Asians' facility with math and technical tasks. The 4 percent of respondents in Los Angeles and the 2 percent in Boston who criticized Asian hard skills (see table 4.4) were invariably speaking of problems with English. Of course, in a number of businesses serving immigrant communities, bilingualism, or even speaking the immigrant language, is instead a plus. A manager at a Boston-area public-sector agency noted both sides of this coin: "If you're people from a background where English isn't their first language, yeah, they may have trouble communicating with other people if they're not that good with the English language." But he continued:

Well, I think having some [people for whom English is a second language], it's an advantage, because we do realize that [clients] are from everywhere. And being here, we do look for some people with other languages, again being here in this area there's a lot of Hispanic [clients], so we have a certain pool of Hispanics. If a person gets a call and they don't speak the language, they have a difficulty, we can transfer it to a person who speaks Spanish.

Criticisms of Latino, Asian, or immigrant soft skills were relatively rare. Referring back to table 4.4, only 1 percent of respondents said anything negative about Latinos' interaction skills; 5 percent faulted Latinos' motivation. The overall average for Latino motivation is a bit misleading, however, because there are so few Latinos in Detroit and Atlanta. In Los Angeles and Boston the percentages criticizing Latinos' motivation were 9 percent and 7 percent. Fewer than 1 percent of the surveyed managers said negative things about Asians' soft skills.

Detractors of Latinos' soft skills often echoed themes that we heard more often in descriptions of blacks. Some managers complained of Latino pride or prickliness. For instance, the owner of a Boston-area factory commented:

I had a manager in here and the way he tells them to do things, they thought it was disrespectful, the way he was talking to them. They wanted to see "please" and "thank you" and kind of "kiss my fanny"-type of an attitude. They pretty much thought that the way the authority was delegated by that person, it would have been different if it had been a white person who was going to do the same job.

Motivation issues came up at the same plant, where a manager described Latinos as "more slow-paced because of their background and the countries they came from [that] don't have the hustle and bustle of the United States." Although managers at this plant reported problems with first-generation immigrant Latinos, we more commonly heard praise for the new immigrants' work ethic, coupled with complaints that succeeding generations did not necessarily inherit this attitude.[5] A Los Angeles-based manager of contracted hospital housekeepers identified young, native-born Latina women as the group with the worst ethic, stating that he had encountered high levels of workers' compensation fraud in this population. "There is an issue of respect" with native-born Hispanics, much as with African Americans, stated a manager at a Los Angeles–area utility.

Outnumbering the negative comments about Latinos and Asians were laudatory statements about their work habits. Closely related were the recurrent paeans to the immigrant work ethic—primarily applying to Latinos, Asians, and Afro-Caribbean migrants in the cities in question. It was not always easy to tell whether employers were praising Latinos or Asians as a group or were praising their immigrant workers (whom these two groups disproportionately represent). When it was not obvious whether a respondent was referring to Latinos or Asians, on the one hand, or immigrants who happened to be Latino or Asian, on the other, we coded *both* a preference for Latino workers or Asian workers *and* an affirmation of a stronger work ethic among immigrants in tables 4.4 and 4.5.

As table 4.4 shows, over 13 percent of all respondents asserted that Latinos are preferred workers (more than six times as many as expressed this view of blacks), and more than 7 percent felt this way about Asian workers. The percentages were much higher in Los Angeles, where there are relatively more Latinos and Asians than in other cities, and higher as well in Boston, where racial diversity is also greater than in Detroit or Atlanta. The firm-level counts in table 4.5 make the point even more forcefully. Over 16 percent of firms have a plurality of respondents who favor Latino workers, and close to 13 percent of firms have a plurality of respondents who prefer Asians. The chorus who sang the praises of immigrant workers included 13 percent of our respondents, and at almost 16 percent of firms, half or more respondents agreed that immigrants were superior to native workers. Again, this opinion was heard most often in Los Angeles and Boston. When we consider the 13 percent with positive comments as a percentage of those who commented at all on the relative work ethic of immigrants and natives, the results are far more dramatic: 92 percent of those making any comment rated immigrants as more committed. The same was true in the smaller SSRC sample, in which 81 percent of Detroit respondents who ventured an opinion agreed that immigrants have a stronger work ethic than native-born workers, as did 88 percent of Los Angeles respondents. This bodes ill for less skilled African American workers, particularly in Los Angeles, since they increasingly compete with immigrant workers for jobs.

As with blacks, those employers who rate Latinos, Asians, and immigrants as better workers are bestowing a mixed blessing. Since a key issue is willingness to work where natives might turn up their noses, these firms turn out to offer below-average wages. At firms where at least one respondent or at least half of respondents pronounced Latinos better workers, the hourly starting wage averaged 24 and 27 cents less, respectively, than at other firms. Businesses where at least one manager lauded Asians paid 36 cents per hour less than others, and when half of the managers or more jumped on the bandwagon, the gap widened to 93 cents. Praise for the immigrant work ethic, similarly, came with a wage penalty of 39 cents (when at least one manager spoke up) to 96 cents (when half or more did so). One Los Angeles manufacturer made this connection explicit. When asked why most of his workforce was Latino, he explained that as a small business, "We have to have a competitive edge, and our edge is our prices are lower." He added, "All of my guys, practically, start at five dollars an hour," while "some of the competitors that we deal with pay fifteen an hour." This should not surprise us, since immigrants are often comparing their current situation with peasant agriculture, maquiladora-type export assembly jobs, or even low-intensity warfare back home.

Praise for Latino and Asian workers typically focused on motivation, with managers sometimes attributing these groups' high levels of commitment to their recent immigration:

> Spanish people are more willing to work. They are willing to work longer hours. I think the ones that I've known are very dedicated to their jobs. (*Boston-area metal-finishing shop*)

> Your Asian workforce, because it's the newest immigrant in the country, and what I've seen with them is they have a completely different work ethic. You need them for seventy-two hours a day, they'll be there for seventy-two hours a day. (*Boston-area factory*)

If anything, employers were even more positive about Asians than Latinos, as this comment by a Boston-area factory trainer indicates: "[Hispanics] take a lot of pride in what they do, but they also can get very insulted. As a spectrum I see the Asians on the high end of work ethic and working hard and privately and quietly. I probably see Hispanics on the other end because of that pride in their culture."

Some employers compared immigrants favorably to native whites.

The remarks of two white Boston-area managers are striking in this regard:

> *Respondent:* [The Latinos] work pretty well. They're trying to support their family.

> *Interviewer:* Would say you have more problems in getting the white people to work?

> *Respondent:* Absolutely. I mean, not that we won't hire them, but we will look twice before we hire just a regular white guy for a floor job. (*factory*)

> The Cape Verdean guys back there [in the kitchen] are my hardest workers. These guys are absolutely fantastic workers. When I was younger in all restaurants, you always had young, white, American boys washing dishes. Now, you know, I almost try to stay away from them in a way because they're so lazy at times. I get Cape Verdean kids in here and they bust their butt. You know, I get these white kids in here, they're young, sixteen, seventeen, eighteen years old, and they think they're just going to hang out and just be lazy all day. (*restaurant*)

However, in other cases whites are not applying for the jobs in question, so employers compared immigrants favorably to blacks alone. The maintenance supervisor at a Boston-area facility compared *immigrant* blacks to African Americans, and concluded that West Indian immigrants "seem to be a little bit harder workers, will give you a little bit more," whereas "the native black expects a lot more for doing a lot less." The personnel director of an Atlanta-area laundry expressed a strong opinion on the merits of Latino immigrants versus African Americans:

> [Hispanics] have a much higher work ethic [than blacks]. Hispanics, while they are employed with you, are very good employees. They're diligent. They do their job. They don't complain as much. [Blacks are] more vociferous than Hispanic people. If we are going to have complaints or we're going to have people not coming into work, it's going to be more predominantly black than it is Hispanic.

In fact, a supervisor at this laundry expressed concern at the prospect that prosperity in Mexico would cut off their labor supply, since blacks don't stay in the jobs and whites don't even apply:

> *Respondent:* The only thing that really bothers us [supervisors] right now is how they say that Mexico is going to start paying

more money and all of this kind of stuff. If we didn't have Mexican people that come in and want jobs like they do now, I believe we'd be in trouble. Because we do not get black people that will come to work and stay here.

Interviewer: Or white people?

Respondent: Oh there's no—you can forget white people, period.

At a Los Angeles garment factory, the manager drew similar conclusions when he compared workers by race and ethnicity: "I think the work ethic for Hispanics is better than it is for blacks," he stated. "Asians are very good workers." Whites, on the other hand, were simply out of the picture for these jobs: "Whites, they wouldn't do the type of job in the back. That's a rarity, especially in Southern California, to see a member of the Caucasian race working in the plants. They just don't have the stamina or the, you know, humility to do that type of job."

In this context, African Americans have fewer opportunities than whites, but higher expectations than immigrants do. A Los Angeles warehouse's operations director quoted black workers as saying, "I'm paraphrasing it: 'You expect me to do that for what? You're not paying me enough for doing what you want me to do'"—and contrasted this with "hard-working" immigrant Latinos.

Customer reservations about dealing with Latino or Asian employees came up far less frequently than for blacks. Nonetheless, customer bias is an issue for these ethnic groups as well, as the examples of an Atlanta supermarket and a Los Angeles car dealership illustrate:

I think in today's world we get more complaints from customers about Hispanics and Orientals than we do blacks. Years ago we used to get complaints when we had "too many blacks" in a particular store. You don't hear that today, but you sure as hell hear about the fact that "You've got nothing but slant-eyes working in this store," or, "All those damn Mexicans are everywhere."

Unfortunately, I've had people come up to me and say, "I want a Caucasian salesperson. I don't want to talk to a Chinese salesperson." I think it's more that than it is the ability of my salesperson.

The Silent Majority: Employers Who Denied Racial Differences

It is important to note that the largest group of respondents consisted of those who did *not* describe differences by race within the workforce.

Based on context, some of these answers appear to be sincere, whereas others were almost certainly offered as the socially desirable answer. As one Boston-area public-sector respondent wryly remarked, "we have to be so politically correct these days." Certainly a number of respondents were uncomfortable with the question, as in the case of this clerical supervisor at an Atlanta-area educational institution:

> *Interviewer:* A number of the people that we have talked to in the area have commented on the differences between black and white workers. Could you comment on that?
>
> *Respondent:* [whispers inaudible words]
>
> *Interviewer:* But it's confidential.
>
> *Respondent:* I know, I know. I guess you hear me hedging a little. It just depends on the individuals. But this has been one of our problems. The . . . a lot of it is the . . . and it's not true, it's not true, blanket . . . definitely it's not, but unfortunately in the majority of the cases we have problems that tend to be minority. I am going to close my door in case anyone comes down the hall.

A few managers referred to equal employment opportunity laws in ways that seemed to indicate discomfort at drawing racial distinctions. "That's a loaded question," said another Boston-area public-sector manager; "you know, the direction of your question was towards, for lack of a better term, 'protected populations,' and I cannot articulate any particular reason why those populations and/or employees would have any more of a hurdle with regard to their work that I know of."

Moreover, many respondents gave mixed responses, at some points delineating racial differences and at other points denying them. Consider this Atlanta-area restaurateur, who offered a detailed indictment of black job applicants:

> When you have white people come in the door [they usually] are more qualified than some of the black people that come in off the street. Because most of the time, black people that come in off the street, they've had sixteen jobs in the last two months just because they're never satisfied with what they have. You never know if they're telling you the truth. Whereas white people, nine out of ten times theirs are pretty much what they write down. A white person will come in dressed in a tie, whereas a black person will come in dressed in, you know, rags. Have four earrings in each ear. In this business you want someone that comes to the table that's

not going to intimidate you. You want somebody that's going to look presentable, have good communication skills.

But at the end of this speech, he insisted, "I love my black employees as much as I love my white employees. They do just as much a job, you know." In this case, the respondent is distinguishing between black applicants and the black employees he has actually hired; in other cases, the logic underlying apparently inconsistent statements is far less clear.

Within the majority group who did not describe racial differences, there were four general categories of responses. First were the respondents who appeared uncomfortable or irritated with the question, or simply wanted to get the topic over with. These interviewees gave the minimal answer, "no," to the question about differences among groups of workers, and to the interviewer probes that often followed a clipped answer of this kind. Such flat denials were frequent, but more numerous was the second class of replies: "it all depends on the individual." For example, the human resource manager from a Boston-area instrument manufacturer stated:

> You might see certain traits or tendencies in individuals, but you can't necessarily say it's based on their race or something like that. So, I don't think it would be fair to make those generalizations. I don't want to sit here and say, "Asians make good workers," and things like that, because it depends more on the individual than the particular racial group.

The manager of a financial services office in Los Angeles gave a similar response:

> I have an Asian lady working for me now. She's a very hard worker. Very dedicated, very dependable. But I've had Asians work with me that were not. The same in the black community and Hispanic. I've had it work both ways. The young lady that worked for me straight out of high school for six years was Hispanic background. Never had office experience in her life. Excellent. And yet I had Hispanics work for me that were lazy, didn't have an interest in the job. So I personally don't think it's too much on the ethnic background as it is the personal individual.

Quite often, this response was phrased not as an answer to the question, but rather as an assertion that color-blind procedures are used at the firm—"we don't consider race, we look at the individual." As the facilities manager at a large Atlanta factory put it: "I'm just color-blind. I know there's a black, white, Asian, Latin, Indian, Korean, whatever the case is. But I just look at them as individual people, simple as that."

In some cases, it appeared that "it depends on the individual" was given as a socially desirable response, since the circumstances of the firm suggested something different. For example, the manager of a contract cleaning firm in Boston offered: "Well, my personal feeling from watching people do this work for twenty years, and when we sold the company before, we had ten thousand cleaners going out every night, okay, so we see a lot of people. And to me, it's not that segment of society, it's the individual."

But earlier, he had indicated that twenty years ago the cleaning crews were almost entirely Portuguese immigrants, and now because the second-generation Portuguese don't want these jobs, the crews are virtually all Latino.

One variant of "it depends on the individual" was a group of employers who dismissed the question of differences between groups of workers by recounting their experience with a successful black (or Hispanic or Asian) employee. Others avoided the question by saying they had no black applicants in recent memory (or, less often, no white applicants), often because of the distance of the firm from the central city or because "blacks just don't apply for these jobs."

Third were the respondents who stated that different groups have different cultures, not necessarily different levels of skill, and that it is management's responsibility to deal with diversity. Here a personnel official at a Boston-area public agency starts out by saying "it's individual," but then goes on to talk about how the office manages diversity: "I really think it's individual rather than looking at the race. In every race, you're gonna find something different. Someone who may not fit. We try to discourage stereotyping in here, too. So we celebrate the different ethnic groups on a regular basis and that's one of the things, we have a committee."

But some respondents who proclaimed the importance of recognizing and respecting diversity voiced what appeared to be very conventional stereotypes at another point in the interview. For example, the Asian human resource director at Anytown College in the Los Angeles area asserted: "Sure, work ethics. I think it has to do with their cultural background. And that's why I think we're talking more about how to deal with diversity, how to value diversity. Because if you don't understand one culture from the other, you tend to have within your workforce problems." Later in the interview, however, he stated, "And you've got your African Americans who think that 'Oh well, they owe it to me, and therefore I can do whatever I want.'"

The final type of "no difference" reply was "there may be some differences out there, but we screen [or train] so effectively that we do not see such differences among our candidates [or employees]." Most public-sector agencies fell into this category. Respondents from these agencies indicated that the need to pass the relevant civil service tests for a job in their organization resulted in slates of candidates, all of whom could do the job.

For example, at a government agency in Massachusetts the personnel manager declared:

[Differences by race or ethnicity don't] have a whole heck of a lot to do with it. No, a black kid has to be as motivated as a white kid to go up and take these courses on his own. To go up to [a particular level of] training, to become a [category of specific competence in this training] and that kind of thing. He's got to be as motivated as a white person to be attractive to us. And so by the time we get people, the standard is so high it is foolish for us to do anything less. The black, white, age doesn't, I mean, whatever we've got in that pool, they have to meet that standard.

A Los Angeles public agency manager emphasized training rather than selection:

People skills? It's pretty across the board, as far as them being able to deal with the public and supervise. I think it's just the constant training at [name of the agency]. We take them when they're seventeen and eighteen, and just keep them here forever, so they're homegrown, and that's it, you know. And maybe that's why we don't see [such differences].

This type of reply was not exclusive to the public sector. After having been asked why the private-sector company for which he worked had developed such a good reputation as a place for African Americans to succeed, this Los Angeles personnel official stated:

Well, because of the programs we have. That we do take affirmative action seriously. We have great training programs. But it's not just for one ethnicity. Everybody goes through those programs. You really come in and you really do get trained well. And the [company] has continued an atmosphere, environment for people to succeed.

Based on these comments by the "silent majority," we suspect that negative employer views of black workers, and most likely of Latinos and Asians, are more widespread than the numbers in our tables would suggest. Those who cited cultural rather than skill differences, or stated that through screening or training they garner well-performing workers from all racial groups, offered explanations that square their denial of racial differences with the widely known differences in workforce outcomes by race. But most of the silent majority answered the question about racial differences among workers with variants of "no" or "it depends on the individual." These are the answers one would expect of someone giving the socially desirable response to shut off further discussion. While we acknowledge that some managers who told us "it depends on the individual" were most likely stating a sincere, deeply held belief, we suspect that others were not.

The views of the "silent majority" conclude our first look at employer perceptions of racial groups in the workforce. We have simplified by stressing commonalities in employer attitudes, and by examining quite varied managers together as a single group. Now it is time to devote more attention to variation in employers' stated perceptions.

Dimensions of Variation in Employer Perceptions

We examine variation in two ways. First, we consider how employer attitudes toward racial groups, particularly blacks, differ according to the *gender* of the workers being discussed. It turns out that managerial perceptions of black men and Latinos differ in many cases from their view of black women and Latinas. Second, we examine the attitudes of *different groups* of managers: by race, by position within the business, and by the type of job for which they are hiring.

Gender Within Race in the Eyes of Employers

Past research leads us to expect that employers will view black women and black men in distinct ways. An extensive literature—not primarily focused on the workplace—explores stereotypes of black men and black women. As we have noted, stereotypes of black men often include laziness, violence, and hostility. Black women are often stereotyped as welfare-dependent, single mothers, and dominating or pushy. Indeed, a common view blames many of the problems of African Americans on widespread single motherhood (Collins 1990; Mullins 1994).

If such stereotypes are prevalent, it should not be surprising to find that many employers refer to them in judging the employability of black men and women. Joleen Kirschenman (1991) found that 39 percent of Chicago-area employers rated inner-city black women as more desirable workers than their male counterparts, whereas only 10 percent expressed a preference for inner-city black men; the remainder did not report seeing any difference between the two groups. Interestingly, employers typically linked both positive and negative perceptions of black women to single motherhood. Positive views of black women tended to emphasize their high level of motivation and commitment, attributed by many employers to their economic role as main supporters of their families. Employers who criticized black women as workers, on the other hand, stressed their unreliability due to their child care obligations. Ivy Kennelly (1999), using a subset of the data analyzed in this chapter (she examined employer interviews from Atlanta, one of the four cities in the larger data set), confirmed Kirschenman's finding of two-sided employer judgments of black women workers keyed to an image of the African American woman as single mother. Unlike Kirschenman, Kennelly found that equal numbers of employers described black women as committed and as unreliable.

Our findings from the four-city sample of face-to-face interviews are generally consistent with Kirschenman's and Kennelly's results. Specifically, we likewise find employer views characterizing black women as single mothers. However, we also find a set of additional employer assessments of the difference between black men and women that are not anchored in single mother, absent father stereotypes: black women as more educated and skilled than black men, black women as better at relating to others, and, conversely, black women as touchier than black men. In addition, we encountered a small number of employers who distinguished between Latino and Latina workers, most often by criticizing the "macho" attitude of the former.

In the interests of truth in advertising, we wish to note that in the in-depth surveys, we learned much more about the distinctions employers drew between black and white workers than about those they drew between black women workers and black men workers. This is due to the structure of the questionnaire itself. Interviewers were instructed to probe first for employer perceptions of racial differences, then gender differences in general, and finally gender differences within race. Because many employers were uncomfortable with these lines of questioning, interviewers had the discretion to cut the series of queries short if they concluded that continuing it would be fruitless and might jeopardize responses to the rest of the survey. As a result, employers spoke directly about differences between black men and women only in a small minority of cases—about one in nine. In coding responses, we did not count employers who simply addressed differences in physical strength ("Women can't lift cases of Coke all day") or commented on workers' gendered preferences for particular jobs.

As table 4.4 shows, about 4 percent of respondents characterized black women as superior to black men; about 1 percent stated the reverse. When we recalculate these proportions as a percentage of those who expressed an opinion about the *relative skills* of black men and women, they amount to 36 percent who rated black women better than black men and 10 percent who stated the reverse. These rankings are strikingly similar to those found by Kirschenman (1991)—in both cases indicating a strong preponderance of rankings placing black women above black men.

Employers who identified black women as better workers than black men sounded three main themes. The most frequent one, echoing Kirschenman's and Kennelly's findings, pointed to black women's motivation. For instance, the white male manager of a chain restaurant in the Los Angeles area commented: "The black female tends to work more and harder than the black male. Where the black male tends to slack off, not work. They're the ones who would say, 'Ten-minute break,' or, 'I need a cigarette.' You know, 'I need to get out,' or, 'I need this particular weekend off.'"

A number of employers expressed this superior motivation in terms of being willing to put up with more or settle for less (a pattern also noted by Kennelly). For example, a white male supervisor at a Detroit-area steel plant said, "Sometimes the [black] women are more aggressive," and went on to explain that by "aggressive," he meant able to get beyond "feel[ing] uncomfortable working with white males." He added, "They're accepted because they are aggressive and they are willing to do the job and they don't expect someone else to do their job for them." The human resource director at the same plant, also a white man, commented on the fact that black women "strive" for jobs paying $6 an hour, whereas black men do not. And a white male plant manager in the Atlanta area commented that men, black and white, see the order processor job as "beneath them," whereas women tend to be more content in it. Given comments like this, one might expect that employers who describe black women as better workers than black men might offer lower starting wages—like employers who view blacks as better workers than whites. However, the difference turns out to be negligible (employers who spoke more highly of black women in any way paid, on average, 7 cents an hour more than those who did not; those who specifically lauded black women's superior motivation paid 9 cents an hour less).

Once more echoing Kirschenman and Kennelly, employers argued that black women are more motivated than their male counterparts because they are the main or only sources of support for their families, evoking images of the single mother or matriarch. At Peachtree Foods, an Atlanta-area grocery store, the personnel director stated: "[black] women are the main force in the workplace. And I don't know what's going on with the [black] men—boy, they must be staying at home or something. There are more I know of that the female of the household is the main worker."

The white male owner of a downtown Detroit store agreed: "[black women are better workers] I think because they probably have a child at home that they have to provide for and they have a commitment to it. A woman has a lot more commitment to their family than a man does."

He contrasted black men, who "have a defeated attitude, totally."
And a black man who supervises Jack's Junkyard in the Detroit area
observed that black women "have learned over a period of time that if
you want to have something solid to rely on you'd better rely on yourself and be able to support yourself, because they found out over time
you cannot rely on that man to be there to take care of you."

A second theme voiced by employers who expressed a preference for
black women over black men was black women's higher education and
skill levels. Respondents described black women as having "better communication skills, better work skills in everything," and being "a hell of
a lot sharper" and "very impressive" compared to black men, who
"tended to be less skilled, less educated." These views match up with
the greater presence of black women (relative to black men) in jobs requiring added skilled tasks or credentials, as we saw in the previous
chapter.

Finally, a few managers rated black women's interaction skills as
better. "I think black women are more aggressive, I mean, more outgoing and more people-oriented as a whole," remarked the human resource director at a Detroit-area manufacturer. Black men, on the other
hand, were more often described as hostile and even potentially violent,
as we described earlier in this chapter. The manager of the Peachtree
Foods store near Atlanta—himself a black man—summed up all three
themes by declaring: "I would say that normally the [black and white]
females are smarter. I would say that they're probably a little easier to
work with. Flexibility, being able to adjust." He contrasted black men
within his hiring pool, whom he described as "more trend-binding" and
"into the rappers."

Only a very small number of employers rated black men above
black women. None referred to hard skills. Instead, they voiced the flip
side of the interaction and motivation issues. In terms of interaction,
the white male site manager at a home maintenance service complained
that women are overly sensitive to perceived discrimination and harassment, and "your real challenge is when you have an ethnic minority
person of the female persuasion." At a Detroit food manufacturer whose
workforce is 80 percent black, the white male personnel manager said
that "guys will say 'Fuck you' and that will be the end of it. Girls will
talk behind your back and start these little cliques." As for motivation,
while, as noted earlier, a number of employers described women as willing to settle for less, the front desk supervisor at a Boston-area hotel
observed that young women, black and white, "seem to have incredible
attitude these days." He attributed this attitude problem, which had led
him to fire a number of women, to frustration at inability to move up
fast enough in the workplace. Finally, while employers invoked the image of black women as single mothers to explain these women's com-

mitment to a job, they also pointed to it as a source of unreliability—due to "baby and boyfriend problems," as one Atlanta manager put it. A white male middle manager at a Boston-area health care facility opined:

> You have a lot of single mothers who struggle to survive and that to maintain a full-time, forty-hour position, the kids issues that come up and the disturbances about their work, calling in sick or not being able to make it to work on time and those type of things. Those issues that come in, and I would find more in the black population.

While few employers commented specifically on the disruptive effects of black women's child care responsibilities, many others made such comments about women in general or single mothers in particular.

The comparison between Latino men and Latina women came up less frequently in the interviews. When it did, most often the balance tipped toward women, as with blacks. Some employers contrasted "proud" or "macho" Latino men (easily offended and demanding "respect") with more submissive Latina women. At a public agency in Los Angeles, a white female personnel official remarked: "The [Latino] men tend to want to boss the women. And to order them around, even though they're working at the same level. I can't help thinking it has to do with the machismo. Because it has been with the Latin males that we have, that this problem has come up."

And a white male warehouse manager in Los Angeles rated Latino men more willing workers than blacks, but not on a par with Latinas: "I think in general the blacks tend to make sure that you're not pulling the wool over their eyes. A little more the jailhouse lawyer kind of attitude. Hispanic women are extremely hard-working. And Hispanic men kind of like a spectrum of all of those things."

At a Los Angeles accounting firm, however, the white male CEO pointed to the effect of family demands on Latina data entry workers, echoing the "babies and boyfriends" comment about African American women: "If I've noticed any difference, I'd say I've noticed that the Hispanic women spend more time dealing with personal issues. Their children and their families and stuff like that, and consequently don't get as much production."

In summary, when managers compared men and women *within* the categories of black and Latino, the comparisons primarily redounded to the disadvantage of men. This is consistent with the fact that the presence of most tasks and credential requirements is associated with a greater probability that a woman will be hired within any given racial group (including whites), as we saw in the previous chapter. However, it would be misleading to suggest that women have unambiguous advan-

TABLE 4.6　Effects of Child Care Constraints on Women's Employment, by Race and Ethnicity

	Total	White	Black	Latina	Asian
In the past twelve months, has a concern about your child care needs caused you to					
Not look or apply for a job	31.6%	33.4%	20.6%	34.2%	26.0%
Turn down a job you were offered	12.5	15.2	8.8	10.5	8.4
Not participate in school or a training program	19.2	24.0	18.0	14.1	13.5
Quit or be fired from your job	11.4	11.4	6.1	12.7	20.6
Hourly wage penalty associated with answering yes to at least one of the above	−10.2	−15.0	−8.7	−9.7	−7.7
	N = 2,238–41	N = 278–395	N = 445–782	N = 328–765	N = 151–287

Source: Multi-City Study of Urban Inequality Household data analyzed by authors; wage penalty data from Browne, Tigges, and Press 2001.
Note: For women with a child under eighteen in Atlanta, Boston, Detroit, and Los Angeles, surveyed from 1992 to 1994. "Quit or be fired" and wage penalty are calculated based on number who worked in last twelve months; others are based on all women with children. Wage penalty data control for education, experience, and a variety of other factors. The low end of each range of sample sizes shows the number of women employed in the last twelve months; sample sizes for the first three variables in the table were all quite close to the high end.

tages relative to men in our data. In the Employer Survey data, women are still paid less—with a starting wage disadvantage of 10 percent or so, even after controlling for race, ethnicity, human capital, and other factors affecting pay, and a significantly slower rate of wage growth (Hertz, Tilly, and Massagli 2001). In the Multi-City Study Household data, women are four times as likely to report sexual harassment as men, and more than three times as likely to say that they have experienced gender discrimination in promotions or pay raises.

In addition, although relatively few employers commented on child care demands as an employment handicap for women, this issue deserves a closer look. Child care constraints have become more important because mothers of young children increasingly seek paid work: as of 1995, 55 percent of mothers aged fifteen to forty-four were in the labor market *within a year of giving birth* (U.S. Department of Commerce 1997). The Multi-City Study Household Survey offers a look at how child care handicaps women's labor force participation. As table 4.6 shows, child care requirements prevented almost one-third of women from seeking a job (compared to only one man in twelve—not shown), prompted one in eight to turn down a job, and caused one in ten job-holding women to quit or be fired (see Press 2000 for a more detailed analysis of Los Angeles data). Women who reported any kind of child care constraint suffered an hourly wage penalty of 10 percent relative to other women, after controlling for education, experience, and other factors affecting wages (Browne, Tigges, and Press 2001). White, Latina, and Asian women cited child care constraints more often than did black women, but these handicaps are severe for every racial and ethnic group.

How Different Groups of Managers Perceive Workers of Color

We now slice managers up into three sets of categories: race or ethnicity, position within the firm, and type of job being discussed. Our goal is to determine whether managers' perceptions of the skills of various racial groups differ systematically across these categories. We expect employer comments to be shaped by several things:

- The degree of contact they have with each group
- Their degree of sympathy with each group
- The degree to which they are concerned about each type of worker performance

In particular, we expect the race of managerial respondents to have two kinds of effects on their perception of their own racial or ethnic group. The *salience* effect suggests that managers who are members of a racial group are particularly likely to notice the strengths and weaknesses of other members of that group (in part, no doubt, because they are particularly likely to manage employees from that group, given patterns of workplace segregation). This will make black managers, for instance, more likely to make negative statements about black workers *and* more likely to make positive statements about them. A second effect, the *ethnic loyalty* effect, suggests that managers will tend to view workers from their own group more favorably than will managers from other groups. We do not pass judgment on the relative accuracy of in-group and out-group perceptions.

The two effects sometimes work in the same direction and at other times in different directions. Both salience and ethnic loyalty lead to the prediction that members of a racial group should be especially likely to say that workers from this group are better workers. Table 4.7, which shows employer perceptions by race of respondent, demonstrates that this is true. Black, Latino, and Asian respondents were particularly likely to state that workers of their own race or ethnicity are "better workers."

However, when it comes to perceiving negative qualities of one's own group, the salience and ethnic loyalty effects work in opposite directions. For black managers, ethnic loyalty appears to be the stronger effect. Black managers criticized black skills less often than the average manager. This is particularly true when it comes to soft skills: black respondents were only about two-thirds as likely to say negative things about blacks' interaction and motivation. On the other hand, Latino and Asian managers were actually *more* likely to identify certain shortcomings of their own groups. Latinos criticized Latino hard skills and motivation more often than other respondents did; Asians disproportionately faulted Asian hard skills. The numbers of Latino and Asian managers are quite small (and even the number of black managers is none too large), so we must interpret the findings with some caution.

Perhaps the most striking finding emerging from this breakdown by manager's race is that managers of color *do* find fault with their own racial group. This is surely due in part to the influence of dominant white attitudes and to attempts by managers of color to distance themselves psychologically from their co-ethnics. There is no reason to expect black or Latino managers to be immune to widespread racial stereotypes. However, we would expect managers of color to be more resistant to such attitudes, so this evidence also suggests that white managers' negative assessments of the hard and soft skills of minority workers are based in part on real differences in performance.

Table 4.8 reports respondent perceptions broken down by the re-

TABLE 4.7   *Variation by Race of Respondent: Percentage of*
             Respondents Reporting Particular Perceptions in
             Face-to-Face Interviews

	White	Black	Latino	Asian	Total
Employers who said					
About blacks					
Blacks have lagging hard skills	22.1	17.9	6.3	7.1	20.3
Blacks have lagging interaction skills	16.1	10.3	6.3	7.1	14.6
Blacks have lagging motivation	34.3	23.1	37.5	42.9	33.4
Black women are better than black men	4.3	5.1	6.3	0.0	4.0
Black men are better than black women	1.4	0.0	0.0	0.0	1.1
Blacks are better workers	1.8	2.6	0.0	0.0	1.7
About Latinos					
Latinos have lagging hard skills	5.7	0.0	12.5	7.1	5.4
Latinos have lagging interaction skills	1.4	0.0	0.0	0.0	1.1
Latinos have lagging motivation	5.4	0.0	12.5	14.2	5.4
Latinos are better workers	13.2	12.8	25.0	7.1	13.4
About Asians					
Asians have lagging hard skills	1.8	0.0	0.0	7.1	1.7
Asians have lagging interaction skills	0.0	0.0	12.5	0.0	0.6
Asians have lagging motivation	0.4	0.0	0.0	0.0	0.3
Asians are better workers	6.4	10.3	0.0	28.6	7.4
About immigrants					
Immigrants have a stronger work ethic	13.2	12.8	25.0	0.0	13.1
	N = 280	N = 39	N = 16	N = 14	

Source: Multi-City In-Depth Employer Survey.

spondent's position within the firm. We expect a manager's position to matter for a couple of reasons. Top executives, human resource managers, and frontline supervisors differ in their degree and type of contact with entry-level workers. They also differ in their objectives and con-

TABLE 4.8   *Variation by Position of Respondent: Percentage of*
Respondents Reporting Particular Perceptions in
Face-to-Face Interviews

	Executive or Owner	Human Resources	Supervisor	Total
Respondents who said				
About blacks				
Blacks have lagging hard skills	16.0	25.0	20.4	20.3
Blacks have lagging interaction skills	9.6	17.4	17.4	14.6
Blacks have lagging motivation	30.4	30.4	37.9	33.4
Black women are better than black men	4.0	4.3	4.5	4.0
Black men are better than black women	0.8	1.1	1.5	1.1
Blacks are better workers	4.0	1.1	0.0	1.7
About Latinos				
Latinos have lagging hard skills	4.0	6.5	6.1	5.4
Latinos have lagging interaction skills	0.8	0.0	2.3	1.1
Latinos have lagging motivation	7.2	3.3	5.3	5.4
Latinos are better workers	16.0	8.7	14.3	13.4
About Asians				
Asians have lagging hard skills	1.6	2.2	1.5	1.7
Asians have lagging interaction skills	0.0	2.2	0.0	0.6
Asians have lagging motivation	0.0	0.0	0.8	0.3
Asians are better workers	7.2	6.5	8.3	7.4
About immigrants				
Immigrants have a stronger work ethic	12.8	7.6	17.4	13.1
	N = 125	N = 92	N = 132	

Source: Multi-City In-Depth Employer Survey.

cerns, with top executives more focused on bottom-line profit, human resource managers concerned with the ease of recruiting and retaining workers, and supervisors striving for ease of management (Tilly and Tilly 1998).

The results in table 4.8 appear to reflect these differences. Top executives, who have the least contact with entry-level workers, were in general least likely to criticize any of the groups of workers. This seems analogous to the salience effect. But another pattern diverges from the salience effect based on degree of contact: the executives were more likely than other managers to describe blacks and Latinos as better workers. Differing managerial concerns may be at work here. Recall that employers who rated blacks and Latinos better workers tended to pay below-average wages, suggesting that they are praising the willingness of these workers to settle for less. Executives, with more of an overview of the business's environment than other managers, may be particularly aware of these wage issues. On the other hand, personnel managers and supervisors are likely to worry less about keeping wage costs down and more about dealing with the rough edges of a low-wage workforce.

Human resource managers were more likely than others to grumble about hard skills and interaction skills. This makes sense, since human resource managers—unlike the other two groups—come directly into contact with the entire applicant pool, and screen applicants primarily through interviews (which assess interaction) and tests (which assess hard skills). Finally, frontline supervisors, who must deal day to day with motivation issues such as attendance and tardiness, were more sensitive about motivation than the other groups. They more often complained about black workers' motivation and more often praised immigrants for a strong work ethic.

How do employer perceptions vary with the type of job in question? In table 4.9, we have divided jobs according to occupation (blue-collar, clerical, service) and low or high levels of customer contact. Two of the job categories may appear puzzling. "Blue-collar, customer contact" includes jobs such as delivery drivers and equipment installers; "service, no customer contact" consists mainly of cleaners. We added a category for "big-ticket," commission-based salespeople (including those selling appliances, autos, real estate, and travel services) because it seemed inappropriate to group them with the cashiers in the "service, customer contact" group. Note that several of the samples are quite small, limiting the inferences we can make about these particular groups.

We expect respondents to cite problems with a particular skill most often in settings where that skill is in demand—once more, a type of salience effect. Employer concerns about hard skills meet this expectation, matching up with the hard-skill requirements we described in chapter 3. Managers overseeing blue-collar jobs, where we saw basic skill needs are increasing, and clerical jobs, where computer literacy is increasingly required, were the ones most likely to complain about hard-skill problems. However, for Latinos and Asians in particular, managers of service jobs with no customer contact were particularly likely to find fault with hard skills. In fact, this is the only job type in which

TABLE 4.9   Variation by "Sample Job" Being Discussed: Percentage of Respondents Reporting Particular Perceptions in Face-to-Face Interviews

	Blue Collar, No Customer Contact	Blue-Collar, Customer Contact	Clerical, No Customer Contact	Clerical, Customer Contact	Big Ticket Sales	Service, No Customer Contact	Service, Customer Contact	Total
Respondents who said About blacks								
Blacks have lagging hard skills	20.7	25.0	25.0	18.0	11.1	6.3	23.0	20.3
Blacks have lagging interaction skills	10.3	6.3	18.8	19.7	11.1	18.8	14.0	14.6
Blacks have lagging motivation	37.9	43.8	29.2	23.0	27.8	62.5	30.0	33.4
Black women are better than black men	8.0	6.3	2.1	3.3	0.0	0.0	4.0	4.0
Black men are better than black women	1.1	0.0	0.0	0.0	5.6	0.0	2.0	1.1
Blacks are better workers	1.1	0.0	2.1	1.6	0.0	0.0	3.0	1.7

(Table continues on p. 136.)

TABLE 4.9   *Continued*

About Latinos							
Latinos have lagging hard skills	4.6	18.8	6.3	4.9	0.0	12.5	5.4
Latinos have lagging interaction skills	1.1	0.0	0.0	0.0	5.6	0.0	1.1
Latinos have lagging motivation	8.0	0.0	6.3	3.3	5.6	12.5	5.4
Latinos are better workers	18.4	37.5	0.0	8.2	11.1	31.3	13.4
About Asians							
Asians have lagging hard skills	0.0	6.3	2.1	1.6	5.6	6.3	1.7
Asians have lagging interaction skills	0.0	0.0	0.0	1.6	0.0	6.3	0.6
Asians have lagging motivation	1.1	0.0	0.0	0.0	0.0	0.0	0.3
Asians are better workers	8.0	6.3	4.2	4.9	5.6	12.5	7.4
About immigrants							
Immigrants have a stronger work ethic	24.1	25.0	4.2	3.3	11.1	18.8	13.1
	N = 87	N = 16	N = 48	N = 61	N = 18	N = 16	N = 100

Source: Multi-City In-Depth Employer Survey.

blacks trade places with Latinos and Asians, receiving *less* criticism. These are predominantly jobs as cleaners in which, as we saw in chapter 3, basic English literacy is at a growing premium.

The results for interaction skills are surprising at first glance. On the whole, complaints about interaction are no greater in jobs that involve customer contact than in jobs with no such contact. But recall that many of the criticisms of black and Latino interaction skills stressed hostility or touchiness toward *managers*. And indeed, in cases where workers do their jobs fairly independently, with little contact with managers (the delivery drivers of "blue-collar, customer contact," as well as commission salespeople), complaints about blacks' interaction skills were at a minimum.

Motivation is the flip side of the coin. Managerial criticisms of workers' motivation (and praise of the immigrant work ethic) are greatest in jobs where close supervision is difficult: delivery drivers and janitors, as well as, to a lesser extent, other blue-collar jobs. In these jobs, managers must rely on higher degrees of worker self-motivation to get the job done. Although this is also true of commission sales (where complaints about motivation are infrequent), in that case the commission itself provides a strong incentive to produce. In the category of service jobs without customer contact (cleaners and the like), complaints about black and Latino motivation are nearly twice as great as in other job categories. This job poses a particularly daunting combination: it is difficult to monitor, and pays very low wages.

Finally, where do managers describe various racial groups as *better* workers? Latinos and Asians are most often prized in blue-collar and service jobs. These are the jobs in which low-skill immigrants with few alternatives are likely to be willing workers (as confirmed by the fact that managers of these jobs also are most likely to salute the immigrant work ethic). Many such jobs require limited training but high levels of attention to detail and tolerance of unpleasant working conditions. In such jobs, those not literate in English can be guided by oral instructions from bilingual supervisors.

The highest incidence of positive views of blacks occurred in service jobs with customer contact. Less educated African Americans presumably provide a relatively motivated workforce for such retail and fast food jobs, especially in Atlanta and Detroit, where immigrants are few and the main alternative workforce for such jobs consists of young whites unlikely to take the jobs seriously. There is a second, smaller group of employers who praise black workers in clerical jobs, suggesting that these jobs provide another niche, for black women in particular. In all these cases, positive employer opinions may stem in part from views of certain jobs as appropriate or suitable for certain groups.

Stereotypes and Reality

It is of considerable interest how much employers' perceptions—particularly the frequent negative perceptions of black workers—stem from stereotypes and how much from reality. We use the word *stereotype* in a different way than many social psychologists do. Social psychologists often define any belief about a group's traits or behavior as a stereotype (Bobo and Massagli 2001; Brown 1995). By that definition, all of the many generic statements by employers about racial groups in this study constitute stereotypes. Rupert Brown (1995) defended this broad definition by arguing that it is difficult to prove such views true or false—especially in instances where "beauty is in the eye of the beholder." We are interested, however, in a narrower and stronger definition: beliefs that exaggerate or distort reality, and that make managers less sensitive to individual differences within a group.

The problem, of course, is that we have no independent source of information about the skills or qualities of the applicants and workers with whom employers have come into contact. However, we do have recourse to some internal and external evidence that can help us evaluate employer perceptions. Based on this evidence, a case can be made that these perceptions combine outright stereotypes, cultural gaps that separate managers from workers of color, and genuine worker shortcomings. Some of the genuine shortcomings, in turn, result from hostile or unrewarding workforce settings.

A first source of evidence is employers' own descriptions of how they formed opinions about black workers. Employers indicated that they base their perceptions of various race and gender groups on their experiences with past and present employees, on their impressions of applicants, and on more general impressions from the media and from experiences outside work.[6] By far the largest group of employers referred to experience with their own employees. The immediacy of these observations rendered them objective in the minds of many employers. Stated a store manager: "I think [black men] feel things should be given to them and not earned. And because of that, they don't earn the right to keep jobs. Now, someone would say I may have an attitude problem, but I just look at pure facts. I mean, with the people that I've had work for me."

Several employers drew inferences from their experiences at different prior locations. Earlier, we quoted a Detroit-area public-sector custodial supervisor who spoke of the poorer quality of workers in his present location compared to his previous location, farther from Detroit. Two Los Angeles employers relied on a comparison of locations to inform their judgments, the first a manufacturing human resource manager, the second a store manager:

The big problem with the inner-city male is transportation and, to some degree, the motivation to work. I have been in organizations in Glendale, on the other side of the city, and our stability there was not as high.

I was at Culver City before I went to this store, and it seems like we had a very high turnover in that area and it was a very, very busy store and it was probably 95 percent black. And I think there is a different work ethic.

Quite a few employers described the applicant pool as a basis for assessments about minority workers. They raised issues such as the number of blacks and Hispanics who failed skill tests, the inability of some applicants to fill out an application properly, or applicants' unfamiliarity with the conventions of the pre-employment interview.

The media also figured prominently in managers' comments. An Asian manager at Financial Research Associates in the Los Angeles area gave her ranking of racial groups from best to worst (white, Asian, Latino, and black), and then said:

When we hire, we don't look for ethnicity or anything, but if I had my perfect world and I could do these things legally, I'd probably hire them in that order, and I think it's only because of my own experiences and what you see in the media and what the media pushes. . . .

I'm just thinking about the welfare. You know, every time I see the news and you see black women and Hispanic women having four or five kids, not even thinking about the system and abusing the system, when there are other people that are really in need of that funding and they can't get it because they're too honest.

Although few respondents directly cited the media as the source of their judgments, as this manager did, a number referred to the media in their discussion, and for others the influence of the media seemed apparent. Consider the response from this supervisor at a Detroit-area manufacturing plant:

Interviewer: Do you think people's prejudices have increased since the seventies?

Respondent: Yeah. What happens to make it the way it is? I guess if you watch the news, it's very depressing, and I don't like to watch the news anymore. I don't like to hear about two-year-old kids getting shot with a gun. I don't like to hear about five kids getting burnt up in a house because the woman was living there with two other families and none of them have husbands and there are fifteen kids in the house. These are the things that work on our minds and it makes it very difficult for us to say, "Yeah, it's okay for black people to live next door and it's okay to associate with them." It makes it very difficult to get in that frame of mind by what we see on the TV and in the news, so it's hard. I think it's worse now than it's ever been.

Again, the impact of the media was evident in these two comments by white Detroit-area manufacturing managers:

We have a lot of guys out there with cocaine in their pocket and Uzis in the trunk.

I think a lot of [the difficulty black men face in the labor market] is based on their inability to complete schooling early on, for whatever reason. I don't know a lot of the statistics of the black race, but I do see that. I think that is a good fact. It's going to take unfortunately a heck of a long time to fully eliminate discrimination. We hear about it in the news still, and it's a shame.

A few managers from firms in white areas referred to contact with blacks (or other minorities) outside the workplace. For example, a white manager of a real estate firm in Atlanta gave this account:

Interviewer: Currently there's all white workers here, is that correct?

Respondent: Yeah, we have, as far as agents are concerned. To be honest, I have not been in a situation where I've supervised that many blacks. I've taught a lot of black ones in real estate classes that I teach.

Interviewer: Do you notice differences in your classes?

Respondent: Yes, very definitely. I find that generally the white students will study harder and not give up as easy as the black students seem to.

And a white male insurance manager outside Detroit reported, "I am involved and attend an urban church and we [work] with the homeless and the retarded and people of that nature, [and] unless something is done to help these black males, it is just a sorry situation."
Those managers who spoke at length often wove together information from a wide variety of personal experiences inside and outside the workplace, combined with general knowledge shaped by the media. For

instance, the white owner of a small manufacturing shop in a Los Angeles suburb related:

> [Forty years ago in Los Angeles] the workforce was Caucasian, and the lower end of the workforce, the labor end, was black. Through civil rights and so forth, the black community elevated themselves into positions that weren't there [previously]. . . . As that workforce disappeared and the great migration from the Latin countries [took place], it became a Latino environment. We put an ad in the paper, we would have had very few Caucasian applicants. Even very few black applicants.
>
> It seems that the black kids maybe just don't want to work. Why should they take an entry-level job when they can make more on some sort of welfare, unemployment, or dealing drugs? We have a lot of poor people in the city, a lot of homeless, people asking for money. I was in the L.A. airport a while back and a black man walks up to me and says, "Hey, man, I need five bucks." It is a "gimme" attitude. I can remember as a kid a man coming into my father's store and saying, "I need money, can I sweep the floors for fifty cents?" But that is not the way it is anymore. Now it's "can you spare a quarter?" or "can you spare a dollar?" Nobody wants to work for it.

In short, managers, like anyone else, draw on a variety of sources to form their opinions of various racial groups as workers. Those relying particularly on the media risk being influenced by sensationalized images of African Americans and Latinos as gang members or welfare mothers. But employers who cite firsthand observations of their applicants or workforce are not necessarily immune. As noted in the literature review at the outset of this chapter, those who hold stereotypes tend to give more weight to information that confirms the stereotypes than to information that challenges them. Nonetheless, employer accounts based on direct observation do suggest that some of the generalizations have some basis in reality.

Examining individual employer statements about blacks reveals some that are self-evidently stereotypical and others that are consistent with evidence from outside the study. Characterizations of black men, as a group, as "lazy" or "scary" are clearly inaccurate. Or consider this assertion by a white male utility manager in the Los Angeles area: "I'm no doctor, but I'm convinced, having dealt with grievance and unrest, that black men, and to some extent black women, do not deal with stress physically as well as some other races."

As Irene Browne and Ivy Kennelly (1999) documented for Atlanta, a minority of black women are single mothers, and their rates of absenteeism and lateness due to child care issues are less than those of white women (and not as different from black or white men as might be supposed). Certainly, the notion that the typical black mother is a teenager is greatly at odds with reality. One black male manager, the supervisor at Detroit-area Jack's Junkyard, even described the typical black single mother as "probably eight to nine or ten years older than the kids are," a patently ridiculous image. We are particularly skeptical of employer criticisms of blacks' motivation, and bring some additional data (from sources other than the employer surveys) to bear on this issue in the concluding chapter of this book.

In addition, certain managers charged that *other* managers harbor stereotypical views: "People have a tendency to look toward, even if they don't voice it, they deal with their stereotypes. It's easy to identify someone as a female or identify someone as black male or a white male. And so whatever it is that they have of their expectations of those people, they will project that."

In particular, some managers claimed that their peers engage in statistical discrimination, or generalize from a visible but unrepresentative subset of blacks: "I think that many employers may feel that because of the large numbers of black males who are in prison and have problems, that there is a tendency for those who are out and in the workforce to do mischievous things. That's unfortunate."

Some respondents, such as this black female manager at a Detroit-area utility, contended that employers hold blacks and Latinos to a different standard than whites:

> When blacks and Hispanics and whomever come into the work group and they are not part of the majority, then one thing they need to know is that they cannot always do what they see others doing, and that is key. That is a lesson that needs to be taught. I think the rules aren't always the same, and it may not always be intentional. A lot is institutional and a lot of it is people just not understanding others.

This last statement raises the issue of cultural gaps that impede communication across race, class, and age divides.

On the other hand, some employer statements match up with data from sources beyond this study. This is clearest with respect to hard skills. Blacks and Latinos do not, on average, get as much education as whites. On average, black women do attain higher educational levels than black men (Harrison and Bennett 1995).

But the vast majority of employer statements about soft skills are neither self-evidently stereotypical nor easily verifiable. As we have noted, assessments of soft skills are inevitably subjective. We suspect that many, perhaps most, employer criticisms of blacks' interaction and motivation are exaggerated. Many employers who made apparently "reasonable" statements swerved into stereotypes at some point in the discussion—for example, sweepingly associating blacks with single motherhood, welfare, or crime. However, we also suspect that many negative managerial perceptions of blacks' soft skills have some basis in actual worker behavior. A variety of other research, including ethnography (Wilson 1987; Anderson 1990), surveys (Wilson 1987), and focus groups (Jobs for the Future 1995a, 1995b), reports that many young black men in U.S. inner cities really do act "tough" and that they really are skeptical of what legitimate jobs offer, and find other alternatives attractive. Harry Holzer and Robert LaLonde (2000) found higher turnover rates for young black men than for their white counterparts.

These research examples highlight a second problem with soft skills, beyond the bias that enters any judgment about them: suitable interaction and motivation depend on context. Elijah Anderson (1990) cautioned that though young, inner-city black men may lag in the skills most sought by employers, they possess a wealth of other soft skills needed to survive and thrive in dangerous environments. In fact, the soft skills most suited to inner-city survival may include suspicion of strangers and a threatening mien—qualities unwelcome on most jobs.

The workplace context itself shapes the soft skills workers exhibit. Holzer and LaLonde found that when they controlled for wage level and occupation, young black men's turnover rates were similar to or lower than those for whites—reversing the relationship they found when not taking job quality into account. Sociologists have likewise argued that successful job performance depends on the degree to which a workplace is welcoming or hostile (Vallas 1990; Darrah 1994). As we saw earlier in this chapter, quite a few managers attribute racial differences in performance to differences in wages, job quality, management style, or management failure to figure out how to communicate with and motivate workers from varied racial groups. Low expectations of black workers, as for students, may become a self-fulfilling prophecy.

Attitudes and Action

One-third of the respondents in the face-to-face interviews denigrated the motivation of black workers, yet not one admitted to avoiding hiring blacks altogether. To do so would be to admit illegal behavior. Even so, are negative attitudes toward black workers associated with reduced hiring of blacks? To the extent that employers themselves linked attitudes to action, they described it in nonracial terms. They talked about carrying out geographically restricted recruiting and hiring (we will examine this in chapter 5). They discussed preferential use of certain recruiting or screening methods, such as hiring through personal networks (we will look at this in chapter 6). To round out this chapter, we turn away from *how* employers discriminate, in order to come up with some rough estimates of *how much* negative attitudes correspond to actual employer actions. Qualitative data are best suited to understand the "whys and hows" of behavior. Measuring behaviors, on the other hand, is better done with quantitative data. To explore connections between employer perceptions and their hiring decisions, we once more tap the Telephone Survey data, as well as analyzing numerical summaries of the face-to-face interviews.

Quantitative Evidence from the Telephone Survey

Direct measures of employer perceptions in the Telephone Survey—ratings of the last worker hired, degree of agreement with generalizations about the quality of various groups of workers—yielded limited results, as we described earlier in this chapter. When we look *indirectly* at the associations among certain variables and hiring outcomes, however, we do find some added indicators of employers' disposition toward different groups.

One, albeit indirect, window onto the influence of attitudes on hiring is the ratio of new hires to applicants by racial, ethnic, and gender group. Table 4.10 presents the ratio of the percent of latest hires by race, ethnicity, and gender (for blacks) to the corresponding group's percentage of applicants.[7] Businesses hire a greater proportion of "white and other" applicants than of black male, black female, or Latino applicants.[8] In almost every instance, the ratios are smallest for black males, and in several cases the difference between the ratio for black males and other groups is startling. Some of these differences result from differing qualifications in the applicant pools. But the divergence between central-city and suburban ratios suggests that there is something more going on as well. Compared to their urban counterparts, suburban firms hire a smaller proportion of black male and female applicants. Again, the disparity is largest for black males. The contrast in the probability of hiring a black between city and suburban firms is even more striking, because central-city jobs on average require higher levels of skill and set higher requirements than jobs in the suburbs (see chapter 3). As blacks have lower levels of hiring credentials, lower levels of education and test scores, on average, than whites, we would expect the hiring ratios to be higher in the suburbs.[9]

These hiring ratios differ across the four cities as well. Black men show the lowest ratios in Los Angeles and Boston, but the sharpest contrast between city and suburb in Detroit. Black women fare most poorly

TABLE 4.10   *Hiring by Race and Gender: Ratio to Application*
            Rates by Race and Gender

	Primary Central City	Suburbs	Other Central Cities
For all metro areas			
Ratio of firm's latest hires to applicants for			
Black men	0.62	0.51	0.60
Black women	0.89	0.68	0.74
Latinos	1.01	1.12	1.02
White and other	1.18	1.09	1.00
	N = 1,038	N = 1,925	N = 547
Atlanta			
Ratio of firm's latest hires to applicants for			
Black men	0.65	0.74	0.65
Black women	0.89	0.82	0.83
Latinos	0.89	0.85	0.82
White and other	1.25	1.08	1.08
	N = 366	N = 275	N = 166
Boston			
Ratio of firm's latest hires to applicants for			
Black men	0.55	0.58	0.54
Black women	0.59	0.41	0.68
Latinos	1.12	1.09	1.07
Asians	0.62	0.60	0.60
White and other	1.15	1.00	0.97
	N = 207	N = 523	N = 159
Detroit			
Ratio of firm's latest hires to applicants for			
Black men	0.63	0.41	0.45
Black women	0.97	0.70	0.67
Latinos	0.42	0.87	1.38
White and other	1.39	1.07	1.34
	N = 177	N = 496	N = 131
Los Angeles			
Ratio of firm's latest hires to applicants for			
Black men	0.53	0.40	0.77
Black women	0.80	0.65	0.51
Latinos	1.11	1.12	0.95
Asians	1.05	0.94	1.00
White and other	0.93	1.19	0.64
	N = 288	N = 631	N = 91

Source: Multi-City Telephone Employer Survey.

in Boston, and again the contrast of city to suburb is largest in Detroit. Latinos show much less distress on these indicators than do blacks, except in Detroit, where the Latino population is very small. Such contrasts between city and suburb, and among metropolitan areas, seem unlikely simply to reflect differing qualifications among applicant pools. Instead, employers in general in Boston and Los Angeles, and suburban employers in Detroit, appear to be more likely to discriminate against black job seekers. Part of the greater disadvantage faced by black men in Boston and Los Angeles, and the smaller gap in Atlanta, is likely due to the fact that in the early 1990s, when the survey was conducted, unemployment remained quite high in the former two areas, but was comparatively low in Atlanta.

The Telephone Survey data give another piece of suggestive evidence that racial attitudes, not just straightforward skill assessments, shape employer hiring decisions. Analyses of these data by us and others show that larger firms are much more likely to hire blacks, controlling for a large number of other factors (see chapter 6 in this volume; Holzer 1996; and Holzer and Neumark 1999). But the larger the firm, the greater the skill requirements. If a skill gap were the primary reason for not hiring blacks, large firms would hire fewer blacks. It is likely that closer contact among employees and owners, in small firms, as well as use of less formal hiring procedures, gives rise to a greater influence of attitudes in hiring.

If an employer worries about the ethnocentric attitudes of his or her customers or current employees (and table 4.3 showed that the incidence of such reports of ethnocentrism hovered around 20 percent), then she may be hesitant to hire employees whose race or ethnicity doesn't match. To test this, we use logit equations to estimate the effect of reporting such ethnocentrism on the likelihood that the employer's last hire was black. We employ two alternative sets of control variables to take into account the pool from which the employer hires. First, we control for the percent of the population that is black in the relevant portion of the metropolitan area (the central city or the rest of the area, depending on where the business is located), as well as the average distance of black people in the metropolitan area from the business in question.[10] Second, we control for the percent of the employer's applicants who are black (or black men, or black women, when looking at hiring these race or gender subgroups). We also control for the starting wage, to take into account the labor market segment in which the employer hires and the size of the firm as a control for institutional differences in hiring practices.

Results are in table 4.11.[11] Employer concerns about customer ethnocentrism do seem to matter, especially for black men. If an employer

TABLE 4.11   *Logit Analysis: Reported Customer or Employee Ethnocentrism and Probability of Hiring a Black Person (z-Statistics in Parentheses)*

	Odds Ratio, Probability that the Most Recent Hire Is		
	Black person	Black man	Black woman
Forms of ethnocentrism with demographic controls			
Customer ethno-centrism	1.04*	0.73*	1.37*
	(2.65)	(−1.67)	(1.88)
Employee ethno-centrism	1.05	1.07	0.99
	(0.38)	(0.41)	(−0.04)
	N = 1,995– 2,005	N = 1,993– 2,003	N = 1,993– 2,003
With applicant pool controls			
Customer ethno-centrism	0.88	0.63*	1.06
	(−0.86)	(−2.23)	(0.30)
Employee ethno-centrism	0.96	0.79	1.05
	(−0.31)	(−1.28)	(0.29)
	N = 1,875–93	N = 1,897– 1,914	N = 1,993– 2,003

Source: Multi-City Telephone Employer Survey.
Note: Results are shown as odds ratios, signifying the ratio of the estimated probability of hiring someone from a given group when the employer answers yes to an ethnocentrism question to the estimated probability when the answer is no. All regressions control for the firm size and starting wage. Demographic controls include the percent black in the relevant portion of the metropolitan area and the business's average distance from black people in the area. Applicant pool controls include the percent of the applicant pool from the group in question. Missing values reduce the number of usable observations to the sample sizes shown.
*Coefficients significant at 10 percent or above.

reports that her customers prefer to be served by people of their own race, she is only three-quarters as likely to hire a black man compared to employers who do not report such customer sentiments. When we ask how likely she is to hire a black man *given black men's share of the applicant pool* (instead of the controls based on demography of the area), this fraction drops below two-thirds and becomes even more statistically significant.

Interestingly, we find the opposite effect for black women. An employer who notes customer ethnocentrism is one-third *more* likely to hire a black woman than are other employers. In assessing the overall impact on the probability of hiring a black person, the black female effect predominates slightly, so that businesses where a manager reports customer biases are 4 percent more likely than other businesses to hire

147

a black person. However, when we control for the composition of the applicant pool, the effect on black women diminishes and fades into insignificance, and the overall impact on black hiring becomes negative and insignificant. One possible interpretation is that the analysis is *not* detecting a customer preference for black women. Rather, it may be that customer racial biases are strongest in traditional "women's" jobs, where large numbers of black women apply. Once we take this skewed applicant pool into account, the customer-preference effect for black women disappears—but consumer prejudice continues to dampen hiring of black men.

Employee ethnocentrism, based on reports that employees want to work with people of the same race or ethnicity as themselves, does not have any statistically significant effects on black hiring. There is a substantial, negative estimated effect on the hiring of black men when controlling for the applicant pool, but it does not achieve statistical significance (and there is no negative effect at all when area demography controls are used).[12] However, employee biases are associated with a significantly reduced probability of hiring a white person and a significantly elevated chance of hiring a Latino (not shown). Apparently managers report employee ethnocentrism particularly when there is a Latino workforce—consistent with statements we heard in the face-to-face interviews from employers whose workforce had evolved into an ethnic enclave of Hispanic employees.

In yet another analysis of the Telephone Survey data published elsewhere (Moss and Tilly 2000), we investigated the degree to which employers adjusted their hiring patterns in the face of tighter labor markets. Much other research has indicated that as unemployment rates rise or vacancy rates fall, employers move down their queue of preferred workers. In this situation, they are more likely to hire people of color, who typically rank relatively lower than whites in employers' estimation. We examined this connection using, as our key indicator of labor market tightness, the duration of the longest vacancy for a job not requiring college. We also used the local area unemployment rate in our investigation. First, we estimated the influence of these measures of labor market tightness on the employment chances of white men and women, black men and women, Latinos, and Asians. We added a host of control variables to rule out hiring effects other than those resulting from labor market tightness.

Our results indicate that tight labor markets, measured by duration of longest vacancy, increase the probability of hiring a black person—specifically, a black woman. This gain appears to come primarily at the expense of Latinos, whose probability of hire falls when the duration extends. A one-month increase in the duration of the longest vacancy corresponds to an increase in the probability of hiring a black woman of

13 to 14 percent (depending on the specification), or about 1.6 percentage points (since black women represent only 12 percent of hires); the estimated increase in black hiring overall is 8 to 9 percent (about 1.9 percentage points). This is comparable to the effect of a 1 percentage point decrease in unemployment, which is associated with a 12 percent increase in the odds of hiring a black woman and an 11 percent increase in the probability of any black hire.

We were also interested in the *processes* through which a tightening labor market changes hiring outcomes. For example, we posited that as the labor market heats up, employers alter their attitudes toward less preferred groups in the workforce. Our attitude measures came from employer answers to questions asking, "How often would you hire someone who . . . ?" (where the categories of applicants included a welfare recipient, someone with a criminal record, someone from a government program, someone unemployed for a year or more, someone with only short-term, part-time experience, or hiring someone less qualified because you need workers badly). We estimated a two-stage model: stage one is the influence of labor market tightness on employer attitudes, and stage two the effect of attitudes on hiring. However, most of the estimated effects do not achieve statistical significance. Two statistically significant coefficients do bear out the expected relationship at both stages of the model. First, employers are more willing to hire people with criminal records when the time to hire is longer, and those employers more prepared to hire an ex-convict do hire more black men. Second, employers are more likely to settle for less qualified workers when vacancies last longer, and those who resort to hiring less qualified workers are hiring fewer whites (although the positive point estimate for hiring *more* black women falls short of significance).

One interpretation of these findings about the racial impact of labor market tightness is that they are consistent with a racial queue in employer preferences: whites and Asians most preferred, then Latinos, black women, and black men. Perhaps micro-labor market tightness in the settings we are studying most strongly affects the boundary between Latinos and black women in this ranking. The paucity of significant findings on the effects of employer attitudes suggests either that our measures of such attitudes are inadequate or that labor shortages act through some different channel.

Attitudes and Action in the Face-to-Face Survey

The face-to-face interviews elicited more negative statements about workers of color than did the Telephone Survey. How does the hiring at firms whose respondents express negative attitudes toward minorities compare to firms whose respondents do not? We limit our attention to the hiring of blacks; manager comments about other racial groups were much rarer.

We see (at least) two possibilities, a priori, for the nexus between attitudes and hiring. Each suggests a different sign for the relationship. First is the possibility that "familiarity breeds contempt"—a variant of the salience effect we described earlier. Employers who hire blacks in relatively larger numbers may feel more willing to voice their perceptions, whether those perceptions are accurate or not. They may be more willing to criticize blacks because they believe their views are based on direct observation, or simply because they think more about black workers than managers who have little contact with a black workforce. They also have closer experience with any skill gaps, deficient work habits, or cultural differences that *do* exist, and therefore may hold more deprecatory attitudes than other employers. And businesses that hire more blacks may offer worse jobs, inducing worse behavior in their workforce. If any of these relationships hold, there should be a positive correlation between professing pejorative attitudes and hiring minorities. The other possibility is "avoidance": a negative attitude about black employees' skills and conduct at work fosters a reluctance to hire blacks. If this were the dominant pattern, we would expect a negative correlation between hiring and attitudes.

We started by conducting an analysis along these lines with the smaller SSRC sample, using the percentage of employees who were black (divided by the percentage black in the metropolitan-area population, to take into account cross-city demographic differences) as the dependent variable (Moss and Tilly 1995). Negative employer views of black men are generally associated with *higher* proportions of black men employed, though only one such association reaches statistical significance, at the 10 percent level. This is weak evidence for the "familiarity breeds contempt" hypothesis, and is also consistent with no relationship at all between employer perceptions and hiring. However, the small (fifty-eight observations) and unrepresentative SSRC sample is not particularly suited to statistical analysis. Analyzing the Multi-City Study sample promised to give a better fix on any connections between attitudes and action.

To probe the link between employer attitudes and hiring outcomes in the larger Multi-City Study data set, we regressed the race of the last hire on the racial attitude variables that were relevant for the particular group, using a logit specification. Since every firm contacted in the Face-to-Face Survey was first interviewed in the Telephone Survey, we use the race and gender of the last person hired in the sample job *as reported in the Telephone Survey* as the measure of hiring outcomes.[13] As in the statistical analysis of customer and employee biases, we controlled for the percent of the population that is black in the surrounding portion of the metropolitan area, as well as the business's average distance from black residents in the area. In addition, we once more controlled for starting wage and firm size.

To our surprise, the results (table 4.12) yield stronger support for the notion that "familiarity breeds contempt." Blacks are more likely to be hired where one or a plurality of managers knocked black hard skills or interaction skills.[14] Black women in particular have a greater chance of being hired where business criticized blacks' interaction skills. And businesses where a plurality of managers complained about black motivation are more likely to hire black men. All these relationships are

TABLE 4.12   *Logit Analysis: Reported Employer Perceptions of Blacks and Probability of Hiring a Black Person (z-Statistics in Parentheses)*

	Odds Ratio, Probability that the Most Recent Hire Is		
	Black Person	Black Man	Black Woman
Negative Views of Blacks			
Hard skills			
At least one manager	2.62*	1.72	2.21
	(1.80)	(0.92)	(1.46)
Plurality of managers	4.22*	2.52	2.38
	(2.47)	(1.53)	(1.52)
Interaction			
At least one manager	2.87*	0.88	3.43*
	(1.83)	(−0.19)	(2.07)
Plurality of managers	3.44*	1.25	3.27*
	(1.98)	(0.34)	(1.94)
Motivation			
At least one manager	1.65	2.14	1.02
	(1.02)	(1.29)	(0.04)
Plurality of managers	1.62	4.09*	0.55
	(0.91)	(2.23)	(−1.02)
	N = 90	N = 90	N = 90

Source: Multi-City Telephone Employer Survey.
Note: Results are shown as odds ratios, signifying the ratio of the estimated probability of hiring someone from a given group when the employer answers yes to an ethnocentrism question to the estimated probability when the answer is no. All regressions control for the firm size and starting wage, the percent black in the relevant portion of the metropolitan area, and the business's average distance from black people in the area. Missing values reduce the number of usable observations to the sample sizes shown.
*Coefficients significant at 10 percent or above.

statistically significant, and the effects are large: the probability of hiring a black person is more than doubled in some cases, more than quadrupled in others.

There is no evidence for avoidance, since only two negative relationships between negative attitudes and the probability of hiring someone black are estimated (out of eighteen relationships investigated), and neither one is statistically significant. Should we conclude that employers holding negative perceptions of blacks do not discriminate against blacks in hiring? No, these results simply mean that any such discrimination is dominated in our data by effects that link critical views with more frequent hiring of blacks. The other quantitative results we have presented suggest that racial discrimination is alive and well. We also cannot tell from these results which of the "familiarity breeds contempt" connections leads to an association between negative views and increased hiring. Do managers with black employees form negative perceptions based on accurate observation of these employees? Do these managers offer worse jobs and observe poor work habits that result from poor working conditions? Are employers with more black employees simply more willing to express criticisms that are privately held by a wider range of businesspeople? We suspect, based on the content of the face-to-face interviews, that each is true to some extent.

In reviewing the literature early in this chapter, we noted that the connection between expressed racial attitudes and actual discriminatory actions is far from straightforward. Studies have shown discrimination by people who did not state prejudicial views, and failure to discriminate by people who did voice biases. Only the most carefully designed experiments reveal a clear link between attitudes and action (Duckitt 1992). Statistical analysis of our face-to-face interviews adds to the evidence that there are many possible relationships between stated attitudes and an action such as hiring.

Conclusion

Let us step back and summarize what we have learned about employers' perceptions of racial groups in the workforce, starting with results from the Telephone Survey. In terms of numerical performance ratings, employers rate black and Latino men marginally lower than their white counterparts. Few are willing to endorse a sweeping statement that some jobs are better suited to certain racial or ethnic groups, but about 20 percent agree that inner-city workers are poorer performers. Around 20 percent each also report racial biases among their customers, employees, and other employers in their line of business.

In the face-to-face interviews, an even more substantial minority of respondents, 46 percent in total, criticized blacks' hard or soft skills, with black workers' motivation a particularly frequent target. They typically attributed African Americans' shortcomings as workers to the pernicious influences of single motherhood, the welfare system, or the inner-city environment. A smaller group faulted Latinos' skills, and an even smaller set knocked Asians as workers. In both these latter cases, positive comments—often favorably referencing the immigrant status of many workers in these ethnic groups—outnumbered negative ones. A few employers did tout blacks as superior workers. At businesses where managers praised Latinos, Asians, immigrants, or African Americans, average wages fell markedly below the sample's overall average. This suggests that an important basis for such praise was these workers' willingness to work hard at substandard jobs—an inference that is supported by managers' statements at these businesses as well. More generally, positive or negative evaluations were often influenced by the alternative workforces employers looked to as comparison groups. A "silent majority" denied the presence of systematic racial differences in the workforce—in terms that ranged from a flat "no" without elaboration, to explanation of how the business irons out differences through diversity management, screening, or training. We suspect that many of this "silent majority" chose not to state perceptions that they actually held. Going beyond managers' own views, small numbers of employers in the face-to-face interviews described racial preferences by customers or employees, in some cases—especially in retail—describing efforts to keep the racial composition of their workforce from deviating too far from the makeup of their customer base.

Within characterizations of black workers, employers ranked black women above black men far more often than the reverse in the face-to-face survey. These more positive evaluations of black women embraced three themes: black women are viewed as more motivated than their male counterparts (in many cases precisely because they are viewed as single mothers providing the sole source of support for their children), black women are seen as possessing more education and skills, and black women are perceived as interacting better with supervisors, coworkers, or customers.

Managers' views also varied depending on the manager's own race and ethnicity, his or her position within the firm, and the type of job in question. The most consistent results were various versions of what we have called the salience effect. Those in a position in which they were more likely to come into contact with a particular racial group, or be concerned about a particular workforce issue, were also more likely to utter negative statements (and in some cases, positive statements as well) about that group or issue. Human resource managers complained about the hard and interaction skills they see in applicants; supervisors focused on the lack of motivation they must deal with every day; top executives said more about the cost savings associated with a low-wage workforce. Complaints about hard skills, interaction, and motivation matched up, more or less, with the jobs in which these qualities were at a premium. Beyond the salience effect, laudatory assessments of particular racial groups were most common in jobs that are typically seen as "suitable" for them. The salience effect was also somewhat offset by ethnic loyalty, at least in the case of black managers.

We can take only limited steps to evaluate the accuracy of employers' perceptions of black workers. Managers responding to the face-to-face survey pointed to a variety of sources of evidence for their perceptions, ranging from direct contact with this workforce to media images. A few managers voiced self-evidently exaggerated stereotypes, and others described the biases they saw among the managerial ranks. We conclude that the statements include a mix of stereotypes, cultural gaps that block communication between black job seekers and predominantly white employers, and real differences in work performance by race. The real differences, in turn, are due in part to the contexts in which many blacks work. In this limited-skill section of the world of work, black workers often encounter low wages, tedious or unpleasant tasks, and hostile or insensitive supervisors. Touchiness and lack of commitment to the job are not surprising where such conditions prevail.

Finally, we are concerned about the link between employer attitudes and hiring actions. The Telephone Survey provides a variety of indirect evidence pointing to racial discrimination. A black applicant is less likely to get hired in the suburbs and in a small business, even though skill requirements are lower in these settings than in central cities and larger firms, respectively. Employers reporting that customers prefer workers from their own racial group have a reduced probability of hiring a black man. When businesses face a shortage of applicants, they are more likely to hire a black woman than otherwise.

In the face-to-face interviews, on the other hand, we were surprised to learn that negative perceptions of black workers were linked to increased probability of hiring a black worker. Perhaps we should not have been surprised, since the pattern echoes the salience effects we found when comparing the views of subsets of managers. A range of explanations are possible for this association, including greater willingness to state views of black workers among managers who have direct contact with them, actual skill shortcomings that once more are most visible to those who employ more black workers, and black workers' concentration in worse jobs that stimulate worse work habits.

Having considered the images employers hold of black, Latino, and Asian workers, we turn next to a closely related topic: How do they view the inner city and the inner-city workforce? Although "inner city" and "minority" are clearly linked, employers' discussion of the inner city raises new issues such as fear of crime, new decisions such as where to locate a business, and new differences among the four cities in our study.

5

EMPLOYERS VIEW THE INNER CITY

I worked downtown in a [grocery chain] store, and it was a nightmare. It was so difficult working inner city to find anybody that's a good person. Maybe one out of twenty people was a halfway decent, moral person. (*white grocery-store manager in a very white, suburban, affluent suburb of Atlanta*)

I ran a hotel in Cobb County [a very white, suburban, affluent county] for a while, and it was just a nightmare. They opened a Wendy's down the street. We lost over half of our housekeeping staff in one week. (*white hotel manager in downtown Atlanta*)

Metropolitan areas are big. Transportation options are limited, especially for those with few financial resources. So in determining who has access to jobs, it matters greatly *where* within a metropolitan area employers locate (whether as a startup, a new branch, or a relocation). It also matters *from where* employers hire. These business decisions depend on the spatial distribution of land and other costs, customers, and relevant workers.

Location and hiring decisions, however, also rest crucially on how managers *perceive* different sub-areas within the metropolitan region and the people who live in them. In this chapter, we posit that employers' perceptions of different areas of the city or suburbs as places to locate and from which to recruit, like their views of a person's skills, are tinted by their perceptions about race. Because of the degree of racial and ethnic segregation in most U.S. cities, our four included, we should not be surprised that employers distinguish areas of the city, in part, by their racial makeup. But there is more than just race. Employers' views and, as a consequence, their decisions about locating in and recruiting from the city, we argue, are influenced by a compound perception of race and of inner-city life, families, schools, class, and crime. This composite image works to the detriment of inner-city workers of color.

The usual starting point for thinking about how changes in urban geography have affected minority workers is the *spatial mismatch hy-*

pothesis, about which social scientists have written extensively. The theory of spatial mismatch holds that within metropolitan areas, the locations of businesses offering relatively low skill jobs have disproportionately shifted away from the inner city and toward the suburbs. However, due to residential segregation, communities of color—and particularly black communities—have remained concentrated within inner cities, far from the loci of job growth. As a result, inner-city minority—particularly African American—populations, who on average have relatively low skill levels, have suffered heightened joblessness (see, for example, Kasarda 1993; Wilson 1987). While there is growing evidence for the spatial mismatch (Ihlanfeldt, 1999), most analyses simply consider the correlation between location and economic disadvantage, without exploring the causal links. Christopher Jencks and Susan Mayer (1990) posited four distinct mechanisms that could account for lower black employment in suburban than in urban businesses. In the two most commonly discussed mechanisms, distance forms a barrier to black labor supply. First, distance may increase the time and money costs of commuting. Second, information about job openings may diminish with distance. But distance can also be an indicator of racial discrimination, as spelled out in two additional mechanisms that have received less attention. Suburban clienteles, themselves disproportionately white and Anglo, may prefer to deal with workers who are white and Anglo, leading employers to tailor their workforces accordingly. In addition, the employers with a preference for white, Anglo workers may choose to locate in the suburbs.

The first two explanations target space (distance) as a barrier to employment, whereas the second two point to race, and specifically to racial discrimination. Most research on the spatial mismatch has focused on space as a barrier—not surprisingly, since distance is far more readily measurable than discrimination, and policy solutions are more obvious. There is some evidence, particularly in more recent data, that distance and commuting-cost barriers contribute significantly to black labor market disadvantage, especially for younger workers (in addition to Jencks and Mayer 1990, see Holzer 1991; Ihlanfeldt 1999; Moss and Tilly 1991). Recent findings from other researchers with the Multi-City Study of Urban Inequality confirm the importance of space as a barrier (Holzer 1996; Holzer and Ihlanfeldt 1996; Ihlanfeldt 1995).

But a growing body of spatially oriented research spotlights discrimination. Joleen Kirschenman and Kathryn Neckerman (1991) discovered that some Chicago employers used city or suburban school attendance, neighborhood, and even address (for example, whether a person lived in a public housing project) as screening criteria. Employers, they found, used space to refine the category of race, distinguishing among black workers—but on the whole disadvantaging black job seekers. Philip Kasinitz and Jan Rosenberg's (1994) study of the Red Hook neighborhood of Brooklyn found that most Red Hook businesses did not hire local black workers, due to multifaceted discrimination (based on class and location as well as race) and to recruitment through social networks that tended to exclude blacks.

Recent Multi-City Study results also build a case for the importance of discrimination correlated with employer location. Harry Holzer (1996) reported that even after controlling for job skill requirements, suburban employers hire a smaller proportion of black applicants than do urban employers (a result we discussed in chapter 4). David Sjoquist (1996) found that after controlling for distance, blacks in the Atlanta area are less likely to search for work in areas rated by all respondents as more hostile toward potential black residents—despite other evidence that urban black workers who gain jobs in the suburbs earn a wage premium over those employed in the city (Holzer 1996; IhIanfeldt and Young 1994). And Susan Turner (1996), drawing in part on the Multi-City Study Face-to-Face Employer Survey, documented incidents of white suspicion of or hostility toward blacks traveling through predominantly white Detroit suburbs. Turner also reported that despite distance from black populations, some suburban Detroit employers nonetheless hire substantial numbers of black workers.

These findings, plus analysis of our own data, lead us to the following propositions about how urban space affects the job opportunities of workers of color:

- Distance matters, pure and simple. The distribution of jobs, both quantity and type, across city and suburb is a *barrier* for less skilled minority residents.

- The effect of space goes beyond pure distance and spatial mismatch. Space is a *signal*. Employers hold a view of inner-city areas and inner-city residents that is strongly influenced by their views on race. Partially underlying and compounding employers' racial attitudes about inner-city residents of color are stereotypes of a host of inner-city ills.

- These employers' perceptions create a negative view of the quality of inner-city workers' skills, and hence a view of inner-city residents as less desirable workers to recruit. The assessment of inner-city residents is contingent to a degree, however, on the type of job employers are trying to fill.

- Employers' perceptions of inner-city residents add to cost, fear of crime, and other economic factors to create a negative view of the desirability of inner-city business locations.

- Employer perceptions influence actions. At least some employers adopt spatially based recruitment strategies that disadvantage inner-city workers.

- Employers explain their location decisions (typically away from the inner city), in part, on the basis of negative assessments of inner-city workers relative to suburban workers.

Hence, while we acknowledge the importance of spatial mismatch, we stress a different version of the spatial mismatch hypothesis from most analysts. Most analysts posit that firms locate for cost reasons, and distance is what disadvantages inner-city minorities. We argue first that employers are not neutral about inner-city minority workers. Most employers, with important exceptions, prefer non-inner city white workers. Second, employers are not passive. They *recruit* workers. Some recruitment strategies directly work against or steer clear of inner-city minority residents. In addition, some employers appear to locate their businesses to target workers other than inner-city workers of color.

These propositions about the links among space, race, and labor market disadvantage flow very much parallel to those of the previous two chapters on the connections among skill, race, and labor market distress. Some of the arguments closely overlap. This is true, in part, for the obvious reason that racial minorities live predominantly in inner cities. There is more than demographic coincidence, however. Perceptions of space, race, and skill, we maintain, are connected and intertwined. As a result, they are hard to pull apart and assess completely separately. Nonetheless, each piece of the picture has distinct aspects. Employers' views of space place special weight on the effects of inner-city upbringing and education. These dimensions amplify the problem of mixing racial stereotypes with skill judgments, both because they add to the amalgam of stereotypes and, crucially, because they help employers explain and rationalize real and perceived skill gaps of inner-city workers of color and hence rationalize not hiring them. Employers' perception of inner cities as dangerous places, moreover, do influence not just their view of workers who come from the mean streets, but also their perception of desirable business locations.

The rest of this chapter follows the order of our propositions. We weigh each in turn against the evidence we can draw from our quantitative and qualitative data.

Distance Matters: Space as a Barrier

Data from the Telephone Survey of employers allow us to look at the geographic distribution of entry-level jobs in Atlanta, Boston, Detroit and Los Angeles. Table 5.1 shows the distribution of firms in the survey across the four metropolitan areas, and within those metropolitan areas, across the primary central city, suburb, and other central cities and municipalities with a significant minority population. Except in Atlanta,

TABLE 5.1   *Jobs and Vacancies by Primary Central City, Suburb, and Other Central Cities*

	Atlanta	Boston	Detroit	Los Angeles
Percentage of firms				
Primary central city	42.8	18.6	18.0	25.4
Suburbs	37.1	63.2	67.2	64.7
Other central cities	20.1	18.5	14.8	9.9
	N = 584	N = 614	N = 602	N = 730
Percentage of firms reporting a vacancy				
Primary central city	45.0	56.6	49.9	38.9
Suburbs	40.1	39.8	44.5	41.4
Other central cities	45.1	44.7	40.2	49.9
	N = 584	N = 614	N = 602	N = 729
Mean number of vacancies among firms reporting a vacancy (trimmed mean in parentheses)[a]				
Primary central city	21.7 (15.9)	26.2 (9.4)	38.4 (18.8)	36.4 (13.0)
Suburbs	4.4 (4.4)	21.6 (21.0)	6.7 (6.7)	26.4 (13.9)
Other central cities	8.6 (8.6)	7.4 (7.4)	12.0 (12.0)	7.3 (7.3)
	N = 253	N = 269	N = 268	N = 303

Source: Multi-City Telephone Employer Survey.
[a]In many of the cells there was one (or two, in one case) firm that reported an anomalously high value for the number of current vacancies. The mean in parentheses was calculated after deleting the firms that reported a value of two hundred or greater for the current number of vacancies. In almost all cells, there was only one such firm.

entry-level noncollege jobs are concentrated in the suburbs.[1] These findings support our contention, and the findings of others, that the geography of jobs is a barrier to central-city minority workers. Harry Holzer and Sheldon Danziger (2001) use these data, plus the Multi-City Study household data to further explore the potential mismatch between the location of jobs and the location of disadvantaged workers in need of jobs. They conclude that a substantial number of job seekers—between 9 and 17 percent—will have difficulty finding work, even in a tight labor market. They predict particularly high rates of mismatch between jobs and job seekers for blacks, high school dropouts, and welfare recipients.

Although more jobs are located in the suburbs, suburban firms are not more likely to report a current vacancy. A somewhat higher fraction of firms in the central cities report a current vacancy. Further, the mean number of vacancies in the firms that report having one is generally less among firms in the suburbs than either central-city firms or firms in other central-city areas.[2] Holzer reports the vacancy *rate*—the fraction of jobs in the firm that are currently unfilled—and finds that it does not vary substantially across city, suburb, and other (see Holzer 1996, 25–37 and table 2.3).

The number of vacancies is higher in the central city, but the number of unemployed workers and their unemployment rate is higher as well, and further, suburban commuters take a significant number of the available jobs in central cities. Thus, as Holzer has shown, the *effective* level of unemployment, accounting for the size of the labor force and commuting patterns of suburban and city residents, is higher in the central cities (see Holzer 1996, 32–37 and table 2.4). We replicate his results in table 5.2. In this table, we present the ratio of filled jobs, vacant jobs, and unemployed workers, respectively, to the resident labor force in the central city versus the suburbs plus other municipalities, for each metropolitan area. The effective unemployment and the gap between effective unemployment and the number of vacancies are shown as well, scaled by the size of the labor force in the area. Effective unemployment is calculated by assuming that unemployed residents will have the same commute patterns as employed residents, and apportioning the unemployed residents in each area to the central city or outside the central city using the commute pattern of the employed residents. The final line in the table gives the ratio of effective unemployment to job vacancies.

The results in table 5.2 show much more labor market distress in the central cities than in the suburbs and other areas. Effective unemployment is substantially higher in the central cities compared to outside the central city, as is the gap between effective unemployment and job vacancies. The difference is greatest in Detroit, where the central city-suburb distinction is sharpest, and smallest in Los Angeles, where that distinction is hardest to draw. Finally, we should recall the results shown in tables 3.2 and 3.3 (in chapter 3) indicating a relatively higher set of hiring credentials and skill demands among city employers.

These findings add to the evidence of others that the location of jobs is a source of labor market disadvantage for inner-city job seekers. We now look beyond physical distance to the potential disadvantage for inner-city workers in the conceptual maps employers have of their metropolitan areas.

More Than Distance: Employers' Mental Maps of Four Cities

In this section, we explore employers' own definitions—implicit or explicit—of "the inner city" in each of the four areas, as expressed in the

TABLE 5.2   *Ratios of Filled Jobs, Vacancies, and Unemployed Workers*

	Primary Central City	Suburb and Other Central Cities
Atlanta		
Filled jobs/labor force	1.985	0.786
Vacancies/labor force	0.056	0.02
Unemployed, as percentage of labor force	9.2	4.4
Effective unemployment, as percentage of labor force	12.7	3.9
Effective unemployment-vacancies, as percentage of labor force	7.1	1.9
Effective unemployed people per vacancy	2.27	1.95
Boston		
Filled jobs/labor force	1.472	0.816
Vacancies/labor force	0.037	0.021
Unemployed, as percentage of labor force	6.8	6.5
Effective unemployment, as percentage of labor force	10.8	5.8
Effective unemployment-vacancies, as percentage of labor force	7.1	3.7
Effective unemployed people per vacancy	2.92	2.76
Detroit		
Filled jobs/labor force	0.842	0.902
Vacancies/labor force	0.024	0.032
Unemployed, as percentage of labor force	19.7	5.2
Effective unemployment, as percentage of labor force	13.4	7.0
Effective unemployment-vacancies, as percentage of labor force	11.0	3.8
Effective unemployed people per vacancy	5.58	2.19
Los Angeles		
Filled jobs/labor force	0.938	0.88
Vacancies/labor force	0.022	0.019
Unemployed, as percentage of labor force	8.4	6.8
Effective unemployment, as percentage of labor force	8.2	6.9
Effective unemployment-vacancies, as percentage of labor force	6.0	5.0
Effective unemployed people per vacancy	3.73	3.63

Source: Holzer 1996, table 2.4.

face-to-face interviews. We attempt to show that their map of the city is tinged with attitudes about race. As we noted before, we expect employers to see the geography of the city in racial terms, because that is the reality of current racial segregation in U.S. cities. However, the attitudes of employers in our data about different areas of the city go beyond a report on demography.

Views of the business environment and workforce of the inner city, or of minority areas in general, vary in intensity across the four metropolitan areas. For Detroit-area employers the inner city is a crisply defined, ever present part of the map, even when geographically distant. For most Los Angeles and Boston employers, the inner city is remote, in many cases poorly defined, and irrelevant to their business activities. These differences in employers' mental maps are shaped by the social history of each area. The 1967 riots in Detroit etched the city-suburb distinction in stone in the minds of employers, and to many white employers the etching is defined in terms of black and white. The Los Angeles riots in 1965 and 1992 sharply outlined the predominantly black community of South Central as dangerous and undesirable, but the highly multiethnic character of its recent immigration makes the outer boundaries of the inner city diffuse. There certainly is no clear city-suburb distinction in Los Angeles. In the Boston area, decades-old black-white conflicts over school desegregation still resonate in the city, and presumed deficient education has become a strong signal attached to city minorities. But in many Boston suburbs the recent Latino and Asian migrations raise the most immediate spatial-racial issues for employers. And in Atlanta, the north-south, black-white division is an issue for many businesses, but there is not Detroit's degree of disjunction between black population centers and economic activity. We now take a look at each city in more detail.

Detroit

In the hypersegregated metropolis of Detroit, dividing lines between black and white areas play an extraordinarily large role in employers' perceptions of space. More significantly, the line between black and white is closely linked in respondents' minds to other distinctions, such as the city-suburb boundary—particularly the frontiers of Detroit, but also the line between Pontiac and other northern suburbs of Detroit. Indeed, the Asian male manager of a fast food restaurant on the south side of Eight Mile Road, which forms Detroit's northern border, stated, "We are on the [south] side, on the other side, on the black side of the road." His assistant manager noted, "People [on this side] don't go [to] that side that often, and that side['s] people don't come here."

The identification of black versus white with city versus suburb appeared most dramatically when we asked the black male director of a Detroit-based nonprofit social service organization about the differences between Detroit and suburban workers, and he answered—without a trace of self-consciousness—with a discussion of differences between black and white workers.

Interviewer: What do you think of city and suburban workers; do you think there's a difference between the two?

Respondent: You know, I mean, probably kind of foolish not to think that there must be some difference, but the truth is I see just as many goofy white kids as I do goofy black kids.

But short of this, many employers voiced a perception of the distinction between Detroit and its suburbs as a black-white distinction.

Interviewer: Do you see differences even among white employees from the city and the suburbs?

Respondent: Frankly, we don't have that many white people from the city who apply. I don't think there are that many people, at least not in this area.

Interviewer: Do you have black suburbanites apply or is it—

Respondent: Detroit.

Interviewer: Yeah, so when we're talking geography we're also talking race here?

Respondent: (*Pause.*) Yeah. (*white male human resource director of Michigan Utility, located in a suburb*)

A few departed from the typical black-white distinction by bringing Chaldeans or Latinos into the picture—often burdened with stereotypes of their own: "[In southwest Detroit] you have a large Hispanic community and they tend to attract gangs," observed the black male operating manager of Jack's Junkyard located in that area.

Many respondents also implicitly identified the division between black and white turf with distinctions between "good" and "bad" neighborhoods, and (relatedly) between poor neighborhoods and those with working-class or wealthier residents.

Some suburban respondents were extremely concerned about the process of neighborhoods "turning" or "going downhill." Respondents spontaneously raised the subject at one-quarter of suburban sites. In many cases (though not all), their comments on the subject conflated race and class:

I think [compared to Livonia, Southfield, which is an integrated community neighboring Detroit, is] a little less . . . a little more crime . . . a little dirtier out there. It's just kind of going downhill. Do you know what I'm saying? I mean, people are moving out to West Bloomfield and Birmingham. There's a big distinction between Birmingham and Southfield. Because you're getting closer to Detroit, and I think it just gets a little yucky as you. . . . [laughter.] (*white female office manager at the suburban regional headquarters of discount chain ShopKwik*)

In the south end [of Detroit's northern suburbs], I would say it is predominantly black. You see a difference in the neighborhoods—although [in] the south end many of them are still kept up as good as the north—but I do see a difference, there is a different atmosphere. It's almost like the 696 freeway [at the 10 1/2-mile point] is the dividing line, the new Eight Mile Road. I've read that urban blight has most definitely moved north of Eight Mile and it is creeping to the point where the 696 corridor is predicted, and I see it happening myself, has become a new Eight Mile Road. (*white male custodial supervisor for a public agency in a northern suburb*)

People are moving away [from the suburbs near Detroit]. You have a lot of blacks in the cities, It's very easy to make up your mind that you don't want to live in those type of areas because you look around and you see things. I like nice things, I have a nice house, I take care of my yard. I go to areas maybe where there's a lot of blacks and I don't see what I want to see. I wouldn't want to live there. (*white male supervisor at a manufacturing plant located "downriver," in a primarily white area southeast of Detroit*)

In a few cases, respondents equated racial distance with physical distance. In a revealing comment, a white female suburban public-sector manager described her former home of Sterling Heights, which remains less than 1 percent black, as "thirty-five miles northeast of Detroit"; in fact, Sterling Heights is a rectangle extending from six to twelve miles above Detroit. Apparently, Sterling Heights feels far more distant from Detroit than it actually is.

Although city-suburb and black-white contrasts dominated respondents' geographic narratives, other distinctions figured as well. Respondents drew class distinctions among predominantly white suburbs: "North side, that's where all the money is. We're just little guys downriver here, we're just trying to eke out a living, okay?" (White male president of a transportation firm).

Atlanta

When they described the region, Atlanta employers showed a sharp eye for demographic variation:

Atlanta has a big mixture of people everywhere. Whether it's North Fulton County with the upsy-doosy [upper income, tony] people or down near the airport with a lot of those folks called lower-middle class people or even worse. But you have a good mixture all over. You get to South Atlanta, you've got Fayette County and a lot of people that have money. (*County Construction manager*)

[Describing workforces at stores in his retail chain] In Marietta everybody's white. The two stores are in East Cobb, and that's a very white, middle-class, upper-middle-class area. Greenbriar, which is over by the airport, is—everybody's black there, except for the manager, who's white. And our customer base at Greenbriar is 99.9 percent black there. The Greenbriar and East Point area is probably middle-class or upper-middle-class black area. (*owner of chain*)

Atlanta employers are particularly keenly aware of the north-south division, which is, in addition, a black-white division. "The people who live on the north side of town are pretty unwilling to travel to the south side of town," noted a manager with facilities in both areas—adding that this was partly due to distance but also to fear of crossing the race and class divide. But Atlanta respondents also described cognitive boundaries between the inner city, the "outer city," and the suburbs—a three-way division that is uniquely meaningful to firms in Atlanta, among the four cities in our sample. "We define [our stores] as inner city and within the perimeter and outside of the perimeter," said the manager of a fast food restaurant, "and I'm outside the perimeter, but I'm probably more like an inside store [because the workforce is overwhelmingly black]."

Most employers characterized the inner city as "downtown." This space well inside the urban perimeter is sharply distinct from the suburbs well outside the perimeter. There are clear barriers that keep these areas separate, such as the lack of a common transportation system, the use of suburban community papers to recruit versus use of the metro area paper, and the sheer distance between them. But firms, employers, and employees also occupy the space—the outer city—that separates these two extremes. MARTA, the Atlanta public transit system, is accessible to most employees and firms within this area. Employers can recruit from the outer city using either local papers or the main metropolitan newspaper. The distance between many points of residence and employment in the outer city is not severe. A manager at a downtown business commented on the division between the "downtown" and "outer-city" labor markets for low-level jobs:

When you speak of Atlanta, I think there is a vast difference between downtown Atlanta and other parts of Atlanta. Typically people who are

166

looking for secretarial, clerical positions who are not inner-city residents are going to look around the periphery, where there are many offices located and many employment opportunities. They live in Gwinnett County and they don't want to come twenty-six miles all the way downtown when there are plenty of opportunities in their neighborhood. So for low-skilled jobs, people tend to look closer to home for low-paying jobs. If you view that as the truth, then most of our applicants are inner-city residents, for low-paying work and low-skilled jobs.

The outer city is intricately linked with the rest of the metro area. The northern part of the outer city is largely white and is sometimes connected with the suburbs to the north of the city, and the southern part is mostly black and connected with southern suburbs. Employers from the northern suburbs, in particular, demarcate between northern Atlanta's outer-city areas and the northern suburbs.

Boston

As in the other cities, Boston-area employers distinguish between the inner city and other areas. One interesting institutionalization of the city-suburb dichotomy came from a hospital that has "health centers" in low-income, largely minority areas and "ambulatory care centers" in more affluent, primarily white suburbs. When asked about the difference between the two, the manager of an ambulatory care center had not considered it:

Respondent: Those are health centers. I guess I've just never heard them called ambulatory care centers, basically. I wouldn't be able to speak to that, what the dynamics are of all the hiring practices.

Interviewer: But do you know what the difference is, why this is called ambulatory care and that is called a health center?

Respondent: I really wouldn't be able to speak to that.

Interestingly, a health center director confirmed that "some people believe that [a] health center is a place where poor people can go, so as they move up, they don't want to go to the health center." She added, "It's a part of our job to try to change that through education."

The distinction between the city and the suburbs is not so sharp in the eyes of Boston's city and suburban employers as it is in Detroit and Atlanta, but the distinctions clearly reflect race. Respondents often defined Boston's inner city with a list of Boston neighborhoods: "Roxbury,

Dorchester, Mattapan, Jamaica Plain . . . the most inner city of the neighborhoods."

While this black-Latino core of the inner city was well defined in employers' minds, the boundaries were fuzzy and subject to varying interpretations. For instance, a hotel manager in a neighboring city defined Dorchester and Jamaica Plain as not being in the inner city:

> *Interviewer:* Do many of your workers come from the inner-city kinds of neighborhoods of Boston?

> *Respondent:* Well, not inner city, I wouldn't say, no. They come from some pretty rough Boston neighborhoods, maybe. North Dorchester, even Jamaica Plain, to some point isn't exactly Beverly Hills.

For this employer, apparently, only Roxbury and Mattapan—the poorest and blackest of the Boston neighborhoods—were sufficiently "rough" to include in the inner-city category. The human resources chief at a Boston-area manufacturer, however, referred to Dorchester and Jamaica Plain as "communities that were white that are now inner-city and deteriorating."

Furthermore, employers' comments, while mostly negative, were not as starkly racialized or pejorative, either about the inner city as a business location or about workers from the inner city, as were comments from Detroit and Atlanta employers. In contrast to Detroit and Atlanta, and more like Los Angeles, the substantial recent immigration and resulting racial and ethnic diversity in Boston and around the greater Boston area appears to have made the inner city, and black inner-city residents in particular, less important to Boston-area employers seeking low-wage labor. The old manufacturing cities such as Lowell and Lawrence, among others, have become important sources of labor for suburban Boston firms and have inner cities and inner-city problems of their own. It is useful to think of three geographic groups of firms in greater Boston—the firms in the city of Boston, the firms in the suburbs of Boston, and the firms in cities such as Lawrence, Lowell, and Brockton, the particular satellite cities represented in our sample.

Los Angeles

The complex geographic, industrial, and population differentiation of Los Angeles is reflected in employers' views of space. With the exception of South Central, the "black-white, city-suburb, good-bad" distinctions are not particularly vivid for Los Angeles employers. Areas that employers see as highly desirable and highly undesirable are scattered across the landscape. Employers tend to be concerned with their own current locations, not with areas that are both socially and physically distant. Respondents typically described "the inner city" by listing communities; those lists comprised low-income areas inhabited primarily by people of color—always black, sometimes Latino. Relatively few employers explicitly identified space with race—though a Latina, downtown-based public-sector manager described the main difference between the inner-city and suburban workforce as "ethnic makeup" and explained, "The closer to the downtown area, you know, the darker you are." Despite reticence about linking race and space, many employers spoke readily about class markers such as housing costs and general levels of affluence. For instance, at a company we call SoCal Utility, "My salespeople come from everywhere but L.A., because they're paid well. The support people are very much, however, from L.A."

Some managers gave narrow definitions of the inner city as the black-Latino areas in and immediately adjacent to South Central. Broader definitions included downtown or extended the defined area west and/or east. The vice president of a real estate firm based in Santa Monica described the inner city as "the downtown and the immediate surrounding inner city around that," adding, "I hate to go to either one." Perhaps the most expansive definition came from the general manager of a LAX-based airport service company, who stated that his "inner-city" janitorial workforce sweeps "from East L.A., all the way through the South Central, the Watts, Carson, Culver City, Inglewood, Hawthorne, a little in the Torrance area." While suburbanites offered varied definitions of where the inner city begins, in some situations they defined very crisp boundaries. The executive director of a private social service agency stated:

> When we advertise and say "an agency in Pasadena," I think Pasadena has an ... image in people's mind. They say, "Well, I wouldn't mind working in Pasadena." [But] if you know the structure, where you step off of property on three sides and we're in Highland Park. I think if we had said "an agency in Highland Park," people would maybe take a second look. They wouldn't be as anxious to make that phone call. Because of the image of Highland Park.

In response to the interviewer's query, "What's wrong with being in Highland Park?" he responded, "I think people think of Highland Park as being gang-infested. Sort of low-income, sort of on the edge of East L.A." Another example of this name game in the Los Angeles area is Rancho Dominguez. This industrial area with "real good coverage by the police" is essentially in Compton—poor, black, and celebrated in "gangsta rap" lyrics—but the developers evidently chose another name to avoid the connotations of a Compton address. Race and ethnicity are clearly a part of these boundary definitions.

On the other hand, many suburban employers expressed a more diffuse sense of the inner city's location. Indeed, of two respondents at a traditional manufacturing concern in Commerce, a small industrial city in the Los Angeles area, one thought they were doing business in the inner city, whereas the other thought the inner city was elsewhere! At SoCal Utility, a manager reported that technicians think they ought to receive "combat pay" for going into the inner city (in fact, he pays gang members to follow his technicians), but added, "I'm sure you listen to the news like I do. There's no real area now, [the inner city is] just everywhere." "I don't know where the inner city is anymore," reported an informant at a large suburban insurance company.

Most respondents saw the inner city as socially and physically distant, and indeed their discourse about the inner city often referred to "what you see on the news" and "what you read in the papers." Downtown Los Angeles is "the unknown big city" with a "big-city reputation" to the field manager of a Long Beach–based customer service organization. An administrator at Anytown College in Orange County described its isolation from "that" world: "There's the business environment that we're situated within, and that's our business, and then there's L.A. County, which has several concentric rings about it. One is inner-city, which is many miles from here. Then we're suburban—is our classification. So you're asking me about the inner city of Watts, Compton, and that . . . kind of that?" A Santa Monica employer simply professed ignorance about the inner city, saying, "I really don't know too much other because I don't deal much in that area."

However, employers were often keenly aware of workforce demographics in the locations where they *are* doing business. A respondent who hires for a utility company distinguished the racial and ethnic character at the various sites: for instance, the office in Korea Town "used to be Mexican, then became Central American, and now it's almost all Korean." Moreover, despite their distance from it, most employers had opinions about the inner city and could describe what it connoted.

The employer cognitive maps that emerge from the commentaries in all four cities show that employers have a good idea of the racial demography of their metropolitan areas, as we would expect, but further, that this racial picture helps them define and demarcate the inner city. This is significant because in most cases, inner city spells trouble to employers both because race itself often raises a warning flag and because inner-city life carries a set of additional troubling images frequently suffused with race. Our task now is to delineate the specific means by which this negative view of the inner city and its residents generates labor market disadvantage. The first of these is how employers regard inner-city workers as a source of labor.

Perceptions of the Inner City as a Place to Recruit and Hire

In this section we explore employers' assessments of inner-city residents as workers—the scope of these views, how employers explain them, and how some views change with the nature of the job the employer is offering. We detail these perceptions first to understand them better, so that we might determine how mutable they are, and second to form a basis for our argument that the views translate into decisions that hinder inner-city workers in the labor market.

As we indicated earlier in the propositions for this chapter, we see two ways in which employers' perceptions of inner-city workers can harm their job prospects. First, which we explore in this section, inner-city residents appear to be pushed lower on employers' hiring queues than they would be based on skill, race, and ethnicity alone, by added negative images of the inner city. This is true for both city and suburban employers. In the next section, we probe how employers' appraisal of inner-city workers feeds their frequent avoidance of the inner city as a business location.

While we do not aim to repeat ourselves, some of our discussion of employers' images of inner-city workers and the explanations they have for those images will have a familiar ring. In the previous chapter, we indicated that many managers attribute poor black skills to growing up in the inner city. In this section, we show that skill deficits are one dimension of employers' unfavorable view of inner-city workers. Inner-city workers are disproportionately black and Latino, so, in part we are looking at alternate sides of the same coin. Perceptions of skill and images of what it is like to be from the inner city are mixed together and reinforce one another. But we argue that they are not identical. "Inner city" adds ingredients to the pot. Our analytical dilemma of not being able to discuss skill and race, and space and race, completely separately, reflects the connections we found among all these factors in employers' statements.

In our in-depth interviews, respondents spoke to a wide range of spatial issues, mainly in response to two questions focused specifically on space: "How is [this community] as a place to do business?" and "We have heard that [central city], particularly the inner city, is a difficult place to do business; what do you think?" Depending on responses, there were a variety of follow-up probes, notably: "Do you see a differ-

ence between workers from [central city] and workers from the suburbs?" The varied discussions prompted by these questions form a rich
database on employers' perceptions and actions.

How widespread are the negative attitudes toward workers from the
inner city? Our data give us two sources for estimates of the prevalence
of such attitudes: the 3,510 employers in the Telephone Survey (table
5.3, reprising data we looked at in table 4.2) and the 365 respondents in
our sample of 174 employers in the in-depth, Face-to-Face Survey (table
5.4). Tables 5.3 and 5.4 display reported employer views from the two
sources broken down by the location of the employer—primary central
city, other central city, or suburb. We can learn about employer perceptions of the quality of the inner-city workforce from both sources.

Managers were *far* more likely to criticize the inner-city workforce
in the face-to-face interviews. It appears that the conversational style of
the in-depth interviews gave employers added opportunities and incentives to state their views frankly. As with chapter 4's findings on reporting of attitudes in the two surveys, this suggests that despite its smaller
sample size, the Face-to-Face Survey offers a more reliable assay of employer attitudes on sensitive matters such as these.

Table 5.4 demonstrates that negative views of inner-city workers
are widespread. Managers at 48 percent of suburban businesses, and over
60 percent of urban ones, cited workforce quality problems in areas that
they perceive as inner city. These negative statements were somewhat
more frequent than the negative assessments of black workers we re-
viewed in chapter 4. A range of concerns was common to employers in
all four metropolitan areas. As with the employer perceptions of skills
and race that we discussed in the previous chapter, we view these criticisms as a mixture of stereotype, cultural gap, and objective reality. As

TABLE 5.3   *Proportion of Employers Who Say That Inner-City*
Residents Are Weaker Job Applicants or Employees

	Central City	Suburbs	Other Central Cities	All Employers
All four cities	16.6%	15.3%	17.8%	16.1%
Atlanta	19.7	17.3	23.7	19.7
Boston	11.9	14.1	11.2	13.1
Detroit	15.3	16.2	22.2	16.9
Los Angeles	15.6	14.9	15.2	15.1
	N = 712	N = 1,482	N = 421	N = 2,615

Source: Multi-City Telephone Employer Survey.
Note: "Other central cities" also includes any municipality other than the primary central
city that has a black population of 30 percent or more.

TABLE 5.4   *Employers' Attitudes About Inner-City Business Locations and Workers, by Respondent Business Location, from Face-to-Face Interviews*

Percentage of Firms Where Respondents Stated Concerns About	Primary Central City	Other Central Cities	Suburb	Total
Inner-city workforce worse				
At least one respondent	64	62	48	57
Half or more of firm respondents	40	53	37	41
Inner-city workforce better				
At least one respondent	15	15	30	21
Half or more of firm respondents	12	15	24	17
Inner-city crime a problem for business				
At least one respondent	57	65	61	60
Half or more of firm respondents	43	50	55	50
	N = 164	N = 164	N = 164	N = 164

Source: Multi-City In-Depth Employer Survey.
Note: "Other central cities" also include any municipality other than the primary central city that has a black population of 30 percent or more.

we indicated in chapter 4, stereotypes are not always divorced from reality, but they exaggerate or distort that reality. The various components of the mixture of stereotype, cultural distance, and reality cannot readily be pulled apart.

The fact that more city employers than suburban ones criticize the inner-city workforce is consistent with results in table 4.3 on reported ethnocentric preferences. However, this fact contrasts with the lower black hire-to-applicant ratios in the suburbs we saw in chapter 4, which suggest that suburban employers are more discriminatory than those in the city. Jencks and Mayer's hypothesis about discrimination and distance, cited earlier, also predicts more discrimination in the suburbs. As with some of the unexpected results in chapter 4, the explanation may be a type of salience effect. As we will show, many suburban employers don't concern themselves *at all* with the inner city. They don't have employees from the inner city, they do not consider recruiting there, and they do not remotely consider locating there. Part of the correlation between suburban location and lack of negative opinion arises, therefore, because being in the suburbs increases the likelihood that the inner city has been erased as a possibility, either purposefully or because of distance. These employers don't have a negative opinion or much of any opinion. Inner-city workers are much more *salient* to employers in or close to the city, and these employers are more likely to have inner-city residents as employees.

Skills

Employers' evaluation of inner-city workers relative to suburban workers, not surprisingly, often focuses on their skills. When employers speak of the skills of inner-city residents, they use the same dimensions we detailed in chapter 4 to describe the skills of workers of different race, ethnic, and gender groups—hard skills and the soft skills of motivation and interaction. Because the perceptions overlap a great deal, just as the perception of race and inner-city residence overlaps significantly, we offer only a few examples concentrating on specific references to the inner city.

Many negative employer comments spoke to hard skills such as reading, writing, and basic reasoning:

I am kind of amazed at the level of, or lack thereof, of literacy in people, especially people who have graduated from high schools in this area. Especially in downtown. (*hotel manager, downtown Atlanta*)

The residential population here is mostly lower-income, uneducated. And we prefer someone with a little more education, someone who can comprehend how to make food or so forth, and to get a lot of that group in this neighborhood is difficult. (*manager, institutional food service at edge of Boston's inner city*)

The more applicants we've been hiring from the Pontiac and Detroit area[s], the [more the] failure rate [on the company's exam] has increased. (*supervisor, Michigan Utility, in suburbs*)

The population in the inner city of Los Angeles is very different than it is in [suburban community]. Or in any of the outlying areas of Los Angeles. I mean the skill level. I mean, just look at the schools. Look at the statistics of the reading scores and the math scores. It's dismal. If I move to another position, it will not be inner-city Los Angeles, I'll tell you that right now. (*manager of support department, Anytown College in suburban Los Angeles*)

Others deplored inner-city residents' verbal communication skills. Their comments evince the cultural distance between the language of the inner city and elsewhere. "They don't have a language base, a lot of it is [a matter of] just plain, everyday old dialect," a black suburban school personnel official commented. The white personnel manager of a union complained that "it is negative" for inner-city workers to speak "street slang" within her organization. When managers are confronted with this type of communication, a white human resource officer at ShopKwik said, "the initial thought is 'Gosh, you're dumb.'"

Less frequent than employer criticisms of the inner-city workforce's technical skills, but often more emotionally freighted, were negative evaluations of their soft skills or character. For instance, the assistant director of rooms in a hotel in Cambridge (just north of Boston), when asked why the hotel employs no inner-city Boston residents, responded:

> You're looking for a certain individual. You have to have people in that area that show some interest. You can't have somebody standing behind the front desk with a long face on, doesn't want to be there, and looking at their watch every five minutes. Doesn't look good to you [as a guest] when you're paying $159 a night to stay here.

Most suburban employers in Atlanta complained about their own local labor pool, but their concerns about the inner-city workforce eclipsed any worries about suburban workers. A white store manager noted that "it's real difficult [finding enough qualified workers] in this area, when you're competing with the mall." But he added: "It just amazed me, some of the people that I met downtown. But then I guess that's inner city. They were just basically there for the buck. And they came in and they did just as little as they could get by with and then they left, and when they had enough money to satisfy them they were gone."

We heard a similar refrain in Detroit. The Michigan Utility supervisor who talked about higher test-failure rates among Detroit applicants added, "And I don't know that it's all education. I mean, I think it has to do with work ethics, too."

As we have suggested, city businesses' greater readiness to express negative evaluations of the urban workforce is due in part to the fact that their suburban counterparts were less able or willing to express any opinion. For instance, when asked about doing business in the inner city, an employer of clerical workers in Santa Monica, west of Los Angeles, replied:

Respondent: We do very little business with inner-city L.A. So I think I would decline, I wouldn't be able to answer that.

Interviewer: What about people, workforce quality issues?

Respondent: I don't know that I'm qualified to answer that. I mean, simply because I don't have any experience in that area.

I haven't tried to recruit from the inner city. I haven't tried to or not to—it's just the fact that it isn't something that I've been exposed to.

While urban employers more often expressed negative views, their criticisms were rarely sweeping. Indeed, a substantial minority of city businesses gave mixed or even positive evaluations of the inner-city workforce, as we will explore further.

How Employers Explain Problems with the Inner-City Workforce

When employers perceive deficits in the inner-city workforce, the way they explain these deficits to themselves is crucially important. If they view the workforce differences as fundamentally racial in nature, this attitude will put inner-city blacks and Latinos doubly at risk. If they attribute differences to school quality—rightly or wrongly—then education reform may well open doors for job seekers from the inner city. The importance of employers' "folk theories" is not so much what it tells us about the inner-city labor force itself, but rather the information about what it would take to get more businesses to hire urban workers.

Although in the United States at the turn of the twenty-first century, "inner city" generally implies "nonwhite," only a few employers stated outright that the difference between the inner-city and suburban workforces was racial. They typically accounted for differences by linking race to inner-city education, class, family structure, and living environment. As expected, this list of factors overlaps substantially with the set of employer explanations for skill deficits among minority workers that we discussed in chapter 4. Again, we face the dilemma of separately analyzing employers' causal views of the problems with inner-city workers, given that their perceptions, and the reality, of race, inner-city ills, and skill deficits are so knotted together. Overlap is a consequence of the phenomena we are studying. We offer examples here of causal explanations where the discussion is specifically about inner-city workers and remind the reader that this section and the parallel section in chapter 4 are parts of the same story.

An example of the tangle of inner-city education, race, and verbal skills comes from ShopKwik's regional human resource director, speaking in the chain's suburban headquarters:

There is a definite difference [in capability between city and suburban workers]. I guess to a degree it is a black and white thing—but it really isn't a black and white thing, because I don't consider myself prejudiced—but there's a communication. . . . And once again, I do think it goes back to the schools. We don't teach people to speak properly [and that] puts [business] people off.

Or listen to this white male plant manager in Atlanta concerned about the connection he sees between work values and single-parent families: "Somebody just sitting there and listening to this will say, 'You know what you're saying? You're talking about black people because that's primarily what's in the inner city.' And unfortunately, that's true. I can't help it if they don't receive that type of upbringing." Similarly, at Financial Research Associates, which moved from the Los Angeles inner city to a suburban location, a white personnel manager linked a workforce that "didn't care about their jobs" at the former site to "a predominantly black workforce" and "a lot, lot of single mothers."

Some respondents explained their assessment of inner-city Latinos with similar factors. The fabrication manager at a factory located in low-income Lawrence, north of Boston, told us: "A big problem I have is attendance. And that is an inner-city problem, right? Every day I have people out for court appearances. I have guys calling me from jail. The guy is in for domestic problems. Domestic abuse. Weird problems. Inner city-type problems." He elaborated with a complicated causal web of stereotypes involving health, race, family, and education:

> For some reason people tend to be more sickly in this area. The Hispanic people tend to get sick more. [T]he education level and so forth. It's, unfortunately for these guys, related to race. They're probably from a dysfunctional family. They probably never ate good, healthy meals like a lot of us were fortunate enough to eat growing up. And that just carries over into adulthood. So your education is down, your life's guidance was down a little bit, and your nutrition goes down.

More frequently than not, the managers we spoke to dropped race out of the discussion of inner-city workers and focused on the other factors—in some cases explicitly declaring that race was not the critical issue. For instance, a vice president at SoCal Utility explained:

> [Los Angeles is] not our strongest market, certainly not our strongest area to pull workers from. There's clearly a deterioration of the education level in L.A. County. There has been a lot of white flight, and while, you know, that makes it sound strictly like a race issue and it's really a class issue. I think an economic class issue. A lot of people with resources have either moved out of the city or have certainly taken their kids out of the city into private schools and what have you, and so the source pool that we draw from for entry level is quite different.

In addition to education, employers often blamed crime, drugs, single mothers, housing projects, and "welfare mentality"—all racially loaded issues. Along with the schools, family values—and single mothers in particular—came in for special criticism, as Kennelly (1999) has pointed out and as we emphasized in chapter 4. A white male plant manager in the Atlanta area stated:

> When we get into the inner city, in my opinion, work values change because you're talking about people that are primarily raised in a single [-parent] family, very poor environment, don't have a role model that shows them that work is good. That you should do your very best when you do a job, no matter where it is or who it's for. Those type values that were taken for granted years ago. I don't know where you grew up, but I grew up in Griffin, which is south of here. Perfect home. Mother and dad that loved me and showed me right and wrong. Made me work. You don't see a lot of people getting that in the inner city.

The full list of inner-city problems and, hence, markers of a poorer quality worker, came up in each city, but some issues were raised more frequently or more prominently in one city than in the others. The clearest example of this was the negative image of the Boston public schools. Boston area businesses repeatedly cited low-quality public schools as the root cause of the inner-city workforce's weaknesses. The Boston public schools have been a flashpoint for race relations in the city of Boston for many years, even before the confrontation over busing in the 1970s. The schools have become largely minority as white residents have left them for private and parochial schools or fled to the suburbs. The purported crisis of the Boston public schools is thus a crucial way in which employers—including liberal ones reluctant to address racial differences directly—expressed negative views of inner-city workers. Given the demographic trends of the student body and the long history of controversy, it is difficult to separate the issue of educational preparation itself from the issues of race, class, and space that the Boston public schools have come to symbolize.

We repeat that these statements should be taken only for what they are: managers' opinions, not an objective assessment of the state of the schools. Nonetheless, the corrosive negativity of this sampling of comments is noteworthy in its own right. A public-sector manager who hires large numbers of Boston residents summarized a widespread view of race, schooling, and skills:

> I think we have a real problem. I think the problem is centered in the Boston public school system. Clearly, in my opinion, the school system in this city is not producing young people with the educational skills to get into the workforce and, in many cases, perform. In most cases, the white

has gone either to private school or gone almost overwhelmingly to the Catholic parochial school system. Minority kids either went to school in the deep South, where the per capita expenditure for education is as weak as you can imagine, or they graduated from the Boston public school system. In either case, we've had, historically, a much larger failure rate among minority than white.

A personnel director, also from a public-sector agency, emphasized basic skill problems:

I seemed to notice that someone that had come out of the Boston public schools, a lot of times does have a hard time with [our] written skills test. My sense is that anyone that came from a private or parochial school seems to do better than a public school student would do on that written test.

The view from a contract cleaning firm across the river in Cambridge is even more scathing:

The difference in the education [for inner-city workers], I can see it very clearly. And you can have a high school degree from Boston and you can have a high school degree from, let's say Medford, Somerville [other nearby northern suburbs], or somewhere else and the abilities of the people to comprehend and write and read are far greater for the people from Somerville, Cambridge, Medford. And I have a sneaking suspicion on a few I know. I know they have a high school diploma, but I don't know if they can read or write. And if they can, it's very limited. Especially when you're asking for reports. One of the most difficult things is the hazardous material shipments. It's a very costly thing if we make a mistake and if the documentation, if you don't dot the *i* and cross the *t*, then we're subject to a heavy fine.

Though the previous three managers are white, we heard similar complaints from a black woman middle manager at a Boston clinic. Asked why people of color are doing worse in the labor market, she responded:

It has a lot to do with the level of education, of course. And if because of financial restraints or whatever, you cannot afford to hire persons with that level of education, and you need to hire a lower level in order to obtain personnel, then you're going to run into those issues. I think that still more blacks are going to school and staying in school, but still there's a high rate of drop-off, the numbers. If you've ever been in the school system, Boston public schools, anyway, the high schools are a nightmare. Granted, there are maybe twenty percent that are fine and are going to do well and get good grades, but the other eighty percent are just lost. They're just there to be there. When they fill out the work applications, it's unbelievable. They can't spell; they don't know what city they live in.

She distanced herself from the public schools, explaining, "My kids are in parochial school. They've always been in parochial school. We went to parochial school, I went to public school too at the end, but it was nothing like it is now."

In greater Atlanta a number of managers raised inner-city workers' dependence on public transportation in a way that marked these employees as less desirable workers. For example:

> Your labor force [from the inner city] is comprised of a different education level and a different income level. In the city of Atlanta, I have sometimes run ads in the Atlanta paper. And I find that all the employees, if you're not on the MARTA [the Atlanta public transit system] route, are not interested in working for you. (white woman, general manager from a northern suburb)

We will return to the signal of dependence on public transportation in the section on "Employer Perceptions and Hiring."

Employers adduced varied types of evidence in support of their explanations. Some respondents grounded their negative perceptions in concrete experiences, and in some cases quantifiable data such as test scores or turnover rates.[3] More often—especially in the case of suburban businesspeople commenting on the inner city—employers expressed their views as opinions. Again, the fraction that speaks disparagingly of inner-city workers is higher among employers located in the city than among suburban employers (see table 5.4), suggesting that experience is likely to be important in forming opinions. Indeed, this suggests that employer encounters with real hard- and soft-skill gaps most likely contribute much to the observed negative views and to differential hiring patterns as well. However, employers' association of inner-city residence with a list of stereotypes and their at times seamless interchange between inner city and race and class—most notably, low-income black—tell us that businesses' negative attitudes about and reluctance to hire inner-city residents go well beyond the issue of genuine skill deficiencies. Although inner-city does correspond closely to race and class, the generalizations about space, race, and class that many employers express, as we argued in chapter 4, are often inaccurate and unfair.

Dissenting Views of the Inner-City Workforce

Employers' spoken evaluations of the skills of urban and suburban workers were far from monolithic. Whereas 60 percent of employers voiced negative views of the urban workforce, many others simply asserted that there was no difference between urban and suburban workers (not shown). Twenty-one percent instead painted inner-city workers as a *better* workforce in some way. In a number of cases respondents at the same business, and sometimes even the same respondents, gave apparently conflicting assessments.

Why this mix? In many cases, managers volunteered negative views of urban workers, but when asked point-blank whether they saw a difference between city and suburban workers, answered no. We suspect, therefore, that many of these comments simply reflect respondents' attempts to provide socially desirable answers. But some employers' assertions of parity between the two workforces went beyond safe formulas like "there are good and bad people everywhere." And in a small number of cases, employers viewed inner-city workers as more likely to be available for work and more content and committed to jobs—particularly menial or low-paid jobs. These dissenting views merit special attention for what they reveal about who employers think is "right" for which kinds of jobs, and how race figures into that assessment. In chapter 4, we examined the employers who viewed minority and white workers as equally skilled, as well as the employers with positive opinions of workers of color. The "no difference" and positive views of inner-city workers we examine here are parallel and indeed overlapping.

Start by considering managers who judged urban and suburban workforces roughly equal. Their responses fell into similar categories as those from employers who responded "no difference" to the question that we discussed in the previous chapter, Do you see a difference between minority and white workers? Some just stated that they haven't experienced a difference, while others argued that they can screen effectively enough to find satisfactory workers regardless of their geographic origins.

"I know a lot about what it takes to do business there [in the inner city]," remarked a mortgage company manager in the San Fernando Valley, citing experience at another business:

> There really is no demonstrable difference in the productivity in my view, in the availability of people of requisite skills, work habits, or anything like that. There is an ethnic difference, though. You get more African Americans and Hispanics on the other side of the hill. And here in the Valley you get more Asians. But beyond that, there really is no difference.

At SoCal Utility, a respondent who recruits statewide said, "I don't find geographically a huge difference" in skills, and "I have no data to support" the notion of significant differences in attitudes or skills across areas. Her supervisor, however, undermined these statements by saying that in Los Angeles, "We seem to struggle to get the quality that we would need," though San Diego is "an excellent source." She continued, "You know, we were trying to determine whether [the Los Angeles recruiting problems are due to] the salaries, or if it's the level of the education of the people who do reside in the metropolitan area. I think it's just a combination of everything."

At a Los Angeles-area temporary help agency that hires workers in lots of gritty areas, a middle manager commented that any applicant would have to pass its "very stringent testing" and provide "two verifiable references," and concluded, "So I feel that we're always getting the top quality no matter where we're at." Remarkably, the agency used a four-hour battery of tests to fill jobs paying $4.50 to $4.75 (in 1995). The manager clearly saw that her company benefits from a surplus of low-skilled labor:

> There seems to be a lot of people that don't have the proper education that don't have much of a choice anywhere you are in California. I don't see any of our offices having recruiting problems at all. It's just unfortunate that, because of a lack of education, this is where they end up. And it's sad. I see them come in, and they're laughing, and smiling, and happy as can be, and we're handing over this paycheck for maybe two hundred dollars, when I know how hard they worked that week. So maybe they came from a different background, and this is a step forward for them.

In fact, she often brought her son to work so he would understand the importance of going to college.

As table 5.4 indicates, a minority of respondents indicated that the inner-city workforce was better than the suburban workforce. The 21 percent of managers who espoused this view far outnumbered the 2 percent who rated blacks better workers (shown in table 4.4). Most often these statements echoed the temporary agency manager's narrative: the inner city offers an excess supply of low-skilled workers appropriate for certain industries, whereas suburban workers have more alternatives. Such responses occurred in all four metropolitan areas, particularly among businesses offering low-paid or menial work.

At a number of Atlanta-area enterprises that do business in both the North and the (lower-income and blacker) South, we heard a preference for the inner-city option—because inner-city workers need the jobs more and therefore are more committed. For example, a black fast food entrepreneur ran one store in the southern suburbs and another in the North, and described the differences between the two workforces:

Interviewer: When you think about these areas as a place to hire workers, and how difficult it is to get good workers, how does this store [in the southern suburbs] and the other compare?

Respondent: Like night and day. This one, I very seldom have problems getting workers. It is in a black community, more or less, people need to work, and a lot of them want to work, and a lot of them have to work because the income is needed to support the family. And this one has a bus line which is real big. So if somebody from five or six miles down the street wants to work, then they get on the bus and they come. At the other one, first of all I don't have the bus lines. Gwinnett County doesn't have MARTA. Second of all it's in a ritzy area or more affluent area, if you want to define it. People don't really have to work, and the ones that do work are just kind of there because their parents told them to come there.

In a public agency that serves an area ranging from northern to southern suburbs, a black top manager indicated that "in the northern suburbs we find it very difficult finding people living in those areas to take some of the lower-paying jobs" such as driver and custodian.

A manager of drivers at the same agency agreed that workers from the south, which is mostly black, are more willing to take low-paying jobs because they need the money more:

What we find is, we have more applicants in south county, due to the socioeconomic background of south county. You have more individuals that are needing a good job, needing the benefits and are looking for them. I can't say for sure, but I would assume that you've probably got more single parents in south county. You've got more people interested in going to work to try to make a living for their families than you get in north county and the Roswell-Alpharetta area [northern, majority-white suburbs]. (*white man*)

Similarly, at an inner-city Los Angeles warehouse, two human re-source managers mused:

I have heard of distribution centers moving into the [outlying] Ontario area. They're having a very difficult time recruiting.

The labor force isn't there. If we were to move to an outlying area, we find the candidate that comes in for this type of job is primarily black or His-panic, less education. It would be very difficult for them to get to an outly-ing distribution center. Here we have a steady stream of people who are available by bus or by walking in the neighborhood.

In a few cases, employers went beyond lauding the greater availabil-ity of workers in the inner city, to favorably compare their performance with suburban workers. Again, the reason given was inner-city workers' greater need for a job. A white grocery store manager in a suburb "down-river" from Detroit indicated:

> There's a couple of individuals [from Detroit who] are some of my better workers, but they also seem to be the ones that are content doing what they are doing. This is just guessing, but it could be that in the past or as they've grown up, they've never had anything, so for them this is great.

And the proprietor of a sporting goods store in a Detroit suburb noted:

> [City workers] might be more motivated, they might be harder workers, more willing to do things for you. They maybe do menial tasks, you know, take out the trash type of physical labor type of things that some of our suburban employees might be against, or, for instance, "Oh, I don't cut the lawns at home, I'm not going to cut the lawns here" type of thing.

All these compliments are sincere, but backhanded. Most employers who described a superior work ethic attributed it to a desperate need for work derived from the financial exigencies of single parenthood or lack of useful skills, tying a positive evaluation of work ethic to a negative evaluation of city workers' character and family life. Moreover, these comments were largely limited to employers hiring for low-wage retail, service, and manufacturing jobs, meaning that the relevant suburban comparison group was primarily teens and very young adults. The inner-city workforce "lends itself to our business," a cafeteria manager explained, "because obviously you need low-scale, low-wage-scale people to work for you."

We saw in chapter 4 that businesses where managers praise black, Latino, or Asian workers pay lower average wages than those that do not. Does the same wage gap show up for employers with good things to say about inner-city workers? To investigate the pay issue further, we compared average starting wages (for the relevant sample job) for employers who said inner-city workers are better in some way with wages of employers who did not. On average, firms where at least one manager lauded the inner-city workforce paid $1.79 less per hour to entry-level employees than nonlaudatory firms. Firms where a plurality of respondents made such positive statements lagged $2.35 behind in entry-level wages. Thus, firms that praise inner-city workers are likely to be offering wages that non–inner city workers might turn up their noses at. One complication is that businesses that *criticize* inner-city workers *also* pay lower wages than those who do not (by 70 cents to $1.12, depending on whether we look for at least one critic or a plurality of respondents). This is consistent with the fact that urban employers are more likely than suburban ones to have harsh words for the inner-city workforce. However, once we statistically control for businesses' location (primary central city, other central city, or suburb), the "praise" wage penalty remains large ($1.50 to $1.90) and statistically significant, whereas the "criticism" penalty fades into statistical insignificance. It does appear that businesses with good things to say about inner-city workers tend to pay wages unlikely to attract anyone else.

In sum, most employers in all four metropolitan areas viewed the inner-city workforce with a jaundiced eye. The incidence of such responses was higher among employers located in the city, which we suggest is due, in part, to the fact that inner-city workers are more salient to city employers. The city employers are more familiar with the actual skill gaps that exist, and the suburban employers are more likely to have no opinion because they deliberately, or because of distance, have no contact with inner-city workers. Although skill deficits were frequently noted, the range of other attributes attached to the perception of inner-city workers, most notably whether or not they are black or Latino, suggests that inner-city residence broadcasts a negative signal over and above the actual skill level of the individuals involved. The explanations for negative assessments of inner-city workers range over a variety of inner-city ills, but most frequently center on the views of the inner city as a place of substandard schools and single-parent families. And even those few employers who see the urban workforce as superior attribute this to these workers' great need for jobs in areas plagued by a labor surplus. To the degree that inferior education drives the negative view employers hold of inner-city residents, a serious policy commitment holds the promise of leveling up perceptions of inner-city minority workers with those of white suburbanites (Jencks and Phillips 1998). Other sources of employers' image of inner-city residents, such as the effects of single parenthood and race pure and simple, make us less sanguine about achieving parity in the eyes of employers.

Perceptions of the City as a Business Location

An extensive literature concludes that the most important factors driving business location decisions are availability of the desired type of labor, costs, access to relevant markets and suppliers, and amenities of the location (Blair and Premus 1987; Ady 1997). As we would expect, the employers in our surveys focus on these factors as well. In discussing their hesitancy about the city as a place to do business, they indicate concern with the availability of satisfactory labor and the difficulty of recruiting other (suburban) workers to work in the city, crime and safety, customer base, and a set of costs associated with city locations. The most frequently expressed concerns are the ones shown in table 5.4: workforce quality and safety. Our task in this section is to plumb employers' perceptions of these issues to understand how the negative image of inner-city areas *and residents* feeds other economic factors to make the inner city a relatively unattractive place for employers to locate.

Availability of Skills

In the last section, we described employers' primarily negative image of inner-city residents as workers. The goal was to depict whom employers want to recruit and hire, regardless of where the employers are located. We make a closely related but slightly different point here.

Employers' assessment that inner-city residents do not offer a satisfactory labor pool, and hence their decision to seek suburban employees, also affects location decisions, because most employers prefer to recruit locally and most employees prefer to work locally as well. Other factors equal, this will tend to push employer locations out of the city.

We gleaned evidence for this point through the comments of both suburban and city employers. A number of suburban managers coupled dismissal of the inner-city workforce with the belief that more qualified workers living outside the city would be unwilling to commute to inner-city locations. Various employers in the city complained of the difficulty of getting employees to come into the city to work. For several employers the recruiting problem was not posed by entry-level workers. Firms that required technical employees as well as entry-level ones—for example, insurance companies needing accountants and information technology workers—stated that it was particularly difficult to get the higher-level workers to commute to the city.

For example, the human resource manager at a central-city Los Angeles insurance company made it clear that her workforce commuted from farther out:

> We have a heck of a time [filling secretarial jobs] here at headquarters in the downtown area because the [workers] are in demand. If you're highly skilled in those fields you usually find a job pretty close to home, and people are somewhat unwilling to commute into downtown when they can make the same money closer to home.

She estimated the typical travel distance for employees to be fifteen to twenty miles.

A Long Beach-based shipping company manager—whose company had closed down its downtown Los Angeles site—commented, "People don't like to work in the inner city. That's a problem. Who to hire. You might get employees until they realize they work in the inner city and then they back out." And, he added, "If you stay there, I think you have a hard time getting people from the outside, then you have to stay with the locals. And the locals have to increase their education or else [they are] going to be [in] a training program forever. You cannot [just] train. You've got some work to do, you know."

A top manager at a Los Angeles-area rehabilitation center gave a marginally more positive assessment of a hypothetical inner-city location, calling it a "double-edged sword" because one "could generate more unskilled applicants, but it would be more difficult getting professional staff into those areas." However, his coworker in middle management thought they "get a very low quality of work from black people," and a direct supervisor of entry-level workers did not believe he could find the skills required for dishwasher jobs in the inner-city workforce! This combination of managerial views presumably represents a formidable obstacle to hiring inner-city residents, let alone considering operating in the inner city.

In fact, many suburban employers dismissed the urban workforce outright. From his standpoint in the northern suburbs of Detroit, one white lawyer implied that there simply is no clerical workforce living in Detroit, commenting that businesses in the city have a difficult time recruiting clerical workers because, "economically, you have to offer something more to get people down there." A white business service manager who sends staff to businesses across the Los Angeles area said that downtown and the airport are the hardest areas to staff, because they are surrounded by "areas that aren't very nice to live in or very high-priced. And so to get the labor force that we look for, again, we have to hire people that tend to end up having long commutes." Writing off the inner-city workforce in this way surely makes it difficult for applicants with inner-city addresses to get a foot in the door.

The Image of the Inner City

Crime and safety was the most frequently raised employer misgiving about doing business in the inner city. Crime in the inner city is a racially charged image, as some of our employer comments attest. Other sources of reluctance focused more on economic issues less closely connected to race, although some economic concerns follow from perceptions of race and class as well.

As we noted in chapter 4, whites' perceptions of blacks, particularly black men, often include an image of hostility and aggressiveness. A number of social scientists have documented the incidence of such racial attitudes (Bobo and Kluegel 1993; Peffley and Hurwitz 1998; Fiske 1998). Mark Peffley and Jon Hurwitz found that 50 percent of respondents in a 1991 race and politics survey agreed that "most blacks are aggressive or violent." Social psychological experiments also demonstrate white fear of young, black strangers (Saint John and Heald Moore 1995). Other researchers have looked at the relation among racial attitudes, fear of crime, and white flight (Frey 1979; Harris 1997). This research documents the potency and consequences of whites' image of blacks as crime-prone and of inner-city areas where blacks live as fear-provoking.

Employers in all cities expressed concerns about crime, violence, and safety, and the consequent fears of customers, employees, and proprietors. As table 5.4 shows, respondents at about one business in five raised the specter of inner-city crime. Unlike assessments of the skill of inner-city workers, concern about crime was greatest among *suburban* employers. While the inner-city workforce is remote from most suburban managers, urban crime remains salient—because they visit the central city for shopping, entertainment, or sporting events, because they fear that crime will spill over to the suburbs, and because they are constantly exposed to media images of inner-city violence. The much more frequent mentions of crime by suburban managers than by their urban counterparts suggest that suburbanites overstate the dangers of the city.

Employers' comments spelled out these fears. Detroit is "a place that suburban people don't want to go to," observed a manager at a Detroit-based nonprofit. The white assistant director of a public agency in Atlanta's southern suburbs stated that "East Point and College Park area [two southern suburbs] has a fairly high crime rate. And the whole south side of Atlanta is fairly high on blacks, which makes a lot of whites nervous coming down in this area."

Los Angeles's turbulent history gave security concerns a special twist; employers referred to the riots of 1965 and 1992 as lightning rods: "There's been two very volatile occurrences in the inner city over the last twenty to twenty-five years. And the threat of those rekindling themselves is always prevalent." In some cases employers' security concerns focused on theft and vandalism. Employers located within the central cities complained of break-ins. In each metro area, several city employers described how they had secured parking areas and buildings for their employees. The general manager of a construction firm based in the predominantly white northern suburbs of Atlanta lauded the low crime in his area, and drew a contrast with the city of Atlanta: "I have some jobs going on in the city of Atlanta that we are doing at night. And we are having just an incredible problem with vandalism. The trucks, the equipment, is stolen and it inflates our cost of doing business there."

Other managers highlighted customer fears. A suburban Los Angeles hospital respondent said that since the 1992 civil disturbances, a sister hospital in Inglewood was struggling to recruit employees, and "visitors didn't want to visit family members there." Interestingly, she blamed misleading media images. People saw on television that Reginald Denny (the victim of a widely televised attack) received care there, so even though "it's not exactly inner-city," people avoid it as if it were—"but the reason [Denny] was taken there was that it *was* outside of [the besieged area]."

Even manufacturers noted that a location's image is important to customers as well as workers. A producer of burners who has remained within the city of Detroit acknowledged that for both customers and potential employees, the location "does scare them off. I have had people tell me that because of our street name they won't come down here. Some people won't come to buy product or won't come for employment."

Crime and safety concerns were most frequently linked in some way to acquiring employees. For some it was an issue of actual and potential crime among inner-city employees, and for others it was worry that fear of the inner city makes it hard to recruit suburban workers. The white kitchen manager at a chain restaurant in Atlanta's largely black southern suburbs explicitly linked race, crime, and workforce quality:

> The individual area that we do live in, since it's a high black area, you get a lot of people that come in that may be drug dealers, that may be in crime or that are actually looking for a job for a cover-up. When I first came into this store we had people that worked here that were actually dealing drugs in the store. We terminated them, but. . . . It's a very high crime area.

And from his standpoint in a western suburb, a law enforcement agency manager cast a baleful eye on the Atlanta workforce: "Our workers don't come from Atlanta to come out here to work; the criminals come from Atlanta to come out here to steal." The office manager at a law firm located in a northern suburb of Detroit related:

Respondent: I think most of the people here, when we send them on errands and they have to go somewhere in Detroit, they are leery and I know probably the majority of them would feel that they may not want to travel down there.

Interviewer: Has anyone ever said they didn't want to go?

Respondent: Yes, the filer, she did. At one time she was going to go downtown to pick something up, and she said, "I really don't want to go," and we ended up sending one of the [male] attorneys.

Along the same lines, a white respondent at a San Fernando Valley mortgage company said, "it would be difficult for me to drive down there [South Central]." And a manager at a public agency in the Boston area noted:

I have a hard time getting people to work in Roxbury [a low-income, primarily black and Latino neighborhood] if they are not a minority and they've been working other places. Some people are very scared to go to Roxbury. They don't want to work there. I mean, let's face it. You just sit home and you read the newspaper and you hear this one gets shot and that one gets shot through the window and the bus and the car and whatever, and people who have no intention of going to that community aren't going to go. Or if they've never been in that area, they say, "I don't want to go there." So it's always been difficult for me to find people to work in that office unless they are minority. I mean, the entire office is minority except for two white males.

Another Bostonian, directing a single-site medical facility in Boston's black inner city, also commented on recruitment difficulties:

I'm not unaware that this is considered to be a dangerous area. Its reputation far exceeds the reality, but it's certainly been a long-standing concern in terms of patients or employees. There are people who have a problem coming into this area. People [will] respond to an ad, and when they come into the area, they won't work. They won't want to. They're afraid.

Like this respondent, a vocal minority of inner city–based employers protested that their neighborhoods' "reputation" for crime "far exceeds the reality." Confirming the disjunction between urban and suburban employers' views of crime as tabulated in table 5.4, several Detroit employers used words such as "hysteria," "racism," and "overstated" to decry the exaggerated negative views of outsiders. A few even reported that they or colleagues were pleasantly surprised upon working in Detroit for the first time. A number of inner-city employers in Atlanta also defended their turf from suburbanites' negative perceptions about issues like crime. "People have the idea that downtown is a more dangerous place than other parts of Atlanta," remarked the white general manager of an inner-city hotel, "which people should be figuring out is probably not true anymore." And a white administrative specialist at an educational institution in Atlanta's inner city said, "I think that a lot of people have a perception that crime is high. They don't want to be walking around the streets of downtown. I think a lot of it just has to do with ignorance about the city. They're just not exposed to it, so they see what's on the news and that's all they think that downtown is—crime and bad things going on."

These last comments reinforce our judgment that employers' concerns with inner-city safety, while certainly based in part on the reality of a higher incidence of particular crimes, are also stoked in part by stereotype.

What's more, while employers of professional and clerical workers feared their workforces would be rattled by the inner city's image, those hiring for low-paid, often dirty manual jobs *targeted* an inner-city workforce willing to work for less—and viewed crime as simply an incidental part of the package. In chapter 2, we quoted the words of a manufacturing executive in low-income, majority Latino Lawrence, Massachusetts, who uses a 70 percent Latino production workforce. He painted a grim picture of the location, but saw no problem with getting workers:

> *Respondent:* Right now it's an issue for us. It's all crack houses and prostitutes out here. And it's tough for us right now, bringing customers in.
>
> *Interviewer:* What about in terms of getting qualified workers in the area, how is that?
>
> *Respondent:* That hasn't been too difficult. We'll get what we need.

The owner of a small metal-coating firm told a similar story about Haverhill, an old mill city just to the northeast of Lawrence:

> You have to be aware that there's a pretty good drug traffic two or three blocks from here. [Haverhill] has an inner city. It has homeless people, a pretty good-sized drug traffic. But I'm not uncomfortable with it. I really don't have any real problems. I view the workforce as an asset and not really as a problem. They really aren't a problem.

These comments are consistent with the view we noted earlier in this chapter of employers who prefer inner-city workers because they are willing to take jobs that others don't want.

Employers raised a variety of other concerns about doing business in the inner city, or about the city in general. In some cases, these were directly tied to the economic problems of poorer areas, such as the lack of a customer base. The president of a Los Angeles-area bookkeeping and tax service pointed out: "Businesses rely on people to buy things. I think a lot of people in the inner city don't have any money. They're poor. The grocery stores can still make money, but can a beauty shop? That being a discretionary [purchase]. Probably not as well as in a suburb where people have more discretionary income."

One Detroit retailer pointed out that the thin customer base was part of a vicious circle: as businesses closed or pulled out of Detroit, the employees who formed his major customer base evaporated. On the other hand, for a San Fernando Valley mortgage company, a major issue was cultural and social unfamiliarity—despite the fact that all three respondents said the company wants to expand minority lending: "We don't know how to do business in the inner city. We don't have those kinds of skills that's needed. That includes the ability to find quality employees, and the ability to find people in the community that are respected by others. And we've tried. That's not my circle."

Other issues raised include familiar complaints about relatively higher business costs in the city—congestion, parking, traffic and commuting, taxes, unfriendly regulations and government treatment of business. Detroit's city income tax (3 percent on residents, 1.5 percent on nonresident employees) also came in for special criticism. But again, some evidence suggests that suburban respondents in particular were overstating this—and probably other—problems. For example, a manager at ShopKwik's suburban headquarters facility who formerly worked in Detroit recalled the 1.5 percent income tax as "about 10 percent out of your net pay"!

In polycentric, dispersed Los Angeles, location of employers is not pushed away from downtown so much by the relative cost of the city versus suburbs. Instead, there is the pull of many localized agglomerations far from downtown Los Angeles. Notable was Long Beach, where we heard about a film company that had moved to the "New Hollywood," a shipping company that had shut down a downtown office to concentrate its activities, an aerospace firm that described the Long Beach aerospace complex as "big business," and a paper wholesaler-retailer that locates stores near printers.

In some instances, city boosters countered by celebrating the vitality and diversity of the city, and debated the accuracy of many of the criticisms, but these cases were much less frequent. And for many businesses that operate in the inner city—particularly smaller ones—this location is less the result of choice than circumstance. The white kitchen manager of a restaurant in Atlanta's low-income southern suburbs spoke for many small businesspeople in the following exchange:

Interviewer: What are some of the advantages of being in this location, in terms of the workforce specifically?

Respondent: [Pause, and then laughter.] Yeah, I had to think about that one. There's not really any advantages, to be honest.

How Perceptions Translate into Decisions: Hiring and Location

Employers' perceptions of space are important primarily to the extent that they shape their actions—chiefly decisions about business location and recruiting and hiring. We do not observe behavior longitudinally, but we did gather information on the nature, rationale, and consequences of employer decisions. Our evidence for the relation between racially and class-tinged perceptions and actual location and hiring decisions, we believe, makes a reasonable case, but remains primarily indirect.

Employer Perceptions and Hiring

Direct modifications to employers' *hiring* strategies based on their perceptions of space were infrequent in these data. While quite a few employers' perceptual accounts included apparently overt racism, few described active measures to avoid hiring workers from spaces they defined as less desirable. They may, in fact, have steered clear of such measures, since taking them would risk violating antidiscrimination laws. However, we suspect that some employers' silence amounts to the provision of socially desirable answers. Striking evidence of this comes from the Telephone Employer Survey that served as the sampling frame for our in-depth interviews. When asked if they target particular neighborhoods for recruiting workers, 12 percent of employers replied "always," another 17 percent "sometimes," and 15 percent specified "rarely"; a slim majority of 55 percent said "never." But when asked if they *avoid* particular neighborhoods, 90 percent replied "never"—even though targeting some neighborhoods implies neglecting others.

One notable exception to the silence about spatially focused hiring was an employer in an organization in our sample with sites across Fulton County, which reaches from far north to far south of Atlanta, encompassing most of the city itself. This business's human resource chief presented an elaborate series of rationales for why he preferred to hire workers from the north, which he characterized as "wealthy" (and is predominantly white). Citing reasons primarily having to do with a higher rate of desperation "due to the socioeconomic background of south [county]" and lower skill level in applicants from the south (despite the fact that this organization had to train fully every worker they hired in the specialized skills required to do the job), he said that they weeded out 66 to 80 percent of the applicants from the south end, but they hired at least half of the north end applicants. His evaluation of southern applicants may have been based on an objective appraisal of them compared to those from the north. Yet what was notable about his stance was that an applicant's address automatically determined her or his odds of passing the first screening: "So what we basically do is if we have forty applications from the south end, we'll try to screen them down to the best ten." Despite this selectivity in the south, he said, "We are always fighting in north [county] just to get the applications in." Consequently, applicants from the north got at least a stronger look, indicating that in the employment practices of this organization, space was a salient signal of employee desirability and a basis for hiring decisions.

Unlike this employer, who offered an above-market wage and was able to exercise a good deal of selectivity, most employers in every city drew their entry-level employees primarily from the immediate vicinity. Despite this, some employers did discuss selective recruitment strategies that indirectly allowed them to avoid hiring employees from particular spaces. When describing where they found workers to be most desirable, employers sometimes remarked that they relied on local newspaper advertisements in those areas to recruit applicants. For example, a restaurant manager in College Park, a predominantly black southern suburb very close to Atlanta, expressed a dim view of local applicants. Consequently, he recently began to recruit workers from a white suburb about twenty miles farther south: "I try now to run them [job advertisements] in a local paper instead of *Atlanta Journal Constitution* because you can actually select individual areas that you want to interview from. Like right now I have an ad running in the Newnan paper and I've got a really good turnout from it lately."

Many employers in the suburbs sang the woes of public transportation in explaining why they advertised only in specific suburban newspapers rather than in the broader metropolitan dailies. Hiring practices that resulted in mainly white workplaces, some suburban employers asserted, were sometimes an unavoidable consequence of transportation problems for city residents. As one suburban Detroit employer, a maid service, with an all-white staff explained: "I think it's mainly geography. We advertise for our people mostly in the Macomb newspapers, because that's where we get the best results. We don't discriminate, but, because of our distance from the city, where there's a larger black population, we hired from that area, but they find it difficult to get here."

Eventually she discontinued any recruitment from majority-black areas, including the inner city. In a similar vein, the white male owner of a small manufacturing company located in a northern suburb, with only one Detroit resident out of fifteen workers, explained that he has advertised only in suburban newspapers, because "my primary interest was for people who live close to here. I just felt that this was more convenient for people for commuting purposes, and that would be better for both of us."

A number of suburban employers echoed this argument to explain why they advertised only in suburban newspapers, not in the metropolitan dailies. The manager of a suburban car dealership even commented, "I like to hire young people that come from within the area—again, that's one of my qualifiers."

Unprompted, employers in all four cities—including over one-third of Detroit employers—alluded to city residents' difficulties with transportation. The kitchen manager at a restaurant in Atlanta's northern suburbs, contrasting a rural location where she formerly worked, commented: "One thing you couldn't rely on an excuse as far as being late—MARTA didn't run where I'm from. Here, everybody's, like, they have an excuse for being late." Despite his public-sector agency's downtown location, a Boston respondent agreed: "I find that people that rely on the subway have much more of a problem with consistency to getting to work than those that live in the outlying communities." And when inner-city residents do have cars, they often prove an unreliable mode of transportation, because they tend to be old, in poor repair, and in some cases in violation of the law, as this suburban food manufacturer explained: "I can tell you right now that if there are ten people back there from Detroit and ten cars out in this lot, seven of them are illegal. Seven of them don't have the right license plates on 'em, guaranteed most of them don't have insurance on 'em, and I would be surprised if half the people have their licenses."

Since the need for public transportation is so intertwined with the areas where workers live, these perceived difficulties became a space-based signal to some employers about worker reliability, particularly, as we have noted, in Atlanta. At a construction firm in the northern Atlanta suburbs, a white supervisor rather remarkably linked public transportation dependency to welfare dependency:

Respondent: I get a few calls here or there from Atlanta, but most of them are not good candidates. [They always ask:] "Are you on the MARTA line?" It seems prejudiced sometimes to say that you don't want to hire them, but due to two-man crews and job situations, we've got to have people that are flexible and can get to jobs everywhere and be there on time and not worry about set schedules for getting back and forth to work. We do a lot of night work, weekend work, early morning work.

And if you don't have the flexibility of getting yourself around, you affect the schedule of work.

Interviewer: So, really, having your own transportation is important?

Respondent: It's very important. But, like I said, most of the people that we do get replies out of now [from inside Atlanta] are not very good candidates. It just goes back to the old welfare scenario. The people don't have a place to stay. They don't have transportation, and it affects them.

We doubt that the distance-based explanations offered by employers are sufficient to account for workforce composition, especially since other suburban businesses at similar distances stated that city workers had no problem getting to work. The human resource director of Michigan Utility, for example, commented: "I had an open application day, which we didn't advertise—it was just sort of word of mouth and referral agencies—one Saturday. We had a thousand people here, probably forty percent minority, and the majority are from Detroit. We don't have any problem with them getting here."

This utility is a large, high-profile company with better-than-average jobs, and it is possible that some of the other suburban firms with high minority representation are distinct as well in ways that facilitate the commute of inner-city residents. But if so, such distinctions did not reveal themselves in our data.

We must also note that in response to the ways they perceived space in its relationship to class and race, some employers used affirmative action in their hiring practices. A number of employers in each city remarked on how they actively attempted to recruit minority workers from various areas in an attempt to make their workforces reflect the demographic composition of their cities. Some employers used spatial targeting to attain diversity rather than avoid it.

Employer Perceptions and Location Decisions

How do employer perceptions of various areas sway their location decisions? Both the Telephone Survey of employers and the In-Depth Survey asked businesses basic questions about any recent changes in location. The results are broadly similar.

Table 5.5 shows descriptive information from the quantitative Telephone Survey on firms' current and past location, and whether they plan to move in the near future. (Recall that the "other" location category

refers to central cities other than the primary one, and to other municipalities with a population that is at least 30 percent black.) The results
indicate that firms in all areas have an average tenure that is fairly high.
Because the distribution is skewed upward by a relatively small number
of values near one hundred years, we also present the median number of
years in the present location. By either measure, suburban firms have
more recently moved to or opened in their present location. Despite
substantial average tenures, the proportion of businesses that have
moved in the past ten years is also strikingly high: 44 percent across all
businesses and 46 percent for suburban firms in particular. Only about 8
percent of all firms are planning a move, and among those, there is not
much difference across central city, suburb, and other. Almost no firms
in this survey report that they are likely to close in the foreseeable future.

The last panel of table 5.5 addresses the question, For firms that
started out in a given part of the metropolitan area (primary central city,
suburbs), how many moved elsewhere in the metro area, and to where?
(Because this is based on a retrospective question of firms currently located in the metro area, it excludes businesses that moved out of the
area altogether.) Moves out of the primary central city—to either suburbs or other cities in the metro area—totaled 21 percent of firms that
started out there. This is far more common than the reverse move, un-
dertaken by only 1 percent of businesses that started out outside the
central city. Even taking into account that the primary central cities
represent a minority of metro-area business sites (ranging from 20 percent of businesses in Boston to 45 percent in Atlanta), so that even businesses relocating at random would be more likely to move out than in,
there is a strong net flow of relocating business away from these main
cities. On the other hand, the most common moves kept businesses
within the same geographic category; such "stayers," combined with
those who did not move at all, add up to a substantial majority of businesses.

In the In-Depth Employer Survey, 36 percent reported a past move
(with four out of five of the moves after 1979), somewhat fewer than in
the Telephone Survey. Thirty-eight percent reported contemplating or
planning a move, indicating that the much smaller number in the Telephone Survey who stated they are planning a move may be the tip of the
iceberg. Because of substantial overlap between past movers and likely
future movers, a total of 42 percent either had moved or were planning
to do so.

As in the Telephone Survey, most movers stayed within a particular
type of area—for example, moving within the central city or from one
suburban location to another. Table 5.6 examines the smaller 12 percent

TABLE 5.5   *Location Characteristics of Firms, by Central City, Suburb, and Other Central Cities, from Telephone Survey*

	Primary Central City	Suburb	Other Central Cities	All Firms
How long at the present location				
Mean number of years	23.8	19.2	21.0	20.6
Median number of years	14.6	12.0	13.3	12.7
Moved in the last ten years	40.8%	46.0%	40.7%	44.0%
A move is planned	8.2%	9.2%	9.1%	8.9%
Plan not to keep firm open indefinitely	1.5%	1.3%	1.9%	1.5%
	N = 746–805	N = 1,601–1,746	N = 466–67	N = 2,841–2,960

	Did Not Move	Moved But Stayed in Category	Moved to Central City	Moved to Suburb	Moved to Other	Total
Started in						
Central city	66.0%	11.0%		17.0%	5.0%	100.0%
Rest of metro area	89.0%	10.0%	1.0%			100.0%

Source: Multi-City Telephone Employer Survey.
Note: "Other central cities" also includes any municipality other than the primary central city that has a black population of 30 percent or more.

TABLE 5.6   *Firms That Moved, by Original Location and Destination, from Face-to-Face Interviews*

| | As Percentage of Total | Percentage Who Moved | Of Those Who Moved, Percentage Who Moved To | | | |
			Primary Central City	Other Central Cities	Other Suburb	Row Totals
Original location						
Primary central city	42%	22%	—	6%	94%	72
Other central cities	15%	4%	0%	—	100%	25
Other suburb	44%	4%	67%	33%	—	75
Total	100%	12%	10%	10%	80%	172
Column totals	172	20	2	2	16	

Source: Multi-City In-Depth Employer Survey.
Note: "Other central cities" also includes any municipality other than the primary central city that has a black population of 30 percent or more. In this table, "movers" include only those who moved from one type of locality to another (for example, from the primary central city to the suburbs). We include a small number of firms that have not moved but have an explicit plan to move in the near future.

(twenty firms) that crossed from one type of location to another, organized by their point of origin. Confirming the results from the larger Telephone Survey, firms that started out in the central city were almost twice as likely to leave as the average; suburban firms were one-third as likely to leave. Comparing movers' destinations with the original locational distribution of movers and nonmovers combined, we see that though 42 percent of firms started out in the central cities, only 10 percent of movers went there. Conversely, 80 percent of movers went to suburbs without high black populations; only 44 percent of firms started in such suburbs. Table 5.6, like table 5.5, thus documents the flow of firms from central city to suburbs, and particularly to whiter suburbs.

So far the findings reflect well-known U.S. urban trends over the last few decades. The in-depth interviews also gave employers the opportunity to talk about their reasons for moving. Most movers gave standard business reasons that have little to do with perceptions of neighborhoods: needs for a larger space or lower rents or taxes; consolidation of scattered operations after downsizing; need for better access to transportation. But about one in seven of those moving or planning a move (eleven out of seventy-three) raised "inner-city" issues in explaining the firm's decision to move or choice of destination. While this group represents a small minority of movers, their concerns are of interest as one factor in location decisions.

We detailed earlier the major aspects of employers' negative perceptions of the inner city as a business location. The eleven firms that included an inner-city reason in their rationale for a recent move gave similar reasons. We highlight some of these reasons again in this section because they were linked to actual moves. At all firms in this small group, respondents raised issues of crime or related environmental issues of vandalism, trash, and economic class. For example, the white personnel director of a food-processing firm that recently moved from one suburban location to another said that although they looked at sites in Detroit, "we realized that we didn't want to move to Detroit. For all the reasons about Detroit. I mean, I know people myself that own businesses in Detroit. One in particular, the guy was killed walking into his building."

Similarly, a car dealer shifted from Pontiac to a nearby suburb because "we acquired [an additional] franchise, and to get the franchise we had to move to a bigger facility. And plus the area we were in was kind of going downhill, as opposed to a steady, level area like this is. It was becoming—I shouldn't say *slum*, but a lot of low-income people and more problems with vandalism."

And an Atlanta manufacturer was anxious to leave the south side of the city "as quick as possible" due to complaints about "the working environment," including trash in the streets that "looks like crap" and trailers parked on the street illegally for years. He commented that, in contrast, "when you pull off of an expressway and up onto the street that you're headed to on the north side, usually the grass is cut, the bushes trimmed, and there is not a lot of garbage."

Crime, class, and location quality were often linked together in ways that were explicitly or implicitly correlated with race. In Atlanta, for instance, a white personnel officer at a household repair service that moved from the East Point area commented: "See, East Point was starting to get a higher crime rate. The further south you go, the worse it gets." Of course, the racial composition also becomes more black the farther south you go in the Atlanta metro area. In the Los Angeles area, the Anglo owner of a bookkeeping and tax service explained that he had left Bell Gardens, a community that experienced a 61 percent decline in its white population and is now 88 percent Latino, to move to nearby Downey because "Downey is a nicer city than Bell Gardens is, in my opinion. Downey was pulling me because it had a higher economic standard than Bell Gardens did." None of these statements indicates that racial antipathy itself motivated a move, but all represent antipathy toward the *communities* in which blacks and Latinos reside.

One case in the Multi-City Study is particularly interesting. An Asian American manager at Financial Research Associates, which relocated from the LAX airport area to Orange County, over thirty miles away, told us:

Respondent: [At the old LAX office] a lot of them just kind of lived in the Inglewood area, and that office mix was ninety-five percent black. That work environment and that work attitude is night and day from this office. Just coming to work, doing your work. There every rule, every policy was challenged.

Interviewer: Why do you think it was different there from here?

Respondent: The employees, like I said, were ninety-five percent black. It was their culture. I mean, I really truly believe it was their culture.

When the firm decided to move, the manager continued:

They narrowed it down [to] here, this location, and there was a place in Glendale. I said, "We need to [go to] a mall." "Why do you need to go to the mall?" "If I go to the mall, I will let you know, I can tell what kind of clientele shops there. Depending on what kind of clientele shops there, they have to live there, and we'll figure out what kind of work source we're going to have." So the senior vice president and my boss, the vice president, went to the [local] mall. I saw the second floor, so I said, "Okay, I can hire from this place." 'Cause, you know, the people that were walking around it, they were predominantly white, but they still were a mixture of different other races. And the way those people were dressed, you could kind of tell they were educated. They weren't gang-related or street. You could just tell.

This narrative is quite dramatic, but it is also exceptional in our Multi-City Study data. Not surprisingly, therefore, the correlation between making or planning a move and expressing concern about the inner-city workforce is a scant 0.02. The correlation between moving and voicing concerns about crime is a slightly higher 0.04. The Financial Research Associates story is also unusual because the manager explicitly linked workforce issues to race.

The Multi-City Study employer interviews placed less emphasis on exploring the reasons for relocation than our SSRC study, and as a consequence, only a few respondents raised workforce issues in addition to concerns about crime and class in general. In the earlier Detroit-Los Angeles SSRC interviews, we discussed location decisions at more length, including asking a more general question about why respondents think businesses are leaving central cities. The SSRC interviews also gave more focused pictures of what drives relocation in the four industries we sampled. In these discussions, workforce issues came up with some regularity. This was particularly true in the insurance industry, one of the four industries on which we focused. Many of the insurance companies we spoke to indicated that they target a clerical workforce of articulate English-speaking women—including both younger women and married women—whose education includes high school but little more. The employers expressed a desire for employees who, in their minds, will be good with customers, flexible with regard to part-time work, and available at relatively modest wages. They associate these attributes with non-inner city (and, therefore, for the most part, non-minority) women. As this target workforce has gravitated to the suburbs, the insurance companies have followed. The human resource director of one such company told a representative tale:

> We moved down here twenty years ago. For recruiting reasons. We couldn't get people to come into downtown L.A. The turnover was very high in downtown L.A. There were a lot more insurance companies up there. They'd say, Hey, if I didn't get this kind of increase, I am going to work for [another insurer] down the street.

She added that the large demographic changes in the Los Angeles population—the growth of minority, non-English-speaking, and poor groups—had not begun yet at the time the company moved. In fact, the other insurance companies that once competed for workers with her company on Los Angeles's "Insurance Mile" have now moved to the suburbs, "all of them—I don't think any of them are left."

An employment manager from an insurance company that remains in Detroit pronounced, "We've always been committed to the city. We're a major Detroit employer, and we really think that we can't bail out on the city." But, in fact, this company relocated about half its downtown workforce to a suburban site in 1984 "because of recruitment and to attract more people." Even in the downtown office, the workforce remains 50 percent white (compared to 25 percent in Detroit's population), and the typical employee travels 10 miles to work.

But two other insurance companies, both based in Los Angeles, offered striking proof that it is quite possible to field a satisfactory minority workforce within the central city, even in poor areas. One is a black-owned business that makes an explicit commitment to hiring African Americans and remaining located within the community, resulting in a workforce that is 95 percent black. The other is a large, publicly held corporation that employs 88 percent minorities.

The vice president for human resources of the latter company reported that "the company is not experiencing trouble finding qualified people now." She attributed the company's success in recruiting a diverse workforce in part to the downtown location, in part to an employee-centered philosophy that makes it "a very comfortable place for non-Caucasians to work." Wage levels seem to assist these companies in attracting an adequate workforce: entry-level clerical pay at these insurers in 1991 was $13,400 (with a possibility of starting as high as $15,600) and $15,000, respectively, compared with $12,400 offered at another central-city Los Angeles insurance company.

Auto-parts manufacturers in Detroit and Los Angeles, when asked why businesses in general are leaving the central city or in some cases even the metropolitan area, typically offered familiar cost, crime, and related "image" issues and strict regulations (particularly Los Angeles environmental restrictions). But some auto-parts manufacturers are clearly responding to the same kind of target workforce signals as insurers. The employers indicate that they are recruiting from, or employ workers from, outside the city because workers in the central city are less desirable.

In Detroit, many small manufacturing establishments joined the white flight to the suburbs following the 1967 riot. The human resource manager at a small machine shop in a western suburb, when asked why businesses have left Detroit, responded: "Bad image. And the quality of the workforce in the downtown area. Anybody that I've known that has been down there, it's hard to get people to come there. Plus with everybody expanding and moving out here, it makes sense to move your business 'cause the population is growing." When asked what problems her company would face if it was located in Detroit, she amplified: "I wouldn't work there. I think you'd get a problem with the guys that live in the suburbs, going down."

This stems from the fact that the shop's target workforce is primarily white:

Respondent: [Until recently] I wasn't getting black applicants. I don't know if it's just the fact I don't know of anybody [black] who has ever worked in a machine shop. Within the last year, it's picked up quite a bit.

Interviewer: So it's just a question of the industry as a whole; blacks have just started getting into and moving through the industry?

Respondent: I really think so, because from what I used to see, it was primarily a white industry.

203

Similarly, a Los Angeles-area parts producer relocated from downtown to a distant suburb in 1979 in part because "The area was not good, and we had trouble attracting people down there. It was getting difficult for technical people to come to work. The area itself changed. [When the company moved] they brought virtually the whole workforce with them. They lost very few people. The people were glad to come out here to work and get out of there." One result of the move is that "from the EEO standpoint, we are not in compliance [on percentage black]. Part of the reason is that we are way out on the periphery and we can't attract them up here."

The retailers we spoke to in Detroit and Los Angeles in the SSRC study emphasized the customer base rather than the workforce in explaining their suburban locations. One discount clothing chain has only one store in the city of Detroit, operating literally on the northern boundary of the city. The personnel manager in that store said, "From what I've seen, they [the chain] never go inner-city. We're on the borderline of Detroit—[that] was the best way to say they had a Detroit store, without actually being near the inner city."

The chain's decision to avoid the city, in her view, followed from "basically how much the customers are gonna spend." The personnel manager of a suburban store in the same chain linked this back to the crime issue. "When you're in inner city and the crime rate is so high, customers stop coming."

One major retailer from our Multi-City Study made a similar assessment. The head of human resources at the ShopKwik's suburban headquarters, a white woman, stated: "I think the biggest thing as far as the city of Detroit is the perception of crime. And the perception that the labor force has to be imported, that the people there are not able or capable or wanting to work for a living. As an employer, that's basically the perception." ShopKwik appears to have acted on this perception, since it no longer operates any stores within Detroit proper.

Of course, other retailers choose to occupy some of the abandoned central-city niches. For example, the store manager at a Los Angeles clothing discounter, himself Central American, reported, "When we have a new store open, we usually try and open up a store where there's a big concentration of Hispanics, or blacks or Orientals." However, such stores are typically small, low-paying, and less stable than the larger department stores.

The eleven movers in the Multi-City Study sample who attributed their moves (at least in part) to inner-city problems do not tell the full story. We asked about the *most recent* move, but some firms had an earlier history of multiple moves, branch plant closings, and/or shifts of production activity. Respondents at two large manufacturers in the Los

Angeles area, for example, told of shutting down inner-city facilities. "It was never terribly efficient," the white manufacturing director at one of the companies remarked; "I think the work ethic was tough." Asked about finding workers if the plant were to move back, he said, "Well, that would never happen." His counterpart at the other company complained about "the quality of the people—education, work ethic," but noted that the company had just relocated some operations to a suburban Georgia location, where "the skills are not so good" either.

In any case, silence about the inner city does not necessarily imply indifference. As with the case of those suburban firms that did not even consider recruiting from the inner city, for many firms the inner city simply was not on the map of possible locations. For instance, although Detroit is the geographic hub of southeastern Michigan, managers referred to Warren, Troy, and Livonia as "centrally located." The manufacturing human resource manager who called Warren "central" remarked, "We are probably as close to Detroit as you can get"; a law firm's senior partner called Troy "as close to everyone as we could be." The Latina financial controller of a West Los Angeles food manufacturer discussed plans to move to the southeast, near the City of Industry. When asked whether the company would consider South Central Los Angeles, located squarely between these two locations, she was clearly taken off guard:

Interviewer: How about South Central L.A.? Do you know anything about that?

Respondent: No, I just know that it's, kind of like, not safe, a safe area. That's all I know. And again, I don't think it's good for our industry or anything. If it's not safe for the employee, so you would be scared just to go to work.

Interviewer: Do you think there would be hiring issues if you moved to, say, South Central?

Respondent: Definitely. Or maybe the people that would be in the area are not people that you want to work with you.

Finally, what of inner city-based businesses that choose not to move? We found three such groups. First, for smaller businesses and those tied to local clienteles (such as local merchants or banks), relocation is not an option. Second, and related, a variety of employers such as universities, government agencies, and nonprofits have a strong commitment to their locations. As the finance director for a Boston-area nonprofit put it succinctly, "We're a community organization, so we're here because this is the community." The director of a Detroit social service agency gave an explanation along the same lines: "Well, I suppose for our business, because it's a community service business, and in part some of the stuff we do is to serve a distressed community, so it's probably a great place to do business. I mean, you're sitting right in the middle of your kind of customers."

A federal agency had even bucked the outbound tide by relocating a suburban satellite office back into the Motor City. "We'll never leave Detroit," an African American manager at the federal office stated flatly; "Congress doesn't like us to do that."

Even some manufacturers are committed, as with a Boston-area manufacturer that enjoys a strong reputation for social responsibility and whose human resource director commented that costs are higher in the area, but that "this is home. It's where we'll stay."

Third, some low-wage and/or environmentally deleterious industries found inner-city workforces and sites advantageous. This reminds us that business movement toward the inner cities does not necessarily represent a completely desirable trend: for example, a penal institution was one of the small number of firms moving to an inner-city location. The president of a manufacturing firm declared, "We will always be in Atlanta. Our president was born and raised here in Atlanta"—but shortly afterward added, "In order to all of a sudden decide you're going to manufacture somewhere else, you run into a lot of legislative regulations, EPA issues, which now are more and more difficult." The CEO of a Detroit snack food manufacturer, who paid a black workforce from the neighborhood $5.63 an hour in 1994, summed up his situation by saying: "I have this and it works, okay, and I'm able to make a profit at it, so why would I close that up? Even though there is some cost associated with being in Detroit that you may not have in another place."

At a Boston-area home care agency, the branch manager pointed out that the office must be accessible by public transit to the home care workforce, few of whom have cars—and "usually they're from the inner city."

To summarize our findings about firm relocations, in general our data reflect the well-known shift of low-end employment from central cities to suburbs. In our SSRC study in Detroit and Los Angeles, we heard of a substantial number of cases in which the decision to move was linked to inner-city issues. In the Multi-City Study, however, movers raised such issues infrequently, and they primarily spoke of crime rather than workforce quality. This is partly because we delved into relocation less in the Multi-City Study. Moreover, in other cases flight from the inner city predated the most recent move, or the inner city was simply overlooked in relocation decisions. Comments about location from numerous cases in both studies show how many firms think about their present, past, or prospective location in terms of the *suburban* workforce—how hard it is, used to be, or would be to get the good employees to *come down* to the inner city. Despite all this, a mixed group of businesses remain rooted in inner-city areas.

Conclusion

We opened this chapter with a set of arguments about how urban space disadvantages the labor market prospects of inner-city minority workers. We believe the evidence we have marshaled squares with these arguments. The evidence is strong for some of our propositions, less strong for others. Let's run through the arguments by way of concluding this chapter.

Distance matters. The distribution of entry-level jobs, particularly those requiring less skill, favors the suburbs. But beyond the pure barrier of distance, inner-city residents are hurt by the racialized cognitive map employers have of their metropolitan area.

In segregated urban America, race is a crucial factor coloring people's conceptions of space—and employers are no exception to this generalization. For employers in Atlanta, Boston, Detroit, and Los Angeles, racial dividing lines, often closely correlated with class, are important perceptual demarcators. This is particularly true in Detroit, where the city-suburb line is paramount, and in Atlanta, where the north-south divide looms large. In Boston and Los Angeles, where concentrations of people of color and of low-income people are more dispersed and more multiethnic, employers have less crisp conceptions of what "inner city" means, and are more likely to simply ignore low-income, minority areas than to use them as a reference point.

For a substantial minority of employers, these mental maps contain a negative image of the inner city that is tied to race, class, and a variety of perceived urban ills such as crime, family breakdown, welfare dependency, and inadequate education. Such images have some objective basis. Inner cities experience higher relative incidence of all these phenomena. But employer comments are laced with stereotypes, and other employers based in such communities criticize these views as overblown. Nonetheless, for many business decision makers, urban workers are marked as lower quality as a consequence of attending substandard public schools, coming from single-parent families, and being associated with all the other mentioned inner-city problems.

Employers' perceptions of urban business locations are tainted, not only by standard cost concerns, and by visions of crime, and, as important, by the related view that it will be very hard to recruit the preferred

207

suburban workforce to work there. The gap between urban and suburban managers' images of inner-city crime suggests that suburban respondents exaggerate the city's dangers.

A smaller minority of employers described inner-city workers as superior, and an overlapping group spoke of reasons for remaining committed to a city location. The proportions of respondents voicing negative and positive views of *inner-city* workers were greater than the percentages expressing analogous views of *blacks*. Interestingly, this margin of difference was quite large for positive assessments (managers were six to seven times as likely to praise inner-city workers as to laud blacks) and small for negative ones. That asymmetry may reflect the fact that "inner city" encompasses many Latino and Asian workers, whom employers viewed more positively than blacks.

Finally, employers' negative perceptions influence their actions in forming recruiting strategies and in making business location and relocation decisions. Here, our direct evidence is considerably more limited. Perceived crime problems contribute to driving some employers away from black and Latino areas, and lead others to foreclose these communities as potential locations. However, the small number of respondents tying their moves to such concerns is overshadowed by a much larger (and overlapping) group citing traditional locational factors of cost and convenience. Examples of spatially selective hiring policies are even fewer in number. It seems likely that our data have captured only part of the actions driven by negative perceptions of black and Latino communities, and that some respondents are tailoring their responses toward greater social desirability. Further research exploring the link between employer perceptions of space and employer actions within space would help determine how accurately we have captured the true scope of this connection.

6

HIRING PROCEDURES AND THE ROLE OF FORMALITY

The individual presentation is probably the most important source of information, and the most important qualities are their apparent ability to relate to the interviewer and have that extend to relating to customers.

I hate to say this, but a lot of it is gut feeling.

The phenomenon [of discrimination] is very much linked up with that compunction of the private sector with wanting to press the meat before they hire you. There is all kinds of ways that discrimination happens. A lot of it is unconscious.

Employers recruit and screen potential employees in a wide variety of ways, ranging from word-of-mouth networks and casual interviewing to referral from state employment agencies and standardized skills tests. The contrasting views of the employers quoted here as they spoke about interviewing job applicants indicate that the search for the best candidate typically contains important elements of subjective judgment. We hypothesize that more formal techniques reduce the degree of subjectivity and hence the space for prejudice or stereotype in judgments about whom to hire—though, as we will argue, formalized methods are not always leakproof.

In this chapter, we analyze the range of recruiting and screening methods that employers use, and present evidence supporting our hypothesis—demonstrating that formalized recruiting and screening results, other things equal, in a greater chance that a worker of color will get the job. We do this in several stages. First we discuss our hypothesis in more detail, sorting the different techniques of recruiting and screening into those more and less formal, discussing the ways in which formality can affect hiring, and reviewing previous literature that deals with this nexus. We then present our evidence. Quantitative evidence comes first, beginning with simple cross-tabulations of recruiting and screening methods used and the race and gender of the most recent hire.

Following that is a two-stage statistical model of the influence of formality on the race (and, in the case of blacks, gender) of the latest hire. We first estimate the effect of formalized methods of recruiting on the firm's flow of applicants from different racial groups. As a final step in the quantitative analysis, we estimate the impact of formalized methods of screening and the racial composition of the applicant pool on who gets hired.

We then present qualitative findings from both of our sets of in-depth interview data. The qualitative data help us understand why different types of employers rely on different methods and what they think the different methods yield. The qualitative data also allow us to see variations in formality among and within the different techniques, as well as offering a closer look at the boundaries between formal and informal methods. Those boundaries are not always distinct: sometimes formal methods are not as formal as one might imagine! Finally, we zero in on one very important aspect of formality—affirmative action—and examine variations in the use of affirmative action and the range of employer reactions to it.

Recruiting, Screening, and Race

Employers' recruiting and screening methods can affect the chances that inner-city workers of color will be hired—either by design or as an unintended consequence. A key dimension of recruiting and hiring procedures is their degree of formality. Formality in hiring may affect the probability of employment of people of color in several ways. Formal hiring procedures may be more objective, reducing the ambit for biases, stereotypes, or social networks to drive recruitment and selection processes. Businesses may use formal procedures when they require higher levels of skill, or seek to reduce variation in skill levels of new hires. Greater formality in screening may actually be a reaction to higher levels of black or Latino applicants, given many employers' perceptions of black and Latino skill levels. Alternatively, and somewhat more benignly, highly formal screening processes may be adopted by highly visible, well-paying employers, who must select from large applicant pools; such employers may also attract disproportionate numbers of black applicants. Higher levels of public scrutiny and political pressure, and/or higher levels of intrinsic commitment to diversity, are likely to result in more formal procedures.

Viewed from the other direction, particular informal methods of recruiting and screening can spell trouble for inner-city workers of color. Word-of-mouth recruiting will tend to reproduce the workforce that exists. William J. Wilson (1987) argued that joblessness among young blacks is due, in large part, to their isolation from the kinds of social and informal referral networks that link other groups to jobs.

Jomills Braddock and James McPartland's (1987) research confirmed this pattern. They found that to the extent that black high school graduates have *segregated* networks (as proxied by the level of segregation in their high schools), they end up with lower-paying jobs. In addition, employers who use community agencies for referral of applicants employ higher proportions of blacks. They also found that jobs filled by promotion from within are more likely to have *white* employees if the employer approaches employees directly to offer the job or to solicit applications for the job. Jobs are less likely to have white employees if a written job description is posted or circulated.

Among screening techniques, a long literature documents that the quintessential informal screening device, the pre-employment interview, incorporates the racial predilections of the interviewer. For example, Carl Word and co-authors (1974), in a psychological experiment, found that Princeton students treated blacks interviewing for a job differently from whites—offering less eye contact, less forward body lean, and shorter interviews—despite the fact that the applicants were trained to act and respond identically. Word and his collaborators then trained some interviewers to behave in this less responsive fashion toward white applicants. The white interviewees who were treated "like blacks" rated their interviewers as less friendly, and were assessed by outside judges to have been more nervous and to have performed less effectively in their interviews. These findings indicate that, as Robert Dipboye (1982) has suggested, the pre-interview evaluation of a job candidate may become a self-fulfilling prophecy.

In an earlier study using our SSRC data, we found a strong, negative statistical link between the importance of the interview as a screening device and the level of black male employment in a given firm (Moss and Tilly 1995). Kathryn Neckerman and Joleen Kirschenman (1991) also argued that blacks may be less successful or more ill at ease than nonblack job applicants in interview situations. Interviewee concerns about speech patterns, appearance, and past experiences may be sources of tension in interview situations for blacks to a greater degree than for other racial groups. These authors hypothesized that, as a result, inner-city blacks should have greater representation in firms that rely on tests. Using regression analysis on survey data to control for other firm characteristics, they confirmed this correlation.

Harry Holzer's (1996) results, however, raise some questions about these patterns. He did find that use of a pre-employment interview reduces black employment in a univariate analysis. Where motivation, politeness, and English or verbal skills are important factors in assessing the interview, black employment also drops. However, the impact of the latter emphases was not statistically significant in his full, multivariate analysis (which includes up to thirty-eight independent variables, plus industry and occupation dummies; he did not include use versus nonuse of the interview as a variable in the full analysis). And contrary to Neckerman and Kirschenman's finding, Holzer reported that testing *reduces* black employment. Complicating the picture still further, many of these effects cut only against black men, with negligible or positive effects on the employment of black women. Based on these and other results, Holzer concluded that blacks—especially black men—are excluded from jobs primarily due to lack of hard skills, via screening mechanisms designed to measure those skills.

If followed and enforced, affirmative action policies introduce greater formality into recruiting and screening. Most recent studies indicate that affirmative action policies have increased the employment and earnings opportunities of blacks and other minorities (Leonard 1990; Holzer 1998; Holzer and Neumark 1999; the last two references used the same Telephone Survey data we analyze in this chapter and throughout this book). Although affirmative action policy may increase employment opportunities for minorities through a number of channels, one of them certainly may be through encouraging greater use of formal means of recruiting and screening workers.

The past two decades have witnessed a lessening of the pressures on employers to use formal hiring procedures. Union coverage of the workforce has continued to decline, funding and support by elected officials and the general public for affirmative action policy has attenuated, and public-sector employment has shrunk. Two policy trends—devolving more federal responsibilities to the states and increasing reluctance by government generally to intervene in private-sector economic decision making—are likely to reduce incentives for formality in hiring further. Some business initiatives, such as diversity training or minority purchasing requirements, push in the other direction, but the strength of these initiatives is unclear.

At the same time, heightened competitive and shareholder demands have had multiple effects. On the one hand, they have induced many companies to weaken or dismantle the internal labor markets that governed mobility and tenure within them—further propelling the flight from formality (Cappelli et al. 1997). On the other hand, these demands, and many of the organizational and technological changes that have come in response, have heightened the scrutiny employers place on their labor pool for hard and soft skills, as we argued in chapter 3.

The previous chapters in this book built a case for heightened concern about the use of informal recruiting and screening techniques. In chapter 3 we documented the rising demand for skill by employers, in particular the rising demand for soft skills, and explained the blurriness of soft skills and the potential that cultural differences, prejudice, and stereotype will cloud subjective assessment of a candidate's soft skills. The growing demand for soft skills only makes matters worse. Chapter 4 provides evidence that employers see blacks and Latinos as deficient in soft (as well as hard) skills, and in many cases are willing to voice stereotypical negative views of workers of color.

If formalized procedures wane as the pressures to use them are scaled back, the importance of subjective judgments in hiring and recruiting is likely to grow, as is the reliance by employers on networks as a source of employees. To complete the case, it remains for us to confirm that formal methods provide a significant advantage to workers of color. We now turn to this task.

Quantitative Findings

As we will show, several recruiting and screening methods do have disparate impacts by race or ethnicity. Some part of the explanation may be willful discrimination, some part may be a confounding of cultural differences and stereotypes with perceptions of difference in certain types of skills (notably, interaction and motivation skills), and some may be the effect of lower skills and lower access to important job networks on the part of workers of color. The quantitative results reported here directly observe the outcomes but cannot easily distinguish among these different sources of the outcomes. The qualitative evidence is more suggestive about how employer subjectivity can confound skills assessment with stereotyping of different groups.

What Techniques Are Used?

Table 6.1 shows the recruiting and screening method that generated the last hire in firms interviewed for the Telephone Survey. There is not a great deal of variation across primary central city, suburb, or other central cities in the use of recruiting or screening methods. More formal recruiting procedures such as use of newspaper ads or referrals from employment agencies, community agencies, schools, or unions are less likely to be open to social network hiring that could have disparate effects on workers of color. Together, they generated roughly 40 percent of the hires, with newspaper ads accounting for over half that total. The other 60 percent were generated by more informal recruiting procedures, with employee referrals yielding nearly half of this group. To screen applicants, most firms use the more formal device of a written application

TABLE 6.1   *Recruiting and Screening Methods for the Last Employee Hired by City, Suburb, and Other Central Cities*

	Primary Central City	Suburb	Other Central Cities	Total
Recruiting method for the last employee hired				
Newspaper ad	23.9%	28.8%	29.2%	27.6%
Help-wanted signs	4.2	4.6	4.9	4.5
Walk-in	14.1	13.9	12.7	13.8
Referrals from Current employees	26.0	24.8	27.0	25.5
State employment service	1.8	3.1	4.8	3.0
Private employment service	9.6	4.3	4.3	5.7
Community agency	2.2	1.2	1.0	1.4
Schools	3.4	4.6	2.4	3.9
Union	1.2	0.8	0.8	0.9
Other (acquaintances, and so on)	13.5	13.7	11.9	13.4
Used affirmative action in recruiting	56.0	48.5	54.8	51.5
Screening method used				
Interview	87.6	87.1	84.6	86.8
Physical and/or drug test	16.4	10.5	11.8	12.2
Tests or other	49.9	40.2	42.5	43.3
Verify education	34.6	25.4	26.5	28.0
Check criminal record	32.3	29.1	38.9	31.6
Used affirmative action in hiring	36.5	32.6	37.4	34.4
	N = 744, 794	N = 1,714, 1,797	N = 457, 475	N = 2,915, 3,066

Source: Multi-City Telephone Employer Survey.
Note: Recruiting method identifies the one method that yielded the employee hired. Screening method identifies all screening methods used.

and the less formal method of an interview. About half use some form of testing, another formal technique for screening applicants.

In our SSRC study, we did not ask what recruiting or screening method generated the latest employee in the sample job, but we did ask what methods were used generally and which was the most important. The results were comparable to those in table 6.1. Fifty-three percent of the respondents reported relying extensively on employee referrals to recruit. To screen applicants, employers relied most heavily on the personnel interview: 82 percent rated the interview the most important source of information. Slightly more than half used a written test of some kind (ranging from aptitude and specific skill tests to "integrity tests" designed to assess applicant tendencies toward theft). However, just under half required a drug screen, a considerably higher proportion than in this larger, more representative sample.

Among the four industries we sampled in that study, employers in auto-parts manufacture depended most on employee referrals and employers in retail establishments the least. Insurance companies and public-sector agencies were in the middle. The higher the percentage of the firm's workforce unionized, the less likely it used employee referral to recruit. With respect to screening methods, insurance companies in the sample invariably relied most on the interview *and* required a written test. Auto parts and retail employers appeared more inclined than public-sector employers to emphasize the interview, and less likely to administer written tests to applicants. Larger firms relied less on interviews, more on written tests. Unionization was associated with less stress on the interview, but with less testing as well.

The Effect on Hiring

How do the different recruiting and screening methods affect who gets hired? We start with straightforward cross-tabulations and then proceed to a statistical model of the effect of formality on the applicant flow to a firm, and the probability that the firm will hire a member of a particular group.

The race or ethnicity and gender of the latest hire by recruiting and screening method is shown in table 6.2. The numbers in the table are *indices of representation*, as with the tables in chapter 3 showing race and gender by skill requirement. The index is calculated by dividing the proportion of a particular group in the job when each recruiting or hiring screen is used by the proportion of that group in all jobs. For example, looking at the first cell in the table, the index is calculated by dividing the fraction of employees who are white men in a job when a newspaper

TABLE 6.2   Race and Gender of Last Employee Hired, by Recruiting Method and by Use of Hiring Screens

	White Males	Black Males	Hispanic Males	White Females	Black Females	Hispanic Females
Recruiting method						
Newspaper ad	0.910	0.990	0.673	1.267	0.877	0.681
Help-wanted signs	0.835	0.792	1.112	0.855	1.453	1.778
Walk-in	0.851	1.337	1.243	0.786	1.491	1.042
Referrals from						
Current employees	1.008	0.931	1.458	0.922	0.915	1.056
State employment service	0.980	2.297	1.421	0.554	1.094	0.708
Private employment service	0.639	1.010	0.421	1.354	1.094	1.222
Community agency	1.106	2.198	1.673	0.287	1.142	1.319
Schools	1.404	0.653	0.112	0.811	1.500	1.569
Union	1.282	0.386	2.907	0.560	0.774	0.569
Other (acquaintances, and so on)	1.392	0.653	0.916	0.972	0.604	0.958
Used affirmative action in recruiting	0.835	1.089	0.916	1.045	1.189	1.083
Hiring screens						
Written application	0.938	1.088	0.971	0.988	1.087	1.057
Interview	0.987	0.936	0.877	1.056	1.020	1.029
Physical and/or drug test	1.152	1.686	1.143	0.773	0.985	0.764
Tests or other	0.841	0.883	1.050	1.083	1.097	1.117
Verify education	0.873	1.014	0.810	1.033	1.097	1.312
Check criminal record	0.918	1.233	0.832	0.943	1.262	1.090
Used affirmative action in hiring	0.818	1.099	1.052	1.071	1.071	0.993
	N = 627–703	N = 234–76	N = 233–82	N = 832–968	N = 262–95	N = 173–90

Source: Multi-City Telephone Employer Survey.

Note: Recruiting method identifies the one method that yielded the employee hired. Screening method identifies all screening methods used. An index less than one indicates that a given procedure is associated with reduced representation of a race-gender group; an index greater than one indicates the reverse.

ad resulted in the hire by the fraction of white men in all jobs. Proportional representation results in an index equal to 1.

Compared to their rate of representation in all jobs, black men are substantially more likely to be the hire when employers have taken a referral from a state employment agency or community agency. Latino men enjoy a smaller employment boost from these referral sources. These two recruiting methods are used fairly rarely, however, as table 6.1 showed. Again, compared to their representation in all jobs, use of employee referral reduces the representation of white and black women, and improves the representation of Hispanic men. Surprisingly, employee referrals also hurt white men and have only a very small negative effect on black men. Use of affirmative action in recruiting cuts against white men, as expected, but also, to a much smaller extent, against Latino men. Conversely, affirmative action recruiting increases the rate of hire for black men and women and, to a lesser degree, for white and Latina women.

Use of interviews and tests, except for physical tests, is associated with lower rates of hiring of white and black men. Latino men also show a lower representation when interviews are used. Testing raises the rate of hire of black women. Employers appear to be referring primarily to physical tests when they answer the question about physical or drug tests, as there is a clear gender difference in the results. Use of a written application as well as background checks on education and criminal record are associated with higher employment of black and Latina women. Where employers use affirmative action in making the *hiring* decision (as distinct from using it in recruiting), each group except white men and Latino men shows a higher rate of employment. The effects of affirmative action are largest for white and black men (negative and positive employment effects, respectively).

From this table it appears that the relationship between procedural formality and the racial composition of the workforce is not simple. Consider black men in particular. Certain formal methods (recruiting through a state employment service or community agency, written application, verification of education and criminal record, use of affirmative action) increase the chances that a black man will be hired; certain less formal or more subjective procedures (referrals from current employees, pre-employment interview) dampen those chances. But other formal steps (recruitment through schools or union, physical or other test) are associated with *lower* black male employment.

To help sort out the partial effects of different recruiting and screening methods on who gets hired, we developed a two-stage model. The first stage focuses on the *supply* side—the influences, including formal recruiting, on the racial composition of job applicants to the firm. The second stage considers the *demand* side—the influences of this racial flow of applicants, formal screening, and other variables on the likelihood that a person of a particular racial group is hired.

Recruiting techniques modulate the flow of applicants to the firm. We hypothesize that more formal methods of recruiting will result, other things equal, in a higher fraction of workers of color (and females, in the case of nontraditionally "female" jobs) in the applicant flow to the firm. The first set of equations of our model estimates the influence of several sets of variables on the proportion of applicants to the firm from a particular racial group (and in the case of blacks, broken down by gender).

We utilize the following variables that directly measure formality:

- *Use of formal methods of recruiting.* In recruiting for the last vacancy of the sample job, the employer used ads or referrals from government employment agencies, community agencies, schools, or unions (dummy variable).

- *Affirmative action played a role in recruiting activities.* The employer answered yes to the question, "Does affirmative action or equal employment opportunity law play any role in your recruiting activities for this position?" (dummy variable).

We also control for a set of institutional influences on recruiting:

- *Natural log of firm size.* Natural logarithm of total employment in this business at this site. We view this as primarily a proxy for more formal procedures of recruiting and screening that are typical of larger firms. Larger firms also have higher profiles in the community, and therefore may attract a more diverse applicant pool. The logarithmic transformation is used to reduce the undue influence of a small number of very large firms in the regressions; it does not qualitatively alter the results.

- *Percentage of employees unionized.* Proportion of nonmanagerial, nonprofessional employees at this site who are covered by collective bargaining (expressed as a decimal).

Our specification also includes other sets of control variables. First are those that measure the skill level of the job:

- *Skill requirements of the job*, as proxied by dummy variables specifying whether or not the job requires daily performance of the following tasks: reading instructions of one paragraph or more, writing paragraphs or memos, doing arithmetic or other computations, working with a computer (results not shown in the table).

- *Starting wage.* This summarizes job quality, including variation in skill not captured by the four skill requirements just noted.

Next are controls for general demography an employer might expect in his or her applicant pool (results not shown in the table):

- *Average distance of the employer from a particular racial group.* The weighted average of the distances from the firm's own census tract to each other census tract in the metropolitan area, weighted by the fraction of the metro area population from that racial group that lives in each of these tracts. (We thank Harry Holzer for generously providing this variable.)
- *The particular racial group's percent of the population in the portion of the metropolitan area in which the employer is located* (either central city or rest of the metropolitan area).

Finally, we include two other groups of control variables (results not shown in the table):

- Dummy variables for the different metropolitan areas.
- Dummy variables for occupational group of the sample job.

We estimate six equations, one each for whites, blacks, black men, black women, Latinos, and Asians. Our expectation is that formal recruiting and affirmative action influences will have positive coefficients in each equation except that for whites, as will the size of the firm. The average distance of the employer from populations of a particular group should clearly have a negative coefficient. The coefficient on unionization could go either way for each of the groups. More applicants of color may apply if they believe the formal procedures associated with many collective bargaining agreements will be to their advantage. Fewer may apply if they feel the membership or leadership of the union is unreceptive to workers of their group, or if the union is involved in informal word-of-mouth recruiting that tends to exclude members of the group. As already noted, the coefficient on the starting wage could be positive or negative as well.

The results of ordinary least squares regressions of these five sets of variables on the percent of a firm's applicants from each of the six groups are presented in table 6.3. By and large, the coefficients conform to expectation. The use of formal recruiting appears to give an important boost to the flow of black applicants. The effect on the percent of applicants who are white is large and negative. Affirmative action–influenced recruiting has a surprisingly negative and significant effect

TABLE 6.3 Regression Results: Contribution of Formal Methods of Recruiting to the Percentage of a Firm's Applicants from a Particular Race and Gender Group

	Applicant Group					
	White	Black	Black Men	Black Women	Latino	Asian
Coefficient on						
Use of formal methods of recruiting	-6.03*	6.63*	3.71*	2.57*	-0.41	0.62
	(-3.08)*	(3.98)*	(2.86)*	(2.24)*	(-0.34)	(0.92)
Affirmative action played a role in recruiting activities	-1.32	-0.37	-2.30*	2.45*	0.07	1.41
	(-0.73)	(-0.24)	(-1.89)*	(2.28)*	(0.07)	(2.26)
Natural log of firm size	-4.07*	2.64*	1.02*	1.63*	1.02*	0.73*
	(-7.48)*	(5.67)*	(2.81)*	(5.10)*	(3.17)*	(3.91)*
Percentage of employees unionized	-0.02	0.06*	0.08*	-0.01	-0.01	-0.03*
	(-0.87)	(2.46)*	(4.31)*	(-.89)	(-0.41)	(-3.19)*
Starting wage on sample job	2.07*	-1.52*	-.82*	-.94*	-0.74*	0.05
	(7.13)*	(-6.12)*	(-4.26)*	(-5.45)*	(-4.66)*	(0.48)
	N = 1,301	N = 1,335	N = 1,353	N = 1,369	N = 1,507	N = 1,379

Source: Multi-City Telephone Employer Survey.
Note: All regressions control for the percentage of each group in the relevant portion of the metropolitan area, the business's average distance from population concentrations of the relevant group in the area, a set of dummy variables for skills needed on the job, dummy variables for the metropolitan area, and dummy variables for the category of job. T-statistics in parentheses.
*Indicates significant at the 10 percent level.

on black men. It has the expected positive and significant effect on black women and Asians. Formal recruiting methods, as we have measured them, are definitely associated with relatively greater flows of applicants of color.

Large firms clearly attract workers of color, whether through more formalized recruiting channels or via a reputation gained from size. The effect of unions is estimated to be positive and significant in the case of black men and negative and significant in the case of women, although both coefficients are relatively small. The result is an insignificant coefficient on the combined black group. It is quite possible that the unionized jobs in our sample fall outside the typical jobs for which women, including black women, apply. Unionization is also associated with a smaller flow of Asian applicants. Finally, the starting wage appears to have its effect on application flows as an indicator of the skill level of the job. Blacks and Latinos have lower average levels of skill than do whites, and may self-select themselves out or be discouraged by employers from joining the applicant pool for higher-wage, higher-skill jobs. Whites comprise a greater fraction of the applicants for higher-wage jobs.

The second set of equations in our model estimates the impact on the probability that a member of a particular group will be hired of a set of variables that begins with the outcome of the previous set of equations:

- *The proportion of applicants to the firm from a particular racial group.*

The regressions include several variables measuring formality:

- *Requires test.* In screening for the sample job, the employer uses a skills test (including tests of aptitude, job knowledge, math, reading-spelling-grammar, driving, typing, shorthand, or "other," but excluding physical, personality, or interest tests).
- *Requires personal interview.*
- *Requires a written application.*
- *Affirmative action considerations influenced the hire.* The employer responded yes to the question, "Does Affirmative Action or Equal Employment Opportunity law play any role in whom you actually hire [for this position]?"

Again, we control for institutional variables that constrain or influence formality, already defined:

- *Natural log of firm size.*
- *Percentage of employees unionized.*

We also include all the control variables, already defined, that measure the skill level of the job, the demography of the part of the metropolitan area in which the employer is located, each of the different metropolitan areas, and the occupational category of the sample job. We do not show the estimated effects of the control variables in the table.

Our general expectation is that five of the six variables capturing formality and institutional constraints on hiring practices will have positive impacts on the probabilities of hiring any of the nonwhite groups. (We expect use of a pre-employment interview to cut the other way, since it allows greater subjectivity.) However, for two of the variables, the expected outcome is more ambiguous. The fact that an employer uses a test in screening could lead to two opposite predictions. On the one hand, use of a test signifies greater skill requirements, and since on the average blacks and Latinos lag behind whites in skills, this could disadvantage them. On the other hand, testing is a relatively objective screening mechanism that leaves less room for personal bias to enter the selection process, and therefore could act to blacks' (and Latinos') advantage, as Neckerman and Kirschenman (1991) argued. Because we do not have a measure of the relative qualifications of blacks and Latinos, we cannot control for the two possible effects. Our estimate will mix them together.

Similarly, unionization can cut in both directions. Unions have in many cases bargained for formal procedures and due process that presumably aid black applicants who might otherwise be subject to bias. But unions have also sought to give members substantial control over recruiting and hiring; to the extent that these unions have historically been predominantly white, this may tend to exclude black applicants. We also expect a positive coefficient on the percent of applicants to the firm from the particular racial group.

As the dependent variables for these equations are dummy variables, we estimate the equations with a logit specification. We report results only for the key independent variables, and not on the controls for skill or the other control variables. We estimated a set of equations for jobs across all occupational categories. In addition, we estimated a set of equations for each of four broad occupational categories: clerical jobs, service jobs with customer contact, blue-collar and service jobs with no customer contact, and professional-managerial-technical jobs. (Since we have excluded any jobs for which respondents report that college is required, the latter group is weighted toward managers and technicians.).[1] The tables with results for these separate occupational groups are presented in the appendix to this chapter. We note the important highlights from these tables.

Table 6.4 displays the results from the logit equations for each group (across all occupations).[2] The estimated effect of the percent of applicants from a particular group has the expected positive and significant effect in all cases. The results with respect to formality are mixed and much less clear-cut than those from the first stage, application percentage equations. Taken as a whole, though, the evidence favors the contention that formality in screening improves the likelihood that a worker of color will be hired.

The pattern varies considerably by element of formality, occupation, and particularly by gender, however. For example, the expected effect of using tests does not make it over the bar of statistical significance. The estimated effect of using tests is negative for the chance of hiring whites, as the formality hypothesis contends—reducing the odds of hiring a white person by 17 percent—but it fails the 10 percent level of significance. The estimated effect of tests is positive on all other groups except Asians, again conforming to the formality hypothesis. None is statistically significant. (The results on tests from this specification are different from Holzer's [1996] results, in which he found a negative effect of tests on black men.) Within occupations, the negative estimated effect of tests on the probability of hiring a white in jobs requiring customer contact borders closely on statistical significance, but not so in the other occupational categories. This may be because soft skills are particularly important in jobs requiring customer contact, and the assessment of the soft skills of nonwhites is particularly prone to subjective bias.

In general, the weak or insignificant estimated effects of testing may well be the result of a problem we already noted: testing cuts two ways, and we do not have a control variable for different qualifications among minority and nonminority applicants. Therefore, we get a mix of the two possible effects of tests, which may be canceling each other out. That there is no significant estimated effect of testing on the probability of hiring a black may be indirect evidence for different levels of qualifications among minorities and nonminorities. (We thank an anonymous reviewer of an earlier draft of this book for suggesting this point.)

The estimated effects of using personal interviews follow the opposite pattern, as expected, except this time the estimated positive effect on whites is significant at better than the 5 percent level, as is the negative effect on Asians. The person hired is two-thirds more likely to be white if a personal interview was used as a screen. Use of a pre-employment interview cuts (at a statistically significant level) against blacks,

TABLE 6.4   Contribution of Formality and Institutional Constraints to the Probability of Hiring a Member of a Given Group (Logit Results for All Occupations)

	Odds Ratio, Probability that the Most Recent Hire Is					
	White	Black	Black Man	Black Woman	Latino	Asian
Require test	0.83	1.09	1.17	1.03	1.06	0.95
	(−1.43)	(0.53)	(0.80)	(0.15)	(0.34)	(−0.13)
Require personal interview	1.66*	0.71	0.87	0.67	1.22	0.44*
	(2.44)*	(−1.45)	(−0.48)	(−1.34)	(0.76)	(−1.92)*
Require written application	0.79	1.21	1.20	1.06	0.96	0.84
	(−1.24)	(0.81)	(0.59)	(0.19)	(−0.17)	(−0.36)
Affirmative action considerations influence hiring	1.09	0.97	1.30	0.73	1.11	1.03
	(0.61)	(−0.21)	(.132)	(−1.57)	(0.59)	(0.09)
Natural log of firm size	0.88*	1.20*	1.24*	1.18*	1.18	1.18
	(−3.10)*	(3.76)*	(3.72)*	(2.83)*	(1.05)	(1.51)
Percentage of employees unionized	1.00*	1.00	1.00	1.00	1.05*	1.00
	(−1.76)*	(−1.08)	(−0.87)	(−1.24)	(2.69)*	(−0.27)
	N = 1,468	N = 1,500	N = 1,521	N = 1,539	N = 1,604	N = 1,329

Source: Multi-City Telephone Employer Survey.
Note: Results are shown as odds ratios. For yes or no variables, these show the ratio of the estimated probability of hiring someone from a particular group when the answer is yes, divided by the estimated probability of hiring when the answer is no. For continuous variables, the ratio divides the estimated probability when that variable is one unit higher by the estimated probability when it is one unit lower. All equations control for the percent of each group in the firm's applicant pool, the percent of each group in the relevant portion of the metropolitan area, the starting wage of the job, a set of dummy variables for skills needed on the job, dummy variables for the metropolitan area, and dummy variables for the category of job. Z-statistics in parentheses.
*Indicates significant at the 10 percent level.

and in particular black women, in clerical jobs, but surprisingly, improves the chances for blacks, and black men in particular, in managerial, professional, and technical jobs. The estimated effects for use of written applications never muster statistical significance.

Results regarding affirmative action are partially consistent with our expectations about the effect of formality. Respondent statements that affirmative action plays a part in hiring decisions are associated with a greater chance that the person hired will be a black man, but *lower* odds of hiring a black woman (parallel to results reported by Holzer 1998 and Holzer and Neumark 1999), though neither effect reaches statistical significance in the full sample. The positive effect for men is largest and most statistically significant in blue-collar jobs. The negative effect for women packs the greatest punch in service jobs with customer contact. It appears that black women gain from affirmative action at the recruiting stage, whereas black men benefit at the stage of selection. One possible interpretation is that affirmative action in hiring tends to help women, but white women rather than black women in this sample.

Large firms consistently hire more black men and women (as Holzer [1998, 1996] also reports). The effect on blacks is statistically significant in the equations for clerical and blue-collar jobs, with black men driving the coefficient in blue-collar occupations and black women in clerical jobs, not surprisingly.

The effect of unionization is quite mixed. Unionization lowers the probability (but only slightly) of a white hire across all jobs (you have to go beyond the two decimals shown in the table to find the effect) and, within occupations, in clerical and blue-collar jobs. But only Latinos, not other workers of color, benefit from unionization, both when all jobs are considered and within managerial, technical, and professional jobs. Unionization's estimated effect on employment of black men and black women is zero or negative, and significantly negative in customer service jobs. Interestingly, black men are estimated to gain when clerical jobs are unionized. None of these effects is estimated to be large, however.

The formality hypothesis is most consistently borne out for whites. For this group, all the formality variables in both stages of the model (with the notable exception of whether affirmative action influenced hiring) have the expected sign, and most are statistically significant. A majority of coefficients for the other groups have the expected sign, but most fail to marshal statistical significance. It is possible that the advantage of formality to workers of color, which is suggested by the estimated effects on whites, is sprinkled across the nonwhite groups, so that no particular group gains significantly.

225

Qualitative Findings

From the quantitative analysis, we have learned that some types of formality are associated with higher employment of workers of color. Formality does seem to matter. But why, and how? While regression and logit analysis are not designed to answer why and how, analysis of qualitative data can offer important insights.

Formality in hiring procedures varies widely in terms of content, implementation, context, and hence implications. Apparently formal procedures can conceal substantial loopholes; apparently informal procedures can actually be highly structured. A highly formal procedure such as a test can—by design or otherwise—strongly favor one group over another.

Our qualitative data provide illustrations of a variety of dimensions of formality's association with racial representation. We examine the role of formality in recruiting, in screening, and then turn to employers' discussion of the impact of affirmative action laws. To clarify exposition, given the large number of quotes and examples we draw on, we organize each section around several bulleted points.

Recruiting

• Informal recruiting reproduces the current workforce; formality can lead to changed workforce composition.

Informal recruiting privileges employer and incumbent employee networks. For example, a supervisor at a Boston-area manufacturer explained the high number of Asian workers in the plant as follows: "I think [there are] a lot of internal references, so that may have a lot to do with it. I see amongst that group a lot of people trying to help members of their family, friends. Get them a job, get them in the company."

A sizable Los Angeles laundry service, specializing in uniforms, recruits an essentially all-Latino workforce entirely through word of mouth. The owner justified his strategy by saying blacks are less likely to want the jobs he is offering. A second Los Angeles laundry service, this one for restaurant linens, also recruits a majority Latino workforce almost exclusively through word of mouth. Interestingly, this firm offers ten-dollar-an hour jobs and is unionized. The pay and the union setting would lead one to think blacks would apply. The informal recruiting may forestall it.

At an Asian-owned transportation company, a supervisor explained the very small number of black employees as follows:

We don't do much open advertising. We haven't for years, so how would somebody living three blocks down the road know that [this company] was looking for reservations staff? What we generally work from are resumes and referrals. And those are people who already have identified [the company]. So they are looking for us before we're looking for them. Now if I were running a 7-11 or a ninety-nine-cent store, I would be advertising in this area, wouldn't I? And hoping to draw from this area. So it would be quite different.

Word-of-mouth recruiting clearly amplifies the effect of separation between groups, as this Los Angeles employer opined: "If you have a high population employed in an area like, say, here, a high Hispanic population, blacks through word of mouth are going to tend not to apply here. If there are primarily blacks in an area, Hispanics are going to tend not to apply there."

Another example is the personnel supervisor of an auto-parts firm located next to a black area of Los Angeles, who explained that blacks do not apply because "maybe it's hard with all the Spanish-speaking people. Maybe because they only see Spanish around." The dampening of applications by blacks that results from the cultural divide ultimately may have as large an effect as that of the informal recruitment networks.

While smaller and lower-wage businesses, which these last two firms typify, rely on informal recruitment methods, larger and higher-wage employers use more formal methods. One public agency, for instance, posts jobs at 130 locations, including colleges, libraries, and community organizations. Changing the racial composition of a workforce may require supplementing informal channels with more formal ones—or in some cases, opening new *informal* channels. In a public agency composed of uniformed personnel, the leader of a black employees' group described how, under pressure from a court-ordered consent decree, the agency has supported his group's outreach efforts:

Word of mouth, they [whites] have a thousand [job holders]. Those are good recruiters, like even though we [black job holders], on the job we're recruiters, they have more recruiters. 'Cause they're basically on the job, you know. And I think the department has come around quite a bit now. They give us permission to help out. Give us time off to do recruitment. Reassign guys from the [job site] to do this here [at the headquarters of the black employees' group].

A private-sector example was reported by a human resource specialist from a Los Angeles-area location of a large national retail chain. She indicated that informal recruiting, which makes up the bulk of their recruiting, does not generate sufficient black applicants for their company goals. They adopt formal advertising to increase the flow of black applicants:

> It's not cost-efficient, actually, to advertise in the newspaper. We really don't need it for recruitment. The reason we advertise in the black newspaper is because I have a hard time drawing in people that are qualified from that area. That's actually the only reason that we invest in that. It's part of the affirmative action plan. It's something that the company believes in, and it's obviously very beneficial for your sales to have a diversified workforce for people who come in.

But other employers told of adding formal recruiting mechanisms precisely to *move away* from current minority workforces. As we noted in chapter 4, the personnel officer of a retail store in Detroit has become concerned that his workforce has become "too black" (for their desired customer marketing strategies) because of their reliance on walk-ins and employee referrals, and is trying other recruiting methods to attract white employees. Similarly, personnel officers in a distribution warehouse in Los Angeles were trying to improve the quality of their applicants by recruiting through local schools and organizations, such as the Catholic Charities, to get a pool other than the local walk-ins and employee referrals.

• Informal recruitment has different effects at different employers.

Informal recruiting does not always favor white employment, nor cut against black employment. In many cases, informal networks preferentially draw in workers of color. A Boston home care provider serving low-income, largely minority neighborhoods has historically recruited mainly via referrals from clients (who suggested neighbors or friends to provide care to them), and consequently has a workforce weighted toward black women. In fact, in this case, rising skill and certification demands have since shifted recruiting toward training programs—but this more formal recruiting is yielding *fewer* black employees.

Targeted informal recruiting can have different effects from laissez-faire reliance on walk-ins and employee referrals. The manager of a contracted maintenance team has used employee referrals among the existing black employees to shift his workforce more toward blacks because he feels less contented with the female Hispanic workforce he currently employs.

Informal recruiting can complement formal recruiting to bolster the flow of black applicants. Michigan Utility, in the Detroit area, has a very good record of minority representation and uses extensive formal recruiting channels. The director of human resources noted, however, that the number of black employees in the sample job is even higher than their affirmative action target, and he attributes this to word-of-mouth referrals from existing black workers: "They know our work, they know what we expect, and we get a lot of people that way."

- There are typically loopholes in nominally formal recruiting.

One uniformed public service agency, for example, advertises in major dailies as well as community newspapers from communities of color, sends notices to community organizations, and posts jobs with the state employment agency. Nonetheless, a manager commented that candidates for the dispatcher job—our sample job—are typically found by informal means: "We'll get calls from somebody who is a [current employee in this job] who'll say, 'Gee, I worked with, I know this kid.' We find that the informal public safety network is quite often the best way to go."

Similarly, at a Boston-area hospital, the recruiter for clerical jobs noted that managers often locate candidates on their own and refer them to human resources. Indeed, a supervisor of clericals related: "If I have a position for an ambulatory practice secretary, then they should send me somebody that they think their qualifications fit that. Doesn't always happen that way, but I also do sort of go through the back door and sort of get resumes on my own and I interview, and if I like them then I send them to human resources."

She went on to state that her most effective recruiting source is "a referral from people I know," and that racial diversity is not a high priority. In fact, she made disparaging remarks about the self-presentation and skills of nonwhite secretaries.

At another uniformed public agency, a manager observed: "The process by which [location] gets its [uniformed public servants] is so convoluted and archaic that we tend to draw from those areas where there are a larger number of people who share the knowledge of how to get that job"—meaning the neighborhoods where incumbent workers live. In this case, complex formal procedures benefit those who learn about the procedures via informal means.

Screening

- Interviews are subjective, and may fail to give a true assessment of skills.

Our data amply document the subjectivity of the pre-employment interviews. As in the case of an Atlanta-area manufacturer-installer of yard equipment, managers often boast of knowing "how to read people," even though they acknowledge that "sometimes it's a gut feeling." (We should note that this employer is one of the only employers in our Atlanta sample with an entirely white workforce!) The phrase "gut feeling" was used repeatedly by respondents in the SSRC and Multi-City Study surveys to describe the informal judgments made in interviews. As the director of human resources for an Atlanta-area manufacturing plant indicated in response to the question of how you gauge an applicant's soft skills: "Right now it's truly a personal evaluation. We are looking into getting a testing application, where we can measure that more effectively. But right now it's truly a gut feeling." The percent of workers who were black in this plant was well below average for Atlanta.

On the other hand, at a public agency grappling with issues of affirmative action:

> We don't place a great deal of emphasis on interviews. We do not have an interview board or panel because the consent decree requires that we have very detailed reasons for rejecting a candidate, so we have to be on sound footing, and the results of an interview really aren't that—you know, it's too subjective. We want to really document why someone's not suitable.

This agency uses interviews only when needed to probe discrepancies in the information an applicant has provided.

In general, not only does the public sector rely much less on personal interviewing to judge applicants, but many public-sector officials with whom we spoke approach interviewing with a very different attitude than their private-sector counterparts. For example, the civil service of a Detroit-area local government no longer conducts pre-employment interviews, according to one official, because interviews were not really used for decision making and could have been interpreted as leading to discrimination. The official stated that in the hiring process in this public-sector setting, people's "fit" is not an issue: if they can show that they could satisfactorily do the job, an agency can make them fit. He argued that private-sector reliance on the interview is discriminatory (completing the quotation at the beginning of the chapter):

> The phenomenon [of discrimination] is very much linked up with that compunction of the private sector with wanting to press the meat before they hire you. There is all kinds of ways that discrimination happens. A lot of it is unconscious. We are past the point where, on a mass basis, people are doing overt discrimination intentionally, but we still have it out there. [People] don't examine their practices and question whether the impact of what they do is in fact racist.

Echoing the same sentiment, a public-sector human resource official in Los Angeles commented: "Woven into that [the interview assessment] is all of the individual interviewer prejudices, how they see the job, how they evaluate the candidate, and how they present it. You cannot get away from that."

• Formal screening procedures reduce subjectivity.

When considering formal *screening*, some of the same patterns emerge as with formal recruiting. While some firms rely on the pre-employment interview, others base their decisions largely on testing, formal credentials, and other, more objective criteria. Civil service systems mark one extreme, but many private-sector employers use very formal selection methods as well. When an Atlanta insurance company hires clerical workers, for example, a representative explained: "We're looking for high school graduates. For a data-entry type of person, they would have to have strong keyboard skills or keyboard capabilities. We do a number of tests, data perception as to whether they can recognize a series of numbers or letters in sequence and follow that logically." This company conducts interviews as part of the evaluation process. But the interview itself is structured to be relatively objective:

> Basically, if we had a position, we would look at the skills required of that position and we would interview for those skills. To a lesser extent, we are looking at the behavior-type of performance traits as to how they do the job. If it is a new hire, a trainee kind of thing, they are likely not to have had much work experience for that level position. So we are going to be looking for them to demonstrate to us how they may have in the past been able to use those skills, whether it was leading a Girl Scout troop or what it may be. We introduced behavioral interviewing two or three years ago in terms of trying to find means of interviewing for specific skills. We are not interviewing for traits; basically we are looking for performance and what have they done in the past that should predict the future.

Likewise, in a Boston-area public-sector agency, even though the interview is the key screen, it is carefully structured:

Interviewer: What part of the process is the most important in making decisions?

Respondent: It's certainly the interview process. That has to be handled with care, and it has to be completed thoroughly and fairly. Everybody should be asked the same questions. Everybody should be treated the same. And you don't spend two minutes with one applicant and an hour and a half with another. And from the notetaking that goes on during our process, the teams will rate how the applicant did, and it turns into really a relative ranking amongst the applicants.

Of course, "behavioral interviewing" and the like do not preclude the potential for cultural and racial biases to enter into the decision making. Nonetheless, compare these descriptions of the interview process with that provided by County Construction in the Atlanta area, which employs relatively high skill workers: "You've got to play it by ear as far as listening to them [and deciding] are they a 'buller.' Do they sound like they're just bulling you, swift talkers? Or are they quiet, sit there and listen to you and ask questions? It's kind of just a feeling that you have to get."

In some cases, including well-paid public-sector jobs, formal recruiting essentially requires formal screening. Respondents at some Boston-area public agencies spoke of thousands or even tens of thousands of applicants signing up for civil service exams!

In other cases, rising skill demand has engendered more formal screening. The automobile assemblers and parts manufacturers around Detroit illustrate the point. As described in chapter 3, most told of the need for a new type of worker with more technical and more soft skills. New methods of testing applicants were being instituted, the result being more objectivity and better-qualified workers, as one manufacturer explained:

Respondent: So the applicant now goes to the MESC [state employment service] office and takes a little mini-test.

Interviewer: So you no longer have any say personally?

Respondent: That's correct. They took all of that away. I love it. Historically these facilities have been very family-oriented, okay? And you had people that were fifteen- to twenty-year employees that had sons and daughters who maybe were not college material, and "how about my daughter, she's pregnant and married and her husband is out of a job?" kind of thing, so there was a tendency to hire those kinds of people and accept those kinds of referrals. The only problem with that is you can get into a bind where someone says, "Well, you hired his son or daughter—why isn't mine or his nephew or cousin or . . . " It's just a big mess.

232

Interviewer: Are you getting a higher-caliber worker?

Respondent: I think so.

The reduction of subjectivity can reduce racial bias, or help achieve diversity goals. For example, the regional coordinator for hourly staffing of a large utility firm in California indicated that the tests given applicants were the most important criteria in judging their qualifications, and went on to say, "This is probably going to blow a stereotype. The people doing best on the test are African American females."

The director of human resources for Michigan Utility provided further support for the contention that testing can provide objectivity that in turn helps develop a diverse workforce. He indicated that a greater number of minorities fail the tests. But, because of active recruiting, attractive jobs, and careful testing, they are successful in meeting diversity objectives:

Interviewer: I think a lot of employers anticipate, without experience, that it would not work out if they had twenty-five-percent minority workers. What's interesting here is that although you say there are differences, you're still able to recruit.

Respondent: I think the ability to recruit appropriately, and the test, frankly, really helps. We get a higher caliber—it doesn't matter, male, female, minority—we get a higher caliber. But certainly, that minority candidate coming in has to meet that minimum requirement, which is a pretty high requirement.

• Informal screening procedures often disadvantage black applicants.

Our own earlier research and other literature argue that particular reliance on the interview disadvantages black applicants because of the subjectivity involved. An Atlanta greeting card store manager offered an interesting perspective on this. He started by stating that black applicants do not know how to apply for a job:

Blacks, from what I see, do not have the knowledge for seeking a job. They've not been trained in high school. They just don't seem to know how to apply for a job. They don't know how to dress. They simply answer questions yes and no. They don't ask about the job. They don't seem interested. They don't show up on a timely basis. That just seems like a bad way to apply for a job.

233

But moments later, he added that many of these "poor" applicants are actually qualified for the job: "They're fine once they get the training. In fact, you know, I maybe sound like I'm putting the young black kids down, but the group we have right here—they were all greenhorns then, and they're very good right now."

Other respondents likewise complained about inner-city applicants' interview skills, and suggested that the schools might prepare students better for job interviews. It is interesting that the statements made were not about job skills, but interview skills, suggesting the perception that job and interview skills were part of the same thing—a mixture of attitude, appearance, and personal relations.

• Formality in screening does not eliminate subjectivity altogether.

As with recruiting, there are always loopholes. Where formal and informal procedures coexist, the formal screens may be dead letters or may constitute only initial hurdles—as in a correctional institution where, despite a written test, a manager stated that the most important criterion is an assessment of how well applicants are likely to deal with prisoners, via an interview and tour of the facility. And, according to the human resource director at a Boston-area manufacturer, supervisors often use the human resources department as a foil to avoid hiring the below-par children of valued employees!

Even in civil service environments constrained by consent decrees, there are loopholes to be found. The black employees' leader in uniformed public service, cited earlier, claimed: "As a matter of fact, we found out that they skipped over a guy last time, and what they had to do is hire an extra guy to make up for what they did on the previous list skipping over people. There's still a lot of nepotism. Still getting away with it, you know. So there's a lot of nepotism still going on, a lot of chiefs' sons."

And a white human resource official in a different public service agency revealed that the agency's special youth trainee program has become an alternate access route to jobs—a route that "becomes subverted as a way around affirmative action, to be quite honest. Yes, it was done so that, again—this is very confidential—it is a way to have politically connected people bypass the veteran/nonveteran and affirmative action standards. In the worst case, the formality of the process is simply subverted. A large Detroit manufacturer has been administering a skills test aimed at eleventh-grade proficiency in math and language. A supervisor admitted (off the record—when the tape recorder had been shut off) that some time previously, when mostly white men were hired, supervisors would give test answers to people they wanted to hire.

In less blatant cases, some discretion appears to be injected into a formalized screening process. The manager at a public-sector university bookstore described the process by which candidates reach him via a very formalized interview and testing process:

Respondent: Individuals go for a written exam, and those that pass the exam go for interviews from a panel. [The supervisor is then given a ranked list of three candidates.]

Interviewer: Is that a constraint, a problem?

Respondent: Yes, it is a problem, but it is a solution to a larger problem and therefore I think it is an acceptable problem. If I were a private business and I wanted to hire somebody, I would just hire somebody. I can't do that, so what I have to do is I have to influence to the best of my ability the oral examinations and make sure that the panel that's being assembled reflects my values. So it just means that I have to jump through a few more hoops. It does not impede my ability to get a quality staff. It just means I have to play the game a little bit more. I have been able to influence the panels.

- Formal selection methods can be adopted to screen blacks and other people of color in, but also to screen blacks out.

The uniformed public service agencies under consent decree offer laboratories for such changes. In one such agency, the human resource chief pointed to the elimination of test components that created blatant insider advantages—such as questions testing knowledge of specific equipment used on this job. But again, the leader of the black employees' group had something to add. He acknowledged positive changes: for example, validation of the screening procedure has led to less weight on the written exam and greater weight on the physical tests, which more accurately reflects job demands and aids black applicants. But he complained that, "I think [the agency is] upgrading the job in a subtle way, by them trying to screen us [blacks] out."

The personnel director at a Detroit-area manufacturer indicated that the firm received thousands of applications for fifty jobs. Of the first group of applicants winnowed to take the test, one hundred were tested, only twelve passed, and none of them were black men (one was a black woman). He explained that no black men passed the test because "there tended to be lesser completion of high school, lesser ability to use the skills by just looking at how applications were filled out or not filled out."

And a large manufacturing facility outside Boston, which had never tested applicants for blue-collar jobs, began aptitude testing when the surrounding area's population tilted toward people of color. Other changes surely contributed to this shift: there was a growing labor surplus, and skill requirements were being upgraded. Nonetheless, the timing is suggestive, especially in connection with comments like this one from a plant operations executive:

> I mean, these people come from a very different background. We have a strong welfare system. Coming into a factory every day and building and assembling things, they're not necessarily fun jobs all the time. And so, when people can maintain a certain standard of living, and they don't have to do that, then what kind of work ethic would people come here with? So, we have to be very careful in our screening to be sure that people are motivated.

Affirmative Action

- Affirmative action typically contributes to formality in recruiting and screening.

Many of the examples just cited illustrate this point. Some respondents made the point explicit. For example, at Anytown College in the Los Angeles area, several steps have been taken as part of the affirmative action effort to formalize the screening process. The director of institutional research and planning noted, in response to a question about changes in the hiring process: "Over the course of time, they have been tightened. They have made sure that anybody who's involved in the process has training on affirmative action."

The director of human resources at the college then described how the interview process has also been formalized as part of the affirmative action program:

> We do have an affirmative action representative who actually sits in on all interviews. And what they [the interviewing managers] have to do is to submit to me a list of questions that they're going to ask the candidates, and I approve those before the interviews. The questions all have to be job-related, and those questions have to be asked of all candidates. Now, they can ask follow-up questions to the questions that they've asked, but they can't add any new questions.

- Affirmative action is most developed in large firms and in the public sector.

The coefficient on firm size in our regression and logit analyses was typically significant with a sizable effect on the flow of applicants of color, and the probability of a black, black male, or black female hire. In the qualitative data, the large firms and the large public-sector agencies stood out for their affirmative action programs and for the training and other support efforts that enhance the results of affirmative action.

The firm-size effect captures the size and federal contracting thresholds in affirmative action/equal employment opportunity (AA/EEO) regulations. In addition, it reflects the visibility of large firms. It also reflects management approaches that differ according to scale. At one Boston-area federal agency, for example, the division chief remarked:

> We have to be very conscious and cognizant as a federal employer that we have guidelines and mandates that we have to follow. I mean, I have a full-time EEO officer, and she has two or three people who work for her. Well, I think in a large company you have that. Being in a medium to a smaller company, you may not have a full-time EEO officer that helps you look to see if your workforce represents the community.

The effect of size is important in the private sector as well. The customer service operations manager at a Los Angeles branch office of a large firm reported:

> [Company name] has always been on the leading edge of diversity, and you'll see that we've done this for many, many years. There's a magazine called *Black Enterprise* that [company name] is continually written up [in] as one of the best companies for black people to work for because of the programs we have. That we do take affirmative action seriously. We have great training programs.

In Detroit, the human resources director at a plant of one of the big three auto makers commented on the difference between the big auto manufacturers and the small auto-supplier firms:

> Because of the size of the corporation, we would be more attuned to various laws, both federal and state. We are more susceptible and more . . . sensitive, I guess. We look at demographics, the ability of the workforce around the location, what lives in the city, what's close by. We have a responsibility as a citizen of the city to hire the people that live here.

Among the respondents at public-sector agencies whom we interviewed, almost all spoke of well-developed affirmative action programs, EEO officers, and often a complement of training programs to sustain the affirmative action effort.

The mission of public-sector agencies filters down through the organization. A government official in Detroit put it very forcefully:

> I think that we feel as government that this is a responsibility that we have, whereas for [the] private sector it is a pain in the ass that they have to deal with. And they have to do things to get their EEO reports looking halfway good and comply, but they don't have the same basic attitude that we have in government.

In fact, public-sector affirmative action efforts may spill over as benefits to the private sector. A general manager at a Los Angeles–area government agency indicated how such benefits can occur.

> We set up a training program which was unique in the nation for inspectors. It was very big for affirmative action. We found that the private sector could not provide a cross section for affirmative action. It just could not do it. And so when we created the training program, we were able to feed into the system very skilled people because they got three, four, and five years of training. And so when they went into the full-time job, they were quite skilled. Unfortunately, we also lost a lot of those people because other agencies, as soon as our people would graduate, were trying to grab them up.

• Employer attitudes toward affirmative action vary widely.

Some employers openly opposed affirmative action, at least in its present form. The white male CEO of a Boston-area health care facility made this clear: "I'm anti-affirmative action, I have to tell you that. I don't know of a better way, having said that. But I think basically I'm against it. Because it's reverse discrimination."

White male officials in the public agencies under consent decree, while agreeing that diversity is needed, voiced particularly bitter opposition to what they, too, saw as reverse discrimination. At one such agency, a manager even grumbled darkly: "I think everyone is entitled to apply for a job. And I think everyone should be given consideration. [But] to be given a blanket, specialty protection . . . I don't think so. I think that's continuation of divine right that ended in the [revolution that overthrew the] French monarchies in 1793."

A number of respondents indicated that while they try to abide by their affirmative action goals, affirmative action has a chilling effect on the willingness to hire minorities because firing a minority is so difficult. The response of a branch manager for a mortgage sales company in Los Angeles typified this attitude.

Respondent: One of the things as an employer that we kind of under our breath [are] saying [is that] it's much more difficult to fire a black person than it is to fire a female person. I think at this company, if we're going to do that, we take extra care that we're documenting and following the laws that we have to.

Interviewer: Do you think that kind of worry puts some people off from hiring them in the first place?

Respondent: Absolutely, absolutely.

But other managers, including some white males, spoke in support of affirmative action. In some cases, this viewpoint was relatively self-serving—for example, the personnel manager for a Boston-area candy manufacturer that hires immigrants into low-wage jobs, who boasted, "We are *the* affirmative action, equal opportunity employer, you know. Everybody set their model after us, and we don't even need quotas." In other cases, it appeared to reflect a sincere conviction that government-enforced affirmative action is still needed, as for the African American human resource director of a Boston area home care provider.

Well, if we look at reversing affirmative action, then [minorities will] never catch up. There will be, in the year 2000, more women and minorities in the workforce or eligible to be in the workforce. Yet people who are in charge of major corporations and things are white males, okay? So nothing has changed.

One public-sector official, the Asian male human resources director at Anytown College, defended affirmative action as follows:

The whole thing about affirmative action, and you read about it in the press, [is] that we have quotas and that we hire the unqualified. That's absolutely not true. We don't have quotas and we don't hire the unqualified. In fact, if you look at our demographics, if you look at our statistics, you'll still find we don't, for example, still mirror the community that we serve.

He went on to note the legal problems that might well result if affirmative action were abolished:

Boy, if you look at how serious people are on the dismantling of affirmative action programs, it could [have] an effect and [it] might not be okay. And the reason I say that is, if we still have Title 6, Title 7, and all of those federal laws on the books and the executive orders, we still have a requirement, then, to adhere to equal employment opportunity. What you're going to have is a lot more lawsuits from people of color or the historically underrepresented [groups] because you don't have an affirmative action program.

· Conclusion

Despite some unanswered questions and puzzles, this chapter's empirical results provide a message that is, on the whole, fairly coherent. The quantitative findings demonstrate that in many cases, formality in recruiting is associated with higher levels of black employment and lower levels of white employment. Formal methods of screening lower the likelihood of hiring whites, but we do not find that this translates to a boost in hiring for blacks. Again, this may be due to our inability to control for different levels of qualifications among minority and non-minority applicants.

The qualitative findings reveal some of the whys and hows of this relationship, including the numerous loopholes and unintended consequences in formal hiring procedures. Although the quantitative results for the effects of affirmative action are ambiguous and not very strong, the qualitative results suggest the importance of affirmative action, both as a stimulus for formality and as a framework that shapes formality to aid the employment of African Americans.

However, affirmative action is under attack and in retreat—despite, in our view, being needed as much as ever. Any policy proposals in this area must consider how to move beyond defensive, rear-guard actions in order to revitalize affirmative action. In our final chapter, we lay out a portfolio of policy proposals, including ones designed to address the current dilemma of affirmative action.

Appendix

TABLE 6A.1   *Contribution of Formality and Institutional Constraints to the Probability of Hiring a Member of a Given Group Logit Results for Clerical Occupations*

	Odds Ratio, Probability that the Most Recent Hire Is					
	White	Black	Black Man	Black Woman	Latino	Asian[b]
Require test	1.05	1.18	3.64	1.13	0.32*	
	(0.13)	(0.35)	(1.09)	(0.27)	(−1.72)*	
Require personal interview	3.91*	0.23*	0.12	0.28*	4.38	
	(1.80)*	(−2.11)*	(−1.48)	(−1.90)*	(1.46)	
Require written application	1.02	0.95	a	0.71	0.36	
	(0.04)	(−0.08)		(0.53)	(−1.23)	
Affirmative action considerations influence hiring	0.95	0.97	2.31	0.88	1.90	
	(−0.14)	(−0.06)	(0.78)	(−0.28)	(1.11)	
Natural log of firm size	0.86	1.22	0.78	1.24*	1.26	
	(−1.17)	(1.48)	(−0.89)	(1.73)*	(1.23)	
Percentage of employees unionized	0.98*	1.00	1.02*	0.99	1.02*	
	(2.32)*	(0.49)	(1.68)*	(−0.88)	(2.47)*	
	N = 222	N = 232	N = 199	N = 240	N = 252	

Source: Multi-City Telephone Employer Survey.
Note: Results are shown as odds ratios. For yes or no variables, these show the ratio of the estimated probability of hiring someone from a particular group when the answer is yes, divided by the estimated probability of hiring when the answer is no. For continuous variables, the ratio divides the estimated probability when that variable is one unit higher by the estimated probability when it is one unit lower. All equations control for the percent of each group in the firm's applicant pool, the percent of each group in the relevant portion of the metropolitan area, the starting wage of the job, a set of dummy variables for skills needed on the job, and dummy variables for the metropolitan area. Z-statistics in parentheses.
*Indicates significant at the 10 percent level.
a"Require written application" is perfectly collinear with not hiring a black man for a clerical job.
bBoth unionization and the city dummy for Los Angeles are perfectly collinear with not hiring an Asian. This removed too many observations from the Asian equation, making estimation impossible.

TABLE 6A.2 *Contribution of Formality and Institutional Constraints to the Probability of Hiring a Member of a Given Group Logit Results for Service Jobs with Customer Contact*

| | Odds Ratio, Probability that the Most Recent Hire Is | | | | | |
	White	Black	Black Man	Black Woman	Latino	Asian
Require test	.63	1.05	1.25	0.88	1.51	0.48
	(−1.53)	(0.15)	(0.63)	(−0.34)	(0.96)	(−0.77)
Require personal	2.49*	0.66	0.88	0.81	0.98	0.11*
interview	(1.81)*	(−0.83)	(−0.23)	(−0.37)	(−0.03)	(−2.52)*
Require written	0.96	1.09	0.74	1.59	1.17	0.39
application	(−0.10)	(0.19)	(−0.57)	(0.79)	(0.26)	(−0.97)
Affirmative action						
considerations	1.12	0.58*	1.10	0.41*	2.71*	0.40
influence hiring	(0.39)	(−1.65)*	(0.27)	(−2.13)*	(2.35)*	(−0.78)
Natural log of	0.82*	1.13	1.20*	1.14	1.27*	1.27
firm size	(−2.04)*	(1.24)	(1.63)*	(1.21)	(1.69)*	(0.96)
Percentage of						
employees	1.01	0.99*	0.99*	0.99*	0.99	a
unionized	(1.58)	(−2.65)*	(−2.04)*	(−1.80)*	(−0.77)	
	N = 380	N = 387	N = 392	N = 394	N = 413	N = 275

Source: Multi-City Telephone Employer Survey.
Note: Results are shown as odds ratios. For yes or no variables, these show the ratio of the estimated probability of hiring someone from a particular group when the answer is yes, divided by the estimated probability of hiring when the answer is no. For continuous variables, the ratio divides the estimated probability when that variable is one unit higher by the estimated probability when it is one unit lower. All equations control for the percent of each group in the firm's applicant pool, the percent of each group in the relevant portion of the metropolitan area, the starting wage of the job, a set of dummy variables for skills needed on the job, and dummy variables for the metropolitan area. Z-statistics in parentheses.
*Indicates significant at the 10 percent level.
ªPercentage of employees unionized is perfectly collinear with not hiring an Asian.

TABLE 6A.3   *Contribution of Formality and Institutional Constraints to the Probability of Hiring a Member of a Given Group Logit Results for Blue Collar*

| | Odds Ratio, Probability that the Most Recent Hire Is | | | | | |
	White	Black	Black Man	Black Woman	Latino	Asian
Require test	0.89	1.38	1.28	2.34	1.04	0.48
	(−0.46)	(1.05)	(0.78)	(1.34)	(0.15)	(−1.19)
Require personal	1.76*	0.55	0.59	0.50	1.39	0.63
interview	(1.72)*	(−1.45)	(−1.27)	(−0.74)	(0.90)	(−0.64)
Require written	0.82	1.39	1.18	1.58	0.92	0.78
application	(−0.61)	(0.71)	(0.33)	(0.51)	(0.22)	(−0.32)
Affirmative action						
considerations	1.08	1.49	1.81*	0.48	0.64	1.85
influence hiring	(0.30)	(1.28)	(1.88)*	(−1.01)	(−1.40)	(1.04)
Natural log of	0.91	1.18*	1.33*	1.03	1.00	1.17
firm size	(−1.30)	(1.84)*	(2.87)*	(0.13)	(−0.02)	(0.87)
Percentage of						
employees	0.99*	1.00	1.00	1.00	1.00	1.00
unionized	(−1.65)*	(0.43)	(0.10)	(0.44)	(1.36)	(−0.32)
	N = 484	N = 496	N = 501	N = 202	N = 524	N = 444

Source: Multi-City Telephone Employer Survey.
Note: Results are shown as odds ratios. For yes or no variables, these show the ratio of the estimated probability of hiring someone from a particular group when the answer is yes, divided by the estimated probability of hiring when the answer is no. For continuous variables, the ratio divides the estimated probability when that variable is one unit higher by the estimated probability when it is one unit lower. Z-statistics in parentheses. All equations control for the percent of each group in the firm's applicant pool, the percent of each group in the relevant portion of the metropolitan area, the starting wage of the job, a set of dummy variables for skills needed on the job, and dummy variables for the metropolitan area.
*Indicates significant at the 10 percent level.

TABLE 6A.4   *Contribution of Formality and Institutional Constraints to the Probability of Hiring a Member of a Given Group Logit Results for Managerial, Professional, and Technical Jobs*

	Odds Ratio, Probability that the Most Recent Hire Is					
	White	Black	Black Man	Black Woman	Latino	Asian
Require test	0.76	0.95	0.88	0.98	1.64	2.15
	(−1.10)	(−0.16)	(−0.26)	(−0.04)	(1.47)	(0.87)
Require personal interview	0.76	2.59*	8.72*	1.18	0.87	1.24
	(−0.63)	(1.66)*	(1.86)*	(0.27)	(−0.26)	(0.16)
Require written application	0.56	1.33	1.56	1.17	1.45ª	
	(−1.48)	(0.56)	(0.58)	(0.29)	(0.67)	
Affirmative action considerations influence hiring	1.11	0.97	0.76	0.97	1.10	0.84
	(0.42)	(−0.09)	(−0.55)	(−0.10)	(0.30)	(−0.22)
Natural log of firm size	0.88*	1.20*	1.22	1.16	0.97	1.24
	(−1.59)*	(1.95)*	(1.39)	(1.42)	(−0.23)	(0.74)
Percentage of employees unionized	1.00	1.00	0.99	1.00	1.01*	1.00
	(−1.15)	(−0.15)	(−1.15)	(0.49)	(2.14)*	(−0.37)
	N = 382	N = 385	N = 391	N = 399	N = 415	N = 207

Source: Multi-City Telephone Employer Survey.
Note: Results are shown as odds ratios. For yes or no variables, these show the ratio of the estimated probability of hiring someone from a particular group when the answer is yes, divided by the estimated probability of hiring when the answer is no. For continuous variables, the ratio divides the estimated probability when that variable is one unit higher by the estimated probability when it is one unit lower. Z-statistics in parentheses. All equations control for the percent of each group in the firm's applicant pool, the percent of each group in the relevant portion of the metropolitan area, the starting wage of the job, a set of dummy variables for skills needed on the job, and dummy variables for the metropolitan area.
*Indicates significant at the 10 percent level.
ªBoth "require written application" and the dummy for Detroit are perfectly collinear with not hiring an Asian.

7

THE MORAL OF THE TALE: DESIGNING BETTER LABOR MARKET POLICIES

EMPLOYERS' testimony, as sifted in the preceding chapters, outlines the contours of profound disadvantage for low-skilled workers, and specifically for blacks and Latinos with limited skills. This disadvantage prevails even in the jobs requiring no more than a high school education, which we have made the subject of our study. The obstacles of inadequate skills, spatial isolation, and continuing discrimination and miscommunication loom large.

What can be done to remedy these problems, and who should do it? The roots of labor market disadvantage are deep. They include residential segregation, an unequal educational system, institutional discrimination, and the continuing restructuring of industries and jobs in the United States. While all of these obstacles must be confronted, we limit our attention to a narrower and more immediate set of steps. Our objective is to draw the policy lessons that follow more or less directly from our employer interview findings. These are the policy areas in which we have something distinctive or definitive to offer.

Government, in its various levels, is typically called on when businesses are unable or unwilling to solve a problem on their own. So in this chapter we particularly stress the role of government. However, we acknowledge the inherent limits on what government can accomplish in the deregulated, privatized labor market of the United States today. We acknowledge as well current political constraints on government involvement in the labor market—most notably, the widespread hostility toward government-imposed restrictions on business and the backlash against programs aiding disadvantaged groups seen as "undeserving." Consequently, we pay attention to possible actions by private employers and nonprofit agencies, and explore nongovernmental approaches to carrying out key interventions. We also consider what arguments might move the public to support a more active government role in the labor market.

We start by reviewing our main findings. Next we cast an eye back on our research approach, and reflect on its strengths and weaknesses, as well as key areas for additional research. This assessment of what we still do *not* know is a crucial step in policy formulation. We then present employer views in key public policy areas, based on the telephone and face-to-face interviews. Finally, we turn to our own policy recommendations.

What We Learned from Employers' Stories

We structured our investigation with four basic questions. Here we summarize what we learned about them.

How Do Skill Demands Affect Workers of Color?

Skill demands are rising, though the putative need for advanced technical and computer skills—the "digital divide"—is overblown. What employers primarily seek in entry-level jobs are increased command of basic skills, on the one hand, and higher levels of soft skills (interaction and motivation), on the other. Employers most often score soft skills as their top need in the jobs we studied. Both of these factors generate labor market disadvantage for minority entry-level workers. Job tasks such as using computers, writing paragraphs, and interacting with customers knock down the likelihood that black and Latino job seekers will land the job. The situation is worst for black and Latino males. Hiring requirements such as a high school diploma, experience, or references have the same effect. Jobs with few requirements are spare in numbers and offer low wages.

Soft skills are thorny to analyze purely as skills. Assessment of applicants' and workers' soft skills contains an irreducible element of subjectivity. Further, performance of soft skills is influenced by the social context of the workplace. We argue that employers' assessments of soft skills are closely intertwined with racial prejudices, and we analyze both sets of perceptions as an amalgam.

How Do Employers Perceive Workers of Color?

In face-to-face interviews, nearly half our respondents criticized blacks' hard or soft skills. They most often criticized blacks' work ethic. Many employers blamed these perceived skill deficits on single motherhood, the welfare system, or the inner-city environment, including city public schools. Smaller numbers of employers described Latino workers in negative terms, but such comments were outnumbered by positive ones, often citing the "immigrant work ethic." The same was even more true of managers' views of Asians. Positive views of immigrant workers—and of African Americans, for that matter—were most common among low-wage employers, indicating that part of what they are saluting is these workers' willingness to settle for less. The racial images reported by employers varied by workers' gender, the type of job being discussed, and the respondent's race and position within management. Employers' characterizations of racial and ethnic groups consist in part of fallacious stereotypes, in part of cultural gaps, and in part of accurate perceptions of performance differences. The true differences, in turn, result in part from low wages and harsh management in many jobs occupied by blacks and Latinos. We find some links between attitudes and hiring decisions. In the Telephone Survey data, customer racial biases appear to dampen the willingness of employers to hire blacks, and smaller firms and those in the suburbs are less likely to hire blacks as well. Our Face-to-Face Survey data surprised us on this score. Firms in which respondents criticized black workers' skills tended to hire more of them. We attribute this to a mix of reasons: managers in closer contact with blacks think more about blacks' skills, see actual skill gaps more clearly, are more willing to discuss their perceptions of black workers—whether accurate or not—and tend to offer lower-end jobs that induce poorer work habits.

How Do Employers View the Inner City as a Place to Recruit Workers and a Place to Do Business?

Our quantitative and qualitative data are consistent with the theory of spatial mismatch between inner-city workers and jobs: firms providing jobs with modest skill requirements are increasingly moving to, or opening up in, the suburbs. But our data suggest that versions of the spatial mismatch hypothesis that simply attribute businesses' shift to the suburbs to cost minimization do not tell the whole story. Employers in general express negative views of inner-city workers and of the inner city as a place to do business. The ways in which employers describe inner-city workers conform in great measure to their descriptions of workers of color, as we would expect. Connected to racial perceptions are perceptions of a host of inner-city problems—above all, crime—that compound the stereotypes of race and help explain the shortcomings of minority workers, in employers' eyes. In short, as with assessments of

247

skill, employers' views of neighborhoods and their residents are closely entangled with perceptions of racial and ethnic groups.

How Do Different Recruiting and Screening Procedures Lead to Advantages for Some Groups and Disadvantages for Others?

Quantitative results indicate that formal methods of recruiting appear to help blacks in the hiring process. Our evidence for formal means of screening is too weak to draw conclusions about the effects on blacks, but indicates that formal screens reduce hiring of whites. In-depth interviews reveal a wide variety of recruiting and screening strategies and show how subjective assessment methods, particularly for judging soft skills, can be. They also demonstrate that managers often find ways to introduce managerial discretion into apparently formal hiring procedures. The qualitative data also point up the importance of continuing attention to affirmative action policies, something we take up in this chapter.

Listening to the Stories Employers Tell

In this book, we have tried to bring something to debates about race, skill, and hiring that is typically in short supply: interdisciplinary, in-depth, qualitative field research. Though we have drawn on other sources as well, the "stories employers tell"—the face-to-face, in-depth interviews—were unique. These interviews unearthed important insights, but also encountered serious limitations. On the positive side of the ledger, talking to employers face to face helped a great deal in forming a picture of how employers perceive the world. Holding actual conversations rather than multiple-choice sessions and allowing employers to answer in their own words proved far more effective at getting them to talk about race and employment than have other types of surveys.

On the minus side, the time-consuming nature of these interviews (which constrained the number we were able to conduct) and the significant influence of each interviewer's style limit the degree to which we can carry out generalizable statistical analyses. In this book, we have relied primarily on the larger and more uniformly administered Telephone Survey of employers for statistical results. In addition, though we learned about employer perceptions and actions, it proved difficult to learn about the relationships between the two. And though face-to-face conversations offered a better tool for learning about employers' views of race and ethnicity, we still encountered our share of implicit (and some explicit) refusals to discuss the issue, as well as what appear to be quite a few answers proffered because they were socially desirable.

In-depth interviewing of employers can and should be extended to a number of related questions. Our study focuses on the initial hire, but the same method could fruitfully be applied to learn about retention and promotion of workers. Employers told us that retention is a major hurdle for many inner-city workers when they are able to obtain jobs; it is important to find out why and how. Face-to-face employer interviews could also shed light on hiring in higher-level jobs. In the Multi-City Study Household Survey, higher proportions of college-educated blacks than less educated blacks reported experiences of discrimination in pay or promotion. The black-white wage gap for young men has widened most among college-educated men. Others have used interviews with middle-class African Americans themselves to study discrimination (Feagin and Sikes 1994), but employer interviews could provide a highly informative added perspective. Added analysis of employer views of gender differences within racial groups would also be highly fruitful.

Other research methods could help move beyond some of the limitations of the in-depth interview. As much as employers like to talk about what they think and do, they do not want to talk about discriminating. To get a better fix on employer actions, additional audit studies (sending out testers of different races with matched qualifications to apply for jobs) could be one important source of information. Constructing longitudinal employer-employee data sets would be another potential source. Such data sets would link administrative data on employees from the Social Security or Unemployment Insurance (UI) systems to the information about their employers from Census Bureau's Standard Statistical Establishment List and the quinquennial Economic Censuses. The Longitudinal Employer Employee Data (LEED) file based on Social Security Administration data, discontinued in the 1980s, is an example of such a data set. Recent analyses have also linked UI data to business establishment data to examine earnings and turnover (Lane, Stevens, and Burgess 1996; Burgess, Lane, and Stevens 1997). Given the huge amounts of data involved and confidentiality concerns, the federal government itself would have to play a major role in creating data sets of this sort.

While improved statistical analyses can help us learn more about what employers are actually doing, learning more about employer perceptions—where they come from and how they translate into action—depends on moving in the other direction, toward even deeper engagement with individual employers. Detailed case studies and ethnography, both involving sustained interaction with managers and workers, hold out the prospect of establishing a more thorough understanding of employers' world views.

Despite their limitations, the stories employers tell have revealed a lot about race and skill in the American workplace. The stories point to severe problems in the U.S. labor market, but they also point to solutions.

"We're from the Government and We're Here to Help You"

Before floating our own policy proposals, let's take a look at employers' views of public policy on labor markets. Employers, like the rest of the U.S. public, generally evince fairly cynical views of government action. This came across to some extent in the Telephone Survey, but was abundantly clear from the In-Depth Interviews.

In the Telephone Survey, some responses appear to demonstrate relatively benign employer attitudes toward government policies, but a closer look at their actions reveals a much cooler stance. As table 7.1 shows, overwhelming majorities of 90 percent or more stated they "definitely" or "probably" would hire a welfare recipient and someone from a government training program or who received a GED (high school equivalency) rather than a high school diploma. But if we move from a hypothetical question to one about current activities and ask whether employers are taking active steps (rather than asking whether they would exclude an applicant solely due to involvement with a government program), the percentage of employers answering yes drops dramatically. Only 51 percent of employers report that affirmative action or Equal Employment Opportunity law (AA/EEO) play "any" role in their recruiting, and a minority of 45 percent state that AA/EEO plays a role in hiring. If we are concerned about opportunities for workers of color, this glass is starting to look half empty.

When we move from asking a general question about the employer's practices to asking specifically about the last hire, there is yet another drop-off in reported engagement with public institutions. Presumably, the key avenues for affirmative action recruiting for less skilled jobs would be outreach through public schools, state employment agencies, and community agencies. However, the combined percentage of employers who actually recruited applicants through these avenues is a minority of 45 percent. What's more, only 8 percent of the people finally hired originated from one of these sources. Compare the 28 percent who responded to newspaper ads, 26 percent found through referrals by other employees, and 18 percent who were walk-ins or responded to a "Now Hiring" sign (see table 6.1). And when we view the schools, state em-

TABLE 7.1   *Employers' Interactions with Public Policy and Public
Institutions*

	Percentage Answering Yes	Sample Size
"Would you . . .?"[a]		
accept an applicant who is on welfare	91.8	N = 2,846
accept an applicant who was in a government training program, or had a GED instead of a diploma	96.7	N = 2,998
"At your company, would you say . . .?"[b]		
affirmative action or EEO plays a role in recruiting	51.4	N = 3,020
affirmative action or EEO plays a role in hiring	34.5	N = 3,001
"In making your last hire, did you . . .?"		
ask for referrals from schools	34.8	N = 3,084
This method generated the employee hired	*3.9*	*N = 3,035*
ask for or accept referrals from the state employment service	35.4	N = 3,063
This method generated the employee hired	*3.0*	*N = 3,035*
ask for or accept referrals from a community agency	26.8	N = 3,084
This method generated the employee hired	*1.4*	*N = 3,035*
ask for referrals from any of the above	45.4	N = 3,089
One of these methods generated the employee hired	*7.9*	*N = 3,035*

Source: Multi-City Telephone Employer Survey.
Note: Sample sizes exclude "don't know" or "refused" responses.
[a]"Definitely" or "probably" coded as yes; "probably not" or "absolutely not" coded as no.
[b]The questions asked if "affirmative action or Equal Employment Opportunity law play any role" in recruiting or hiring. An added 2.9 percent said AA/EEO "sometimes" plays a role in recruiting, and 4.4 percent said it "sometimes" plays a role in hiring ("sometimes" was volunteered as a response to this yes or no question).

ployment service, and community agencies separately, only a quarter to a little over a third of businesses utilize each of these sources. Private employment agencies, which supplied more than 5 percent of successful applicants, overshadowed state and community agencies, which together accounted for only just over 4 percent.

The subjects of these interview questions are not completely parallel. Nonetheless, it is striking that in spite of their declared openness to hiring people coming out of government programs, only a slim majority of employers apply affirmative action, and a minority draw on public and community institutions for hiring. The bottom line is that firms' actual practices entail fairly limited engagement with government policies and institutions.

The in-depth interviews spotlight some of the employer views behind these actions. Because our interviews focused primarily on workforce issues, we got an especially large earful about public schools and welfare. Boston-area employers were particularly likely to condemn the city public school system, as we saw in chapter 5. But managers in the other three areas joined the chorus as well: "It is scary to see an application filled out sometimes by people that theoretically have graduated from high school in the city of Atlanta." In Detroit: "I find it a little amazing that there are some people that, they don't even have a high school education but have a high school diploma." And in Los Angeles: "I think our educational level is horrible. It's certainly the ability to write. Grammatically we are just dropping right off the cliff. But it's also analytical thinking, problem solving, logical thought processes."

In fact, after complaining about "the California schools," another Los Angeles-area respondent went on to say, "I'm going to imagine that all big cities probably have similar problems." Some employers condemned the decline of American education as a whole, but a somewhat greater number had positive things to say about the school systems in many suburban communities. So the problem with public schools, at least in metropolitan-area employers' minds, is above all a big-city problem.

Employers reserved their most corrosive criticism for welfare. They defined *welfare* broadly to include Aid to Families with Dependent Children (not yet replaced with the Temporary Assistance to Needy Families block grants at the time of our interviews), food stamps, Medicaid, unemployment insurance, and a variety of other cash and in-kind support programs. Their repeated refrain is that welfare undermines the work incentive. "[They figure], hell, why should they work when they can receive the same thing by not doing anything and getting welfare," the owner of an Atlanta-area fast food restaurant declared. The CEO of a Detroit food-manufacturing firm made a similar complaint about his workforce:

> They have a terrible work ethic, for the most part. They are most interested in leaving here and going to get their forty-ounce bottle or going to get their bag of pot or whatever it is that they do. Because they are on the ADC, because they are on all these other social kinds of services, they don't seem to mind when they don't work.

Not surprisingly, as these examples illustrate, low-wage employers experienced and reported the effects of the welfare system most directly.

No other single policy came in for the same amount of ire as public schools and welfare, although worker abuse of workers' compensation did come up repeatedly, especially in California ("a cancerous problem," growled the general manager of a garment plant). But employers blasted a variety of government regulations, ranging from local to national. At a local level, managers castigated Detroit ("they're permit-happy as hell"), but also gentrifying communities such as the so-called People's Republics of Cambridge and Santa Monica that stringently restrict industrial development. At the federal level, a number of managers deplored the effects of the Family and Medical Leave Act (FMLA), which requires employers to grant workers twelve weeks of unpaid leave for medical or family needs. A top manager at a large manufacturing facility northwest of Boston, for instance, railed:

> We recently have gotten into this FMLA, family medical leave thing, and we've seen a big jump in absences. People are taking advantage of that. Okay, the government wants to put in something and people take advantage of it—constant incompetency of government understanding of human nature. And it's very frustrating to people who are asked to compete with people from Taiwan and Malaysia, who wouldn't do that.

Taxes came up surprisingly infrequently, though they did come in for some criticism. All in all, the most frequent form in which employers expressed views on public policy was through scorchingly negative comments.

Our Policy Recommendations

Our own policy recommendations challenge the negative views of government expressed by many employers, though they also build on insights and suggestions of some respondents who moved beyond complaints to formulate alternatives.[1] Despite our strongly held views about welfare reform (see Albelda and Tilly 1997) and school reform, we limit our discussion here to policy options that the employer interviews helped illuminate. We base these policy recommendations in part on added policy-focused employer interviews and a focus group of exemplary employers in the Boston area, organized by the research and policy organization Jobs for the Future.

The Importance of Race and Ethnicity

Perhaps the most important theme from the stories employers tell, cutting like a searchlight across our findings, is the continuing importance of race and ethnicity. Returning to the dichotomy between impersonal market forces and racial discrimination that we posed in the first chapter, we must conclude after reviewing the evidence from employers' testimony that our labor market has important elements of both. African Americans and Latinos face formidable obstacles that go well beyond skill differences. Although employers express negative views of black, Latino, and inner-city workers in terms of hard and soft skills, some of the negative freight is clearly stereotype. Another portion flows from cultural chasms between white and black, suburban and urban, college-educated and less educated workers. A young, inner-city African man who has not finished high school and a middle-aged, suburban, college-educated white manager speak different "languages" in terms of dress, work expectations, body language, and conventions of interaction—as well as vocabulary and syntax. For soft skills in particular, the boundaries between bias, cultural gaps, and objective skill deficits are singularly difficult to define, let alone measure. Managers' negative perceptions of inner-city neighborhoods— as crime-ridden and lacking an adequate workforce—are also exaggerated, at least according to many of the employers who *do* carry on business in inner-city locations. And such invidious characterizations of the inner city are racialized. They are tied to the presence of concentrated populations of blacks, Latinos, and, in fewer cases, Asians.

In short, as we have repeatedly emphasized, race and skill, and race and location, are woven closely together in the typical employer's-eye view of the urban world. In some ways, race is becoming increasingly important. In particular, the growing stress on soft skills opens the door wider for biases and stereotypes to weigh in the hiring process, and on location decisions as well. This tells us that skill- or location-based policies that fail to address race are likely to fall short of the mark. Providing added training programs for black and Latino job seekers will not easily dissolve the suspicion that many employers harbor. And employers' unease may block access by workers of color to the critically important training that takes place on the job. Similarly, new transportation systems such as vanpools to crack inner-city isolation will have limited effects if suburban businesspeople remain chary of the urban minority workforce. Policies to dissipate stereotypes, and to constrain employers' ability to act on them, are necessary complements. We do not dismiss the importance of standard policy tools, but we focus here on what added policy insights grow most directly out of our findings.

Since we and others with similar views are unlikely to have the ear of Congress in the near future, we propose policies that could be effective on a relatively small scale—as initiatives of a single state legislature, an adventurous federal agency, or even in many cases a private foundation interested in pointing a different direction for labor market policy. For the most part, the proposed policies are scalable: they can work equally well at a large scale. And given the likely uphill struggle ahead, we prioritize a small number of programs, with attention to their likely success in building political support for additional action, as well as their likely impacts on the workforce.

Content of Training Programs

What advice can we offer to those designing training programs? First of all, at least some soft skills can be learned. The 1991 U.S. Department of Labor Secretary's Commission on Achieving Necessary Skills (SCANS) and subsequent efforts to promote national skill standards (Bailey and Merritt 1994) have highlighted the importance of social skills—but have also emphasized that these are indeed *skills* that can be learned, rather than simply innate qualities. The SCANS report, for example, identifies "interpersonal skills" as one of five main competencies. The fact that this idea has entered the national policy debate on training is a positive indication. To the extent that employers accept this view (for which there is considerable evidence; see Cappelli 1995), they may be more willing to train for such skills rather than simply screening for them. Of course, the elastic category of soft skills also includes items that are *not* worker skills—cultural gaps and employer biases—and it is counterproductive to insist that worker training must and will erase these barriers as well. The appropriate balance between training prospective workers and training and regulating employers can be informed by social science, but also must be shaped by our expectations and values as a society.

A number of other training-related themes emerged from the in-depth interviews, and particularly from the added discussions with exemplary employers in the Boston focus group. Perhaps the broadest consensus point was that effective training programs for young people with limited education must teach work-readiness. Some of the elements of work-readiness identified by employers are obvious, but others less so. The list includes:

- How to fill out an application and conduct a pre-employment interview
- Appropriate dress and grooming
- The basic rules of the world of work: attendance, punctuality, calling when unable to come to work (these are some of the desired behaviors we have classed under the "motivation" aspect of soft skills)
- Handling conflict
- Code-switching (altering demeanor and speech as demanded by the situation)

255

The last two elements are critically important. Black workers and, to a lesser extent, Latinos face significant numbers of employers who view them through negative stereotypes. As a young African American man reported in one of the focus groups cited in chapter 1, "corporate racism" was the aspect of the workplace for which he was least prepared. Short of outright bias, misunderstandings are common. But if blacks and Latinos react with anger, they play into stereotypes of defensiveness and hostility. Skills in conflict resolution help them avoid this trap. Similarly, the ability to switch between a style of interaction appropriate to inner-city streets and one appropriate to corporate suites is a tremendous asset. In chapter 4, we quoted a black human resource official at a Detroit-area insurance company who told us: "You are one thing up to the point of entering the business world, but then you are something else. I'm not the same person I was fifteen years ago. I had to take on certain thoughts and attitudes, whether I liked it or not."

Recommending that training programs include code-switching raises again the question of the policy balance between training of workers and retraining of employers. Is it solely the responsibility of the victims of discrimination to head off conflict and switch codes of behavior and communication? Certainly not. Managers need special education and training to communicate effectively with a diverse workforce. We discuss policies that might help shape the training of managers later in this chapter. In the good society, managers, workers, and consumers would all do their best to meet each other halfway. In our imperfect society, however, training in code-switching is necessary self-defense for workers of color in many settings.

In addition to basic work-readiness, there is widespread agreement among our interviewees that training programs must also have a "values" component. The exemplary employers in the Boston focus group said that programs must instill self-esteem and a work ethic— adding that families and schools once did this, but have had less and less success. Other managers concurred. Employers emphasized "pride," but in the sense of pride in doing a good job, combined with deference to authority. A Boston-area hospital food service manager even complained explicitly about training programs that "build false confidence in kids— like they're special, they're elite."

We agree that training programs should seek to impart and reinforce work-friendly values. However, a lagging work ethic is greatly overemphasized as a cause for labor market disadvantage. Katherine Newman (1999), in her insightful ethnography of young African American and Latino workers in Harlem fast food restaurants, points out that these marginally employed members of the working poor voice utterly mainstream sentiments about the importance of work. Furthermore, the conviction that today's workers do not manifest the work ethic of yore is probably as old as capitalist labor markets themselves. In a statement cited by Seymour Martin Lipset (1990, 61), the British Parliament of 1495 complained in a public decree that "diverse artificers and labourers waste much part of the day in late coming unto their work, early departing therefrom, long sitting at breakfast, at their dinner and noon meal, and long time of sleep in the afternoon." Employers who bemoan shirkers at the dawn of the twenty-first century are carrying on a tradition at least five hundred years old!

To be sure, young people just starting out in the world of work typically do not share the devotion to work (or at least resignation to its demands) of their elders. But such youthful restlessness is not unique to the inner city. If anything—as many of our respondents pointed out—it may be more acute among the children of the middle class. To the extent that inner-city residents show lower levels of respect for the norms of paid employment, this may be more the result than the cause of low-quality jobs and hostile managers.

For one useful window on this issue, we can examine the average levels of *reservation wages*—the minimum wage level acceptable to a given worker. Comparing reservation wages with actual wages gives a barometer of how willing a group of workers is to do what is needed in the world of work. Harry Holzer (1986) analyzed reservation wages of young black and white men, based on data from the National Longitudinal Survey of Youth and from the National Bureau of Economic Research's 1980 survey of inner-city youth in Boston, Chicago, and Philadelphia. He summarized his findings as follows.

Reservation wages for young black men are quite similar to those of whites. However, the reservation wages are higher than the wages offered by jobs in which black youth are actually employed. Observed wages for young white male job holders are higher, so in this sense blacks' reservation wages are above opportunities to a greater degree than those of whites. Nonetheless, black men are more likely than their white counterparts to accept lower-wage jobs; they report that they view these jobs as temporary. The chief result of blacks' larger gap between reservation wages and actual wage offers is that young black men remain unemployed longer than white men. That is, black men believe they are worth more than the market is offering, but reluctantly—and with some delay—settle for less. Their expectations would doubtless appear more reasonable were it not for the fact that the labor market discriminates against them.

More recent survey data from William Julius Wilson's Chicago Urban Family Life Study and the Multi-City Study of Urban Inequality Household Surveys, while not strictly comparable, do not suggest further rises in reservation wages of blacks relative to whites, nor relative to actually received wages (table 7.2). In fact, if anything, black men's wage expectations have grown more modest over time relative to the wage offers available to them. In any case, while relative escalation of black reservation wages—if there was evidence for it—could help explain black disemployment, it could not help explain the widening black-white wage gap. Higher reservation wages should lead to *increased* average wages among employed persons, either because wages adjust to lower supplies or because the fraction of employed persons who are employed at the lowest wages declines.

Table 7.2 also extends the analysis to women, and to Latinos and Asians of both genders. To the extent that the 1987 Chicago data and the 1990s four-city data are comparable, they certainly do not point to a significantly rising reservation wage for any of these groups. And although in a few cases (including some Latina women, in addition to the black men already noted), nonemployed people of color report a reservation wage higher than the one they actually received on average, for the most part reservation wages are low compared to actually available wages. In the most recent data, white men's average desired wage exceeded their average received wage by about the same amount as Latinas and black men.

In short, the reservation wage data indicate that among the workers of color suffering the greatest disadvantages in the labor force, the work ethic is neither dramatically different from those of whites, nor significantly deteriorating over time. Work-related values are a key part of any training program, but training designers should steer clear of the patronizing assumption that inner-city workers are less oriented to these values than others. In addition, for workers of color, a training program may need to teach the painful lesson that, due to discrimination, they may have a difficult time receiving what they are actually worth in the labor market.

Moving from values to mechanics, the employers in the Boston focus group also stressed that for any training program, follow-up after placement is very valuable. Retention is in many ways a more critical issue than initial hiring. Though one public-sector manager in the Boston focus group objected to follow-up as a "crutch," he was outnumbered by positive comments from others. "Changing attitudes and behaviors is not always a few months' thing," another public-sector manager responded. "Most people that I know, they go and get a job and then they're in shock." In an individual interview, a Boston-area fast food manager elaborated: "There needs to be somebody, somewhere helping these people, saying, 'This is what you need to do.' Especially [during] the first few months." However, a hospital manager noted that employers themselves must take major responsibility for handling these problems—"Don't just say, 'The program's doing it.'"

The importance of follow-up is a subset of a broader point about training programs for disadvantaged populations: the most successful programs are those that build and maintain long-term relationships with both trainees and employers. This appears to be the key to the success of programs such as San Jose's Center for Employment Training (Meléndez 1996) and San Antonio's Project Quest (Osterman and Lautsch 1996). Long-term relationships with trainees—participants in Project Quest training programs typically are involved for two years—provide the opportunity to provide more training and socialization, as anyone who has been a student or a teacher in a two-year or four-year college knows. Equally important, long-term relationships mean that a community-based agency can give both participants and employers ongoing support—and can hold both groups accountable. When a trainee stumbles, the agency can offer counseling and help negotiate with the employer, but can also press that trainee to fulfill his or her commitments. Similarly, an agency with long-standing ties to a business can advise that employer and help locate needed services, but can also hold the employer's feet to the fire to come through on hiring and promotion goals.

Form of Training Programs

How should training be organized? Learning about work starts with primary education, and we must address preschool and kindergarten through twelfth grade education with financing reforms assuring some kind of equity in educational resources. However, the employer surveys don't offer much insight into how to restructure the earlier years of education. They do suggest that one important step is to extend school-to-work program models that link high school education and the workplace. In focus groups of young men of color from the Boston and New York inner cities, participants agreed that the hardest step in employment was "getting a foot in the door." Employers, in focus groups and interviews, expressed serious concerns about young, inner-city men's work readiness. Their concerns focused on soft skills such as work ethic and etiquette, as much as or more than harder skills such as literacy and numeracy. School-to-work initiatives can help address the concerns of disadvantaged young people and employers alike. They give young people work experience and a foothold in the work world, backed up by structured instruction. In addition to teaching work-readiness, they offer employers a "safe," supported way to learn how to manage a workforce

TABLE 7.2 Reservation Wages and Actual Wages, by Race and Ethnicity

1979–1980, Men Aged Fourteen to Twenty-One, Nationwide (National Longitudinal Survey of Youth)

	Nonemployed Men		Employed Men	
	White	Black	White	Black
Mean reservation wage	$4.59	$4.47	$6.01	$5.40
Mean received wage	$4.75	$4.00	$5.13	$4.26
Ratio of reservation wage to received wage	0.97	1.12	1.17	1.27
Ratio of group's reservation wage to white reservation wage	1.00	0.97	1.00	0.90

1980, Black Men Aged Sixteen to Twenty-Four, Boston-Chicago-Philadelphia Inner Cities (National Bureau of Economic Research)

	Nonemployed	Employed
Black men		
Mean reservation wage	$ 3.61	$4.44
Mean received wage	$ 3.98	$4.34
Ratio of reservation wage to received wage	0.91	1.02

1987, Parents Aged Eighteen to Forty-Four, Chicago (Urban Poverty and Family Structure Project)

	White	Black	Mexican	Puerto Rican
Men				
Mean reservation wage (jobless)	$9.34	$5.81	$7.23	$6.18
Mean received wage (employed)	$14.63	$8.91	$7.92	$7.96
Ratio of reservation wage to received wage	0.64	0.65	0.91	0.78
Ratio of group's reservation wage to white reservation wage	1.00	0.62	0.77	0.66
Women				
Mean reservation wage (jobless)	$6.60	$5.52	$5.29	$5.30
Mean received wage (employed)	$11.98	$7.33	$5.23	$6.15
Ratio of reservation wage to received wage	0.55	0.75	1.01	0.86
Ratio of group's reservation wage to white reservation wage	1.00	0.84	0.80	0.80

1992 to 1994, Workers Aged Sixteen to Twenty-Four, Atlanta-Boston-Detroit-Los Angeles (Multi-City Study of Urban Inequality)

	Nonemployed Men				Employed Men			
	White	Black	Latino	Asian	White	Black	Latino	Asian
Mean reservation wage	$ 8.93	$5.85	$5.97	$7.49	$ 9.00	$6.54	$6.98	$ 6.83
Mean received wage	$ 8.69	$5.45	$6.34	$8.5	$10.07	$8.49	$8.38	$11.14
Ratio of reservation wage to received wage	1.03	1.07	0.94	0.88	0.89	0.77	0.83	0.61
Ratio of group's reservation wage to white reservation wage	1.00	0.66	0.67	0.84	1.00	0.73	0.78	0.76
	N = 26	N = 26	N = 20	N = 16	N = 69	N = 56	N = 89	N = 18

	Nonemployed Women				Employed Women			
	White	Black	Latina	Asian	White	Black	Latina	Asian
Mean reservation wage	$ 5.40	$5.47	$5.42	$4.89	$ 8.42	$5.78	$6.15	$ 7.66
Mean received wage	$ 6.08	$5.87	$5.17	$7.69	$ 9.45	$7.40	$8.44	$ 9.79
Ratio of reservation wage to received wage	0.89	0.93	1.05	0.64	0.89	0.78	0.73	0.78
Ratio of group's reservation wage to white reservation wage	1.00	1.01	1.00	0.91	1.00	0.69	0.73	0.91
	N = 39	N = 93	N = 102	N = 21	N = 54	N = 68	N = 57	N = 15

Sources: National Longitudinal Survey of Youth and National Bureau of Economic Research data from Holzer 1986, Urban Poverty and Family Structure data from Tienda and Stier 1991, Multi-City Study of Urban Inequality data calculated by authors.

that many of them view with suspicion. A recent Chicago study confirmed that African American youth, in particular, benefit from training programs with operational ties to industry (Lundgren-Gaveras and Rankin 1995).

The challenges confronting school-to-work programs serving disadvantaged young people are far greater than those facing programs serving a more typical mix of vocationally oriented high school students. Both employers and the young men in focus groups agreed that poverty, discrimination, and racial tension, and the lure of the drug trade and other illicit economic activities, all undermine young people's commitment to school and to legitimate employment. Teaching inner-city workers to code-switch and reinforcing work-oriented values are very resource-intensive processes, requiring close interaction of young people with role models at work and school.

There is a vast existing "second-chance" training system designed to assist adults (particularly younger ones) who have dropped out of or not benefited from schooling. Calling this a "system" may be somewhat misleading, since in reality it is a welter of programs with different funding sources, mandates, and clienteles—some oriented to welfare recipients, others to immigrants, still others to displaced workers, and so on. The second-chance system could be far more effective if parts of it were retooled to combine training and work experience, and to extend follow-up after placement. Much of the second-chance system consists of classroom instruction followed by placement, with little if any contact between the program and the worker after placement. But for all the reasons that we just advanced in favor of school-to-work models, this traditional second-chance model often will not successfully place disadvantaged workers, and will do little to prevent them from rapidly turning over, whether through quitting or being terminated. A model combining instruction and work experiene—including, where possible, workplace-based training—can help overcome these problems. Again, follow-up, counseling, and support for workers *after* placement will be particularly valuable. To make this work, the rewards directed to agencies must emphasize job duration (or upward mobility) and continuing labor market success, not just placement.

Affirmative Action:
The Carrot and the Stick

The quantitative findings in chapter 6 demonstrate that in many cases, formality in recruiting and screening is associated with higher levels of black employment—particularly black male employment. The qualitative findings reveal some of the whys and hows of this relationship. The qualitative results highlight the importance of affirmative action, both as a stimulus for formality and as a framework that shapes formality to aid the employment of people of color. Affirmative action is designed to offset past discrimination, so the fact that we find *ongoing* racial and ethnic discrimination makes its implementation especially urgent.

But affirmative action—at least as we have known it—is in the process of being rolled back. Court decisions, executive actions, and plebiscites alike have reduced or threaten to reduce its reach. Antidiscrimination enforcement, a major spur to affirmative action, has fallen off. Economists John Bound and Richard Freeman (1992) noted that "the number of employment discrimination suits was roughly constant in the 1980s at about 9,000 per year after having risen rapidly; the number of class action suits fell; and most employment discrimination cases involved termination rather than hiring. The EEOC [Equal Employment Opportunity Commission], which monitors Title VII, reduced its staff by 20 percent from 1979 to 1985." Since Bound and Freeman wrote, employment discrimination suits by individuals have climbed significantly, but civil rights litigation by the federal government—the lawsuits that assist low wage workers who typically cannot afford to retain a lawyer—continued to decline (Sniffen 2000; U.S. Equal Employment Opportunity Commission 2000). In fact, a recent *Wall Street Journal* article reported that white males' opposition to affirmative action has cooled, because they no longer see affirmative action as a serious threat: "The rise of women and minorities in some companies has slowed or even halted. . . . Many white men are finding affirmative action less of an obstacle to getting jobs and promotions than they expected" (Kaufman 1996). At the same time, less formal, more subjective recruiting and screening methods are growing in importance in the workplace as employers view soft, social skills as increasingly critical. Based on our evidence, this two-pronged retreat from affirmative action and formality is likely to further harm employment of blacks and Latinos, especially among men.

What can be done? We believe that government must not abdicate its enforcement role. But clearly, we cannot simply advocate that the clock be turned back to a stronger affirmative action policy that has proved politically vulnerable. Instead, we urge what we call an *evangelistic* approach to affirmative action—going beyond traditional monitoring and enforcement functions to implement policies that help make a case for affirmative action, and facilitate compliance. Such evangelization should be directed particularly at small and medium-sized businesses, those least likely to be pursuing affirmative action in any substantial way.

Specifically, we advocate three new kinds of affirmative action policy steps—focusing here on the key issues at the low-skill section of the labor market that we have been studying. First, *link affirmative action rhetorically and programmatically to strengthened education and training programs.* Widespread skill deficits among black and Latino workers compound the damage of discrimination, and contribute to stereotypes and statistical discrimination. To make the rhetorical link, those of us advocating for affirmative action must emphasize that discrimination is not the only labor market problem facing workers of color, and that affirmative action is not a stand-alone policy. Rather, it is one of a package of programs that together can begin to reverse labor market inequality. Programmatically linking the education and training system to affirmative action means institutionalizing education and training providers as reliable sources of affirmative action hires. The tiny 1 percent of hires who were referred by community agencies testifies to the current weakness of the link between such agencies and employers. Making the link more robust will take action from both sides. Another programmatic link is to engage firms that receive public benefits in quasi-contractual first-source agreements, which bind these businesses to advertise and recruit first—at least for certain types of jobs—with local training providers or community organizations.

A second step is to *make affirmative action/equal employment opportunity more user-friendly, and help those who want to do the right thing.* Somewhat surprisingly, some of the biggest boosters of affirmative action are big businesses. The business media provide varied evidence of this corporate viewpoint. In a *Wall Street Journal* op-ed, Heather Mac Donald (1996) lamented business opposition to the so-called California Civil Rights initiative (CCRI), barring affirmative action in state-funded programs, which was passed in 1996:

> The CEOs of such firms as Chevron, Hughes Aircraft, and Atlantic Richfield issued ringing endorsements of affirmative action, clearly targeted at the CCRI debate. And many big companies, including Pacific Bell and Southern California Edison, conducted internal "education" campaigns explaining the need for diversity policies. Kaiser Permanente sent a letter to all its member physicians and employees warning of the initiative's dangers.

Despite the outrage on the *Journal's* editorial pages, the advertising pages may provide an even more telling piece of evidence. That same year, a Kodak ad in the *Wall Street Journal*, nearly full page in size, showed a smiling woman manager with this message:

> She likes her staff *diverse* . . .
> her associates *respected* . . .

her team *motivated* . . .
her policies *flexible* . . .
her work relationships *win-win* . . .
and her documents from Kodak.

The reference to Kodak aside, the message is clearly that diversity is hip and forward-looking, a characteristic of leading-edge companies. A 1994 special supplement in the *Boston Globe*, "Working Together: Exploring Diversity in the Workplace," sends the same message. The lead-off headline reads "Retaining a Diverse Workforce Is [a] New Goal" (*Boston Globe* 1994). Businesses give a variety of reasons for embracing diversity. Most important, of course, is the demographic shift that means people of color and women will account for a growing share of the workforce, and that people of color will constitute a larger share of consumers as well. Quite a few large businesses welcome affirmative action as a predictable, orderly alternative to the potential chaos of widespread individual litigation and intergroup dissension, much as some businesses welcomed the Wagner Act as an alternative to civil war on the shop floor. The globalization of markets for many companies spells even greater diversity in the customer base, and diversity within the business may better arm the company to contend with diversity outside. Social responsibility, public image, and compliance with equal employment opportunity laws are also factors.

At the same time, "diversity chic" does not necessarily translate into effective affirmative action practices. In our interviews, we saw that publicly expressing antipathy toward particular racial groups has become socially unacceptable. But stereotypes of the skills and qualities of blacks, Latinos, and others continue. Only a slim majority of employers state that they practice affirmative action in recruiting, and a minority adheres to it in hiring. In addition, public statements of commitment to diversity may coexist with private slurs and egregious discrimination—as in the case of Texaco, which paid $176 million to settle racial discrimination charges in 1996. Political conservatives have also mounted an offensive against businesses that take a public stand in favor of affirmative action. After AT&T's retreat—due to a firestorm of criticism—from participation in drafting the Civil Rights Act of 1991, few corporations will be willing to take high-profile individual roles. Even more fundamentally, diversity remains a secondary concern for most businesses. In a 1992 survey of businesses following the Los Angeles riots of that year, 44 percent stated that adapting to workforce diversity was "important but not a priority," and another 20 percent rated it "not very important" in their plans for the next two years. This was not because they saw themselves as paragons of diversity management. Fifty-five percent graded themselves as "average" in this area, and another 13 percent admitted they were "poor" or "very poor" (Rigdon 1992).

While enhanced enforcement of equal opportunity laws is called for as one response to this situation, there are also ways to exploit and promote the notion that managing diversity well is a desirable business practice. One possible model for this would be a Diversity Management Extension Service. The idea is that disadvantaged workers need to learn new skills—but so do the managers who employ them. Toward this end, the extension service model should be applied to diversity management. The U.S. Department of Agriculture's Agricultural Extension Service has helped make this country's agriculture the most productive and successful in the world. In the last several years a number of states have begun to adapt this model to manufacturing, establishing industrial extension programs; the federal government has also experimented with industrial extension.

Extension services vary, but the main elements of the model typically include the following activities:

- Offer businesses a variety of types of training and consulting, ranging from classes to customized problem solving. The staff involved can go beyond those of the extension service itself to include other experts. Extension services particularly target small and medium-sized businesses, which are less likely to have the in-house capacity to self-educate and problem-solve. They often provide services based on a fee and/or a competitive process. (Some extension services have pots of money, and encourage consortia of businesses to make funding proposals for extension activities.)
- Conduct research and gather information about best practices. Diffuse this knowledge through a variety of channels.
- Contribute to developing higher education curricula in the area of interest, to better prepare managers or specialists. (The Agricultural Extension service was originally based out of the land grant agricultural colleges.)

Would businesses make use of such an extension service? We know that some businesses (mostly larger ones) currently use consultants to assist them with diversity issues. Mark Wallace, president of the diversity management consulting company J. Howard & Associates, estimated in 1994 that companies spend $100 million to $200 million per year on such consultants (Shao 1994). But in a survey conducted by the American Society for Training and Development, *0 percent* of the seventy-four companies surveyed viewed workplace diversity programs as "highly effective." Of those who voiced an opinion, 40 percent called such programs "moderately effective," 34 percent labeled them just "effective," and 26 percent branded them "ineffective" (Shao 1994). Clearly, substantial numbers of companies are looking for help in this area, and equally clearly, many of them are dissatisfied with the help they are getting. An extension service can help fill this gap—not by displacing private-sector consultants, but by complementing them, helping to set standards, and speeding the diffusion of knowledge and techniques. Recalling our findings in chapters 4 and 6 that smaller firms hire fewer blacks than larger firms do, the focus of extension programs on small and medium-size firms would be all the more helpful.

Still broader business participation can be encouraged by aggressive marketing, and by linking this extension service (directly or via referral) to other, better-known services available to businesses. In addition, business "ownership" of the program can be heightened by involving employers in its design. Particularly potent is a combination of regulation and extension: the Massachusetts Toxic Use Reduction Act has used that combination to induce businesses to develop production technologies that generate fewer toxic by-products. It makes sense to start with experimental pilot programs to determine what approaches work best, before rolling out a national-scale program. The U.S. Equal Employment Opportunity Commission's recent release of a report assessing best EEO practices in the private sector (U.S. Equal Employment Opportunity Commission 1997a) is a very positive step in this direction.

Third, we can *use policy to demonstrate why affirmative action is still needed*. Policies should help make the case for affirmative action. One appropriate tool for this is audit studies. As we noted in chapter 1, audit studies, originally pioneered to test for housing discrimination, send out trained pairs of testers—from different racial and ethnic groups, but with identical qualifications—to apply for jobs. Recent audit studies have demonstrated that identically qualified African Americans and Latinos get fewer job offers than non-Latino whites (Bendick, Jackson, and Reinoso 1994; Fix and Struyk 1993). Following the release of these studies, the Massachusetts Commission Against Discrimination (the state-level equivalent of the EEOC carried out its own audit study of retailers, at the end of which it publicized findings and announced its intention to prosecute one company.

Many employers acknowledge that racial and ethnic discrimination persist, but others—along with much of the white public—view such discrimination as a thing of the past (even though they themselves may engage in it!). Audit studies, which send testers matched on everything but race to apply for jobs, sound a powerful wake-up call: unlike standard statistical studies, they expose to public view the smoking gun of discrimination. The optimal policy strategy is probably to conduct small audits targeted to particular geographic areas and industries. The point is not to document discrimination scientifically; earlier studies have adequately done that. The point is to bring home the seriousness of the problem, and to spur employer reflection about their own employment practices. It is important to keep in mind that audit studies capture only one portion of employment discrimination: they focus on screening, skipping over the targeted recruitment that often excludes workers of color. And by controlling for everything but the race of the applicant, they remove the effects of class and inner-city residence, which our findings suggest are quite important. Nonetheless, the evidentiary impact of such studies should encourage employer participation in affirmative action, including participation in projects like an extension service.

These steps to strengthen affirmative action are potentially useful, even in the absence of affirmative action enforcement, though they will be much more effective in combination with that stick. Importantly, all three of these steps can be carried out—at various scales and to various degrees—by any level of government: federal, state, or local. In fact, in some form they can be carried out by nongovernmental organizations. Training programs typically rely on federal Workforce Investment Act funds, but have harnessed the nonprofit sector's innovations. Workplace audit studies have so far been chiefly a foundation initiative (from the Rockefeller Foundation). Even individual businesses have begun to use testers, if only "to test their own employees before they are tested by watchdog groups" (Wynter 1998, B1). Thus, even if the government continues to back off from a commitment to deal with these issues, the measures we outline offer possible continued leverage points for workplace diversity. Encouragingly, however, the federal Equal Employment Opportunity Commission itself recently made a quiet decision to experiment with audit studies (U.S. Equal Employment Opportunity Commission 1997; Wynter 1998).

Although public support for affirmative action is currently lukewarm, survey data indicate that there are beliefs to build on. In the four metropolitan areas of the Multi-City Study, large majorities agree that blacks and Latinos face "a lot" or "some" job discrimination. A smaller majority believes that Asians face such discrimination, and only about one-quarter of respondents agree that whites do (see table 7.3).

As many others have noted, the degree of support for affirmative action recorded in surveys depends crucially on how the question gets asked. In the Multi-City Study Household Survey, solid majorities favor "special job training and education assistance" to remedy "past disadvantage" for blacks, Latinos, and Asians (see table 7.4). However, when asked about "special preference in hiring and promotion" for the same

TABLE 7.3   *How Much Job Discrimination Various Racial and Ethnic Groups Face: A View from the Four Cities*

	A Lot	Some	A Little	None	
Blacks					N =
	35.6%	42.9%	14.5%	7.0%	8,642
Latinos					N =
	31.1	47.0	15.0	7.0	8,591
Asians					N =
	10.7	43.9	30.4	15.0	8,392
Whites					N =
	3.6	19.5	31.5	45.4	7,146

Source: Multi-City Study of Urban Inequality Household Survey, calculations by authors.

groups, favorable respondents dwindle to a minority. Along similar lines, pollster Louis Harris (1996) reported that in 1996, 55 percent of Americans said that they support "affirmative action—without strict quotas," down only slightly from the average of 60 percent who expressed support over the preceding twenty-five years. Harris also pointed out that though the California Civil Rights Initiative, dismantling state-sponsored affirmative action, did pass, one important reason was that Californians were confused by the phrasing of the initiative ("The state will not use race, sex, color, ethnicity, or national origin as a criterion for either discrimination against, or granting preferential treatment to, any individual or group . . . "). When asked before the passage of the initiative, "Would you still favor this proposition if it would outlaw all affirmative action programs for women and minorities?" the percentage supporting the measure plunged from a majority of 78 percent to a minority of 31 percent. And in November 1997, affirmative action opponents hit a major bump in the road to rollback, in Houston, Texas. Here a CCRI-like initiative was defeated, due in part to opposition from the Republican political establishment and the Greater Houston Partnership, the city's main business organization (Feagin 1998). The reason that Houston and statewide elites lined up in favor of affirmative action is not hard to discern: the city of Houston is already only one-third white, and demographers project that by 2010 Texas as a whole will have a majority of Latinos, African Americans, and Asians.

The point is not that winning support for stronger measures to remedy racism in the workplace will be a cakewalk. But where anti–affirmative action conservatives have attacked "preferences" and "quotas" to mobilize support for their view, supporters of a comprehensive program against discrimination and disadvantage can use a combination of evidence and policy linkages to make the case for theirs. Using evidence

TABLE 7.4   *Degree of Support for Special Programs for Various Racial and Ethnic Groups*

	Strongly Favor	Favor	Neither Favor Nor Oppose	Oppose	Strongly Oppose	
Training and educa-tional assistance for						
Blacks	24.2%	41.3%	20.8%	10.1%	3.6%	N = 8841
Latinos	23.4	40.0	22.7	10.6	3.3	N = 7300
Asians	16.3	37.8	29.6	12.3	4.0	N = 7285
Special preference in hiring and promo-tion for						
Blacks	8.0	20.1	31.1	27.6	13.3	N = 8823
Latinos	7.4	20.6	32.7	26.7	12.6	N = 7297
Asians	4.5	17.9	36.3	28.4	13.0	N = 7283

Source: Multi-City Study of Urban Inequality Household Survey, calculations by authors.

means, for example, proliferating audit studies to demonstrate that racial and ethnic discrimination are still setting back black and Latino job seekers. Using policy linkages means connecting up strengthened equal employment opportunity enforcement, assistance for businesses of goodwill (as through a Diversity Extension Service), and beefed-up real-world training—all as part of a "high road" labor market package. This is an uphill battle, but it can be won.

New Roles for Business, Government, and Intermediaries

The traditional model of public policy affecting business is straightforward: government regulates, business complies. But the policy suggestions in this chapter point to a wider range of models, and new roles for business, for government, and for a variety of labor market intermediaries that don't fall into either camp. On the business side, our findings and the growing discourse of "diversity management" imply that management, in addition to workers, needs to build up its soft skills. Employers mentioned the following elements of good management of disadvantaged workers, particularly those of color:

- The key element is commitment at the top of the organization; without that, the remaining items on the list are unlikely to be implemented
- Building a management team that is itself diverse
- Managing in a way that is sensitive to cultural differences

270

- Concentrating on building mutual trust between managers and workers
- Re-educating frontline managers when needed (for example, via diversity training)
- Clearly communicating and implementing expectations
- Using pay and opportunities for mobility as motivators
- Some employers stated that team methods of management can help resolve tensions and conflict among different groups in the workforce.

The growing importance of soft skills also raises four other issues for businesses, and especially for human resource managers. First, the drive for increased social skills places the human resource function at the center of business strategy. Manager after manager told us that altered skill requirements formed a key part of the response to intensified competitive pressures. In this context, hiring, training, and retention become strategic issues, if they were not before. A second issue: demands for greater soft skills pose a choice between screening and training. Most managers appear to believe that qualities of interaction and motivation are not responsive to training, so that employers must screen for them at the outset. But as we noted earlier, the social psychological literature indicates that training *can* enhance "attitude" (Cappelli 1995), and some of our respondents stated this as well. Skill development can be a viable alternative to screening, and provides greater opportunities for disadvantaged workers.

The effect of compensation on soft skills represents a third, related issue. It is well known that offering above-average pay can help attract superior workers, improve morale and motivation, and strengthen retention; economists call this phenomenon "efficiency wages" (Akerlof and Yellen 1986). Leonard Schlesinger and James Heskett of the Harvard Business School (1991), in a series of business case studies, found that higher wages form part of a virtuous circle for some service employers, leading to lower turnover and greater customer satisfaction. Thus, again, soft skills are not simply fixed characteristics of individuals, but depend on the employment situation. Our respondents drew two opposite conclusions from this, however. Some adopted above-market wages as part of a package designed to elicit improved worker motivation. Others concluded that since they could not afford to raise pay or otherwise improve working conditions, they were doomed to a workforce with poor attitudes. Essentially, the latter group believed that the costs of the virtuous circle exceeded the benefits.

Finally, while the managers we interviewed spoke in terms of skill upgrading, much of the change also appears to involve simply eliciting

271

greater employee effort. Businesses are seeking more emotional labor (Hochschild 1983) from their workers—for example, by asking that cashiers be more "fast, fun, and friendly," or requiring clerical workers to interact directly with customers. Employers are also trying to select or create a more cooperative, self-monitoring workforce that has internalized the norms of the business rather than responding only to management pressure (Edwards 1979). This changing configuration of skill demands embodies a potential contradiction. On the one hand, managers wish to empower workers, shifting responsibility downward and shortcutting traditional lines of authority. On the other hand, managers seek greater influence over worker behavior, including employees' attitudes. In the short run, human resource managers can use careful recruiting and training to pursue the two objectives simultaneously. But in the long run, there is a trade-off. As employers make this choice, along with the others we have highlighted, there is a strong public interest in encouraging them to take the high road, empowering workers, developing worker skills, offering higher compensation, and nurturing diversity.

This public interest must be served in part by government. Government as regulator—for example, enforcing laws against discrimination—remains irreplaceable. But government, at its various levels, must also take on less accustomed—though not entirely new—roles. Government can serve as teacher and consultant in a Diversity Extension Service. Government can partner with business to develop new transportation options for isolated inner-city workers. Governments from local to national can also help build and strengthen business networks. For example, Katherine Newman (1999) has proposed "hiring consortia" that would link small businesses with limited promotion opportunities, such as the fast food restaurants she studied, with larger businesses that possess internal job ladders. Small businesses could offer trained, experienced workers to their larger counterparts; in turn, the opportunity of stepping onto a job ladder could provide a powerful incentive for the small businesses' employees to stay on the job, learn skills, and apply themselves. While businesses could in principle organize such consortia on their own, there are common difficulties in organizing business coordination where the benefits are widely shared. Some businesses will tend to be "free riders," skimming off the benefits of such arrangements without committing resources to organize the activity. The fear or reality of free-rider effects can scuttle collective business activities. Government can serve as an honest broker, as well as providing rewards to participants or penalties to free riders.

The hiring consortium model is one example of the huge potential role of labor market intermediaries that are neither for-profit businesses nor government agencies. Many such intermediaries are nonprofit agencies, but a much broader range of actors have stepped forward to play this role in various settings. The Cleveland Chamber of Commerce has taken a leading role in mobilizing local businesses to develop shared training curricula and standards. In San Francisco, the Hotel Employees and Restaurant Employees union has helped the major hotels to create training programs, and runs a temporary agency that places union members in short-term catering jobs at the hotels. Our findings in chapter 6 suggest that, more broadly, unions can help enforce formality in hiring that enhances blacks' chances of being hired—although some unions use their power over hiring to perpetuate racial exclusion instead.

Intermediaries can play a key role in training, since training involves a classic free-rider problem. Businesses that train workers in widely useful skills risk losing the worker—and therefore losing their training investment—to other businesses that then become free riders. As a result, businesses provide far less training than they should, even from the perspective of business. Intermediaries can coordinate business training efforts, as the Cleveland Chamber of Commerce has done, so that businesses can feel assured that their contribution to training is commensurate with the rewards they reap. To exert the maximum impact on disadvantaged workers, nonprofit employment and training agencies—and other counterparts, including community groups and unions—must build their capacity as labor market brokers. Many employers have expanded their use of for-profit temporary agencies and subcontractors, as a way of screening workers—even for permanent jobs. To the extent that not-for-profit employment and training agencies serving disadvantaged young workers can develop a reputation for placing good workers, they can get a piece of this growing business.

In principle, employers should be willing to pay nonprofit agencies for such labor supply services. In practice, this will depend on the cost and quality of the labor supplied relative to other alternatives. But fees should be explored, and might even heighten employer interest. As one business aphorism puts it, "If I can get it for free, it can't be worth much." It is important to note that the brokering role places employment and training agencies in a conflicted situation, especially when businesses are paying customers. On the one hand, the agencies seek to help the young people facing the greatest labor market hurdles. On the other hand, they seek to offer employers reliable workers; there is a strong incentive to "cream"—select the best workers who are already work-ready—in order to meet this need. The agencies will have to wrestle with this contradiction, handling multiple programs in ways that offer young people intensive assistance and allow them mobility—without jeopardizing the agency's track record as a broker.

Efforts to place disadvantaged workers will not be equally successful in all times, places, and industries. Businesses are most likely to make use of such brokering services under three types of circumstances:

- The businesses are socially conscious (or at least image-conscious). This could be due to a range of factors, from top management leadership to threats of a discrimination lawsuit.

- The businesses offer low pay and few benefits, and are having trouble attracting and retaining good workers. (Once more, this places the employment and training agency in a difficult situation: many of the most interested employers will be those offering lousy jobs!)

- There is a labor shortage affecting a particular industry or geographic area. From time to time, as in the late 1980s and early 2000s, labor shortages become widespread across the country, but they do not endure—sooner or later, recession hits.

These circumstances limit the initial scope of any socially targeted employment brokering program. But once a critical mass of workers from a community has found jobs, informal referral networks can supplement formal brokers. Most people find jobs through people they know, especially at the entry level—so that jump-starting these informal networks may be the most important accomplishment of an employment and training agency.

Once more, government can facilitate this intermediation—by subsidizing or enforcing participation, by serving as a broker, or by directly creating the intermediary. The German youth apprenticeship system, which joins together schools, business associations, and unions with government oversight, is a highly successful example of one way this might work.

A Last Word

Having traveled the long road from research questions to policy agenda, we close with a warning but also a note of optimism. Numerous obstacles are conspiring to lock less skilled workers, particularly less skilled blacks and Latinos, out of jobs in the new century. Discrimination is a continuing factor that plays out in new ways as well as old. Rising skill demands, the growing weight put on soft skills, declining formality in recruiting and hiring, waning affirmative action pressure, and the ongoing flow of businesses to the suburbs translate into serious setbacks for workers of color. But new approaches to workforce policy—approaches that can be taken on by nonprofit and private-sector actors as well as the government—offer a very real promise of enhancing skills, curtailing discrimination, and helping open the way to a more inclusive workplace. The "stories employers tell" can have a happy ending—if we make it happen.

Appendix A

Multi-City Telephone
Employer Survey

Number of observations: 3,510
Location(s): Atlanta, Boston, Detroit, and Los Angeles metropolitan areas
Time period: 1992 to 1995
Sampling frame: Roughly equal samples were drawn from each area, based on two sampling frames: 2,206 cases were drawn from regional employment directories provided by Survey Sampling, Inc. (SSI), a commercial vendor, based primarily on local telephone directories; 1,304 cases were drawn from the current or most recent employer reported by respondents in the corresponding Multi-City Study of Urban Inequality Household Survey for each metropolitan area.
Selection criteria or strata: SSI sample is a probability sample stratified by firm (or, technically, establishment) size as reported by SSI. The sample was drawn 25 percent from firms with one to nineteen employees, 50 percent from firms with twenty to ninety-nine employees, and 25 percent from firms with a hundred or more employees. The effect of this stratification is roughly to weight a firm's probability of being drawn by the number of employees at the firm. The household-linked sample is stratified only by city. It is a probability sample for Atlanta and Detroit, but overrepresents early respondents from Boston and Los Angeles.
Weights: Weights are designed to replicate actual job distribution in each metropolitan area.
Other comments: See Holzer 1996 and http://www.icpsr.umich.edu for additional description.

Social Science Research Council
In-Depth Employer Survey

Number of observations: Interviews with seventy-five managers at fifty-six firms
Location(s): Detroit and Los Angeles metropolitan areas
Time period: 1991 to 1992
Sampling frame: Sampled from Yellow Pages and suggestions by contacts in the four metropolitan areas. Not designed to be a probability sample.
Selection criteria or strata: Four industries: auto parts manufacturing, retail stores, insurance carriers, and public-sector agencies
Weights: No weights.

Multi-City In-Depth Employer Survey

Number of observations: 365 interviews with managers at 174 firms
Location(s): Atlanta, Boston, Detroit, and Los Angeles metropolitan areas
Time period: 1994 to 1996
Sampling frame: Sampled from household-linked portion of Telephone Survey
Selection criteria or strata: Stratified to include businesses that had and had not experienced three types of change over the previous ten years: relocation, changing skill requirements in the sample job, and organizational change
Weights: No weights.

Multi-City Study of Urban Inequality
Household Survey

Number of observations: 8,916
Time period: 1992 to 1994
Location(s): Atlanta, Boston, Detroit, and Los Angeles metropolitan areas
Sampling frame: U.S. Census of Population, 1990
Selection criteria or strata: Samples differed by city: Atlanta (1,528), Boston (1,820), Detroit (1,543), Los Angeles (4,025). Samples were clustered probability samples stratified by income and race of census tract. Racial composition of the samples differed by city: Atlanta and Detroit drew black-white samples, Boston drew a black-white-Latino sample, and Los Angeles drew a black-white-Latino-Asian sample.

Weights: Weighted to replicate actual populations of the four metropolitan areas, scaled so that the weights of the four areas are equal.

Other comments: See Bobo, O'Connor, and Tilly 2000 for added analyses and discussions of these data. http://www.icpsr.umich.edu has an additional description.

Appendix B

DESCRIPTIVE STATISTICS OF VARIABLES

Means, Standard Deviations, and Sample Sizes for Variables from the Multi-City Telephone Employer Survey

Variable	Mean	Standard Deviation	Sample Size
Talk face to face with customers	0.589	0.492	3,137
Talk on the phone with customers	0.516	0.500	3,139
Read instructions	0.539	0.499	3,119
Write paragraphs	0.295	0.456	3,137
Do arithmetic	0.63	0.483	3,127
Use computers	0.504	0.500	3,133
Job requires high school diploma	0.706	0.456	3,143
Job requires general experience	0.681	0.466	3,142
Job requires specific experience	0.608	0.488	3,141
Job requires references	0.720	0.449	3,152
Job requires vocational or other training	0.746	0.435	3,152
Report a change in skills	0.398	0.489	3,132
If report a change in skills			
Skills risen	0.963	0.189	1,235
Skills declined	0.370	0.483	1,235
Of those reporting a rise in skills, the change due to			
Basic reading, writing, numeric	0.292	0.455	1,181
Social and verbal	0.266	0.442	1,181
Both	0.239	0.426	1,181
Other	0.178	0.383	1,181
The skill change was a result of			
New technology	0.831	0.375	1,185
Computers	0.717	0.450	1,185
New products	0.469	0.499	1,185
Higher product quality	0.625	0.484	1,184
New services provided	0.662	0.473	1,184
More customer contact	0.564	0.496	1,185

Continued

Variable	Mean	Standard Deviation	Sample Size
Organizational change	0.771	0.420	1,185
Last hire was a white man	0.243	0.429	2,921
Last hire was a white woman	0.300	0.458	2,921
Last hire was a black man	0.104	0.306	2,921
Last hire was a black woman	0.117	0.322	2,921
Last hire was a Hispanic man	0.098	0.298	2,921
Last hire was a Hispanic woman	0.071	0.256	2,921
Supervisor performance rating	77.6	14.9	2,791
Some tasks are performed better by men, others by women	0.168	0.374	3,042
Some tasks are performed better by members of some ethnic or racial groups	0.048	0.215	3,094
Customers prefer to deal with employees of their own race or ethnic group	0.207	0.405	2,675
Employees prefer other employees of their own race or ethnic group	0.240	0.427	2,699
Employers in your business prefer employees of their own race or ethnic group	0.220	0.414	2,449
Any of the types of ethnocentrism	0.329	0.470	3,152
Proportion of applicants white	0.480	0.371	1,984
Proportion of applicants black male	0.183	0.236	2,609
Proportion of applicants black female	0.145	0.213	2,099
Proportion of applicants Hispanic	0.156	0.254	2,308
Proportion of applicants Asian	0.058	0.124	2,112
Firm size	374.9	1,790.9	3,117
Starting wage	8.33	3.58	2,837
Proportion white in the relevant portion of the metropolitan area	0.810	0.157	3,510
Proportion black in the relevant portion of the metropolitan area	0.146	0.162	3,510
Proportion Hispanic in the relevant portion of the metropolitan area	0.118	0.140	3,510
Proportion Asian in the relevant portion of the metropolitan area	0.041	0.034	3,510
Employer's average distance from black populations	17.13	7.66	2,494
Employer's average distance from Hispanic populations	20.47	7.01	2,494
Employer's average distance from Asian populations	18.86	6.27	2,494
Percentage of firms reporting a vacancy	0.445	0.479	3,142
Mean number of vacancies among firms reporting a vacancy	10.00	20.28	1,362

Continued

Variable	Mean	Standard Deviation	Sample Size
Proportion of employers who say inner-city residents are weaker applicants	0.157	0.364	2,615
How long at the present location	21.25	23.40	2,849
Moved in the last ten years	0.438	0.496	1,467
A move is planned	0.082	0.274	2,968
Plan not to keep firm open indefinitely	0.015	0.120	2,959
Recruiting method for the last employee hired			
Newspaper ad	0.269	0.443	2,923
Help-wanted signs	0.046	0.209	2,923
Walk-in	0.148	0.355	2,923
Referrals from			
Current employees	0.251	0.434	2,923
State employment service	0.035	0.184	2,923
Private employment service	0.053	0.224	2,923
Community agency	0.014	0.117	2,923
Schools	0.042	0.201	2,923
Union	0.008	0.089	2,923
Other (acquaintances and the like)	0.132	0.338	2,923
Used affirmative action in recruiting	0.526	0.499	3,075
Screening method used for the last employee hired			
Written application	0.818	0.386	3,141
Interview	0.870	0.336	3,143
Physical and/or drug test	0.518	0.500	1,059
Tests or other	0.441	0.497	3,041
Verify education	0.282	0.450	2,899
Check criminal record	0.322	0.468	2,853
Used affirmative action in hiring	0.357	0.478	3,055
Percentage of employees unionized	0.159	0.331	2,943
Used formal methods of recruiting	0.734	0.440	3,136
Accept an applicant who is on welfare	0.514	0.500	2,906
Accept an applicant who was in a government training program, or had a GED instead of a diploma	0.556	0.497	3,061
Firm is in Atlanta	0.288	0.453	3,510
Firm is in Boston	0.253	0.435	3,510
Firm is in Detroit	0.229	0.420	3,510
Firm is in Los Angeles	0.288	0.453	3,510
Clerical job	0.165	0.371	3,425
Customer service job	0.246	0.431	3,425
Blue-collar job	0.271	0.445	3,425
Other job	0.309	0.462	3,510

Source: Multi-City Telephone Employer Survey.

Means, Standard Deviations, and Sample Sizes for Firm-Level
Variables from the Multi-City In-Depth Employer Survey

Variable	Mean	Standard Deviation	Sample Size
Most important qualities sought			
Any mention			
Hard skills	0.248	0.434	125
Interaction skills	0.392	0.490	125
Motivation	0.360	0.482	125
First mention			
Hard skills	0.536	0.501	125
Interaction skills	0.560	0.498	125
Motivation	0.512	0.502	125
Either soft skill	0.840	0.368	125
Employer perceptions of workers			
About blacks			
Blacks have lagging hard skills			
At least one respondent	0.337	0.473	172
Half or more of firm respondents	0.262	0.440	172
Blacks have lagging interaction skills			
At least one respondent	0.267	0.442	172
Half or more of firm respondents	0.186	0.389	172
Blacks have lagging motivation			
At least one respondent	0.506	0.500	172
Half or more of firm respondents	0.395	0.489	172
Black women are better employees than black men			
At least one respondent	0.076	0.265	172
Half or more of firm respondents	0.064	0.245	172
Black men are better employees than black women			
At least one respondent	0.023	0.150	172
Half or more of firm respondents	0.018	0.133	172
Blacks are better workers			
At least one respondent	0.035	0.184	172
Half or more of firm respondents	0.023	0.150	172
About Latinos			
Latinos have lagging hard skills			
At least one respondent	0.099	0.299	172
Half or more of firm respondents	0.052	0.222	172
Latinos have lagging interaction skills			
At least one respondent	0.017	0.129	172
Half or more of firm respondents	0.012	0.109	172
Latinos have lagging motivation			
At least one respondent	0.099	0.299	172
Half or more of firm respondents	0.058	0.234	172
Latinos are better workers			
At least one respondent	0.203	0.402	172
Half or more of firm respondents	0.163	0.369	172

Continued

Variable	Mean	Standard Deviation	Sample Size
About Asians			
Asians have lagging hard skills			
At least one respondent	0.035	0.184	172
Half or more of firm respondents	0.023	0.150	172
Asians have lagging interaction skills			
At least one respondent	0.012	0.109	172
Half or more of firm respondents	—	—	172
Asians have lagging motivation			
At least one respondent	0.006	0.077	172
Half or more of firm respondents	—	—	172
Asians are better workers			
At least one respondent	0.134	0.341	172
Half or more of firm respondents	0.128	0.334	172
About immigrants			
Immigrants have a stronger work ethic			
At least one respondent	0.192	0.394	172
Half or more of firm respondents	0.157	0.364	172
Employer perceptions of neighborhoods			
Inner-city workforce worse			
At least one respondent	0.573	0.495	164
Half or more of firm respondents	0.415	0.493	164
Inner-city workforce better			
At least one respondent	0.207	0.405	164
Half or more of firm respondents	0.171	0.376	164
Inner-city crime a problem for business			
At least one respondent	0.604	0.489	164
Half or more of firm respondents	0.500	0.500	164
Firm moved	0.116	0.321	172

Source: Multi-City In-Depth Employer Survey.

Means, Standard Deviations, and Sample Sizes for Respondent-Level Variables from the Multi-City In-Depth Employer Survey

Variable	Mean	Standard Deviation	Sample Size
Employer perceptions			
About blacks			
Blacks have lagging hard skills	0.203	0.402	350
Blacks have lagging interaction skills	0.146	0.353	350
Blacks have lagging motivation	0.334	0.472	350
Black women are better employees than black men	0.040	0.196	350
Black men are better employees than black women	0.011	0.104	350
Blacks are better workers	0.017	0.129	350
About Latinos			
Latinos have lagging hard skills	0.054	0.226	350
Latinos have lagging interaction skills	0.011	0.104	350
Latinos have lagging motivation	0.054	0.226	350
Latinos are better workers	0.134	0.341	350
About Asians			
Asians have lagging hard skills	0.017	0.129	350
Asians have lagging interaction skills	0.006	0.077	350
Asians have lagging motivation	0.003	0.055	350
Asians are better workers	0.074	0.262	350
About immigrants			
Immigrants have a stronger work ethic	0.131	0.337	350

Source: Multi-City In-Depth Employer Survey.

NOTES

Chapter 1

1. Critics raised a number of objections to the use of the term *under-class*. The word is used to refer to a wide range of overlapping but nonequivalent phenomena: geographic concentration of poverty, persistence of poverty, "deviant" behaviors. What's more, there is little evidence that any of these phenomena marks a group with sufficient internal coherence to be labeled a "class" (Gans 1992; Hughes 1989). And many of the behaviors and indicators associated with the "underclass" either have declined recently (crime, teen childbearing, lags in educational attainment) or are so widespread in the society as to defy a class label (single motherhood) (Jencks 1991). Finally, the term *underclass* has the potential to stigmatize a broad set of low-income people—regardless of whether their poverty is persistent, concentrated, or associated with nonmainstream behaviors. For all these reasons, most social scientists have stopped using the term.

Chapter 2

1. Harry Holzer supervised the collection of 3,213 responses. Our colleague Joleen Kirschenman and we oversaw an additional 297 interviews.

2. The codebook and further information on the telephone survey are available on the Inter-university Consortium for Political and Social Research (ICPSR) website: www.icpsr.umich.edu.

3. Our segregation indices come from Reynolds Farley and William Frey (1994). This segregation index is Otis Dudley Duncan and Beverly Duncan's (1955) index of dissimilarity.

4. Where not otherwise specified, the source for statements about demographic change in Atlanta is Truman Hartshorn and Keith Ihlanfeldt 2000.

5. These numbers refer to the Standard Consolidated Statistical Area (SCSA).

6. The numbers in this paragraph refer to the Massachusetts portion of the New England Consolidated Metropolitan Statistical Area, which is the area described in table 2.1 and the area from which the employer samples were drawn.

7. Where not otherwise specified, the sources for statements about demographic and industrial change in Los Angeles are Philip Moss and Chris Tilly 1993b and David Grant 2000. The underlying data source for both is the U.S. Census of Population. We thank David Grant for conducting the census analyses reported in Moss and Tilly 1993b.

8. Community descriptions are from Camille Zubrinsky and Lawrence Bobo 1995. Proportions reporting that a family from a given racial and ethnic group would be unwelcome are calculated by the authors.

Chapter 3

1. In our analyses, we count references to spoken communication skills as soft skills; excluding them does not substantially alter the quantitative or qualitative findings we report.

2. Most studies tracking returns to education have sought to analyze the rise in earnings inequality in the last several decades. The goal was not to understand the nature of skill change, but to assess the contribution of rising skill demands to the widening gulf between high- and low-wage workers.

3. Specifically, in Telephone Survey cases not linked to a Multi-City Study Household Survey respondent, the sample job was the last entry-level job for which the employer had hired. In cases linked to a household respondent (and in the face-to-face interviews, which were limited to these cases), the sample job was the job held by the household respondent. In both cases, if the manager responding to the survey was not able to comment on this particular job, we asked instead about the largest job category requiring no more than a high school education, and defined this category as the sample job.

4. As Harry Holzer notes, the use of computers can be quite varied and potentially ambiguous in interpretation. The range might include the simple tasks of operating a grocery store checkout scanner or meal-ordering machine in a fast food restaurant, to word processing, to more technical computer use (Holzer 1996, 46, n. 4). Our qualitative findings, to be discussed, drive this point home.

5. As demand for and the return to skill increase, we are likely to see a supply response. To the degree they can, both white and non-white young people will invest in getting more skill as they have done increasingly in the last two decades. Demand shifts tend to occur more rapidly than supply shifts, so that the labor market difficulties we attribute to increasing skill demand may continue to worsen for some time. (We thank Harry Holzer for this point.)

6. Given small sample sizes in the SSRC study, the differences in proportions shown in the first panel of table 3.8 should be interpreted with some caution.

7. The emphasis by employers in both qualitative and quantitative surveys on greater literacy and numeracy (among employers that reported increased skill demands) is consistent with other recent studies. See Mishel and Teixeira (1991), Osterman (1995), Cappelli (1993), and Murnane and Levy (1996).

8. Our SSRC survey data on the auto parts manufacturing industry comes from twenty-one interviews covering nineteen firms. Four of the firms did not produce parts for the automobile industry. Their products and processes were sufficiently related to the firms that did produce auto parts to make the information from these interviews comparable. The firms varied widely in the typical skill level of their production process. One required essentially no skill other than taking metal parts on and off traveling racks, while another firm produced exactingly machined parts for the space shuttle.

9. As part of the SSRC study, we spoke to managers at five retail clothing chains—comprising a total of twenty interviews with twenty-four informants at fifteen sites. Although we conducted one interview at a chain that sites small stores in underserved low-income and minority areas, our main focus was on the other four chains, which run larger stores aimed at a working- and middle-class customer base.

10. In the SSRC study, we spoke to human resource officials at eight insurance companies, including companies specializing in life, property and casualty, and health lines. We revisited two of the companies, for a total of ten interviews.

11. The SSRC survey included fifteen interviews with respondents in public-sector agencies, public utilities, public-sector hospitals, or who were involved with service providers contracted to public-sector facilities, including hospitals and museums. Our interviews covered twelve sites.

12. In this section, we analyze the race, ethnicity, and gender of the most recent hire in the firm. Many of the issues we raise about skill, attitudes, and screening procedures pertain as well to em-

ployer decisions *after* the point of hire. For example, decisions to train, to promote, or to fire may be affected by skills, perceptions, and procedures as well. Our data limit us to hiring outcomes.

13. We calculate the representation gap by subtracting the index of representation for whites from the index of representation for a given racial group, within gender (for example, the index for Latino men minus the index for white men).

Chapter 4

1. The question was asked slightly indirectly. The standard wording was, "We have heard from other managers that they see differences between _____. Have you seen such differences?"

2. We assume that some of the differences across metropolitan areas reflect a different climate of racial attitudes, some reflect less willingness to speak candidly about race, and some reflect interviewer effects across the cities (since there were different interviewers in each city).

3. These opinions usually came in response to the question, "We know from other research that blacks and other minorities are doing worse than whites in the labor market. Why do you think that is?"

4. This finding comes from our colleague Ivy Kennelly, who has done extensive analysis of the attitudes regarding single mothers of the Atlanta employers in this survey. See Ivy Kennelly (1999) and Irene Browne and Ivy Kennelly (1999), who review some of the same data.

5. Two decades ago, Michael Piore (1979) noted that the children of immigrants often viewed their parents' jobs as unacceptable, because their frame of reference was now the United States and not the home country of their parents.

6. We did not directly ask employers to state the basis for their perceptions, but as they discussed the perceptions these patterns emerged.

7. The Telephone Survey asked for the percent of applicants who are black men and black women, and the percent who are Hispanic and Asian; the latter two were not broken down by gender.

8. We are not able to separate white applicants from "others" due to the questionnaire design, but "others" represent only 6 percent of the workforce and 2 percent of the most recent hires, so "white/other" is primarily white.

9. On the other hand, one possible reason for lower hires-to-applicants ratios for blacks in the suburbs is that workers who get mul-

tiple job offers tend to accept the offer closest to home, all else equal. Since blacks are concentrated in the cities and whites in the suburbs, blacks will more often accept urban jobs and whites will more often take suburban jobs when multiple jobs are offered. (We thank Keith Ihlanfeldt for pointing this out.)

10. The variable is the weighted mean of distances of census tracts centroids from the business, with the number of black people in each tract as the weights. (We thank Harry Holzer for providing this variable.)

11. Results are shown as odds ratios, signifying the ratio of the estimated probability of hiring someone from a given group when the employer answers yes to an ethnocentrism question to the estimated probability when the answer is no.

12. The coefficient does attain significance (at the 10 percent level) in some specifications with fewer controls (not shown).

13. An alternative hiring outcome variable is the race and gender breakdown reported for all employees in the sample job in the face-to-face interviews themselves. However, we believe this is reported less accurately than the characteristics of the last hire, and it also reflects historic hiring (and layoff) practices as well as current ones, making it less suitable.

14. As in table 4.11, results are shown as odds ratios, signifying the ratio of the estimated probability of hiring someone from a given group when the employer answers yes to an ethnocentrism question to the estimated probability when the answer is no.

Chapter 5

1. Harry Holzer notes that the geographic distribution of jobs from this survey accords with the distribution from the 1990 census, but with some exceptions that may be due to different choice of the central city-suburb border in this survey and in the census, and differential response rates across the area. In particular, the fraction of jobs in Atlanta's central city is somewhat larger for the survey than for the census, Holzer also discusses the geographic distribution of jobs broken down by industry (see Holzer 1996, 21–25).

2. In table 5.1 we report the mean number of vacancies among the firms in each cell. In many of the cells, there was a firm that reported an unusually high value for the number of current vacancies. In almost all cells, there was only one such firm. Recognizing the possibility that the anomalous high values are either mistakes or so atypical as to distort the results, we also report a trimmed mean with the very high values deleted (a value of 200 or greater was used as the cutoff, and again there was only one such firm per

cell in almost every instance). Because a very large fraction of firms report no vacancies, the median number of vacancies in each cell is fairly small and ranges across the cells from a low of 2 to a high of 6.

3. Test scores are lower, on average, among lower-income blacks and Latinos (Jencks and Phillips 1998), although turnover rates, once wages and occupation are controlled for, are similar or lower for blacks (Holzer and LaLonde 2000).

Chapter 6

1. We suspect that respondents did not always answer the college requirement question accurately, since the jobs reported as not requiring college include a small number of professionals such as engineers, lawyers, and even one physician. For the current research, however, we took these responses as our guideline for inclusion or exclusion from the sample.

2. Results are shown as odds ratios. For yes or no variables, these show the ratio of the estimated probability of hiring someone from a particular group when the answer is yes, divided by the estimated probability of hiring when the answer is no. For continuous variables, the ratio divides the estimated probability when that variable is one unit higher by the estimated probability when it is one unit lower.

Chapter 7

1. This section draws in part on Tilly 1995, which was produced for Jobs for the Future (Boston), with funding from the Annie E. Casey Foundation.

References

Ady, Robert. 1997. "Symposium on the Effects of State and Local Public Policies on Economic Development." *New England Economic Review* (March/April 1997): 77–82, discussant's comments.

Aigner, Dennis J., and Glen G. Cain. 1977. "Statistical Theories of Discrimination in the Labor Market." *Industrial and Labor Relations Review* 30(2): 175–87.

Akerlof, George, and Janet Yellen, J., eds. 1986. *Efficiency Wage Models of the Labor Market*. Cambridge: Cambridge University Press.

Albelda, Randy, and Chris Tilly. 1997. *Glass Ceilings and Bottomless Pits: Women's Work, Women's Poverty*. Boston: South End Press.

Allport, Gordon. 1954. *The Nature of Prejudice*. Reading, Mass.: Addison-Wesley.

Anderson, Elijah. 1990. *Street Wise: Race, Class, and Change in an Urban Community*. Chicago: University of Chicago Press.

Arrow Kenneth. 1972. "Models of Job Discrimination" and "Some Mathematical Models of Race in the Labor Market." In *Racial Discrimination in Economic Life*, edited by Anthony H. Pascal. Lexington, Mass.: Lexington Books.

———. 1973. "The Theory of Discrimination." In *Discrimination in Labor Markets*, edited by Orley A. Ashenfelter and Albert Rees. Princeton, N.J.: Princeton University Press.

Bailey, Thomas, and Donna Merritt. 1994. "Making Sense of Industry-based Skills Standards." Unpublished paper. Institute for Education and the Economy, Columbia University, New York (January 1994).

Bayor, R. 1988. "Roads to Racial Segregation." *Journal of Urban History* 15(1): 3–21.

Becker, Gary S. 1957. *The Economics of Discrimination*. Chicago: University of Chicago Press.

Bendick, Marc, Jr., Charles W. Jackson, and Victor A. Reinoso. 1994. "Measuring Employment Discrimination Through Controlled Experiments." *Review of Black Political Economy* 23(Summer): 25–48.

Bennett, Phillip. 1991. "Welcome to L.A." *Boston Globe*, Sunday Magazine, October 13, 1991.

Berman, Eli, John Bound, and Zvi Griliches. 1994. "Changes in the Demand for Skilled Labor Within U.S. Manufacturing: Evidence from the Annual Survey of Manufacturers." *Quarterly Journal of Economics* 109(2): 367–97.

Berman, Eli, and Stephen Machin. 1999. "SBTC Happens: Evidence on the Factor Bias of Technological Change in Developing and Developed Countries." Paper presented at the National Bureau of Economic Research Summer Conference, Labor Studies, Cambridge, Mass. (July 1999).

Best, Michael. 1990. *The New Competition: Institutions of Industrial Restructuring*. Cambridge: Harvard University Press.

Blair, John P., and Robert Premus. 1987. "Major Factors in Industrial Location: A Review." *Economic Development Quarterly* 1(1): 72–85.

Blumer, Herbert. 1958. "Race Prejudice as a Sense of Group Position." *Pacific Sociological Review* 1(1): 3–7.

Bobo, Lawrence, and James R. Kluegel. 1991. "Whites' Stereotypes, Social Distance, and Perceived Discrimination Toward Blacks, Hispanics, and Asians: Toward a Multiethnic Framework." Paper presented at the 86th Annual Meetings of the American Sociological Association. Cincinnati (August 23–27, 1991).

———. 1993. "Opposition to Race-Targeting: Self-Interest, Stratification, Ideology or Racial Attitudes?" *American Sociological Review* 58(4): 443–64.

Bobo, Lawrence, James R. Kluegel, and Ryan A. Smith. 1997. "Laissez-faire Racism: The Crystallization of a 'Kinder, Gentler' Anti-black Ideology." In *Racial Attitudes in the 1990s: Continuity and Change*, edited by Steven A. Tuch and Jack K. Martin. Greenwood, Conn.: Praeger.

Bobo, Lawrence, and Michael Massagli. 2001. "Racial Identity, Stereotypes, and Perceived Group Competition." In *Urban Inequality: Evidence from Four Cities*, edited by Alice O'Connor, Chris Tilly, and Lawrence Bobo. New York: Russell Sage Foundation.

Bobo, Lawrence, and Susan Suh. 1995. "Surveying Workplace Discrimination: Analysis from a Multiethnic Labor Market." Presented at the Multi-City Study of Urban Inequality Research Conference on Searching for Work, Searching for Workers. Russell Sage Foundation, New York (September 1995).

Borjas, George. 1994. "The Economics of Immigration." *Journal of Economic Literature* 32(4): 1,667–1,717.

Boston Globe. 1994. "Working Together: Exploring Diversity in the Workplace." Special section (March 7, 1994).

Bound, John, and Laura Dresser. 1999. "The Erosion of the Relative Earnings of Young African American Women During the 1980s." In *Latinas and African American Women at Work*, edited by Irene Browne. New York: Russell Sage Foundation.

Bound, John, and Richard Freeman. 1992. "What Went Wrong?" The Erosion of Relative Earnings and Employment for Blacks." *Quarterly Journal of Economics* 107(1): 201–32.

Bowles, Samuel, and Herbert Gintis. 1995. "Why Do the Educated Earn More? Productive Skills, Labor Discipline, and the Returns to Schooling." Unpublished paper. Department of Economics, University of Massachusetts at Amherst.

Braddock, Jomills Henry, II, and James M. McPartland. 1987. "How Minorities Continue to Be Excluded from Equal Employment Opportunities: Research on Labor Market and Institutional Barriers." *Journal of Social Issues* 43(1): 5–39.

Brown, Rupert. 1995. *Prejudice: Its Social Psychology*. Oxford: Basil Blackwell.

Browne, Irene, and Ivy Kennelly. 1999. "Stereotypes and Realities: Images of Black Women in the Labor Market." In *Latinas and African American Women at Work: Race, Gender, and Economic Inequality*, edited by Irene Browne. New York: Russell Sage Foundation.

Browne, Irene, Leann Tigges, and Julie Press. 2001. "Inequality Through Labor Markets, Firms, and Families: The Intersection of Gender and Race-Ethnicity." In *Urban Inequality: Evidence from Four Cities*, edited by Alice O'Connor, Chris Tilly, and Lawrence Bobo. New York: Russell Sage Foundation.

Burgess, Simon, Julia Lane, and David Stevens. 1997. "Jobs, Workers and Changes in Earnings Dispersion." Center for Economic Policy working paper 1714. London School of Economics.

Cain, Glen C. 1986. "The Economic Analysis of Labor Market Discrimination: A Survey." In *Handbook of Labor Economics*, vol. 1, edited by Orley C. Ashenfelter and Richard Layard. Amsterdam: North-Holland.

Cappelli, Peter. 1993. "Are Skill Requirements Rising? Evidence for Production and Clerical Workers." *Industrial and Labor Relations Review* 46(3): 515–30.

———. 1995. "Is the 'Skills Gap' Really About Attitudes?" *California Management Review* 37(4): 108–24.

———. 1996. "Technology and Skill Requirements: Implications for Establishment Wage Structures." In *Earnings Inequality*, special issue of the *New England Economic Review* (May/June).

Cappelli, Peter, Laurie Bassi, Harry Katz, David Knoke, Paul Osterman, and Michael Useem. 1997. *Change at Work*. New York: Oxford University Press.

Card, David, and Thomas Lemieux. 1999. "Can Falling Supply Explain the Rising Return to College for Younger Men? A Cohort-based Analysis." Paper presented at the National Bureau of Economic Research Summer Conference, Labor Studies. Cambridge Mass. (July 1999).

Carré, Françoise, and Chris Tilly. 1998. "Part-time and Temporary Work: Flexibility for Whom?" *Dollars and Sense* 215 (January/February): 22–25.

Chafets, Ze'ev. 1990. *Devil's Night, and Other True Tales of Detroit*. New York: Random House.

Cheng, Lucie, and Philip Q. Yang. 1996. "Asians: The 'Model Minority' Deconstructed." In *Ethnic Los Angeles*, edited by Roger Waldinger and Mehdi Bozorgmehr. New York: Russell Sage Foundation.

City of Detroit. 1978. *The Overall Economic Development Program*. Detroit: City of Detroit.

Clifford, Frank, and Anne C. Roark. 1991. "Racial Lines in County Blur But Could Return." *Los Angeles Times*, May 6, 1991, p. 1.

Collins, Patricia Hill. 1990. *Black Feminist Thought: Knowledge, Consciousness, and the Politics of Empowerment*. New York: Routledge.

Conrad, Cecilia A. 1999. "Soft Skills and the Minority Work Force: A Guide for Informed Discussion." Washington, D.C.: Joint Center for Political and Economic Studies.

Corcoran, Mary, Colleen M. Heflin, and Belinda I. Reyes. 1999. "Latino Women in the U.S.: The Economic Progress of Mexican and Puerto Rican Women." In *Latinas and African American Women at Work*, edited by Irene Browne. New York: Russell Sage Foundation.

Corcoran, Mary, and Sharon Parrott. 1999. "Black Women's Economic Progress." In *Latinas and African American Women at Work*, edited by Irene Browne. New York: Russell Sage Foundation.

Darden, Joe T., Richard Child Hill, June Thomas, and Richard Thomas. 1987. *Detroit: Race and Uneven Development*. Philadelphia: Temple University Press.

Darity, William A., Jr., and Patrick L. Mason. 1998. "Evidence on Discrimination in Employment: Codes of Color, Codes of Gender." *Journal of Economic Perspectives* 12(2): 63–90.

Darrah, Charles. 1994. "Skill Requirements at Work: Rhetoric vs. Reality." *Work and Occupations* 21(1): 64–84.

Davis, Mike. 1990. *City of Quartz: Excavating the Future in Los Angeles*. London: Verso.

DiNardo, John E., and Jörn-Steffen Pischke. 1996. "The Returns to Computer Use Revisited: Have Pencils Changed the Wage Structure Too?" Cambridge, Mass. National Bureau of Economic Research working paper S606 (June).

Dipboye, Robert L. 1982. "Self-Fulfilling Prophecies in the Selection-Recruitment Interview." *Academy of Management Review* 7: 579–86.

Doeringer, Peter, Philip Moss, and David Terkla. 1986. *The New England Fishing Economy: Jobs, Income, and Kinship*. Amherst: University of Massachusetts Press.

Dougherty, Laurie. 1993. "Towards on Overview of the Economic History of the Greater Boston Consolidated Metropolitan Statistical Area Since World War II." Unpublished paper. University of Massachusetts at Boston, Boston Urban Inequality Research Group Summer Project.

Duckitt, John. 1992. *The Social Psychology of Prejudice*. New York: Praeger.

Duncan, Otis Dudley, and Beverly Duncan. 1955. "A Methodological

Analysis of Segregation Indexes." *American Sociological Review* 20(2) (April): 210–17.

Edwards, Richard C. 1979. *Contested Terrain: The Transformation of the Workplace in the 20th Century*. New York: Basic Books.

England, Paula. 1992. *Comparable Worth: Theories and Evidence*. New York: Aldine.

Farley, Reynolds, and William Frey. 1994. "Changes in the Segregation of Whites from Blacks During the 1980s: Small Steps Toward a More Racially Integrated Society." *American Sociological Review* 59(1): 23–45.

Farley, Reynolds, Howard Schuman, Suzanne Bianchi, Diane Colasanto, and Shirley Hatchett. 1978. "Chocolate City, Vanilla Suburbs: Will the Trend Toward Racially Separate Communities Continue?" *Social Science Research* 7(4): 319–44.

Farley, Reynolds, Charlotte Steeh, Tara Jackson, Maria Krysan, and Keith Reeves. 1993. "Continued Racial Residential Segregation in Detroit: 'Chocolate City, Vanilla Suburbs' Revisited." *Journal of Housing Research* 4(1): 1–38.

Feagin, Joe R. 1998. "Shifting Racial Tides in Houston." *Dollars and Sense* 215 (January/February): 7.

Feagin, Joe R., and Melvin P. Sikes. 1994. *Living with Racism: The Black Middle Class Experience*. Boston: Beacon Press.

Ferguson, Ronald F. 1996. "Shifting Challenges: Fifty Years of Economic Change Toward Black-White Earnings Equality." In *An American Dilemma Revisited: Race Relations in a Changing World*, edited by Obie Clayton, Jr. New York: Russell Sage Foundation.

Fiske, Susan T. 1998. "Stereotyping, Prejudice, and Discrimination." In *Handbook of Social Psychology*, edited by Daniel T. Gilber, Susan T. Fiske, and Gardner Lindsey. New York: Oxford University Press.

Fix, Michael, and Raymond Struyk. 1993. *Clear and Convincing Evidence*. Washington: Urban Institute Press.

Ford, J. Kevin, Kurt Kraiger, and Susan L. Schechtman. 1986. "Study of Race Effects in Objective Indices and Subjective Evaluations of Performance: A Meta-analysis of Performance Criteria." *Psychological Bulletin* 99(3): 330–37.

Freeman, Richard. 1976. *Black Elite: The New Market for Highly Educated Black Americans* (Report prepared for the Carnegie Commission on Higher Education). New York: McGraw-Hill.

Freeman, Richard B., and William M. Rodgers III. 2000. "Area Economic Conditions and the Labor Market Outcomes of Young Men in the 1990s Expansion." In *Prosperity for All? The Economic Boom and African Americans*, edited by Robert Cherry and William Rodgers. New York: Russell Sage Foundation.

Frey, William, II. 1979. "Central City White Flight: Racial and Nonracial Causes." *American Sociological Review* 44(3): 425–48.

Fry, John P., and Paul G. Whitmore. 1972. "What Are Soft Skills?" Paper presented at the CONARC Soft Skills Conference, sponsored by the U.S. Continental Army Command. Fort Bliss, Tex. (December

12–13, 1972). Published in Paul Whitmore and John Fry. 1974. *Soft Skills: Definition, Behavioral Model Analysis, Training Procedures.* HumRRO professional paper 3-74. Alexandria, Va.: Human Resources Research Organization.

Gaertner, Samuel L., and John F. Dovidio. 1986. "The Aversive Form of Racism." In *Prejudice, Discrimination, and Racism,* edited by John F. Dovidio and Samuel L. Gaertner. New York: Academic Press.

Gans, Herbert. 1992. "Fighting the Biases Embedded in Social Concepts of the Poor." *Chronicle of Higher Education,* January 8, 1992, p. A6.

Gardner, Howard. 1983. *Frames of Mind: The Theory of Multiple Intelligences.* New York: Basic Books.

Grant, David M. 2000. "A Demographic Portrait of Los Angeles County, 1970–1990." In *Prismatic Metropolis: Inequality in Los Angeles,* edited by Lawrence Bobo, Melvin Oliver, James Johnson Jr., and Abel Valenzuela Jr. New York: Russell Sage Foundation.

Greenhaus, Jeffrey H., Saroj Parasuraman, and Wayne M. Wormley. 1990. "Effects of Race on Organizational Experiences, Job Performance Evaluations, and Career Outcomes." *Academy of Management Journal* 33(1): 64–86.

Hacker, Andrew. 1992. *Two Nations: Black and White, Separate, Hostile, and Unequal.* New York: Ballantine.

Handel, Michael J. 1994. "Skills and Work in America in the Twentieth Century." Unpublished paper. Department of Sociology, Harvard University.

———. 1997. "Computers and the Wage Structure." Unpublished paper. Department of Sociology, Harvard University.

Harkess, Shirley, and Carol Warren, 1994. "The Good Worker: Race and Gender in a 1970s Southern City." *Sociological Perspectives* 37(2): 269–92.

Harris, David R. 1997. "The Flight of Whites: A Multilevel Analysis of Why Whites Move." University of Michigan Population Studies Center Research Report no. 97-386. April 1997.

Harris, Louis, 1996. "The Power of Opinion." *Emerge* 7(5 March) 49–52.

Harrison, Bennett, and Jean Kluver. 1988. "Re-assessing the Massachusetts Miracle: An Analysis of Postindustrial Regional Restructuring." Unpublished paper. Department of Urban Studies and Planning, Massachusetts Institute of Technology.

Harrison, Roderick J., and Claudette Bennett. 1995. "Racial and Ethnic Diversity." In *State of the Union: America in the 1990s,* edited by Reynolds Farley. *Vol. 2: Social Trends.* New York: Russell Sage Foundation.

Hartshorn, Truman, and Keith R. Ihlanfeldt. 2000. "Growth and Change in Metropolitan Atlanta: A Historical Perspective." In *The Atlanta Paradox,* edited by David Sjoquist. New York: Russell Sage Foundation.

Hauser, Robert M., and Min-Hsiung Huang. 1997. "Verbal Ability on Socioeconomic Success: A Trend Analysis." *Social Science Research* 26(3): 331–76.

Herrnstein, Richard, and Charles Murray. 1994. *The Bell Curve: Intelligence and Class Structure in American Life*. New York: Free Press.

Hertz, Thomas, Chris Tilly, and Michael Massagli. 2001. "Bending the Rules? Race, Ethnicity, and Gender Effects in a Rule-Bound Model of Hiring and Wage-setting." In *Urban Inequality: Evidence from Four Cities*, edited by Alice O'Connor, Chris Tilly, and Lawrence Bobo. New York: Russell Sage Foundation.

Hill, Richard Child. 1984. "Economic Crisis and Political Response in the Motor City." In *Sunbelt/Snowbelt: Urban Development and Regional Restructuring*, edited by Larry Sawers and William K. Tabb. New York: Oxford University Press.

Hinojosa-Ojeda, Raul, Martin Carnoy, and Hugh Daley. 1991. "An Even Greater 'U-turn': Latinos and the New Inequality." In *Hispanics in the Labor Force: Issues and Policies*, edited by Edwin Melendez, Clara Rodriguez, and Janis Barry Figueroa. New York: Plenum.

Hinojosa-Ojeda, Raul A., and Rebecca Morales. 1992. "International Restructuring and Labor Market Interdependence: The Automobile Industry in Mexico and the United States." In *U.S.-Mexico Relations: Labor Market Interdependence*, edited by Jorge Bustamente, Clark W. Reynolds, and Raul A. Hinojosa-Ojeda. Stanford, Calif.: Stanford University Press.

Hochschild, Arlie R. 1983. *The Managed Heart: Commercialization of Human Feeling*. Berkeley: University of California Press.

Holzer, Harry J. 1986. "Black Youth Nonemployment: Duration and Job Search." In *The Black Youth Employment Crisis*, National Bureau of Economic Research, edited by Richard Freeman and Harry J. Holzer. Chicago: University of Chicago Press.

——. 1991. "The Spatial Mismatch Hypothesis: What Has the Evidence Shown?" *Urban Studies* 28(1): 105–22.

——. 1996. *What Employers Want: Job Prospects for Less Educated Workers*. New York: Russell Sage Foundation.

——. 1998. "Employer Hiring Decisions and Antidiscrimination Policy." In *Generating Jobs: How to Increase Demand for Less-Skilled Workers*, edited by Richard Freeman and Peter Gottschalk. New York: Russell Sage Foundation.

Holzer, Harry J., and Sheldon Danziger. 2001. "Are Jobs Available for Disadvantaged Workers in Urban Areas?" In *Urban Inequality: Evidence from Four Cities*, edited by Alice O'Connor, Chris Tilly, and Lawrence Bobo. New York: Russell Sage Foundation.

Holzer, Harry J., and Keith Ihlanfeldt. 1996. "Spatial Factors and the Employment of Blacks at the Firm Level." Paper presented at the Multi-City Study of Urban Inequality conference on "Residential Segregation, Social Capital, and Labor Markets." Russell Sage Foundation, New York (February 8–9, 1996).

Holzer, Harry J., and Robert J. LaLonde. 2000. "Job Change and Job Stability Among Less-Skilled Workers." In *Finding Jobs: Work and Wel-*

fare Reform, edited by Rebeca Blank and David Card. New York: Russell Sage Foundation.

Holzer, Harry J., and David Neumark, 1999. "Are Affirmative Action Hires Less Qualified? Evidence from Employer-Employee Data on New Hires." *Journal of Labor Economics* 17(3): 534–69.

Howell, David R. 1997. "The Collapse of Low-Skill Wages." *Public Policy Brief: Institutional Failure and the American Worker.* 27. Annandale-on-Hudson, N.Y.: The Jerome Levy Economic Institute of Bard College.

Howell, David R., Margaret Duncan, and Bennett Harrison. 1998. "Low Wages in the U.S. and High Unemployment in Europe: A Critical Assessment of the Conventional Wisdom." Working Paper 5. New York: Center for Economic Policy Analysis, New School for Social Research (rev. August).

Howell, David R., and Edward N. Wolff. 1991. "Trends in the Growth and Distribution of Skills in the U.S. Workplace, 1960–85." *Industrial and Labor Relations Review* 44(3): 486–502.

Hughes, Mark Allen. 1989. "Misspeaking Truth to Power: A Geographical Perspective on the 'Underclass' Fallacy." *Economic Geography* 65(3): 187–207.

Hurwitz, Jon, and Mark Peffley. 1997. "Public Perceptions of Race and Crime: The role of Racial Stereotypes." *American Journal of Political Science* 41(2): 374–401.

Ihlanfeldt, Keith. 1995. "Information on the Spatial Distribution of Job Opportunities Within Metropolitan Areas." Paper presented at Multi-City Study of Urban Inequality conference on "Searching for Work, Searching for Workers." Russell Sage Foundation, New York (September 28–29).

——. 1999. "The Geography of Economic and Social Opportunity Within Metropolitan Areas." In *Governance and Opportunity in Metropolitan America*, edited by Alan Altshuler, William Morrill, Harold Wolman, and Faith Mitchell. Washington D.C.: National Academy Press.

Ihlanfeldt, Keith, and Madelyn Young. 1994. "Intrametropolitan Variation in Wage Rates: The Case of Atlanta Fast Food Restaurant Workers." *Review of Economics and Statistics* 76(3) 425–33.

Jackson, Susan E. 1991. "Team Composition in Organizational Settings: Issues in Managing an Increasingly Diverse Workforce." In *Group Process and Productivity*, edited by Stephen Worchel, Wendy Wood, and Jeffrey A. Simpson. Newbury Park, Calif.: Sage.

Jencks, Christopher. 1991. "Is the American Underclass Growing?" In *The Urban Underclass*, edited by Christopher Jencks and Paul E. Peterson. Washington, D.C.: Brookings Institution.

Jencks, Christopher, and Susan Mayer. 1990. "Residential Segregation, Job Proximity, and Black Job Opportunities." In *Inner City Poverty in the United States*, edited by Laurence E. Lind and Michael McGeary. Washington, D.C.: National Academy Press.

Jencks, Christopher, and Meredith Phillips. 1998. "America's Next Achievement Test." *The American Prospect*, September-October (40): 44–53.

Jenkins, Richard. 1986. *Racism and Recruitment: Managers, Organisations, and Equal Opportunity in the Labor Market*. New York: Cambridge University Press.

Jobs for the Future. 1995a. "The Club Focus Group," April 18. Unpublished focus group transcript. Boston, Mass.: Jobs for the Future.

———. 1995b. "STRIVE Focus Group," April 22. Unpublished focus group transcript. Boston, Mass.: Jobs for the Future.

Johnson, James, Melvin Oliver, and Lawrence Bobo. 1994. "Understanding the Contours of Deepening Urban Inequality: Theoretical Underpinnings and Research Design of a Multi-City Study." *Urban Geography* 15(1): 77–89.

Kasarda, John D. 1993. "Inner-City Concentrated Poverty and Neighborhood Distress: 1970 to 1990." *Housing Policy Debate* 4(3): 253–302.

Kasinitz, Philip, and Jan Rosenberg. 1994. "Missing the Connection: Social Isolation and Employment on the Brooklyn Waterfront." Working paper. Michael Harrington Center for Democratic Values and Social Change, Queens College, City University of New York.

Kaufman, Jonathan. 1996. "Mood Swing: White Men Shake Off That Losing Feeling on Affirmative Action." *Wall Street Journal*, September 5. 1996, pp. A1–A9.

Kennelly, Ivy. 1995. "'That Could Come from Lack of Nurturing': Employers' Images of African-American Women." Master's thesis, Department of Sociology, University of Georgia, Athens.

———. 1999. "'That Single Mother Element': How White Employers Typify Black Women." *Gender and Society*, 13(2): 168–192.

Kilbourne, Barbara S., Paul England, and Katherine Beron. 1994. "Effects of Changing Individual, Occupational, and Industrial Characteristics on Changes in Earnings: Intersections of Race and Gender." *Social Forces* 72(2): 1,149–76.

Kirschenman, Joleen. 1991. "Gender Within Race in the Labor Market." Presented at the Urban Poverty and Family Life Conference. Chicago (October 10–12, 1991).

Kirschenman, Joleen, and Kathryn M. Neckerman. 1991. "'We'd Love to Hire Them, But . . .': The Meaning of Race for Employers." In *The Urban Underclass*, edited by Christopher Jencks and Paul E. Peterson. Washington: Brookings Institution.

Klitgaard, Thomas and Adam Posen. 1995. "Morning Session Summary of Discussion." *Economic Policy Review*, Federal Reserve Bank of New York 1(1): 33–34.

Kodrzycki, Yolanda K. 1996. "Labor Markets and Earnings Inequality: A Status Report." In *Earnings Inequality*, special issue of the *New England Economic Review* (May/June).

Kraiger, Kurt, and J. Kevin Ford. 1985. "A Meta-Analysis of Ratee Race

Effects in Performance Ratings." *Journal of Applied Psychology* 70: 56–65.

Krueger, Alan B. 1993. "Have Computers Changed the Wage Structure? Evidence from Micro Data." *Quarterly Journal of Economics* 109(1): 33–60.

Lane, Julia, David Stevens, and Simon Burgess. 1996. "Worker and Job Flows." *Economics Letters* 51: 109–13.

Laslett, John H. M. 1996. "Historical Perspectives: Immigration and the Rise of a Distinctive Urban Region, 1900–1970." In *Ethnic Los Angeles*, edited by Roger Waldinger and Mehdi Bozorgmehr. New York: Russell Sage Foundation.

Lee, Gloria, and Ray Loveridge, eds. 1987. *The Manufacture of Disadvantage: Stigma and Social Closure*. Philadelphia: Open University Press.

Leonard, Jonathan. 1990. "The Impact of Affirmative Action Regulation and Equal Opportunity Law on Black Employment." *Journal of Economic Perspectives*, 4(4): 47–63.

Levine, David I., ed. 1999. "Symposium: (Attempts at) Replication of *The Bell Curve*." *Industrial Relations* 38(3): 245–406.

Levine, David I., and Gary Painter. 1999. "The NELS Curve: Replicating *The Bell Curve* Analyses with the National Education Longitudinal Study." *Industrial Relations* 38(3): 364–406.

Lichter, Michael, and Devon Johnson. 1997. "'You Know How *They* Are': The Construction of Employers' Racial Attitudes and Preferences." Paper for the Annual Meetings of the American Sociological Association, Toronto, Canada (August 9–13, 1997).

Lipset, Seymour Martin. 1990. "The Work Ethic—Then and Now." *The Public Interest* 98: 61–69.

Lukas, J. Anthony. 1985. *Common Ground: A Turbulent Decade in the Lives of Three American Families*. New York: Knopf.

Lundgren-Gaveras, Lena, and Bruce Rankin. 1995. "The Effect of Program versus Client Characteristics on Employment Wages of Job Training Partnership Act (JTPA) Program Graduates." Unpublished paper. Boston University School of Social Work and Center for the Study of Urban Inequality, University of Chicago.

Mac Donald, Heather. 1996. "Race Still Matters to California Companies." *Wall Street Journal*, November 11, 1996, pp. A16–A20.

Majors, Richard, and Janet Mancini Billson. 1992. *Cool Pose: The Dilemmas of Black Manhood in America*. New York: Touchstone.

Marshall, F. Ray. 1974. "The Economics of Racial Discrimination: A Survey." *Journal of Economic Literature* 12(3): 849–71.

Massey, Douglas, and Nancy Denton. 1993. *American Apartheid*. Cambridge, Mass.: Harvard University Press.

McConahay, John B. 1986. "Modern Racism, Ambivalence, and the Modern Racism Scale." In *Prejudice, Discrimination, and Racism*, edited by John F. Dovidio and Samuel L. Gaertner. New York: Academic Press.

Meléndez, Edwin. 1996. *Working on Jobs: The Center for Employment*

Training. Boston: Mauricio Gastón Institute, University of Massachusetts at Boston.

Mishel, Lawrence, Jared Bernstein, and John Schmitt. 1997. "Did Technology Have Any Effect on the Growth of Wage Inequality in the 1980s and 1990s?" Unpublished paper. Washington D.C.: Economic Policy Institute, April (rev. December).

———. 1999. *The State of Working America 1998–1999*. Ithaca, N.Y.: Cornell University Press (Economic Policy Institute).

Mishel, Lawrence and Ruy A. Teixeira. 1991. *The Myth of the Coming Labor Shortage*. Washington D.C.: Economic Policy Institute.

Moss, Philip. Forthcoming. "Earnings Inequality and the Quality of Jobs: What We Know, What We Don't Know, and How We Should Look." In *Corporate Governance and Sustainable Prosperity*, edited by William Lazonick and Mary O'Sullivan. New York: Macmillan.

Moss, Philip, and Chris Tilly. 1991. "Why Black Men Are Doing Worse in the Labor Market: A Review of Supply-Side and Demand-Side Explanations." Working paper. New York: Social Science Research Council Committee on the Urban Underclass.

———. 1993a. "A Turn for the Worse: Why Black Men's Labor Market Fortunes Have Declined in the United States." *Sage Race Relations Abstracts* 18(1): 5–45.

———. 1993b. "Why Aren't Employers Hiring More Black Men?" Final Report to the Committee for Research on the Urban Underclass of the Social Science Research Council. Department of Policy and Planning, University of Massachusetts at Lowell.

———. 1995. "Skills and Race in Hiring: Quantitative Findings from Face-to-Face Interviews." *Eastern Economic Journal* 21(3): 357–74.

———. 1996. "'Soft' Skills and Race: An Investigation of Black Men's Employment Problems." *Work and Occupations* 23(3): 252–76.

———. 2000. "How Labor Market Tightness Affects Employer Attitudes and Actions Toward Black Job Applicants: Evidence from Employer Surveys." In *Prosperity for All? The Economic Boom and African Americans*, edited by Robert Cherry and William Rodgers. New York: Russell Sage Foundation.

Mullins, Leith. 1994. "Images, Ideology, and Women of Color." In *Women of Color in U.S. Society*, edited by Maxine Baca Zinn and Bonnie Thornton Dill. Philadelphia: Temple University Press.

Murnane, Richard J., and Frank Levy. 1996. *Teaching the New Basic Skills: Principles for Educating Children to Thrive in a Changing Economy*. New York: Free Press.

Murnane, Richard J., John B. Willet, and Frank Levy. 1995. "The Growing Importance of Cognitive Skills in Wage Determination." *The Review of Economics and Statistics*. 77: 251–66.

Murphy, Kevin M., and Finis Welch. 1993. "Industrial Change and the Rising Importance of Skill." In *Uneven Tides: Rising Inequality in America*, edited by Sheldon Danziger and Peter Gottschalk. New York: Russell Sage Foundation.

Neal, Derek A., and William R. Johnson. 1996. "The Role of Premarket

Factors in Black-White Wage Differences." *Journal of Political Economy* 104(5): 869–95.

Neckerman, Kathryn M., and Joleen Kirschenman. 1991. "Hiring Strategies, Racial Bias and Inner-City Workers." *Social Problems* 38(4): 801–15.

Newman, Katherine S. 1999. *No Shame in My Game: The Working Poor in the Inner City.* New York: Knopf and Russell Sage Foundation.

O'Connor, Alice, Chris Tilly, and Lawrence D. Bobo. 2001. *Urban Inequality: Evidence from Four Cities.* New York: Russell Sage Foundation.

O'Neill, June. 1990. "The Role of Human Capital in Earnings Differences Between Black and White Men." *Journal of Economic Perspectives* 4(4): 25–46.

Osterman, Paul. 1995. Skill, Training, and Work Organization in American Establishments. *Industrial Relations* 34(2): 125–46.

Osterman, Paul, and Brenda Lautsch. 1996. "Project Quest: A Report to the Ford Foundation." Cambridge, Mass.: MIT Sloan School of Management.

Paajanen, George. 1997. "Measuring 'Soft' Skills: Instruments Designed for Employers and Job Candidates." Paper presented to Anne E. Casey Foundation Jobs Initiative Working Meeting. Philadelphia (June 10–11, 1997).

Paajanen, George E., Timothy L. Hansen, and Richard A. McLellan. 1993. *PDI Employment Inventory and PDI Customer Service Inventory Manual.* Minneapolis: Personnel Decisions International.

Peffley, Mark, and Jon Hurwitz. 1998. "Whites' Stereotypes of Blacks: Sources and Political Consequences." In *Perception and Prejudice: Race and Politics in the United States,* edited by Jon Hurwitz and Mark Peffley. New Haven, Conn.: Yale University Press.

Pettigrew, Thomas F., and R. W. Meertens. 1995. "Subtle and Blatant Prejudice in Western Europe." *European Journal of Social Psychology* 25(1): 57–75.

Phelps, Edwin. 1972. "The Statistical Theory of Racism and Sexism." *American Economic Review* 162(4): 659–61.

Piore, Michael J. 1979. *Birds of Passage: Migrant Labor and Industrial Societies.* New York: Cambridge University Press.

Porter, Michael E. 1994. "The Competitive Advantage of the Inner City." Unpublished paper. Harvard Business School.

Press, Julie E. 2000. "Child Care as Poverty Policy: The Effect of Child Care on Work and Family Poverty." In *Prismatic Metropolis: Inequality in Los Angeles,* edited by Lawrence Bobo, James H. Johnson, Melvin L. Oliver, and Abel Valenzuela. New York: Russell Sage Foundation.

Pryor, Frederic L., and David L. Schaffer. 1999. *Who's Not Working and Why: Employment, Cognitive Skills, and the Changing U.S. Labor Market.* New York: Cambridge University Press.

Reimers, Cordelia. 2000. "The Effect of Tighter Labor Markets on Unemployment of Hispanics and African Americans: The 1990s Experience." In *Prosperity for All? The Economic Boom and African Americans*, edited by Robert Cherry and William Rodgers. New York: Russell Sage.

Rigdon, Joan E. 1992. "Work-force Diversity Stirs Little Concern." *Wall Street Journal*, May 22, 1992, p. B1.

Rusk, David. 1999. *Inside Game, Outside Game: Winning Strategies for Saving Urban America*. Washington, D.C.: Brookings Institution Press.

Rutheiser, Charles, 1996. *Imagineering Atlanta: The Politics of Place in the City of Dreams*. London: Verso.

Sabagh, Georges, and Mehdi Bozorgmehr. 1996. "Population Change: Immigration and Ethnic Transformation." In *Ethnic Los Angeles*, edited by Roger Waldinger and Mehdi Bozorgmehr. New York: Russell Sage Foundation.

Sackett, Paul R., and Cathy L. Z. Dubois. 1991. "Rater-Ratee Effects on Performance Evaluation: Challenging Meta-analytic Conclusions." *Journal of Applied Psychology* 76(6): 873–77.

Saint John, Craig, and Tara Heald Moore. 1995. "Fear of Black Strangers." *Social Science Research* 24(3): 262–80.

Sanchez, George J. 1993. *Becoming Mexican American: Ethnicity, Culture, and Identity in Chicano Los Angeles, 1900–1945*. New York: Oxford University Press.

Schlesinger, Leonard, and James Heskett. 1991. "The Service-Driven Company." *Harvard Business Review* 69(5): 71–81.

Scott, Allen, and Mark Drayse. 1991. "The Electronics Industry in Southern California: Growth and Spatial Development from 1945 to 1989." *Review of Regional Studies* 21(1): 1–14.

Sears, David O. 1988. "Symbolic Racism: Profiles in Controversy." In *Eliminating Racism*, edited by Phyllis A. Katz and Dalmas A. Taylor. New York: Praeger.

SEMCOG (Southeast Michigan Council of Governments). 1984. "Major Economic Activity in Southeast Michigan." Map. Detroit: SEMCOG.

Shao, Maria. 1994. "Diversity Training: What Is It? Who Does It?" *Boston Globe*. Special section, "Working Together: Exploring Diversity in the Workplace," March 7, 1994.

Sharpe, Rochelle. 1993. "Losing Ground: In Latest Recession, Only Blacks Suffered Net Employment Loss." *Wall Street Journal*, September 14, 1993, pp. A1, A12–13.

Shellenbarger, Sue. 1993. "Work-force Study Finds Loyalty Is Weak, Divisions of Race and Gender Are Deep." *Wall Street Journal*, September 3, 1993, p. B1.

Sherif, Muzafer. 1967. *Group Conflict and Cooperation*. London: Routledge and Kegan Paul.

Simpson, George E., and John M. Yinger. 1985. *Racial and Cultural Minorities: An Analysis of Prejudice and Discrimination*, 5th ed. New York: Plenum.

Sjoquist, David. 1996. "Social Mismatch and Social Acceptability." Paper presented at the Multi-City Study on Urban Inequality conference. Russell Sage Foundation, New York (May 30, 1996).

Smith, James P., and Finis R. Welch. 1989. "Black Economic Progress After Myrdal." *Journal of Economic Literature* 27(2): 519–64.

Smith, William J. 1997. *Trends in Atlanta's Employment Profile*. Atlanta: Research Atlanta, Inc., School of Policy Studies, Georgia State University.

Sniffen, Michael J. 2000. "Workplace Bias Suits by Individuals Tripled in 1990s." *San Francisco Chronicle*, January 17, 2000, p. A3.

Soja, Edward, Rebecca Morales, and Goetz Wolff. 1983. "Urban Restructuring: An Analysis of Social and Spatial Change in Los Angeles." *Economic Geography* 59(2): 196–230.

Steele, Claude M., and Joshua Aronson. 1995. "Stereotype Threat and the Intellectual Test Performance of African Americans." *Journal of Personality and Social Psychology* 69(5): 797–811.

Tajfel, Henri, and John C. Turner. 1986. "The Social Identity Theory of Intergroup Behavior." In *Psychology of Intergroup Relations*, edited by Stephen Worchel and William G. Austin. Chicago: Nelson-Hall.

Task Force on Reconstructing America's Labor Market Institutions. 1999. "The Evolving Wage Structure." *Blueprint* 2(2): 1,4.

Tienda, Marta, and Haya Stier. 1991. "Makin' a Livin': Color and Opportunity in the Inner City." Paper presented at the Urban Poverty and Family Life Conference. Harris Graduate School of Public Policy Studies, University of Chicago (October 10–12, 1991).

Tilly, Charles. 1998. *Durable Inequality*. Berkeley: University of California Press.

Tilly, Chris. 1995. "Putting Employers in the Picture: Engaging Employers in Employment/Training Programs for Disadvantaged Youth and Young Adults." Report to Jobs for the Future, Boston.

———. 1996. *Half a Job: Bad and Good Part-Time Jobs in a Changing Labor Market*. Philadelphia: Temple University Press.

———. 1997. "Arresting the decline of good jobs in the U.S.A.?" *Industrial Relations Journal* 28(4): 269–74.

Tilly, Chris, and Charles Tilly. 1998. *Work Under Capitalism*. Denver: Westview Press.

Tsui, Anne S., Terri D. Egan, and Charles A. O'Reilly III. 1992. "Being Different: Relational Demography and Organizational Attachment." *Administrative Science Quarterly* 37(4): 549–79.

Tsui, Anne S., and Charles A. O'Reilly III. 1989. "Beyond Simple Demographic Effects: The Importance of Relational Demography in Superior-Subordinate Dyads." *Academy of Management Journal* 32(2): 402–23.

Turner, Susan. 1996. "Barriers to a Better Break: Wages, Race, and Space in Metropolitan Detroit." Paper presented at the Multi-City Study of Urban Inequality conference on "Residential Segregation, Social Capital, and Labor Markets." Russell Sage Foundation, New York (February 8–9, 1996).

U.S. Department of Commerce. U.S. Bureau of the Census. 1988. *City and County Data Book*. Washington: U.S. Government Printing Office.

———. 1994. *City and County Data Book*. Washington: U.S. Government Printing Office.

———. 1997. *Fertility of American Women: June 1995*. Current Population Reports, P20-499. Washington: U.S. Government Printing Office.

U.S. Department of Labor. U.S. Bureau of Labor Statistics. 2000. "Nonagricultural Payrolls" and "Labor Force Statistics from the CPS." Web site, http://data.bls.gov.

U.S. Equal Employment Opportunity Commission. 1997a. "Best Practices of Private Sector Employers: Executive Summary." Web site, http://www.eeoc.gov/task/prac2.html. December 22.

———. 1997b. "EEOC Announces Pilot Projects to Test for Employment Discrimination." Web site, http://www.eeoc.gov/press/12-5-97.html. December 5.

———. 2000. "EEOC Litigation Statistics, FY 1992 Through FY 1999." web site, http://www.eeoc.gov/stats/litigation.html.

Vallas, Stephen. 1990. "The Concept of Skill: A Critical Review." *Work and Occupations* 17(4): 379–98.

Waldinger, Roger. 1997. "Black/Immigrant Competition Reassessed: New Evidence from Los Angeles." *Sociological Perspectives* 40(3): 365–86.

Waldinger, Roger, and Mehdi Bozorgmehr, eds. 1996. *Ethnic Los Angeles*. New York: Russell Sage Foundation.

Wayne State University (Center for Urban Studies/Michigan Metropolitan Information Center) and SEMCOG (Southeast Michigan Council of Governments). 1991. *1990 Census Community Profiles for Southeast Michigan*. Vol. 1: Macomb, Oakland, and Wayne Counties. Detroit: Wayne State University and SEMCOG.

Wharton, Amy. 1993. "The Affective Consequences of Service Work: Managing Emotions on the Job." *Work and Occupations* 20(2): 205–32.

Wicker, Allan W. 1969. "Attitudes versus Actions: The Relationship of Verbal and Overt Behavioral Responses to Attitude Objects." *Journal of Social Issues* 25(4): 41–78.

Wilson, William J. 1978. *The Declining Significance of Race: Blacks and Changing American Institutions*. Chicago: University of Chicago Press.

———. 1987. *The Truly Disadvantaged: The Inner City, the Underclass and Public Policy*. Chicago: University of Chicago Press.

Word, Carl O., Mark P. Zanna, and Joel Cooper. 1974. "The Nonverbal Mediation of Self-Fulfilling Prophecies in Interracial Interaction." *Journal of Experimental Social Psychology* 10(2): 100–20.

Wynter, Leon E. 1998. "Testing for Discrimination Gains Wider Acceptance." *Wall Street Journal*, July 1, 1998, p. B1.

Zubrinsky, Camille, and Lawrence Bobo. 2000. "Prismatic Metropolis:

Race and Residential Segregation in the City of Angels." In *Prismatic Metropolis: Inequality in Los Angeles*, edited by Lawrence D. Bobo, Melvin Oliver, James Johnson Jr., and Abel Valenzuela Jr. New York: Russell Sage Foundation.

Index

Numbers in **boldface** refer to tables and figures.